Business School Leadership and Crisis Exit Planning

The European Foundation for Management Development (EFMD) is the largest international accreditation body for business schools, with more than 950 members across 92 countries, including the world's highest-ranked schools. A not-for-profit, mission-led institution, the EFMD plays a central role in shaping a global approach to management education, emphasizing the development of socially responsible leaders. As part of EFMD's fiftieth anniversary celebrations, its President, Professor Eric Cornuel, has edited this volume, featuring contributions from leaders in management education, including the presidents and deans of the top business schools from across the world. Each contribution will address the challenges and dilemmas facing business schools today, with respect to four key themes: the "higher purpose" of business schools; the social impact of business schools; the internationalization of business schools; and crisis management within business schools, with a special focus on the impact of COVID-19. This volume is also available via Open Access.

PROFESSOR ERIC CORNUEL is the President of EFMD Global. Having graduated from Sciences Po Paris and HEC Paris, he completed his Ph.D. in management at Paris Dauphine University. He has held management positions and taught at various management schools in Europe and Asia, including HEC Paris and the Catholic University of Louvain. He has received several awards, including, in 2018, the Magnolia Award from the city of Shanghai, and the French national order of the Légion d'honneur. He has published several books and academic articles. His latest co-authored book, *The Institutional Development of Business Schools*, was published by Oxford University Press. Eric is a fellow at numerous academic institutes, and sits on boards and advisory boards of several international organizations, including China Europe International Business School (CEIBS), the Globally Responsible Leadership Initiative (GRLI), HigherEd, and International Teachers Programme (ITP).

Business School Leadership and Crisis Exit Planning

Global Deans' Contributions on the Occasion of the 50th Anniversary of the EFMD

Edited by

ERIC CORNUEL
European Foundation for Management Development

CAMBRIDGE
UNIVERSITY PRESS

CAMBRIDGE
UNIVERSITY PRESS

University Printing House, Cambridge CB2 8BS, United Kingdom

One Liberty Plaza, 20th Floor, New York, NY 10006, USA

477 Williamstown Road, Port Melbourne, VIC 3207, Australia

314–321, 3rd Floor, Plot 3, Splendor Forum, Jasola District Centre, New Delhi – 110025, India

103 Penang Road, #05–06/07, Visioncrest Commercial, Singapore 238467

Cambridge University Press is part of the University of Cambridge.

It furthers the University's mission by disseminating knowledge in the pursuit of education, learning, and research at the highest international levels of excellence.

www.cambridge.org
Information on this title: www.cambridge.org/9781316514450
DOI: 10.1017/9781009083164

© Cambridge University Press 2022

First published 2022

A catalogue record for this publication is available from the British Library.

ISBN 978-1-316-51445-0 Hardback

Contents

Figures

Tables

Contributors

Frank Bournois has been the executive president and dean of École Supérieure de Commerce de Paris (ESCP) since 2014. He is the chairman of the Programmes Committee of the Conférence des Grandes Écoles, a board member of the European Foundation for Management Development (EFMD), and an independent supervisory board member of the Mazars Group. As a specialist in executive governance and people management, he has spent his career in businesses, such as Rhône-Poulenc Fibres and Polymers and some of the largest French companies, as well as in French and European universities and schools. Professor Bournois is the author of numerous books and articles on leadership development. Bournois is an officer of the Legion of Honour and of the national Order of Merit.

Eric Cornuel is the president of EFMD Global. Having graduated from Sciences Po and HEC Paris, he completed his PhD in management at Paris Dauphine University. He has held management positions and taught at various management schools in Europe and Asia, including HEC Paris and the Catholic University of Louvain. His achievements have earned him a number of awards, including, in particular, the Magnolia Award of the City of Shanghai, the French National Order of the Légion d'honneur, and several honorary professorships. He has published a number of books and academic articles. His latest coauthored book, *The Institutional Development of Business Schools*, was published by Oxford University Press. Eric Cornuel is a fellow at numerous academic institutes and sits on the boards and advisory boards of several international organizations, including China Europe International Business School (CEIBS), the Globally Responsible Leadership Initiative (GRLI), HigherEd, and International Teachers Programme (ITP).

Gerald F. Davis received his PhD from Stanford and taught at Northwestern and Columbia before moving to the University of Michigan, where he is the Gilbert and Ruth Whitaker Professor of Business Administration and a professor of sociology. He has published widely in management, sociology, and finance. His books include *Social Movements and Organization Theory* (2005), *Organizations and Organizing* (2007), *Managed by the Markets: How Finance Reshaped America* (2009), *Changing Your Company from the Inside Out: A Guide for Social Intrapreneurs* (2015), *The Vanishing American Corporation* (2016), and *Taming Corporate Power in the 21st Century* (2021).

Yuan Ding is the vice president, dean, and Cathay Capital Chair Professor in Accounting at CEIBS. With a PhD degree from Montesquieu University/Bordeaux IV, Dr. Ding is a member of the European Accounting Association, the French Accounting Association, and the American Accounting Association (AAA) and the author of three books on financial reporting and multiple articles in leading journals. In addition to being on the board directorship of several listed firms and financial institutions, he serves on the Steering Committee of the EFMD Conference for Deans and Director Generals; the International Advisory Board (IAB) at Université Paris Dauphine, École hôtelière de Lausanne (EHL), and Bologna Business School; and the Board of the Graduate Management Admission Council (GMAC).

Fernando J. Fragueiro is a full professor who received his PhD in strategic leadership from Warwick University in the UK. He is the academic director of the Business Leadership Chair and the founder and director of ENOVA LEAD: CEO Learning Network in Latin America, both at IAE Business School. He is an advisor of boards and top-management teams on the strategic leadership process, was the president of Austral University (2013–2018) and the dean of IAE Business School (1995–2008), and is a visiting scholar at Harvard Business School.

Santiago Iñiguez is the president of IE University and a recognized influencer in global higher education. His books include *The Learning Curve: How Business Schools Are Reinventing Education* (Palgrave Macmillan), *Cosmopolitan Managers: Executive Education That Works* (Springer), and *In an Ideal*

Business: How the Ideas of 10 Female Philosophers Bring Value to the Workplace (Palgrave Macmillan).

Valery S. Katkalo is the Higher School of Economics (HSE University) first vice-rector and the dean of the HSE Graduate School of Business. Prior to joining HSE, he was the founding dean of Sberbank Corporate University and the dean of the Graduate School of Management at St. Petersburg University, where he has led these organizations to the first-in-Russia Corporate Learning Improvement Process (CLIP) and EFMD Quality Improvement System (EQUIS) accreditations. Professor Katkalo also serves as the EFMD vice president, a member of the EFMD Board, and the chairman of the Education Commission at the Russian Association of Managers. His research on the evolution of strategic management theory and management education has been published in top international and Russian journals. He holds undergraduate and doctoral degrees from St. Petersburg University and has completed a post-doctoral program at the Haas School of Business of the University of California, Berkeley, and executive education programs at Stanford Graduate School of Business and the Massachusetts Institute of Technology (MIT).

Pierre Kletz is a professor in the Faculty of Management at Ben-Gurion University of the Negev (BGU). There, he headed the MBA in Social Leadership program, which he founded in 2010, and the Jack, Joseph and Morton Mandel Institute of Social Leadership, until September 2021. Pierre Kletz received his PhD from HEC Paris School of Management. He holds a habilitation to direct research (HDR) from the Sorbonne. In the 1990s, he was the academic director of the Central and Eastern Europe Centre at HEC Paris. He was also an associate professor at the University François Rabelais (France), where he was the founding director of the Master of Public Management program. In 2006, he joined the Mandel Foundation–Israel and served as vice president until January 2014.

Peter Little, AM (Member, Order of Australia), is an emeritus professor at the Queensland University of Technology (QUT), fellow of the EFMD, and fellow of CPA Australia. Formerly, Little was the director of EFMD Global, a deputy vice-chancellor at QUT, and the executive dean of QUT Business School. Little is also a long-standing EQUIS Peer Review Team (PRT) chair and peer reviewer, a company director specializing in corporate and academic governance, and a regular speaker on leadership in the age of disruption.

Jean-François Manzoni is the president of the International Institute for Management Development (IMD), where he also serves as the Nestlé Professor of Leadership and Organizational Development. His research, teaching, and advisory activities are focused on leadership, the development of high-performance organizations, and corporate governance. The recipient of several awards for teaching excellence, he also received numerous awards for his research and case-writing activities, including for his seminal book *The Set-Up-to-Fail Syndrome: How Good Managers Cause Great People to Fail* (with Jean-Louis Barsoux). A fellow of the Singapore Institute of Directors, Professor Manzoni currently serves on the Board of Keppel Corp., an international diversified group listed on the Singapore stock exchange, and previously served on the board of AACSB International and Singapore's Civil Service College. A citizen of Canada and France, Professor Manzoni received his doctorate from Harvard Business School.

Grzegorz Mazurek is the rector of Kozminski University – the leading business school in Poland – and a full professor of management, specializing in his research in the area of digital transformation strategies, e-commerce, and e-marketing. He is particularly interested in the impact of digital technologies on the higher education sector. He is also the director of the Digital Transformation Research Center – CYBERMAN and a member of the EFMD Advisory Board for the Central and Eastern European region.

Peter McKiernan is a professor of management at the University of Strathclyde, Scotland, and a distinguished professor of management at Brussels School of Governance, Vrije Universiteit Brussel (VUB). He is a past president of both the British Academy of Management (BAM) and the European Academy of Management (EURAM). He is a cofounder of EURAM, the European Management Review, and the Community for Responsible Research in Business and Management. Presently, he is the past dean of the BAM Fellows College and the foundational dean of the EURAM Fellows College.

Enase Okonedo, FCA, is the vice-chancellor of Pan-Atlantic University, Lagos, Nigeria. Prior to this, she was dean of Lagos Business School (LBS), where she was instrumental in transforming LBS into a globally recognized and foremost business school in Africa that has gained global accreditations and rankings. She is a professor of management and holds a doctorate in business administration (DBA) from the International School of Management (ISM), Paris. She also serves on boards in the banking, telecommunications, and power sector and is the president of AIFA Reading Society – a society committed to achieving sustainable education in Africa by promoting and supporting a reading culture.

Barbara Sporn is a professor of higher education management and heads the Institute for Higher Education Management at WU Vienna University of Economics and Business. Professor Sporn served as vice rector for research, international affairs, and external relations at WU Vienna University of Economics and Business from 2002 to 2015. Dr. Sporn works as the director of EFMD Programme Accreditation within EFMD Quality Services. She has published books and numerous journal articles on leadership and organization in higher education, university adaptation and change, international and comparative higher education, and the globalization of higher education systems.

Rajendra Srivastava is the Novartis Professor of Marketing Strategy and Innovation at the Indian School of Business (ISB) and a professor emeritus at Singapore Management University (SMU). He served as dean at ISB and as provost and deputy president at SMU. An active researcher, he is a widely cited thought leader and has received numerous research awards for work on marketing strategy, brand and intangible assets, and the marketing–finance interface. He was inducted as a fellow of the American Marketing Association. He has consulted with over 50 multinationals across five continents.

Daniel Traça is the dean and a professor of economics at Nova School of Business and Economics (Nova SBE) in Lisbon and a visiting professor at INSEAD in Singapore. He previously taught at Solvay Brussels School of Economics and Management and at the Graduate Institute of International Economics (Geneva), among other business schools. Traça has consulted for the

World Bank and the European Commission. He obtained his PhD from Columbia University, New York. He has published articles in several leading international academic journals in the field of globalization and economic development.

Anne S. Tsui is a professor emerita of Arizona State University. She is the 67th president of the Academy of Management, the 14th editor of the *Academy of Management Journal*, the founding president of the International Association for Chinese Management Research, the founding editor of *Management and Organization Review*, and a cofounder of the Responsible Research in Business and Management network.

Peter Tufano is the Peter Moores Professor of Finance at Said Business School at the University of Oxford and served as dean from 2011 to 2021. As dean, he emphasized the role of business and business education in addressing large systemic issues, adopting an approach that encouraged close collaboration across the university. He is part of the founding team of Business Schools for Climate Leadership. He was a professor at Harvard Business School for more than two decades. His research, teaching, and engagements span financial innovation, financial engineering, household finance, and the role of business in addressing climate change.

Foreword

The decision to mobilize a number of deans of some of the most internationally eminent business schools and management faculties to produce the present book – *Business School Leadership and Crisis Exit Planning: Global Deans' Contributions on the Occasion of the 50th Anniversary of the EFMD* – was made in the first half of 2020 as the world sank into the COVID-19 crisis.

A worldwide feeling of uncertainty was emerging that had consequences for both the management and the strategy of business schools, as well as for the future of management education itself.

A strong need was felt for analytical reflection that would not only outline prospects for facing the crisis – the form, intensity, and consequences of which were completely unknown to us – but also create the conditions for exiting it.

From this point of view, the contributions that make up this work perfectly achieve their objective, offering an exhaustive perspective on the issue of crisis management, structured around four major issues that constitute the four major parts of the book:

- Reexamining the purpose of business schools and, more generally, of management education in light of the crisis
- Reexamining the relationship (existential? alienating? legitimizing?) between businesses and business schools
- Taking stock of the uncertainty of the future of business schools through the example of internationalization, which was supposed to constitute a fundamental and inexorable trend in management education but was largely undermined by the COVID-19 crisis
- Studying the peculiarities of how business schools managed the COVID-19 crisis.

These lines of thinking resonate with the most fundamental thoughts and methods of development adopted by the China Europe International Business School (CEIBS) with respect to the COVID-19 crisis. The CEIBS took a proactive role in responding to the crisis from the outset, driven by a proactive desire to make a positive contribution to rethinking the "business school mission" and "practices." As such, the school was not only quick to sign up for this project but also immediately agreed to sponsor it. Producing this compendium of strategic thinking on the problems posed by the COVID-19 pandemic matched our overarching goal to always do our best to make a positive impact on society and bridge the gulf between higher education and social values.

However, this foreword is being written at the beginning of the year 2021. All contributions have been submitted, and the book offers a coherent whole. But one fundamental question arises. Although COVID-19 prompted this book project, it is clear as of the middle of 2021 that the global climate has changed. In China and in Europe, the two places of residence of the two authors of this foreword, we find ourselves much more in the post–COVID-19 recovery period than in a period of crisis management. This is also true for many other parts of the world, such as in North America, Oceania, and so on, even though the intensity and the consequences of the crisis remain, making its disastrous effects felt hard in other parts of the world.

So, isn't this book coming out too late? Wouldn't we do better to wait for a book on the strategies business schools adopt to accompany the growth of a post-crisis period?

On careful reflection, however, the authors of this foreword remain convinced that this work is still profoundly relevant. If we refer to the notion of *event* as defined by Hannah Arendt, the COVID-19 crisis constitutes an "unexpected event." This crisis is the ideal opportunity to explore new approaches to managing operations, and defining good practices, through analyses and new perspectives – all without ever adopting the totalitarian posture of "this is how it should be done" or "it is inexorable." In conclusion, this book thus offers a complete picture of what happened to business schools and how they navigated these uncharted waters. The steps taken by their leadership worldwide pave the way for future reckoning.

The reader of this book, in approaching the rich plurality of its contributions, will thus find useful proposals and thinking, all while turning away from the totalizing analyses of an exceptional event that led to a global crisis.

Prof. Yuan Ding and Prof. Eric Cornuel

Introduction

1 Rationale for the Book and Presentation of the Contributions

ERIC CORNUEL

It seems trivial to note that the coronavirus epidemic has revealed the many deep cracks and dysfunctions running through the political, economic, social, and cultural spheres. It is almost frightening to see how the shockwave generated by COVID-19 affects all areas of life in society.

Thus, it is hardly surprising that our societies are in search of benchmarks, that we ask questions of people whose thinking is likely to enlighten us and help us analyze the present situation and the avenues to explore in the future.

It is extremely interesting to observe how some of the most enlightened analysts do not hesitate to take strong positions on how the COVID-19 crisis is a turning point, after which the world will never be the same again. A recent editorial by Tom Friedman (2020) in the *New York Times* is symptomatic of these radical positions. The title of the article is representative of its content: "After the Pandemic, a Revolution in Education and Work Awaits."

In this article, Friedman draws from many fields to argue for the depth of the revolution underway. His positions on the question of higher education, the question that unites the contributors to this work, are particularly clear-cut and unequivocal. For example, on the issue of continuing education, he says: "In the future, lifelong learning will be done by what I call 'complex adaptive coalitions.' An Infosys, Microsoft or IBM will partner with different universities and even high schools. ... The universities' students will be able to take just-in-time learning courses – or do internships – at the corporations' in-house universities, and company employees will be able to take just-in-case humanities courses at the outside universities" (Friedman, 2020, para. 27).

Just as our society turns to analysts like Friedman for guidance on major issues, our approach in this book consisted of consulting some of the best specialists in our field, management education – namely, some of the most recognized deans on seven continents – to understand how they analyzed this crisis, the possibility of exiting from it, and the conditions for doing so.

Reading these contributions leads one to observe, first of all, that although they do not deny the importance of the challenges and difficulties to be overcome, these deans do refrain from attaching themselves to the doxa that a change in the system of management education is on the doorstep of our societies. In other words, if the word *revolution* is widely overused in the times of COVID-19, the authors who contributed to this work have themselves refrained from participating in its overuse.

The authors of the present volume support deep analyses structured around two elements. First, the observation that the COVID-19 crisis, which was initially a health crisis, being imported into the sphere of management education is an acceleration of underlying trends that were already present but are now unfolding with a rapidity that no one would have suspected before the crisis. Second, a shared concern unites almost all the authors – namely, the need to come out "on top" of this crisis.

Nor is the present work free from lines of division between the contributors – of oppositions, of different understandings of the situation. These contrasts are particularly significant on the issue of school leadership.

Some authors highlight the enormous responsibility of leadership, and also the importance of its role, to find a way out of the crisis and to introduce innovation within their establishments, as well as more broadly within the framework of management education. The fundamental hypothesis of these approaches harkens back to personalist approaches, as the former comes down to recognizing that a leader, and therefore a person, can change the course of things. Far from being deterministic, their stance here is firmly in favor of freedom.

It should also be emphasized that the refusal to recognize a hypothetical revolution or a change of system does not lead to a bland observation that refuses to see the importance of the upheavals in progress. This in no way prevents the recognition that management education institutions are embedded in the social system in which they orbit and are influenced by social changes. For example, a major paradigm shift comes from the progress of the "societal/stakeholder" paradigm within companies, to the detriment of the paradigm of the absolute priority of shareholder value. This new paradigm is incurred by broader societal changes, the new centrality of sustainable development, and the importance of ecology and the long term. It entails essential changes in approach for management education institutions.

Likewise, numerous analyses have pointed out that COVID-19 implies a shift to virtual education, a decline in the increase in foreign students, a change in admission criteria, and so forth. Emphasizing the importance of the role of leadership when faced with these upheavals seems almost obvious. But this approach asks us to go further and consider the social changes that are taking root in societies at the same time as the epidemic in the areas of disruption of family relationships, redefinition of living and working spaces, real estate and town planning, ergonomics, social solidarity, and so forth. These social changes are already affecting business schools and management faculties, both in their missions and in the implementation of their activities. A personalist approach emphasizes the decisive role of the leader in developing and implementing a vision and a strategic approach.

Other authors insist less on the importance of leadership in the face of the COVID-19 crisis, preferring to adopt a deterministic approach. They consider that management education institutions are predetermined, both in their constitutions and in their structures and activities, to meet the need for managerial training and education in a given state of society. Therefore, it is fundamental for management education institutions to develop thinking that establishes the extent to which the COVID-19 crisis is inducing a profound social change. Faced with this question, deterministic contributors themselves split into two camps.

For some, the COVID-19 crisis is first and foremost a health crisis whose effects are felt in companies and in the sphere of management education in a transient manner. As such, the constants and major trends in the economy and society should make it possible to exit this crisis quickly, restoring to business schools and management faculties their entire social role, even though the situation on the health front does not improve in the medium or even the long term. Therefore, the objective is to provide tools to exit the crisis and especially to improve teaching techniques, adapting them to the new ambient context created by COVID-19. Put another way, the current issue for business schools is to improve their teaching techniques so that they can integrate into and continue to find their place in this new context.

Other authors in this volume consider, to the contrary, that the coronavirus has only accelerated developments that were present before the epidemic. Thus, in their view, social changes correspond to long-term trends that made social functioning tend toward an unstable state that COVID-19 established. Business schools must therefore develop thinking on the state of society in order to redefine their place within it and maintain their social utility.

The contributions in this book have been organized into four parts:

- The first group of contributions, Part I, is organized around the theme "Striving for Higher Purpose." These contributions have in common that they are not limited to analyzing the function of business schools and their possible development but present, in parallel, an analysis of the social changes underway and an analysis of the way out of the crisis and the changes that this will imply for business schools.

In Chapter 2, "Crises and Collective Purpose: Distraction or Liberation?," Peter Tufano starts from the observation that the contexts in which business schools operate are becoming more complex because they must now take into account a plurality of stakeholders whose interests are sometimes contradictory and not always unified: this parallels the fact that companies must move from an approach focused on shareholders to a logic of stakeholders. The author poses the question of defining the objectives and the duties to be assumed in order to reconcile these sometimes-contradictory interests. Obviously, this question takes on a particular resonance with respect to the COVID-19 crisis, which often destroys consensus and forces business schools to redefine their duties. The shift from a logic of shareholders to a logic of stakeholders, as underlined by Tufano, is to be compared with the underlying long-term trend mentioned by Santiago Iñiguez in Chapter 3, "From Techne to Paideia: Upgrading Business Education." Because of the increasing complexity of society, this trend requires the education provided in business schools to evolve from training as a company technician (in finance, marketing, etc.) to training allowing for a leadership role at the level of the whole society.

Fernando J. Fragueiro, in Chapter 4, "Educating Business Leaders, but for What Kind of World?," demonstrates a broadly converging perspective. Indeed, in this period of unprecedentedly rapid change in all spheres of society, which is further accelerated by COVID-19, he insists (in resonance with Peter Tufano) on the need to develop the adaptability of schools and, especially in harmony with Santiago Iñiguez, to put students – future leaders – in a position to develop a desirable vision or representation of the world and give them the capacity to contribute to bringing it about.

Chapter 5 by Gerald F. Davis, Peter McKiernan, and Anne S. Tsui, "Multi- and Interdisciplinary Research in a World of Crisis: A Responsible Research Solution," takes a similar perspective to that of Santiago Iñiguez but focuses on the field of research. It insists on the need to develop research that is relevant to the major challenges of the world (in the way business school graduates should, according to Iñiguez, be able to have an impact on the major problems of the world) and, to that end, on the importance of developing research that is both multi- and interdisciplinary but also meets rigorous criteria.

In all of these works, the renewed importance of these approaches in the context of crisis is highlighted.

- Part II, "Going Beyond Business," is more focused on the way in which the changes experienced by companies in their strategies, their structures, their decision-making methods, and their relationships to their environment must influence the approaches and modes of reasoning in force in business schools as much as they influence the teaching provided. Although the points of convergence with the contributions presented in Part I are strong, those contributions stand out because they question the way in which social changes should affect management education, whereas the texts in Part II include companies as a central element of their analyses. They focus both on the way in which social developments affect companies and on the way in which these transformations should influence management education establishments.

Peter Little, in Chapter 6, "The Reshaping of Corporations and Their Governance by Climate Change and Other Global Forces – Implications for Leaders and Management Education," analyzes how the new principles of global governance affect the way companies are managed. He further emphasizes that these principles, which already influence the way companies approach the coronavirus crisis but whose sustainability will go far beyond that, will bring about contextual and regulatory changes and force business schools to rethink the elements of their programs of study in each of the disciplines in which they teach or do research.

Daniel Traça takes the same perspective in Chapter 7, "Transforming Business Schools into Lighthouses of Hope for a Sustainable Future," and elaborates thinking on the changes to come for management education institutions so that they can fulfill their role as agents of transformation in a liberal world facing existential challenges.

Likewise, in Chapter 8, "Rethinking Management Education in Dynamic and Uncertain Markets: Educating Future Leaders for Resilience and Agility," Rajendra Srivastava starts from the observation that our time is experiencing profound changes in all areas of life in society (social, cultural, economic, work, education, health) that are further accelerated by the coronavirus epidemic. Srivastava therefore wonders how business schools can bring new added value to the education of business leaders at this unprecedented moment in human history.

Barbara Sporn, in Chapter 9, "Strategic Continuity or Disruption? Adaptive Structures of Business Schools in Times of Crisis," starts from the observation that the university system, business schools, and all the actors who make up their ecosystem have been confronted with a sudden, unexpected, and deep crisis triggered by the coronavirus – one that has forced schools to rethink their approaches and practices in many areas. Sporn tends to think that business schools, whose great adaptability is proven by their history, will be able to respond to these new challenges but believes that the changes provoked, which are analyzed in this chapter, will be irreversible.

  - In general, and regardless of the sector studied, an examination of the course of events since the start of the COVID-19 crisis highlights a particularly salient element – namely, that internationalization has occupied a central place in all developments and has undergone a total reversal in the way it is viewed. Very quickly, it became clear that international travel was driving the epidemic, and borders, which had been undergoing a process of opening up and even disappearance, were locked down all over the world. In addition, whereas internationalization had been perceived as a phenomenon parallel to development and progress and was generally seen positively, with the coronavirus, it became the object of

powerful distrust, illustrated in particular by the fact that foreign-
ers are felt to be a threat, and a strong sense of the need to limit
internationalization for the common good has arisen. All of this
has obviously had a major impact on management education,
which had made internationalization a central facet of its development, as much to find new students and support the international development of companies by training their managers
as to enrich the quality of exchange in classes, among
other benefits.

It is logical, then, that this book includes the chapters in Part III,
"Internationalization of Business Schools." Thus, Yuan Ding, in
Chapter 10, "Reinventing the Internationalization of Business
Schools in the Post–COVID-19 Era," positions himself in the exact
perspective brought about by this context. He argues that business
schools will have a crucial role to play in rebuilding the post–
COVID-19 world. Thus, they need to better understand how to effectively train business leaders in the art of resilience, recovery, adaptation,
and innovation and provide them with the skills to pull countries and
global businesses out of the storm of COVID-19.

Despite the temporary limitations of international travel and the
return of economic sovereignty, business schools should make the
training of international leaders one of their priorities, and to that
end, they should promote greater pluralism in companies with respect
to both communities and countries.

Enase Okonedo, in Chapter 11, "The Face of Business Education in
Africa Post–COVID-19: Gain or Loss?," explores the impact of
COVID-19 in Africa, knowing that the rapid growth of African economies over the past few decades has highlighted the need for competent, well-trained managers and has contributed to the emergence of
business schools on the continent, either as stand-alone schools or
within universities. However, the COVID-19 pandemic, which was
accompanied by containment measures, upset this nascent market by
causing the emergence, in parallel with those measures, of a plethora of
providers of management education services, often backed by technology companies, financial institutions, and independent trainers.
Okonedo discusses the impact of the COVID-19 crisis on business
schools in Africa, including the risks and opportunities as well as the
ways in which business schools can adapt in this changed environment

by examining their curricula, embracing innovative pedagogy, and evaluating the relevance of their methods.

Finally, in Chapter 12, "Creating a New Major Business School in the Times of COVID-19: The HSE-Moscow Way," Valery S. Katkalo asks how it is possible to create a new business school within a large university, both in the context of COVID-19 and when the competition for a new school that will become a major actor is not only national but also international. He describes a particularly interesting case: the organizational restructuring of the Higher School of Economics at the National Research University to create its Graduate School of Business began in 2019, and with the emergence of the COVID-19 pandemic, it faced critical dilemmas. This has required nontrivial strategic and operational action in putting together the management program portfolio, shifting to e-learning modes, designing new policies for the development of the teaching staff, and training a support ecosystem, as well as a number of other examples of creative leadership – all focused on progressing toward the school's ambitious goal despite the challenges of COVID-19.

 - The last part of the book, Part IV, is entitled "Crisis Management with a Special Focus on COVID-19." Its rationale stems from the understanding that although the coronavirus epidemic relates, above all, to the field of public health, where it has its origins, its consequences have opened up a crisis in the field of management education. However, many of our institutions have developed recognized competence in crisis management and constitute the social places to which other social actors come to develop their own skills. In this context, it is worthwhile to pursue an understanding of how management education institutions have faced this imported crisis, how they have adapted their organizational behavior, and what lessons they have drawn from it. In addition, an underlying question forms the central line of thought in the chapters in this part, and it relates to the specificity of crises. That is, the term *crisis management* covers very different realities in relation to crises. It is clear, then, that the specificities of each crisis determine the modes of response that can be brought to bear on it. Furthermore, it is wrong to assume that there is a toolkit for dealing with any and all crises; each one requires that the work of adapting to it be performed. What is more, these contributions also focused on the specificity of the COVID-19 crisis.

In my Chapter 13, "Going Beyond 'Always Look on the Bright Side of Life' in Management Education Crisis Strategy," I underline the specificities of the way in which management education institutions have faced the COVID-19 crisis in relation to the way which they confronted previous economic and social crises, in particular the crisis of 2008–2009. During this latter period, business schools demonstrated an impressive capacity (and one that has been confirmed during the COVID-19 crisis) to continue to operate under modalities as close as possible to those from before the crisis, yet without questioning the fundamental assumptions of their functioning. Contrarily, a movement based on the recognition by management education institutions that they are, in fact, social actors is now asserting itself. As such, these schools have mobilized the skills of their stakeholders to help other organizations find the means to emerge safely from the COVID-19 crisis.

In addition, I maintain that the COVID-19 crisis has accelerated procedures, behaviors, and approaches that were already emerging in the world of management education. The observation that "the world after" will be different is supported by several contributions. Thus, Frank Bournois, in Chapter 14, "Developing Future Leaders with New Partners: Trends from a Business School Perspective," notes that the current COVID-19 crisis has triggered an unprecedented upheaval on a global scale, even if, from a strictly health point of view, humanity has shown itself capable of joining forces and transcending political borders. Above all, he underscores that this crisis is transforming the management sciences.

Jean-François Manzoni, in Chapter 15, "Leading an (Unusual) Academic Institution through a Crisis: A Personal Reflection," develops a line of thinking that perfectly fits the present work: a reflection on the challenges and opportunities for deans to lead in and through a crisis.

Grzegorz Mazurek also believes in the potential that the COVID-19 crisis has for the progress of management education. In an original contribution titled "'Real Change Comes from Outside': COVID-19 as a Great Opportunity for the Revival of Business Schools and Management Education" (Chapter 16), he analyzes how the recognized shortcomings and dysfunctions of management education (teaching selfishness to the detriment of the general interest, ethereal research that has no impact on the real world, the cost of overpriced studies limiting access to underprivileged social strata, an inability to make and implement decisions, etc.) could be improved thanks to the external shock that COVID-19 represents.

Finally, Pierre Kletz, in Chapter 17, "The Extreme Situation, a Challenge for Management Education," offers an analysis of the situation of schools caused by the coronavirus epidemic, characterizing it as an extreme situation. He shows that the response of educational institutions oscillates between an attitude of coping faced with the new situation that entails a deterioration in the quality of management education and a work of mourning that leads to the recognition that some of the foundations of its development (a virtual absence of competing institutions for education in leadership and management, the continuous increase in international demand for management studies, etc.) are obsolete.

In total, reading the entirety of these contributions devoted to the response of management education institutions to the crisis caused by COVID-19 appears to be extraordinarily invigorating insofar as they oppose the many opinions on the subject that are presented as a panegyric of "making a virtue out of necessity." In such opinions, the way in which business schools have succeeded in reacting to sudden external shocks that have called into question the possibility of carrying out entrance exams, recruiting foreign students, conducting international seminars, teaching within the walls of the institution, and so on, is set up as a paragon of leadership in management education. Obviously, the response of management education institutions has in many cases been remarkable, but according to this new dominant ideology, reactive behavior that responds piecemeal to successive external shocks would constitute the ideal of school management.

Although the chapters in this book do not deny the importance of day-to-day management, they stress the need to focus on the essentials. They point out that even in the face of a shock as powerful as COVID-19, leaders must find the means to take a step back, to continue to define a strategy to be planned in the short and medium terms. Above all, the authors maintain that deans cannot be satisfied with focusing on their schools – or even on the unique field of management education. They insist on the importance of an analytical window onto society that leads to social commitment that determines the projects of their institutions.

We have underscored how the contributors to this book adopt one of two approaches. One comes from a personalist current in which the person can change the course of things, and thus it highlights the importance of leaders, and the other comes from a determinist current, which, on the contrary, insists on the need to analyze the social forces that affect the way of doing business and therefore management education.

It is no less important to highlight that all these contributions have in common that they emphasize the notion of vision as a reference concept and underline, explicitly or allusively, how important it is for leaders of management education institutions to develop and implement a vision.

References

Friedman, T. L. (2020, October 20). After the pandemic, a revolution in education and work awaits. *New York Times*. www.nytimes.com/2020/10/20/opinion/covid-education-work.html.

Striving for Higher Purpose

2 | Crises and Collective Purpose: Distraction or Liberation?[1]

PETER TUFANO

As our colleagues who study management have shown, purpose serves as the bedrock upon which well-aligned organizations rest. Using a less static metaphor, why we exist helps us understand how we should move forward. Typically, an organization's purpose is institution-specific, but COVID-19 and other sustained national and global crises give rise to a sense of *collective* purpose. For the COVID-19 crisis, this collective purpose could be expressed as "Flatten the curve" or, in the UK, "Save lives and protect the NHS." This collective purpose bears no resemblance to our pre–COVID-19 individual senses of organizational purpose.

COVID-19 and its aftermath have tested leaders of all institutions, including business schools. Faced with a massive, externally imposed crisis, how do we prioritize our activities? What do we stop or start doing? The answers to these questions reflect our organizations' sense of individual purpose, as influenced by the broader collective purpose. Sustained existential crises allow us to understand the interplay between collective and individual purpose and the organizational implications of internalizing an externally set collective purpose. Are external crises, and the collective sense of purpose they engender, a force to liberate institutions like ours or are they a distraction?

[1] This chapter is based on the article "Training Leaders to Win Wars and Forge Peace: Lessons from History" (*Business History Review*, 94[4], 807–833), which contains additional material on the five business schools studied here. My thanks to Colin Mayer (dean, University of Oxford's Saïd Business School, 2006–2011), Nitin Nohria (dean, Harvard Business School, 2010–2020), Jordi Canals (dean, Instituto de Estudios Superiores de la Empresa [IESE], 2001–2016), Robert Bruner (dean, University of Virginia's Darden School of Business, 2005–2015), Andrew Pettigrew (dean, University of Bath's School of Management 2003–2008), Ann Harrison (Dean, Berkeley Hass, 2019–present), Gay Haskins, Adrien Jean-Guy Passant, Sandra Epstein, and Geoff Jones for their perceptive comments and encouragement. I would like to especially thank Jeffrey Cruikshank, on whose history of Harvard Business School I draw extensively and who provided detailed and helpful comments.

Were the purposes of business schools solely defined by our customary activities – teaching and research – an external shock like COVID-19 would be a distraction. We would simply move all of our activities online, from teaching to research to professional services, in order to "keep the show on the road." We would feel no need to change what we teach or whom we teach.

But if we strongly adopt the collective, higher purpose – to vanquish COVID-19 and the associated public health, economic, and social ills it has surfaced – might we be led to a completely different direction, as our colleagues in Oxford's vaccine labs have shown? Might we rethink not just how we teach but the content of our curricula, the composition of our student bodies, and how we measure success?

Going beyond COVID-19, the call to "build back better" reflects the judgment that prepandemic "normal" was not ideal and that we need to come out of lockdowns creating new approaches for business to deal with the urgent global problems of social, economic, and national fissures; racial inequality; looming public health crises; and perhaps most importantly, an existential climate crisis. If we internalize these longer-term collective purposes, we might set ourselves an ambitious agenda and, in the process, fundamentally transform ourselves, changing what, who, and why we teach and research.

As a scholar, I know the value of learning from history, not to slavishly repeat the experiences from decades ago but rather to learn from how educational leaders reacted to massive external shocks that gave rise to a sense of collective purpose. Given the relatively short history of business education, there are a number of fruitful periods for studying how business schools navigated between individual and collective purpose in the face of sustained global crises. In the twentieth century, these would include World War I, the Great Depression of the 1930s, and World War II. In this chapter, I examine how business schools behaved – and therefore displayed their purposes – in the most recent of these events, World War II.

In World War II, business school deans found themselves in a changed world: the world became much less certain and predictable; international mobility was restricted; students and faculty were either unwilling or unable to study or teach due to the draft; the student experience was compromised relative to "normal" times; financial budgets were under pressure from falling student numbers due to the draft; typical metrics such as career outcomes of graduates seemed out of place; and top-down university edicts were more frequent and consequential. As the war was coming to an end, the situation was completely different – economies and societies needed to rebuild peace-time economies and absorb hundreds of thousands of returning veterans. In the first half of the 1940s, the collective purpose was "Win the war," a call that was jarring to the more genteel activities of teaching and research – much like "Flatten the curve." In the second half of the decade, "Win the peace" was a more familiar call to action for business schools but still as challenging as "Build back better."

What paths did different schools take when the gap widened between the external mandate of winning wars and their traditional roles of teaching and research? Did they insulate themselves as much as possible from the requirements of the war, or did they fully internalize this externally imposed purpose? If the latter, what were the implications? In this chapter, I look at five leading US business schools in the 1940s and study how they reacted to World War II. How, if at all, did wartime – and the collective purpose of "winning the war" – change what and how they taught and how they conducted research, organized themselves, presented themselves, and made decisions? Can we learn anything from our predecessors from eight decades ago that might help us to better lead our institutions as our societies and economies face our generation's crises?

Identifying Purpose

Words and deeds provide cues to understand how an organization sees its purpose and, in this case, how an organization might internalize a collective purpose. We could examine how the leaders, staff, and employees speak about their work to gauge changes in their conceptions of their purpose. For example, consider how firms are dealing with issues of climate change. Some researchers are studying how organizations are adopting climate-related language in their outward-facing communications. Or we could look at their actions, say, in the form of changes in their carbon footprints.

For this work, I look at both words and deeds, using "modern" authorized histories to gauge how the schools understood and internalized the collective wartime imperative of winning the war. From the current day looking backward, are the war years referenced extensively and seen as critical to the development of the modern institution?

For most schools but one, the answer is a resounding no. Tellingly, as some recount their histories from the present, the war years hardly get any mention. Recognizing that this backward-looking approach may obscure the full impact of World War II on the schools, I contacted each of the current deans of the five schools profiled, asking for additional information that might not have been available in their official histories or current materials.

How can we compare the different ways that organizations internalize collective purpose – and react to crises? As a simple example, in our COVID-19 period, consider how a restaurant's actions might reveal the degree to which it adopts the collective purpose. The restaurant might try to ignore or deny the collective purpose, running business as usual, and shun mask wearing or social distancing. It might comply with externally imposed mandates but otherwise carry out business as usual. It might go a step further and make some changes to its menu to reflect lower likely in-person customers and greater takeout orders. Or it might make major changes to its activities – for example, reconfiguring part of the restaurant into a produce store, transforming itself into a dark kitchen for takeout only, or dramatically changing its menu and pricing – perhaps donating services – to help families suffering from the economic consequences of COVID.

More generally, organizations can react to crises that induce collective purposes in four different manners:

- *Denial*, in which the organization carries out its activities as usual by not taking any particular measures to take account of the crisis or the collective purpose
- *Compliance*, in which the organization obeys externally imposed rules and regulations but does not go further to change its activities
- *Reactive adaptation*, in which the organization goes beyond compliance to make minimal changes to its activities but leaves its core activities intact
- *Transformational adaptation*, in which the organization internalizes the collective purpose and radically changes its activities.

Reactions to World War II at Five Leading American Business Schools

In a related paper on which this chapter is based (Tufano, 2020), I study in depth five of the leading US business schools and their reactions to World War II.[2] I look at American schools not because they were the earliest nor only business schools at the time but, rather, because the earlier continental European schools, largely under Nazi occupation, were often forced to make changes by their occupiers. Their American counterparts had more latitude and management authority to determine how vigorously to adopt the collective purpose of winning the war. The five that I studied – Wharton, Berkeley, Tuck, Chicago, and Harvard – were well established as of 1941, were clearly recognized as some of the leading schools of their time, and demonstrate a full range of responses.[3]

The schools' reactions ranged from simple compliance to reactive adaptation and, in one case, to transformational adaptation, but each story is rich, deserving of far more than a label. In the following sections, I briefly summarize the histories, and then I conclude with possible lessons for leaders of business schools today.

Compliance

In general, modern authorized histories of business schools spend little time discussing the war years, but even by these standards, some schools, such as Wharton, skip over the war years almost entirely. Stephen Sass's history of Wharton (Sass, 1982) suggests that the school endured rather than embraced the collective wartime purpose.

By way of background, during World War II, 50 million American men aged 18–45 were registered for the draft, and 10 million were called into military service (National WWII Museum, New Orleans, n. d.). At the time, business school faculties and students were primarily men, and all students and many faculty were of draft age. Drafts would thus decimate student and faculty numbers at all schools. For example,

---

[2] Other early American business schools include those at Northwestern University (School of Commerce founded in 1908, now Kellogg), Massachusetts Institute of Technology (MIT; originally Engineering Administration in 1914, now Sloan), Babson College (1919), Indiana University (School of Commerce and Finance in 1920, now Kelley), and Stanford Graduate School of Business (1925). The UK business school sector and many of the modern elite European business schools were postwar innovations – for example, INSEAD (1957), IESE (1958), London Business School (1964), Cambridge Judge Business School (1991), and Saïd Business School–Oxford University (1996).

[3] I also examined in less detail other schools (e.g., Columbia, New York University, MIT) whose wartime reactions are similar to the range discussed here.

at New York University (NYU), MBA enrollments fell from 1,196 in 1940–1941 to 1,001, 656, 707, and 1,013 in the 4 following years (Gitlow, 1995, p. 120).

Wharton would suffer a similar decline, as well as a hollowing out of its faculty who were drafted or volunteered. The official Wharton history, *The Pragmatic Imagination: A History of the Wharton School, 1881–1981*, written by Stephen A. Sass and published by the University of Pennsylvania Press in 1982, devotes only about 3 pages out of 342 to the war. The draft reduced student and faculty numbers:

Professors ... left the school's employ and found their way into a great variety of useful positions with the federal government. Wharton, in fact, all but adjourned for the duration of the conflict, and the number of its full time faculty, which had recently totalled 165, fell to 39 by 1944. (Sass, 1982, p. 226)

Those remaining, however, carried out business as usual: "The school continued to train large numbers of students in traditional business subjects, such as accounting, finance, and insurance, and professors and graduates in these areas also found themselves drafted into responsible positions during the war" (Sass, 1982, p. 228). The war seemed to be a pause, not an inflection point. In the immediate postwar period, the school picked up from before, as Sass summarizes: "But as the worlds of affairs and ideas rushed headlong into the future, the Wharton School *resumed its prewar routines*" (emphasis added; Sass, 1982, p. 233).

The scant mention of the war in Sass's (1982) history, and the description of "all but adjourning," teaching "traditional business subjects," and finally, "resuming its prewar activities," tells a consistent story about how Wharton endured the war and complied with the draft, rather than vigorously embracing the collective purpose of winning the war.

Reactive Adaptation: Doing Our Part, Innovating, and Advancing Peacetime Agendas

Although all schools complied with the draft, most went beyond this base level, joining the war effort more actively while still operating under business as usual, as much as possible. Tuck, Berkeley, and Chicago all reflect this approach, running reduced versions of their undergraduate, MBA, and in one case, PhD programs while taking into account that many of their students and faculty members would be called up or would volunteer. They shortened undergraduate programs to allow men to go to war earlier and made minor adjustments to their curricula to enhance teaching on operations and logistics. All did their part, as part of broader university programs, to train officers. Two created innovations specifically aimed at addressing wartime management shortages that would long outlast the war and used wartime to press forward long-planned changes to their peacetime programs.

For example, at Berkeley, the draft reduced the number of undergraduate commerce students (the core business degree) by about a third, to approximately 1,000. The broader University of California system adopted various changes, including pass-fail grades, some refinements in curriculum, and rule changes permitting students to complete a 4-year undergraduate program in 2 years and 8 months (Epstein, 2015, p. 149). Sandra Epstein – the chronicler of Berkeley's history – remarks on the modest changes in the curriculum at the university and the College of Commerce:

The general curriculum did not change, but some courses were added and others received stronger emphasis. For commerce studies, a minor adjustment was made in the area of operations management. What had been a minor area saw new courses added in response to the defense needs of producing essential materials and supplies. Several senior business students joined a Department of Mechanical Engineering course in time and motion study; likewise engineering students took technical courses like Production Management and Control in the College of Commerce. (Epstein, 2015, p. 149)

At Dartmouth University's Tuck School, similar changes took place, including providing training for military personnel. Founded in 1900, Tuck was the first *graduate* school of business in the United States, with a 3+2 model of 3 years of undergraduate education (if a Dartmouth College undergraduate) followed by 2 years of postgraduate business training – including non-Dartmouth College students.[4] The school and university took a joined-up approach when the war broke out. President Ernest Martin Hopkins laid out two goals for the college and its three professional schools: to maintain the liberal arts

---

[4] For a history of the early years of the school, see Broehl (1999).

curriculum for civilian students and to support the war effort (Rauner Special Collections Library, Dartmouth College, n.d.). In effect, two parallel sets of activities took place at Dartmouth – civilian and military. The civilian agenda was much changed from the prewar period:

The College and its three professional schools accelerated their curricula and shifted to three-term, year-round operation. Fraternities closed, Winter Carnival was cancelled, the *Daily Dartmouth* ceased publication and rationing was put in place. Civilian students were outnumbered three to one on campus. Run on military time, with reveille at 6 am and taps at 10 pm, Dartmouth operated like a naval base for the duration of the war. (Rauner Special Collections Library, Dartmouth College, n.d., para. 2)[5]

The majority of students on campus were part of military programs:

Adjusting to the consequent shortage of college-educated commissioned officers, the U.S. Navy developed a way to combine college education with military service: the Naval Indoctrination Training School and the V-12 Naval Training Program. Dartmouth became host to the largest of the Navy's V-12 units. (Rauner Special Collections Library, Dartmouth College, n.d., para. 2)

The V-12 program, launched in December 1942, was designed to train young commissioned officers for the US Navy and Marines (Herge, 1996). Over 130 colleges and universities participated in the program, which trained 125,000 young officers. The program had the added benefit of supplementing the finances of colleges and universities whose students were being drafted. Virtually every major university, including Dartmouth, Berkeley, Chicago – as well as the University of Pennsylvania and Harvard – participated in this program.

World War II was also consequential for the University of Chicago. Although traditional undergraduate, master's, and doctoral programs continued to be offered, after the attack on Pearl Harbor, the university took on the war effort, albeit with a characteristic Chicago approach:

The effects of total war were soon seen throughout the campus. The University agreed to host a variety of military training programs, and by 1942 all available dormitory space had been consigned to military programs.... However, the military training programs of 1942–44 were different from the [World War I] 1918 SATC [Student Army Training Corps] model, which [Chicago's President Robert] Hutchins and other

[5] For additional detail, see Seaton (2008).

university leaders despised. In June 1940 Hutchins had joined with six other midwestern university presidents to write a memorandum outlining the appropriate roles of the university in time of war. The presidents affirmed that the universities should do what they could do best – namely, provide substantive knowledge-based training programs – and not become substitute army encampments. (Boyer, 2015, pp. 301–302)

Perhaps the most far-reaching wartime initiative was the recruitment of refugee scholars from Europe, including Enrico Fermi and Hans Morgenthau, as well as the "Met Lab," which was a joint government–university project connected with the highly secretive atomic bomb project (Boyer, 2015, p. 305).

Adaptive Reactions: War-Specific Innovations

Going beyond participating in government consortia like the V-12 program, both Tuck and Chicago created innovative institution-specific programs to address the wartime needs for management, which have survived nearly eight decades later. Although it is impossible to know if these programs would have been created without the stimulus of the war, they provide examples of how reactive adaptation can have long-term benefits.

During the war, Tuck created the Tuck–Thayer program, combining forces with the Thayer School of Engineering at Dartmouth (Dartmouth Engineering, n.d.). This collaboration between business and engineering was a direct response to war needs to create leaders with backgrounds in both technology and management. The program survives today.

At Chicago, the wartime impetus to train factory managers led to America's first executive MBA (EMBA) program in 1943. This part-time program was explicitly seen as a way to address the wartime shortage of trained managers. Although these first EMBA students' profiles were quite different from those of "traditional" students, the content of their program and faculty were the same as for Chicago's full-time counterparts:

The 52 students comprising the world's first Executive MBA class met two nights per week in downtown Chicago. Many of the students came from iconic Chicago companies such as Marshall Field's, Commonwealth Edison, Illinois Bell Telephone, Walgreen Co., Chicago Tribune, and Spiegel. Some worked at local manufacturing companies that made gears, freight cars, conveyor belts and machinery. They were accountants, plant supervisors, engineers, production managers, purchasing agents and even one librarian. In the early years, students were typically in their 40s or early 50s, with decades of work experience but little formal business education. They attended classes taught by the same faculty as students in the Full-Time MBA Program, unusual for part-time programs of that era. (University of Chicago Booth School of Business, 2018, para. 6)

The EMBA program at Chicago remains an important part of the school's offerings, and the current website celebrates the program's wartime origins.

Adaptive Reactions: Advancing Peacetime Agendas during the War

While wars were fought in Europe, Asia, and Africa, leaders of US business schools and universities used wartime to advance more local conflicts – pressing for change within their organizations. We see this at Chicago, Tuck, and especially at Berkeley.

In the years prior to the war, University of Chicago president Robert M. Hutchins was engaged in a controversial effort to reform undergraduate education at Chicago. With the onset of the war, Hutchins pressed and succeeded in forcing this change:

Early in January 1942, in the aftermath of the American declarations of war on Japan and on Germany, Hutchins suddenly and with considerable drama proposed that the BA degree be transferred from the jurisdiction of the divisions to the College and that it be conferred upon completion of a four-year program in general education beginning with grade eleven, thus making it possible for Chicago to graduate eighteen- or nineteen-year-olds with BA degrees. (Boyer, 2015, p. 253)

This set of changes was accompanied by an adjustment in membership in the college faculty and disenfranchisement of a number of faculty members. The implication of this university-wide innovation was to "effectively eliminate the departments and specializations from the undergraduate curriculum," including the undergraduate business program, to delineate between the undergraduate Chicago experience and the "specialized learning offered and the divisions and the professional schools" (Boyer, 2015, pp. 254–255).

At Tuck, the war years were used to refine the peacetime framing of the school. In 1942, the school changed its name from the Amos Tuck

School of Administration and Finance to the Amos Tuck School of *Business Administration* (Tuck School of Business, n.d.).

Berkeley provides the most dramatic example of reconfiguring peacetime organization during wartime. In the middle of the war, the priorities of its new dean were to split its economics and business administration activities, set up the latter as a "school" rather than a "college," establish the master of business administration graduate degree, and set up joint curricula with engineering and other departments (Epstein, 2015, p. 152). Indeed, in Sandra Epstein's history of the school, the most important activity during the war, receiving far more attention in the volume than war-related activities, was the creation of the School of Business Administration in 1943 and awarding of the MBA degree in 1944.

The issues seem contemporary: wanting greater autonomy within the university, finding a positioning ("business" versus "commerce") that had a more modern ring to it, gaining budget and space for the new school, having control over faculty hiring, and "winning long-sought independence from the Economics Department." The war provided a backdrop for the move:

Having gained departmental status, the groundwork was now laid for conversion of the College to a School, and Dean [Ewald T.] Grether urged that the action be taken quickly. Drawing upon historical precedent, he feared that if the new organizational plan was not adopted, it might again be lost among postwar enrollment pressures, precisely what had occurred after World War I. He also pointed out that failures to adopt those 1915 and 1921 proposals to establish a "school" of business had left the University a quarter of a century behind the times. . . . The timing was propitious since the wartime campus enrollment was smaller. (Epstein, 2015, 158–159)

The leadership at Berkeley used the wartime crisis to forge meaningful institutional change within the university. As the war raged in Europe, North Africa, and Asia, its battles were closer to home. It is as if the war was a diversion that permitted long-standing peacetime institutional changes to move forward.

Berkeley, Tuck, and Chicago each engaged deeply in the war effort through participating in consortia to train military personnel. Tuck and Chicago went further, creating new institution-specific programs to meet the war need that were built upon their existing approaches. All three internalized the collective purpose of winning the war. But in each case, they held on to their peacetime programming, with some modifications. And each used the conditions of wartime – reduced enrollments, distracted colleagues, and leadership transitions – to advance long-sought peacetime agendas. They reacted to the war and internalized it to an extent, but they never lost sight of their peacetime purposes.

Transformational Adaptation

In the book-length histories of Wharton, Tuck, Berkeley, and Chicago, World War II plays a modest role, only receiving a few pages of discussion in each. In contrast, Jeffrey Cruikshank's (1987) history of the Harvard Business School (HBS), *A Delicate Experiment*, devotes 61 of its 285 pages to discussing World War II.

Like the other schools, HBS would experience a substantial reduction in students and faculty due to the draft. Like other schools, HBS would participate in consortium military training. Like Chicago and Tuck, it would create unique programming to address the needs of managers left behind – in effect creating modern non–degree-bearing executive education and a shorter-lived program bringing together unions and management. Like at Chicago and Berkeley, strong educational leaders pushed for institutional change.

But HBS took one quite large step beyond its peers: the faculty voted in December 1942 to stop offering its flagship MBA program and all other peacetime programs. Perhaps most radically, in 1945, as the war was winding down but not yet ended, the faculty voted unanimously not to reinstate any of the prior peacetime programs in what was called the "clean slate resolution" (Cruikshank, 1987, p. 270). In addition, while HBS celebrated faculty who left the school to work for the government as Wharton did, it also brought war-related research onto campus, as Chicago had done. In effect, during the war, HBS stopped being a business school in a traditional sense and focused entirely on the business of winning a war abroad and training those left to run factories at home.

To be clear, HBS faced the same financial and operating pressure as the other schools. Wallace Donham – who served as the dean of HBS from 1919 to 1942 – sought not to repeat the school's experience in World War I, when it lost too many men from the MBA program, lost faculty to the draft, and ran a large financial deficit. While "doing its bit," the school would maintain business as usual as much as possible. Robert McNamara, a young assistant professor at HBS at the start of World War II, described the dean's concerns:

The dean at Harvard was far-seeing, since he recognized that the market for Harvard Business School students was drying up because of the war, the draft, and the desire of individuals of that age to volunteer. Therefore, there would be fewer individuals applying to the Harvard Graduate School of Business. (Watson and Wolk, 2003, p. 6)

In the first year of the war, HBS's activities were similar to those of Tuck, Berkeley, or Chicago. In the months before America entered the war, HBS took tentative steps to prepare. A Reserve Officers' Training Course (ROTC) was established at HBS in April 1941; this did not alter the MBA training but simply added an extra course in defense mobilization.

HBS fairly quickly sought out unique opportunities to contribute to the war effort. The Naval Supply Corps School had been in existence since 1905, in two locations: Philadelphia and Washington, DC. In June 1941, these two merged, and the new Naval Supply Corps School was physically co-located on Soldiers Field Road, sharing the HBS campus alongside the traditional MBA program, "work[ing] more in proximity with each other than together" (Cruikshank, 1987, p. 226). "'We do not teach these officers,' [HBS] Dean [Donald] David noted, 'but we do house and feed them, and we feel fortunate in having this group of outstanding officers living and associating with us here'" (Cruikshank, 1987, p. 226).

At first, HBS tried to maintain its status quo programs, including its flagship MBA. For example, in February 1942, HBS admitted the Navy Supply Corps Midshipman Officer School but merely bolted additional curriculum onto the existing first year of the MBA in a form of curricular co-location.

Moving first from physical to curricular co-location, HBS next made the larger leap to develop customized programs for the military. As McNamara noted, school leadership was acutely aware of the likely impacts of the draft, and as a result, the dean "sent two professors to Washington in an attempt to gain some government contracts for Harvard" (Watson and Wolk, 2003, p. 6). McNamara goes on to describe the creation of the Army Air Force Statistical School (Stat School), a customized program built by HBS faculty to train officers of the Statistical Control Office of the Army Air Forces with instructors drawn from the core HBS faculty.

Although financial pressures might have initially motivated HBS's rapid expansion into wartime efforts, it ultimately chose to fully devote itself to the war, internalizing the collective purpose of winning the war. The decisive rejection of business as usual transpired a year after Pearl Harbor, in December 1942, when the faculty voted to discontinue *all* non-wartime programs – to shut its MBA program, even while Berkeley was working to create one. By 1943, all activities at HBS were devoted to winning the war, training the officers who would lead overseas and the civilians who would lead the factories at home, as well as conducting war-related research.

If this were merely a financial expedient, then we might have expected other parts of the school to be untouched, for example, its general approach to teaching, academic norms, or research activities. Yet all of these seemed to be altered, if only temporarily, during the war. The Stat School became a state-of-the-art program even though its content was a substantial deviation from the school's prewar programs. Although the school was known for its devotion to written case studies, in the war, it adopted a wider variety of teaching approaches, including what we would today call "live cases."

In the war, the school embraced the controversial idea that older executives could be taught. HBS's modern prowess in executive education was a wartime innovation. The prevailing sentiment at HBS and other business schools before the war was that older executives were not clever enough to learn or were too rigid or set in their ways to learn. But someone needed to run the factories. HBS reluctantly embraced this idea and, at first, did not know how to do it. The result, after some missteps, was a formula that survives today and defines executive education: focusing on executives at mid- and senior levels, both nominated by their employers and self-sponsored. What seems obvious today was deeply resisted in its time. One director of an airplane division described potential students as "dummkopfs" (Cruikshank, 1987, p. 236). The program was initially derided on campus as the "retread" program but eventually was acknowledged as critical. According to Cruikshank, "the School's novel concept of executive retraining seemed to be proving itself. Perhaps most important, it was clear that men and women twenty or thirty years out of school could still learn – a dubious assertion, to many, before the retread program" (Cruikshank, 1987, p. 257). This notion of training mid- and senior-level executives defines today's huge executive education activities of major schools. Both Chicago and Harvard saw this need but delivered it in different ways. Chicago stayed close to its academic roots, using the same curriculum as the full-time MBA and creating the executive MBA as a degree-bearing program. Harvard innovated with a non-degree format, now its AMP program, which led the way for the broader executive education market.

Even the research activities of the school were altered during the war, directed to projects that would have a material impact on the winning of the war. There was a pointed concern for the utility of the work, such as the Air Research Program, carried out in conjunction with the aviation industry. In a spirit that characterizes the contemporary impact agenda, the program was evaluated in clear terms: "No matter how thorough a research study may be, it will be of little use if there is no interest in the subject on the part of the public or industry" (Cruikshank, 1987, p. 255). Research that crossed boundaries was also embraced, such as the HBS Fatigue Laboratory, done in collaboration with the Climatic Research Laboratory, combining science, physiology, and behavioral research to determine how airmen would fare in extreme weather conditions. Whereas Wharton's professors left the school to join the government to do applied research during the war, Harvard's model was to bring very applied research inside the school. In both cases, professors made valuable contributions, with the difference perhaps reflecting a judgment of *where* it was appropriate to conduct highly "useful" research.

All of these changes could be interpreted as putting the war purpose ahead of tradition. They were the product of what one junior professor at the time, Dan T. Smith, called "the temporary repression of traditional academic perfectionism" (Cruikshank, 1987, p. 243). Whereas peacetime has the luxury of slow, tested, and careful change, wartime does not. This partial "temporary repression of perfectionism" laid the grounds for modern business education, even though not all of these innovations persisted in the 75 years of subsequent peacetime.

At the conclusion of the war, Wharton, as described by Sass (1982), "resumed its prewar routines" (p. 233). Harvard went in the opposite direction. In February 1945 – well before the end of hostilities – in a 4-hour faculty meeting, the faculty unanimously passed the "Clean Sweep Resolution," which rescinded all previous authorizations of courses (Cruikshank, 1987, p. 270). The faculty members voted that they would not mechanically return to their prewar ways but would determine the future from that day forward. It is nearly impossible to imagine this vote in peacetime. The postwar curriculum drew deeply from the wartime experience.

The mantra of winning the war was replaced with winning the peace. When the war was won, the cessation of wartime production and the large amount of surplus war material meant that the economy could easily go into a tailspin just as the troops returned home looking for jobs, as had happened in the wake of World War I. The clear imperative was to create a stable and growing economy. Dean Donald David acknowledged this in 1945: "Surely the School's wartime record would soon seem incidental and would be quickly forgotten if our efforts on behalf of the men who have won this were any less determined than our efforts in the officer-training program" (Cruikshank, 1987, p. 275).

The Harvard example is one of transformational adaptation. By adopting the collective purpose, first of winning the war and then winning the peace, it fundamentally transformed itself. While others were setting up MBA programs, it shuttered its program. While others maintained their degree formats, Harvard experimented with non-degree courses. While others had their sights on the resumption of the past, Harvard's faculty unanimously voted to abandon it.

Macro-Crises, Collective Purpose, and Business Schools

Although business school campuses of the 1940s and today might project a sense of calm and stability, they – and higher education institutions more generally – are not immune from the crises that plague our economies and societies. In the 1940s, deans and their colleagues were faced with a faraway war and an unavoidable collective purpose. We, too, are subject to wars, pandemics, economic depressions, and climate crises – as well as the implications of national, cultural, and racial divides. When a collective response or purpose emerges in our communities, we choose how we react. In many ways, universities – or more accurately, university students – have been at the forefront of the cultural reactions to macro-crises like wars, as we saw in the US protests against the war in Vietnam in the 1960s or the student protests in Germany against the Nazis in the 1940s, such as the nonviolent White Rose movement (Ray, n.d.).

Although history will, in time, judge how we dealt with COVID-19, eight decades of hindsight allows us to draw a few conclusions – or perhaps hypotheses – from the experiences of our predecessors in World War II and how they internalized the collective purpose of winning a global war.

First, although all schools confronted the war and social imperative, they reacted in different ways. All complied with the requirements of the draft, but organizational reactions ranged from compliance to reactive adaptation to transformational adaptation. All of the schools were strong before the war and continue to this day, so clearly, there was no one "right" answer.

Second, although it is difficult to offer a satisfying explanation of why different schools behaved in different ways, the histories suggest a key role played by the specific leaders of the different institutions. Academia cherishes academic freedom and integrity and tends to embrace concepts of academic democracy. Institutionally, academic democracy is enshrined in bodies such as academic senates or advanced in an extreme way, such as in Oxford's "Congregation" – a 5,500-member "sovereign body" that has the ultimate authority to decide on virtually any matter in the university if 20 members of the university advance the proposal and it receives a majority vote (University of Oxford, Governance and Planning, n.d.). The wartime experiences of the different schools, as recounted in their histories, often deviate from the ideal of academic democracy and involve strong leaders, such as Chicago's President Hutchins, Berkeley's Dean Grether, or Harvard's Deans Donham and David.

As an example, Dean Donham at Harvard piloted the school as it went into the war during his last year as dean after serving for more than two decades of leadership. In May 1942, he was "six weeks from retirement. ... [He] apologized for having taken a series of unilateral actions without adequate faculty consultation, but said that the fluid circumstances necessitated this approach" (Cruikshank, 1987, p. 223). In one amusing exchange, Donham informed a faculty member, "You are volunteering for the job [to work with the government]" (Cruikshank, 1987, p. 226).

The highly deliberative, consultative process of peacetime was replaced with a temporary new model: more rapid, centralized, strategic decision making, granting others closer to the battlefront (classroom) the flexibility to make tactical decisions.

Third, why these leaders made the decisions they did is less clear. Was it national fervor in support of the war or more practical consideration? Secondary research cannot uncover the motivations of these leaders, but there are clues that the decisions were motivated by a range of considerations. Chicago's President Hutchins strongly opposed the war, at least until it started, and so was not a natural person to advance a wartime agenda. Donham's initial concerns were clearly to protect the finances of the school, as indicated in Robert McNamara's reflections. There is a strong parallel in how businesses or business schools might find themselves engaging with climate measures: some might frame this as a moral imperative; others might simply see it pragmatically as good business.

Perhaps most importantly, the five examples present two quite competing yet consistent implications of the power of purpose to maintain or transform an organization.

The first is *individual purpose as anchor*. The histories of Wharton, Berkeley, Chicago, and Tuck display the role of purpose as anchor. Each school held fast to its prewar institutional purposes. While accepting the draft and joining government programs, they never wavered in delivering traditional business programs to a small number of young business students. They kept operating their MBA programs, even with reduced numbers. They kept the content of their curricula largely unchanged. When they innovated, they built directly onto existing programs (Tuck–Thayer), or they maintained the same degree standards as before (Chicago's EMBA). They advanced prewar academic initiatives and continued to fight their domestic university battles, most vividly at Berkeley, while the war raged elsewhere. Their prewar individual purposes anchored them throughout the war.

The second is *collective purpose as liberator*. After a tentative start, Harvard all but abandoned its prewar individual purpose and embraced the collective wartime effort. Innovation flourished in nearly every aspect of the school. For a while, it welcomed new types of students (young and old, business and unions, men and women, those of all races). It created new programs, such as the retread initiative, that bore no resemblance to its prewar MBA. It emphasized new subjects, such as statistics, that had not been at the heart of its curricula and briefly moved away from its case-method approach. It brought onto the campus new research approaches. Ultimately, the faculty voted not to slavishly re-create the prewar past by rescinding all prewar course authorizations. By embracing the demands of the war and accepting "temporary repression of academic perfectionism," the stage was set for the postwar HBS.

I believe these lessons are not only relevant but critical for leaders of business schools and other organizations today. We can never waver from our traditional goals of delivering excellent teaching and research – nor can we abandon academic freedom. Nevertheless, our world faces threats – and opportunities – that arise from pandemics, a climate emergency, and gaping inequality that have given rise to dangerous national, social, and global fissures. As business schools, we can hold fast to our individual purposes, downplay these issues, and reluctantly begin a few initiatives while we carry on largely with business as usual. Or we can use the emerging collective purposes in society – around public health or climate issues – as invitations to transform ourselves.

In our discussions of our purpose at Oxford Saïd, one of my very perceptive colleagues asked a disarming question: What's the purpose of purpose? Although we will always exist to deliver excellent research and teaching – helping advance the careers of students, improving the performance of organizations, and protecting the academic freedom of our scholars – to what end? Would a goal of advancing economic, social, and climate justice be constraining or liberating?

A collective or higher purpose doesn't liberate an organization from the laws of gravity or its financial equivalents. A collective or higher purpose doesn't allow us to deliver poor-quality education or research or fail to train our students for the next steps in their lives. Collective purpose does not and must not silence the important role of critical inquiry in a university. But in our tradition-bound, sometimes inertial institutions, adopting a collective or higher purpose may enable us to unleash innovation that might otherwise be inconceivable and reinvent our institutions as we put ourselves at the greater service of the world.

References

Boyer, J. W. (2015). *The University of Chicago: A history.* University of Chicago Press.

Broehl, W. G. (1999). *Tuck and Tucker: The origin of the graduate business school.* University Press of New England.

Cruikshank, J. L. (1987). *A delicate experiment: The Harvard Business School, 1908–1945.* Harvard Business School Press.

Dartmouth Engineering. (n.d.). *History of Dartmouth engineering.* https://engineering.dartmouth.edu/about/history.

Epstein, S. (2015). *Business at Berkeley: A history of the Haas School of Business.* Berkeley Public Policy Press.

Gitlow, A. L. (1995). *NYU's Stern School of Business: A centennial retrospective.* NYU Press.

Herge, H. C. (1996). *Navy V-12.* Turner Publishing Company.

National WWII Museum, New Orleans. (n.d.). *Research starters: The draft and World War II.* www.nationalww2museum.org/students-teachers/student-resources/research-starters/draft-and-wwii.

Rauner Special Collections Library, Dartmouth College (n.d.). *Dartmouth during World War Two.* www.dartmouth.edu/library/rauner/archives/oral_history/worldwar2/history.html.

Ray, M. (n.d.). White rose. *Encyclopædia Britannica.* www.britannica.com/topic/White-Rose.

Sass, S. A. (1982). *The pragmatic imagination: A history of the Wharton School, 1881–1981.* University of Pennsylvania Press.

Seaton, J. (2008, winter). Engineered for service. *Dartmouth Engineer Magazine, 16–19.* https://drive.google.com/file/d/1wuTTg9QSJ4jJYx4wsRxPDCSTwJ94htVP/view.

Tuck School of Business. (n.d.). *History.* www.tuck.dartmouth.edu/about/facts-and-figures/history.

Tufano, P. (2020). Training leaders to win wars and forge peace: Lessons from history. *Business History Review,* 94(4), 807–833.

University of Chicago Booth School of Business. (2018, February 16). *How the world's first executive MBA program changed business education* [Press release]. https://news.chicagobooth.edu/newsroom/how-worlds-first-executive-mba-program-changed-business-education.

University of Oxford, Governance and Planning. (n.d.). *Congregation.* https://governance.admin.ox.ac.uk/congregation.

Watson, G. M., and Wolk, H. S. (2003). "Whiz kid": Robert S. McNamara's World War II service. *Air Power History,* 50(4), 4–15. https://www.jstor.org/stable/26274484

3 | *From Techne to Paideia: Upgrading Business Education*

SANTIAGO IÑIGUEZ

Introduction

The first business schools, which appeared in the nineteenth century in Europe and then began to proliferate as the Industrial Revolution spread to the United States – notably in the early years of the last century – were set up to train the cohorts of managers needed to fill executive positions at companies (Kaplan, 2014). Their guiding principles can be traced to the Greek philosophical concept of *techne*, a term referring to technical education in classical Athens (Parry, 2020).

The study of management soon developed into an academic discipline within the social sciences, where it has largely been confined to this day (Lamont and Molnár, 2002). But as the principles of management are now increasingly applied to noncommercial activities, it has become clear that business schools need to broaden their teaching to include not just the systems that allow for the efficient running of a company but also to developing leaders at different organizations who can tackle the challenges of an increasingly uncertain and volatile postpandemic world (Christakis, 2020; Galloway, 2020).

If it is to nurture the multitalented leaders we increasingly need in response to these challenges, business education now needs overhauling, and its horizons need broadening. I believe the best way to do this is by loosening the restraints of techne and providing tomorrow's managers with a solid grounding in *paideia*, another Greek philosophical concept that refers to the training of the physical and mental faculties with the goal of producing a broad, enlightened, and mature outlook that is harmoniously combined with cultural development. In other words, the humanities.[1] That said, for this to happen, business schools will have to rethink the way they teach and their research methodology, faculty profile, and learning analytics.

---

[1] Jaeger's (1971) book is a reference on this matter; see also Fotopoulos (2005).

The First Business Schools

As the Industrial Revolution spread throughout Europe and the United States in the late nineteenth century, business schools responded to the needs of large corporations, notably the railroad industry, by teaching a dry combination of economic theory, management techniques, and industrial relations (Wolmar, 2012).

Harvard Business School, which was founded in 1908, sought from the get-go to meet the needs of industry. For example, alumnus George Leighton argued that railroad management ought to be recognized as a science, which meant the men keeping the country's trains running on time required a range of skills: "Management is one of the most versatile of all professions" (Cruikshank, 1987, p. 8). Similarly, Charles Eliot, the president of Harvard University between 1869 and 1909, wrote: "What can I do with my boy? I want to give him a practical education that will prepare him better than I was prepared to follow my business or any other active callings" (Cruikshank, 1987, p. 20). In the end, his son studied landscape architecture in Europe.

Wharton Business School, the first business school in the United States,[2] was set up in 1881. Chief among Joseph Wharton's goals was "to teach economic protection of U.S. global interests," which had already made him a powerful lobbyist for protective tariffs in Washington.[3]

In contrast, the vocational character of France's *commerce écoles* reflects their creation by the country's municipal chambers of commerce, to which they belonged and from which they received funding, some of them still today. Initially, the *écoles de commerce* were not recognized by universities, and it was only with the formalization of studies, and US influence, that their courses were given degree or postgraduate standing (Blanchard, 2009).

In 1959, a major change to business schools and management education took place when a report by the Carnegie and Ford foundations criticized what they saw as the disproportionate emphasis on technical and practical teaching at business schools – reflecting their

---

[2] It is commonly accepted that the first business school was Wharton (1881), although the first MBA program was launched by Tuck Business School at the University of Dartmouth (1900), with the antecedents of the mentioned *écoles de commerce* (Riccoboni, 2010).

[3] See Iñiguez de Onzoño (2011, p. 8).

vocational origins – and recommended a more scientific approach (Iñiguez de Onzoño, 2011, p. 126). In response, business schools at universities such as Carnegie Mellon, Harvard, the Massachusetts Institute of Technology (MIT), and Chicago began to highlight academic excellence, generating research on a par with their other social sciences schools. Since then, we have seen a huge growth in conferences and specialist journals looking at specific aspects of business education, a trend replicated in Europe and around the world (Podsakoff et al., 2005).

The result is a self-perpetuating academic marketplace. As Wharton's P. H. Shoemaker (2008, p. 120) points out: "The field has beefed up its academic standing by promoting faculty with deep scientific roles." That said, he also notes, somewhat critically: "Over time, however, these scholars often took business research in directions no longer comprehensible or relevant to business students and managers" (Shoemaker, 2008, p. 120).

In recent years, however, the nature and the impact of research developed at business schools have been subjected to further scrutiny. Some years ago, the European Foundation for Management Development (EFMD) invited me to chair a commission to define the concept of "research" for the EFMD Quality Improvement System (EQUIS) accreditation standards board,[4] so as to develop criteria to help auditors establish when a school applying for accreditation had developed enough research, in terms of both quantity as well as quality. The first challenge was to tackle business schools' myriad definitions of research based on what they saw as their mission.

We did this by not defining research as simply the output of contributions in academic journals, instead taking a well-known concept from business: research, development, and innovation (RDI), which would include knowledge output – from articles in academic journals to brown books on industries, including teaching materials (case studies, technical notes), books, and articles in professional journals. In effect, working on a case-by-case basis and requiring a customized analysis of the institution in question, its management processes, and its competitive standing. As a result, RDI requirements for the

---

[4] EQUIS has consolidated its status as a leading accreditation system for institution-based business schools, emphasizing connections with the corporate world, international orientation, and academic aspects such as research development and faculty (EFMD Global, n.d.).

accreditation of institutions vary: an executive education center, for example, is required to develop practice-oriented materials, whereas a university-based business school offering PhD programs would produce conventional academic research.

The RDI approach is an up-to-date tool to assess the academic contribution of an accredited school. I wonder, however, whether the scheme has produced its intended objectives.[5] In any case, the framework applied to most management disciplines has been analogous to that common to other social sciences.

The Tension between the Humanities and STEM

Based on a belief that our world is now dominated by digital technology, over the course of the last few decades, a growing number of governments and universities have prioritized science, technology, engineering, and math (STEM) courses, assigning a secondary role to the humanities, not that this hasn't been criticized by many leading academics.[6] Martha Nussbaum, for example, has convincingly argued that the absence of the humanities from curricula has a negative impact on the nurturing of civic virtues and on the development of both creative imagination and critical thinking (Nussbaum, 2010). In line with classical thinking from Aristotle to Cicero, Nussbaum rightly believes that developing global citizens and strengthening our democracies requires a key role for the humanities.[7]

The importance of the humanities in forming the next generation of business leaders and entrepreneurs can be illustrated by comparing the approaches of US and European universities. In continental Europe, they are largely specialized and are still based on the ideas of Wilhelm Von Humboldt: undergraduates attend programs that will prepare them for a specific profession. Thus, mining engineers study subjects

---

[5] Despite new ways of assessing research in terms of its impact in the business community, the inertia at business schools, accreditation agencies, and academic institutions impedes a real transformation. This was evidenced by Bennis and O'Toole (2005): "The system creates pressure on scholars to publish articles on narrow subjects chiefly of interest to other academics, not practitioners" (p. 3).

[6] See, for example, Wexler (2019) or US Department of Education (n.d.).

[7] See Chapter 8 of Iñiguez de Onzoño (2020); see also Nussbaum (2010), as well as Nussbaum (1997), particularly the epilogue, "The 'New' Liberal Education."

like geology from the first day of university and are not "distracted" by other areas (Sorkin, 1983).

At the same time, this narrow specialization is reflected in the structure of university departments, which encourage focused research, the upside of which is a huge leap in scientific knowledge over the last century, matched by exponential growth in academic publications. This approach has created professionals with very specific skills that can be adapted and updated to meet the demands of companies and institutions.[8]

In contrast, many US universities and colleges offer a generalist degree program, typically focused on the humanities and the liberal arts, with specialization only happening at the master's or equivalent level. The evidence shows that one of the many benefits of a business education rooted in the humanities is a honing of students' ability to innovate and their capacity for entrepreneurship. This underpins the arguments of venture capitalist and author Scott Hartley (2017), who questions the division of university programs into the arts and the sciences. At Hartley's alma mater, Stanford University, *fuzzies* is the term used to describe students of the social sciences and humanities; *techies* are those enrolled in engineering and hard sciences. In his 2017 book *The Fuzzy and the Techie*, Hartley points out that despite universities' efforts to keep the two disciplines separate, plenty of technology entrepreneurs have a background in the humanities (Hartley, 2017, pp. 5–6).

The division between the social sciences and the humanities reflects a long-standing acceptance that we must choose one or the other. This approach is instilled in students from an early age and eventually decides students' careers, making it very difficult to move into other professions or areas should they change their minds. I would argue that the time has come to provide young people with a grounding in the natural sciences and the humanities, allowing them to develop the soft social skills that create a more rounded personality.

Among the many people Hartley names in support of this approach are Stewart Butterfield, founder of communications platform Slack, who studied philosophy at the University of Victoria and the University of Cambridge; LinkedIn founder Reid Hoffman, who

---

[8] Specialization deepens the reach of research but may generate the so-called "silo syndrome" among university departments, enhancing isolation. See Tett (2015).

completed a master's in philosophy at the University of Oxford; Peter Thiel, cofounder of PayPal, who studied philosophy and law; Ben Silbermann, founder of Pinterest, who studied political science at Yale; Airbnb founders Joe Gebbia and Brian Chesky, who graduated in fine arts at the Rhode Island School of Design; Steve Loughlin, founder of RelateIQ, who studied public policy; Parker Harris, cofounder of Salesforce, who studied English literature at Middlebury College; Carly Fiorina, former CEO of Hewlett-Packard, who majored in medieval history and philosophy; YouTube CEO Susan Wojcicki, who studied history and literature at Harvard; and Mark Zuckerberg, founder of Facebook, who studied liberal arts at the Phillips Exeter Academy before entering Harvard (Hartley, 2017, p. 5). And last but not least, there's Steve Jobs, who attended the liberal arts institution Reed College; Jobs said, "technology alone is not enough – it's technology married with liberal arts, married with the humanities, that yields us the results that make our heart sing" (Hartley, 2017, p. 7).

There is also evidence that soft social skills help business teams perform more efficiently, as Harvard economist David Deming's research shows. "The fastest-growing cognitive occupations – managers, teachers, nurses and therapists, physicians, lawyers, even economists – all require significant interpersonal interaction" (Hartley, 2017, p. 205). Most of us know from personal experience that many of the most important things we learn are only useful in the long term and guide the formation of our personality, our worldview, our beliefs and principles, and the mental structure that allows us to order and associate the rest of the knowledge we acquire throughout life.

What's more, the value of the humanities is precisely because they are not a technical or applied body of work; they don't teach us how to use machines or apply systems. As well as helping us to develop more abstract capacities, the humanities underpin democratic societies.

A decade ago, during his second, failed, election campaign, Nicolas Sarkozy made the headlines when he asserted that only "a sadist or an imbecile" would have put the seventeenth-century novel *The Princess of Cleves* on the syllabus used to test candidates in a public service entrance exam (Iñiguez de Onzoño, 2017, chap. 9.1). I disagree; after all, why shouldn't officials have to answer questions similar to those asked of nonnationals who wish to acquire French nationality?

I would argue that knowing how to read literature hones skills that are just as useful for civil servants as understanding procedures that will soon be carried out by machines or artificial intelligence (AI). What's more, politicians should always encourage better educational standards rather than making populist appeals to ignorance (Iñiguez de Onzoño and Ichijo, 2018, chap. 1).[9]

"Physics Envy": The Ascription of Management to the Social Sciences

"Institutions are social structures that have attained a high degree of resilience," writes US sociologist William Richard Scott (1995, p. 33), one of the founders of institutional theory, the basis for many academics' research on business phenomena. "[They] are composed of cultural-cognitive, normative, and regulative elements that, together with associated activities and resources, provide stability and meaning to social life. Institutions are transmitted by various types of carriers, including symbolic systems, relational systems, routines, and artifacts. Institutions operate at different levels of jurisdiction, from the world system to localized interpersonal relationships. Institutions by definition connote stability but are subject to change processes, both incremental and discontinuous" (Scott, 1995, p. 33).

The alignment with social sciences methodology in many business schools' research led management guru Sumantra Ghoshal (2005) to note: "Our theories and ideas have done much to strengthen the management practices that we are all now so loudly condemning" (p. 75). He argues that the social sciences have an inferiority complex, what he calls "physics envy," because their assumptions, models, and conclusions are not governed by causal paradigms. Instead, the social sciences' prevailing model is functional, an attempt to explain how individuals behave. What's more, as he points out, there's a reductionist aspect to fitting our behavior to functional paradigms. "[No scientific theory] ... explains the phenomenon of the organized complexity ... [of companies], possibly because companies are not empirically observable natural phenomena like volcanoes or animals ... [and don't] follow any predeterminable pattern" (Ghoshal, 2005, p. 79). The risk of reducing the study of management to the level of scientism has been to downgrade humans to little more

---

[9] See also Prato and Wolton (2018), who provide evidence that the rise of populism may result in political disenchantment, rather than the other way around.

than *homo economicus*, whereby human behavior is simply about meeting basic needs.

Meanwhile, back in the 1970s, the Chicago School's liberalism argued that companies exist solely to maximize shareholders' return on investment.[10] This has led to companies being shaped by institutional theory, with corporate governance based on independent board members, separation of the CEO and the chair's functions, and the provisioning of directors with stock options so as to align their interests with those of shareholders in order to avoid agency theory (Cuevas-Rodríguez et al., 2012). Ghoshal argues that this leads to an amoral theory of business that can encourage questionable behavior. "Unlike theories in the physical sciences, theories in the social sciences tend to be self-fulfilling" (Ghoshal, 2005, p. 77).

Citing Enron and Tyco, Ghoshal (2005) fears a vicious circle in which theory and practice feed off each other. He reminds us to remember that there is always an ideology behind every management theory: "Social scientists carry an even greater social and moral responsibility than those who work in the physical sciences because, if they hide ideology within the pretense of science, they can cause much more harm" (Ghoshal, 2005, p. 87). The solution, says Ghoshal, is better social excellence objectives that reflect the interests of all stakeholders.

Educating Committed Leaders: Bringing Management into the Humanities

I have long advocated that the study of management, or at least a good part of it, should align with the humanities. Experience has taught me that the reasoning behind strategic management has little to do with science: the "golden rules" of management are not written in stone. Although it's true that senior management's decision making is empirical, the underlying assumptions are nevertheless open to question.

After all, decision making in business is not like forecasting the weather: it's a constantly evolving environment, and over the years, we have seen countless times how the appearance of a disruptive

---

[10] A notable representative of the Chicago School is Milton Friedman, whose dictum, "There is one and only one social responsibility of business – to increase its profits," was once taught to managers by business schools everywhere but is now questioned or expanded to include ethical principles. See Friedman (1970).

company like Airbnb can force long-established rivals to change their business models.[11]

Admittedly, many MBA programs now illustrate the complex nature of strategic reasoning through simulations that can outline a wide range of future scenarios based on evaluating alternatives and outcomes (Larréché, 1987; Seaton and Boyd, 2008). Algorithms can simplify the relevant data and then indicate the best likely decision. Which is all well and good, but to be honest, if I were about to make a major investment, I'd choose Warren Buffett over an algorithm any day of the week.[12] Strategic reasoning can be aided by sophisticated algorithms, but there is also an intuitive dimension to choosing one variable over another, of thinking disruptively.[13]

Academics such as Henry Mintzberg have argued convincingly that good management is more an art than a science and that we should temper our belief that it can be taught conventionally and accept that it is best acquired through close and sustained contact with other experienced managers (Mintzberg, 2004).

Veteran campaigners who have long argued that the humanities should play a bigger role in management education have been encouraged in recent years by the growing number of philosophers now focusing their attention on business, thus providing a much-needed complementary perspective. Traditionally, economic thinkers at universities have often been associated with left-leaning political options – and thus not overly welcomed by many companies and business leaders (Tierney, 2011). It's also true to say that philosophers who

---

[11] The literature on disruption in the education sector is abundant, for all: Christensen and Eyring (2011).

[12] Warren Buffett, American investor and philanthropist, is the chairman and CEO of Berkshire Hathaway. His opinions on where to invest and economic forecasts are often published in leading media.

[13] Ed Finn, who has explored the moral dilemmas raised by the use of AI, explains: "The word algorithm frequently encompasses a range of computational processes including close surveillance of user behaviors, 'big data' aggregation of the resulting information, analytics engines that combine multiple forms of statistical calculation to parse that data, and finally a set of human-facing actions, recommendations, and interfaces that generally reflect only a small part of the cultural processing going on behind the scenes" (Finn, 2017, Kindle ed., loc. 359).

In fact, as a number of writers have shown, the configuration of algorithms is not a morally or culturally neutral issue; see Smith and Elliott (2019, Kindle ed., loc. 20).

have studied organizations have usually explored the roles of the state and government as decision makers in society rather than looking at the private sector, despite its growing influence.

That said, most business schools now include ethics in their programs, along with new disciplines such as management or leadership philosophy, driven in part by the appearance of academic journals and professional publications focusing on these issues. At the same time, growing numbers of universities are making connections between philosophy and the business world.

In conclusion, I would recommend that those who are skeptical about the role of the humanities in business education should read Nussbaum (1997, 2010). If we are to nurture managers and entrepreneurs with a global outlook and whose decisions are based on cutting-edge knowledge, who understand the impact of their decisions not just on the business environment but society and the environment, then they must be cultivated and given a solid grounding in the history, art, literature, and culture of different societies: the minimum requirement if they are to lead diverse teams. As CNN's Fareed Zakaria wrote in his 2015 book *In Defense of a Liberal Education*: "Creativity, problem solving, decision making, persuasive arguing and management" are the skills the liberal arts teach us (as cited in Hartley, 2017, p. 14).

The Humanization of Management: Reflections from Thought Leaders

The great Peter Drucker once explained that he owed his impetus to modernize management theory – central to which was the importance of the individual – to John Maynard Keynes. One day in 1934, he was attending a class given by the father of modern macroeconomics at Cambridge University: "I suddenly realized that Keynes and all the brilliant economics students in the room were interested in the behavior of commodities, while I was interested in the behavior of people" (Drucker, 1993, pp. 75–76).

Since then, business schools have continued to come up with and refine theories on corporate governance, the role of the CEO, or what makes a great business leader, but at the end of the day, management boils down to working with people, which makes applying hard-and-fast rules within professional structures pointless, particularly at a time when organizations are thankfully becoming more and more diverse. It cannot be overstressed that the human factor needs to be taken into account regarding how and what is taught at business schools.

For example, the case study, one of the most widely used methods of teaching management, recognizes that it is an organization's people who either create or destroy value. Most business schools now teach students that learning how to see things through the eyes of whomever they're dealing with is as important as economic theory.

Nevertheless, Henry Mintzberg believes that most business schools are still falling short. The problem starts with their raw material. The vast majority of MBA students are too young to learn management. "It's like trying to teach psychology to a person that has never known anybody" (Mintzberg, 2004, p. 9), he says in his 2004 book *Managers Not MBAs*, which foreshadows many of the ideas of a new generation of thinkers and academics who have dominated the debate on management education since. Mintzberg's pioneering work laid the foundations for many increasingly common practices, such as requiring work experience of applicants for MBA programs, in comparison with those applying for a master's in management, which is aimed at students with no professional experience. This is now common practice at business schools, at least in Europe.

The case study, gaming, or projects carried out in real companies appear practical but are dismissed by Mintzberg as pastiches of a much more complex reality. The outcome is students with a skill set that includes the confidence to make decisions quickly, streamline complexity, and tackle technical problems. They may be wizards of strategy, but they can't implement solutions.

Applying the equation "confidence minus competence equals arrogance" (Mintzberg, 2004, p. 74), Mintzberg's most serious charge is that MBA programs produce overconfident graduates who may be skilled in breaking down the mysteries of accounting or marketing but who have no understanding of the reality of business. Unsurprisingly, Mintzberg's statistics on value generation in businesses where the CEO has an MBA, or graduate start-ups and the large number of well-known entrepreneurs who have never been near a business school, have proved contentious. And although I have found Mintzberg's work highly illuminating, I, too, have some cavils with his arguments.

First, my own experience has taught me that management skills can be cultivated in students and young people with no hands-on business experience, for example, in a bachelor's in business administration or a master's in management program. This type of educational environment can create the conditions within which the entrepreneurial spirit can flourish.

Quoting George Gilder, the cofounder of the Discovery Institute, Adrian Wooldridge (2009) of *The Economist* cites the myth that young entrepreneurs are "orphans and outcasts." Clearly thinking about the Bill Gates and Steve Jobs types of this world, who left college to set up their own businesses and who are frequently used to illustrate the irrelevance of university studies in becoming a successful entrepreneur, he talks about "lonely Atlases battling a hostile world or anti-social geeks inventing world-changing gizmos in their garrets" and goes on to say: "In fact, entrepreneurship, like all business, is a social activity. Entrepreneurs may be more independent than the usual suits who merely follow the rules, but they almost always need business partners and social networks to succeed" (Wooldridge, 2009, para. 1 under "Five Myths").

I would also disagree with Mintzberg's (2004) assertion that age and experience are required to fully develop managerial talent and leaders. Perhaps the main challenges for business schools in training young people are identifying young leaders, finding a way to channel their nascent entrepreneurial abilities, and then hooking them up with the main stakeholders in the business world.

Then there is Mintzberg's (2004) criticism of business schools' teaching methodology, particularly the case study, gaming, and simulations: he says the decisions made by students in these situations have no real repercussions. That can also be seen as an upside: take the analogy of a flight simulator used to train pilots. If something goes wrong, nobody dies. Instead, it gives pilots the opportunity to deal with the kind of situations that will probably happen once they earn their stripes. Similarly, cognitive psychology students are introduced to the problem of the map and the territory. A map is a faithful representation of a real territory, but it can never reproduce its aspects in full. Although the journey to knowledge requires maps to help us re-create the geography of a specific territory, we also learn not to confuse the two things (Wuppuluri and Doria, 2018).

Nevertheless, Mintzberg (2004) is correct when he says some business schools fall into the trap of believing that a case study is the same as reality. At the same time, Harvard Business School case studies always include the following footnote: "HBS case studies are developed solely as the basis for class discussion. Cases are not intended to serve as endorsements, sources of primary data, or illustrations of effective or ineffective management."[14] In other words, it's a map, not a territory, and should not be confused with reality.

By the same token, I would say Mintzberg (2004) would be mistaken to believe that the anecdotes told by a veteran manager in a course for senior directors are largely drawn from memory and thus of questionable academic rigor, even if, as in life, many of our ideas and decisions are based on the experiences and emotions shared with us by others. I know from personal experience based on conversations with innumerable MBA graduates that the case studies they took part in have helped them to understand and address many of the situations they have faced. I suspect that the case study, along with other interactive methods used in business schools, may not be perfect but is still the most effective way to teach management skills.

Because business education is one of the most dynamic and responsive sectors in higher education, many of Mintzberg's (2004) suggestions are being taken up by business schools and outlined in the growing body of revisionist literature. This has led many business schools to seek a balance between the teaching of hard and soft skills and to develop students' analytical abilities and emotional intelligence. For directors, this means developing their professional ethics and commitment to social issues, along with a more technical approach to providing functional knowledge and a more general and overarching approach to the world of business.

Recently, Stefano Harney and Howard Thomas (2020) have gone a step further in converging management education and the humanities, aligning themselves with the Carnegie Foundation's 2011 report, *Rethinking Undergraduate Management Education: Liberal Learning for the Profession* (Colby et al., 2011). "Rather than focusing solely on technical business skills, management education would welcome the humanities as the foundation of its curriculum, and the two forms of education, professional and liberal, would be melded into a holistic curriculum. Thus planted at the heart of management education, the liberal arts would by implication also face a very different future"

---

[14] Footnote available in all case studies published by Harvard Business Publishing; see https://hbsp.harvard.edu/cases/.

(Harney and Thomas, 2020, p. 18). In short, an association between business education and the humanities can certainly help generate a more enlightened and ethical managerial profile.

Indeed, given that the bachelor in business administration (BBA) has become the most sought-after program in many universities around the world, the merger of management and the humanities could result in a renewed platform for liberal arts studies.[15]

Some Experiences at IE Business School

In recent years, IE Business School has introduced subjects and sessions dedicated to the humanities in our MBA, master's in management, and BBA programs.

Our goal was twofold: to broaden management studies and free them from the confines of the social sciences to the wider realm of the humanities and sciences, highlighting the interconnectedness of the models, concepts, and theories of a range of disciplines, so as to provide a better understanding of the individual in business. This in turn would help develop well-rounded managers and enlightened directors. We believe that studying history provides key references that enable directors to make better business decisions, on the basis of an understanding of the experiences of the past.

I believe that a grounding in the history of art strengthens our observational and perception skills, which are necessary for making more reflexive or considered decisions, providing a counterbalance to the heuristic approach of most people in the business world. As Drew Faust, the first female president of Harvard University, said: "History teaches contingency; it demonstrates that the world has been different and could and will be different again. Anthropology can show that societies are and have been different elsewhere – across space as well as time. Literature can teach us many things, but not the least of these is empathy – how to picture ourselves inside another person's head, life, experience – how to see the world through a different lens, which is what the study of the arts offers us as well. Economic growth and scientific and technological advances are necessary but not sufficient purposes for a university" (Faust, 2010, n.p.).

---

[15] I owe this idea to my colleague at IE University, Dr. Julian Montaño.

Many business school programs are now overspecialized and thus subject to the silo syndrome whereby academics deal only with same-subject colleagues and students are taught through the narrowest perspective on knowledge. In response, I believe the time has come to include the humanities in business education. By making the humanities a core part of all degree programs, we can cement the learning experience and develop open-minded and well-rounded graduates. This is the spirit that inspired us a decade ago to launch our executive MBA program with Brown University (IE Brown, n.d.).

It is time to bring all the benefits of a classical education to business schools: by teaching modern art, for example, we cultivate skills such as perception and observation that can help managers to take a more measured approach toward risk assessment. At the same time, studying how other societies work can help in leading cross-cultural teams. Critical thinking modules can empower tomorrow's business leaders to question unethical decisions imposed by their bosses.

The counterpart to this alignment of business education and the humanities is to teach management across all university degree programs. In fact, we might as well include management as a core subject at primary school, along with mathematics or literature, which would provide the opportunity for all children to acquire at least the basics of running an organization, a skill they will find useful even if they do not go into business. After all, good management underpins the best professional practice, whether it's a hospital or an architectural practice. If we want tomorrow's graduates, regardless of their area of study, to make the world a better place, then we're going to need them to be able to practice the best and most sustainable management practices.

Conclusions: Some Proposals for "Humanizing" Management

Following my argument in support of the association of management and the humanities, and given the pivotal role that faculty play in the learning process, I would like to provide some proposals that may be key in the implementation of this strategy:

- Restructuring postgraduate management programs so that they include a variety of approaches to research, as well as cultivating a cross-disciplinary mindset in students. Doctoral programs should foster the kind of close and regular contact between students and business leaders that can provide them with firsthand management experience.

- Modifying university tenure systems to encourage partnerships between all departments as a way to overcome the silo syndrome and encourage cross-disciplinary research. Innovation often comes as the result of combining a wide range of subjects.
- Promoting sustainable contact with business leaders, either through membership of boards or through consulting work. Overall evaluation will still emphasize research output, but we need to find a balance that will allow academics to begin incorporating these kinds of initiatives.
- Creating interdisciplinary centers that bring academic departments together with companies to work on projects. As well as producing interdisciplinary research, these centers help develop training programs that address specific issues relating to business management. Business schools' boards and advisory councils should also be aware of the strengths and weaknesses of their respective institutions. These councils are generally made up of businesspeople or alumni who can provide vital feedback about the knowledge required out there in the real world.
- Strengthening ties between research-oriented teachers and practitioners. Until now, such cooperation has usually taken the form of jointly developing teaching material, but it can be extended to other areas. Making this happen should be a key objective of department heads, who can advance joint-research initiatives.
- Establishing ways to access knowledge produced outside the academic environment. Business schools need to take on the role of knowledge hubs, collecting new ideas and models from the wider world, such as consultancies, professional fora, and a wider range of organizations and businesses. There is limitless potential for exchanging ideas and information through knowledge networks and platforms supported by social networks.
- Creating a new platform for the study of the humanities by introducing liberal arts content into the curriculum of BBA and MBA programs.
- Recruiting the support of accreditation agencies such as EQUIS so that a cross-disciplinary approach and a grounding in the humanities are included among their research and teaching criteria.

To conclude this chapter, I would like to praise the job that EFMD has done for the promotion and recognition of best practices in business education, particularly through its fostering of diversity, closeness to the professional world, and international reach. The humanistic approach is also distinctive of most of the EFMD's initiatives and programs, which paves the way for better and sustainable business education in a world with more challenges than ever before.

References

Bennis, W., and O'Toole, J. (2005, May). How business schools lost their way. *Harvard Business Review*, 83(5), 96–104, 154.

Blanchard, M. (2009). From "Écoles de commerce" to "management schools": Transformations and continuity in French business schools. *European Journal of Education*, 44(4), 587–603.

Christakis, N. A. (2020). *Apollo's arrow: The profound and enduring impact of coronavirus on the way we live.* Little, Brown Spark.

Christensen, C. M., and Eyring, H. J. (2011). *The innovative university: Changing the DNA of higher education from the inside out.* Jossey Bass.

Colby, A., Ehrlich, T., Sullivan, W. M., and Dolle, J. (2011). *Rethinking undergraduate business education: Liberal learning for the profession.* Carnegie Foundation for the Advancement of Teaching/Jossey Bass.

Cruikshank, J. L. (1987). *A delicate experiment: The Harvard Business School 1908–1945.* Harvard Business School Press.

Cuevas-Rodríguez, G., Gomez-Mejia, L. R., and Wiseman, R. M. (2012). Has agency theory run its course? Making the theory more flexible to inform the management of reward systems. *Corporate Governance: An International Review*, 20(6), 526–546.

Drucker, P. F. (1993). *The ecological vision.* Transaction Publishers.

EFMD Global. (n.d.). *EQUIS: EFMD quality improvement system.* www .efmdglobal.org/accreditations/business-schools/equis/.

Faust, D. G. (2010, June 30). The role of the university in a changing world [Lecture]. Soundcloud. https://soundcloud.com/the-royal-irish-acad emy/policy-the-role-of-the

Finn, E., ed. (2017). *What algorithms want: Imagination in the age of computing.* MIT Press.

Fotopoulos, T. (2005, January). From (mis)education to Paideia. *International Journal of Inclusive Democracy*, 9(1). www.inclusivedemocracy.org/jour nal/vol2/vol2_no1_miseducation_paideia_takis.htm.

Friedman, M. (1970, September 13). The social responsibility of business is to increase its profits. *New York Times.* www.nytimes.com/1970/09/13/arch ives/a-friedman-doctrine-the-social-responsibility-of-business-is-to.html.

Galloway, S. (2020). *Post corona: From crisis to opportunity.* Random House.

Ghoshal, S. (2005). Bad management theories are destroying good management practices. *Academy of Management Learning & Education,* 4(1), 75–91.

Harney, S., and Thomas, H. (2020). *The liberal arts and management education: A global agenda for change.* Cambridge University Press.

Hartley, S. (2017). *The fuzzy and the techie: Why the liberal arts will rule the digital world.* Houghton Mifflin Harcourt.

IE Brown. (n.d.). *IE Brown executive MBA.* https://emba.brown.edu.

Iñiguez de Onzoño, S. (2011). *The learning curve: How business schools are re-inventing education.* Palgrave Macmillan.

(2017). *Cosmopolitan managers: Executive development that works.* Palgrave Macmillan.

(2020). *In an ideal business: How the ideas of 10 female philosophers bring value into the workplace.* Palgrave Macmillan.

Iñiguez de Onzoño, S., and Ichijo, K. (2018). *Business despite borders: Companies in the age of populist anti-globalization.* Palgrave Macmillan.

Jaeger, W. (1971). *Paideia: The ideals of Greek culture.* Oxford University Press.

Kaplan, A. (2014). European management and European business schools: Insights from the history of business schools. *European Management Journal,* 32(4), 529–534.

Lamont, M., and Molnár, V. (2002). The study of boundaries in the social sciences. *Annual Review of Sociology,* 28, 167–195.

Larréché, J. C. (1987). On simulations in business education and research. *Journal of Business Research,* 15(6), 559–571.

Mintzberg, H. (2004). *Managers not MBAs: A hard look at the soft practice of managing and management practice.* Berret-Koehler Publishers Inc.

Nussbaum, M. (1997). *Cultivating humanity: A classical defense of reform in liberal education.* Harvard University Press.

(2010). *Not for profit: Why democracy needs the humanities.* Princeton University Press.

Parry, R. (2020). Episteme and techne. In E. Zalta, ed., *The Stanford encyclopedia of philosophy,* fall 2020 edition. Stanford University. https://plato.stanford.edu/entries/episteme-techne/

Podsakoff, P. M., MacKenzie, S. B., Bachrach, D. G., and Podsakoff, N. P. (2005). The influence of management journals in the 1980s and the 1990s. *Strategic Management Journal,* 26(5), 473–488.

Prato, C., and Wolton, S. (2018). Rational ignorance, populism, and reform. *European Journal of Political Economy,* 55(C), 119–135.

Riccoboni, A. (2010, June 1). *Who invented the business school?* Business Because. www.businessbecause.com/news/mba-degree/352/who-invented-the-business-school.

Scott, W. R. (1995). *Institutions and organizations.* Sage.

Seaton, L. J., and Boyd, M. (2008). The effective use of simulations in business courses. *Academy of Educational Leadership Journal,* 12(1), 107–118.

Shoemaker, P. J. H. (2008). The future challenges of business: Rethinking management education and research. *California Management Review,* 50(3), 119–139.

Smith, R. E., and Elliott, R. (2019). *Rage inside the machine: The prejudice of algorithms, and how to stop the internet of making bigots of us all.* Bloomsbury.

Sorkin, D. (1983). Wilhelm Von Humboldt: The theory and practice of self-formation (*Bildung*). *Journal of the History of Ideas,* 44(1), 50–73.

Tett, G. (2015). *The silo effect: Why putting everything in its place isn't such a bright idea.* Little Brown.

Tierney, J. (2011, July 24). The left-leaning tower. *New York Times.* www.nytimes.com/2011/07/24/education/edl-24notebook-t.html.

US Department of Education. (n.d.). *Science, technology, engineering, and math, including computer science.* www.ed.gov/stem.

Wexler, N. (2019, January 13). Math and science can't take priority over history and civics. *Forbes.* www.forbes.com/sites/nataliewexler/2019/01/13/math-and-science-cant-take-priority-over-history-and-civics/?sh=1faac474199e.

Wolmar, C. (2012). *The great railway revolution.* Atlantic Books.

Wooldridge, A. (2009, March 12). Global heroes. *The Economist.* www.economist.com/special-report/2009/03/14/global-heroes.

Wuppuluri, S., and Doria, F. A., eds. (2018). *The map and the territory: Exploring the foundations of science, thought and reality.* Springer.

4 | Educating Business Leaders, but for What Kind of World?

FERNANDO J. FRAGUEIRO

Introduction

The mission of most business schools, at least in a generic approach, has been to educate business leaders for the world. However, at the beginning of the third decade of this century, this challenge seems more complex than ever before. Some of the most renowned of these institutions aimed at training leaders of corporations that were flourishing at the end of the nineteenth or the beginning the twentieth century, in a completely different historical context. Two of the most prominent examples are Wharton Business School and Harvard Business School (HBS). The former was founded in 1881, making it the first business school established in the United States; its mission is to *create leaders to change the world* (Wharton, n.d.). The latter was established in 1908, and its mission is to *educate leaders to make a difference in the world* (HBS, n.d.).

Fast-forward one century, and the world is dramatically different, specifically the business world and the education activity. We have never experienced such disruptive and continuous change, mostly due to the digital revolution, which is affecting human life in multiple dimensions: social, cultural, economy, labor, education, and health, among others. The importance of the technological and scientific revolution underway, known as Industry 4.0, is here to stay. Technology will continue to provide society with a drive for change in social dynamics and cultural patterns, with unprecedented speed and global reach.

In such a challenge, adaptation appears to be the natural path to follow. However, because the main purpose of business schools is to educate leaders, and leadership is not about following but anticipating, discovering, and showing the paths to the future, business schools, even those in top positions in the market, are confronted with two crucial challenges: first, the need to reimagine the business world in this new era; second, the need to reinvent and redesign management education for a time of ongoing accelerated disruption in multiple dimensions.

With most of these challenges in mind, at the business leadership chair that I preside, we conducted the study "Business Leadership 2030 in Latin America." The purpose of this initiative is to enhance the quality and effectiveness of business leaders to promote more inclusive and sustainable growth and development in that region. The outputs of this study – with over 100 interviews with presidents and CEOs from six countries in the region (Argentina, Brazil, Colombia, Chile, Mexico, and Peru) – provide some insights relevant to understanding the unprecedented challenges (COVID-19 included) and opportunities we are currently experiencing, from a business leader's view. The central point that is revealed by this study is the multiple consequences emerging from the unparalleled set of ongoing changes – technological, cultural, and social – with strong influences on people and organizations everywhere, both locally and globally.

Some outputs of this study, along with my work on business schools' value propositions and strategies since 1995, inspired this chapter, with the aim of shedding some light on the unmatched challenges business schools confront – and will continue to face – in educating business leaders for the world.

For half a century, the European Foundation for Management Development (EFMD) has played a central role in shaping the global approach to management education, and it has provided a unique forum for information, research, networking, and debate on innovation and best practices. Let's celebrate its 50th anniversary by envisioning business education for the next fifty years.

In that sense, let's start by unveiling the logic behind this radical change while identifying the impact of these transformations to figure out key leadership competencies and how they can be developed in an ever-changing world.

The Dawn of the Era of Accelerations

When Thomas Friedman reflects on today's world, he cites the creation of the first Apple smartphone in 2007 as a turning point, symbolically speaking. At that time, the author argues, we entered "the era of accelerations," driven by technology, globalization, and climate change (Friedman, 2018). That same year, a few new companies were born that would have a profound impact. Together, those companies have changed the way people and machines communicate, create, collaborate, and think.

Twitter was developed on its own platform and started growing on a global scale with its microblogging model; Google launched Android, a platform for mobile devices; Amazon launched Kindle, starting the revolution of the eBook; and Airbnb was created in an apartment in San Francisco.

In the first two decades of this century, the digital and scientific revolution resulted in a radical change of context that affects life and the dynamics of society as a whole. The lengthening of the life span and the coexistence of more generations that have such different world-views also contribute to the new conception of the world.

New dynamics of exchange and development are making their way in this context. These interactive and ecosystemic relationships make it possible to meet people's needs more effectively, if we are able to stop, reflect, think, and create while we keep speeding up our pace of learning. In this context, the task of leading any institution, whether political, social, business, academic, or scientific, and even a family, is being challenged and needs to be revisited.

In a time of disruptive and far-reaching change, an approach to understanding its consequences needs a multilevel perspective: techno-logical, cultural, and sociodynamic. Then, we can find new ways to continue learning at a fast pace in an ever-changing reality.

Scope and Impact of the Technological Revolution

Klaus Schwab, president of the World Economic Forum, referring to the dimension and speed of change, briefly explains that "the unpre-cedented advances that are taking place at once in artificial intelligence (AI), robotics, internet of things, autonomous vehicles, 3D printing, nanotechnology, biotechnology, materials science, energy gathering, quantum computing and other areas, are redefining industries, erasing traditional borders and creating new opportunities" (Herder-Wynne et al., 2017).

A key aspect of the digital revolution is its condition of an inter-connectivity system. One of the effects that runs through all human relationships, work, and life in all its dimensions is that we live "in real time." This leads us to network with other sectors – and with a 360-degree view. The new challenge forces us to establish a new approach to reach all the stakeholders. This relationship begins by identifying the actors; analyzing the opportunity to incorporate them as allies; knowing their interests, potential, and relevance; and defining an action plan related to each one of them (Fragueiro, 2020).

Global Communication, Interconnected Globalization

Globalization is a term that has been widely used to describe modern societies, especially since the end of the twentieth century. In the third decade of the twenty-first century, the digital revolution produced a disruptive acceleration of this process.

Web 2.0 directly influences our social, political, and everyday lives and, of course, the business world. There are new articulations among people, in which individuals can express their opinions because communication 2.0 is interactive, horizontal, public, and universal. The level of exposure becomes absolute and public, which means that companies should try to reinforce the quality of their management and reinvent their communication strategy toward multiple partners to build a better reputation. In this regard, businesses should first identify all their stakeholders and then know their interests and expectations in order to keep up (Fragueiro, 2020).

Interconnection helps to enhance shared information, check data in a global way, and develop integrated and adaptable strategies for the possibilities of each specific environment. Processes are constantly accelerating, and everyone can access massive amounts of data at any time. The new dynamics are quickly interwoven and networked; a co-creation system has definitely come to stay.

The New Ecosystemic Dynamics of Business

Because of the aforementioned effects of communication 2.0, the volume of voices in the market has increased exponentially; therefore, the business world exists in what we can call an *ecosystem*. Nowadays, nothing happens in isolation. This systemic conception has come to stay; it is transversal to all human activities, including business activity. To compete, companies will need to adapt and expand their traditional linear perspective, focused on industries or sectors and with entry barriers, which requires rethinking and discovering new competitive advantages. We are immersed in a broad global ecosystem that integrates companies with governments, civil society organizations, media, countries, multilateral organizations, various institutions, and men and women connected by social networks.

In a context of constant and accelerated change, it is no longer enough to align and inform; it is necessary to add wills in pursuit of a shared purpose. In this new citizen culture, companies must adapt their approach to a more proactive communication involved with the purpose it manifests in public. The members of a community will validate the work and profitability of a company as long as they understand what contributions that company offers to society.

In the current ecosystemic context and network dynamic, to understand others' interests through dialogue and a collaborative approach becomes a critical success factor.

This new way of understanding the world requires a holistic view and systemic intelligence to visualize the "interconnections and interdependencies" of both internal and external stakeholders. A business ecosystem is made up of diverse actors who co-create, and their contributions produce value when they collaborate with each other. The idea is that each of those parties can benefit from the collective effort.

Stakeholder Approach: Systemic Intelligence

Information and relationships become a key source of competitive advantage and provide a view beyond the traditional and narrow focus on short-term shareholder value. The context of interactive, horizontal, public, and universal information and communication, with an ecosystem perspective, broadens the companies' scope by providing them with new opportunities to create value in their interactions with other stakeholders.

With a systemic vision, it is possible to design and execute a strategy that identifies and defines with whom, when, and how to build a coalition with a common purpose, a clear focus, and well-defined objectives.

In other words, the new challenge and opportunity of entrepreneurial leadership in the context of the Fourth Industrial Revolution is to establish a new strategic perspective of relations with stakeholders. It starts by identifying them; analyzing the opportunity to incorporate new ones; knowing their interests and ideologies, potential, and relevance; and defining an action plan for each of them, with all these steps being iterative. Today, more than ever, AI makes it possible to know, in real time, what people need and expect. Products and services have quickly become "solutions" to human needs and aspirations.

In short, stakeholder leadership has become a central challenge for business success in the third decade of the twenty-first century, involving stakeholders from both outside and inside the organization. With external key actors, it is based on a long-term and holistic perspective, achieved through systemic intelligence and collaborative capacity. With collaborators, it is achieved through a purpose embedded in the management and leadership style, complemented by incentives in tune with the defined purpose, values, and culture.

Business Citizenship: The New Demand from Society

In today's ecosystemic dynamics and "all-visible world," both companies and their leaders are called upon to act as role models. They need to contribute profitably with goods and services while managing in a way that adds value to society in general and its institutions, communities, and the environment in particular. This broader approach of value creation for society is now at the core of business leaders' role in this century (Fragueiro, 2020).

In this sense, and enhanced by social media, the reputation of the company and its leaders has become an issue of strategic relevance. Businesses and their leaders are exposed to constant scrutiny, given that everything is visible and subject to the judgment of society.

We are faced with a specific demand that arises from the very nature of the company and its activity: as a social reality, it needs the asset of trust with its stakeholders, and they expect it to exercise a citizenship role.

As a new cultural reality, in order to be sustainable in the long term, within the framework of the Fourth Industrial Revolution, the company needs to explain, communicate, and specify in practice not only the value contributed to each stakeholder but also the different types of value that it creates and contributes to each one of them.

An essential contribution that companies make is that to human development, which usually applies to team members and their families, customers, communities, and citizens in general. In short, companies are the creators and promoters of culture and values. The real culture is shown in the face of difficult decisions, especially in times of crisis.

In the Digital Age, Adaptation Is Key

If you had asked a farmer a hundred years ago what skills his kids would need to thrive, he would not have hesitated to answer that they would need to know how to milk a cow or plant a field – general skills for a single profession that changed slowly. This is how it was for almost everyone throughout human history. In just a few decades, we have witnessed more changes than in the last 300 years.

While many jobs have disappeared, others have been created. Machines have automated much of manufacturing, for example, and they will inevitably automate even more soon. We are currently in the midst of a massive shift. Skills that have traditionally been in demand are now declining. The World Economic Forum's *The Future of Jobs Report 2018* listed things like manual dexterity, management of financial and material resources, and quality control and safety awareness as declining abilities (World Economic Forum, 2018).

Although technology is the engine of transformation, companies and their workers hold the key to change. We need to adapt the talent, develop continuously, and keep pace with technological evolution. Talent will be the clear differentiator in a highly competitive business environment and in an increasingly digital world. People are at the center of the revolution. The challenge of being competitive in the digital age will not be solved by consuming more and more technology or by replacing humans with technology.

Furthermore, humans possess key differential factors that machines do not, a set of skills known as the *four C's*: communication, creativity, critical thinking, and collaboration. These are central to working in teams and are a reflection of the "hyperconnected" world we live in today.

In addition to the four C's, successful entrepreneurs across the globe are demonstrating three additional soft skills that can be integrated into the classroom: adaptability, resiliency and grit, and a mindset of continuous learning. These skills can equip business leaders to be problem solvers, inventive thinkers, and adaptive to the fast-paced change they are bound to encounter. In a world of uncertainty, the only constant is the need for agile adaptation.

The Future of Work: Human and Machine Collaboration

Work can be defined, quite simply, as human skills applied to problems, although it is a concept that has been shifting shape over time. We humans create value by applying our skills to solve problems in the world. There is always a need for problems to be solved and a demand for human skills to satisfy that need. There were plenty of problems to solve in the world before coronavirus, and now we have even more. It is undeniable that the pace of automation has accelerated as a consequence of the pandemic, but companies were already automating processes long before.

Productivity is the main reason companies want to automate workforces. Yet repeatedly, the largest increases in productivity do not result from replacing humans with machines but, rather, from augmenting machines with humans. It all comes down to collaboration. Many car manufacturers, for instance, experienced an increase in productivity when they replaced their traditional – and already automated – assembly-line process with human–robot teams.

It is also worth mentioning that every time a technology goes exponential, a whole set of new opportunities opens up. Taking advantage of these opportunities requires adaptation, which demands workforce retraining, yet the result is a net gain in jobs, not otherwise.

Finally, as AI becomes our user-friendly interface with technology, we will begin to see a major change in the talents required for retraining. For a wide range of jobs, technological fluency and agility will definitely replace mastery in hard skills.

Stakeholder Leadership: The Big Reset

The third decade of the twenty-first century presents a context of constant disruptive change, accelerated by the COVID-19 pandemic. This demands that the leaders of all sectors be able to anticipate and understand the profound transformations that are taking place in the cultural, labor, and educational realms and in all other areas of society. The novelty of the twenty-first century is that the old barriers and defenses tend to disappear, and the creation of value is enhanced by network interaction.

This situation requires leadership with aspiration and permanent transformational capacity. New leaders need to be inspired by a future open to changes that are hard to foresee. At the same time, though, they should be in tune with global trends driven by the digital techno-logical revolution and by its derivatives, such as AI, machine learning, and robotics, as well as data-driven intelligence, in order to discover new trends, human needs, and aspirations, thus creating products and services faster to deliver solutions.

Social dynamics, traversed by technology in everyday life, is adopting new logic: innumerable opinion groups defend humanitarian, social and environmental, and natural resource preservation causes, and all of them are empowered by interactive, public, and universal communication of the networks. This social interaction is in its infancy and already marks a new cultural era that demands more and more transparency and coherence from institutions and their leaders.

The twenty-first century, on the other hand, levels us horizontally: authority no longer appears on thrones or podiums; today, it is acquired by proximity, coherence, and personal example, as well as from the essential knowledge to exercise its function. Leadership in this century is exercised and legitimized in interactions with citizens, team members, colleagues, and opponents or competitors, according to their role in society.

The new leadership paradigm is based on systemic intelligence. Peter Hawkins (2017) suggests the following transitions in order to lead companies by 2030:

1. Moving from *leading my people* to *"orchestrating business ecosystems"*
2. Moving from *heroic leadership* to *"collective and collaborative leadership"*
3. Moving toward leadership driven by a shared purpose and values that create value for all stakeholders

The context of the digital revolution includes the leadership of remote teams, networks, and alliances. Outer leadership must change from an approach based on command and control, centralization, vertical deci-sions, and authority based on hierarchies, all driven and validated from the top, toward a leadership that promotes collaboration, shared or distributed leadership, autonomy and self-organization, empower-ment, decision making at the local level, local interaction, trust, and transparency. In short, emerging leadership thinking includes collab-orative, authentic, servant, and cross-silo leadership.

The Major Leadership Challenge: Integrating Transformation with Collaboration

The personal qualities common to these types of leadership are usually presented as two complementary and even opposed leadership styles: the transformational and the situational and collaborative. However, the context of continuous and disruptive change, combined with the instantaneous and interactive reaction, places leadership in a dilemma. On the one hand, it must have a transformational vision and conviction, capable of projecting, mobilizing, and even anticipating new realities and, thus, inspiring and guiding toward a future of disruption and uncertainty. However, in this era of constant transformation and universally active communication and interaction, it must also possess competencies of situational and collaborative leadership, together with systemic and emotional intelligence, to provide closeness and the perception of individual sentiments and desires to orchestrate a new leading style with different stakeholders, people, teams, and even other institutions.

Let's review some key competencies of these two leadership styles to better understand the challenge ahead. The competencies that follow have been selected from *Leadership – Theory and Practice* (Northouse, 2019), which includes insights from authors like Bass and Avolio, and "Leading Ever-Changing Companies" (Fragueiro, 2020).

Competencies for Transformational Leadership

1. Long-term vision and holistic thinking: systemic intelligence, contextual vision, and full knowledge of trends and their complexities. Identify and distinguish causes and effects.
2. Intellectual stimulation: motivation of creativity and independent thinking of collaborators, allowing taking risks and challenging premises.
3. Ability to inspire and motivate attractive, hopeful, and inspiring communication of a vision, instilling a deep sense of purpose that helps to overcome attitudes of personal interest.
4. Idealistic influence and authenticity: personal integrity and living example of the proposed change. Good guide for collaborators, reliability, credibility, intelligence, coherence of deeds and words. Ability and attitude to rectify.

5. Vision of rupture: conception that the very mission of the role includes radical changes.
6. Desire to excel and willingness to transcend self-interest: ability to create a new development model through a multidimensional change (cultural, relationship with stakeholders, etc.) that seeks to contribute to the common good of society or a group.
7. Strategic vision: clear notion of the context, timing, and stages of the processes and of the various interests of internal and external stakeholders. (Fragueiro, 2020; Northouse, 2019)

Competencies for Situational and Collaborative Leadership

1. Inclusion: creation of value from incorporating the contribution and participation of the greatest number of stakeholders possible.
2. Close communication: clarity, generation of dialogue, consensus building, and ability to negotiate with whoever is necessary at all times.
3. Orientation toward a common purpose: shared, dynamic, and adaptable value proposition. The purpose mobilizes all actors in the ecosystem, energizing all sectors (public, private, and third sector) to achieve shared and mutually beneficial goals.
4. Search for dialogue and collaborative capacity: encouragement for frank conversation and collaboration. Construction of a culture and environment of freedom that facilitates the raising of doubts and allows suggesting and questioning honestly. Generation of agreement when pertinent.
5. Adaptation: ability to distinguish between purely technical and adaptive problems, linked to abilities, knowledge, tastes, beliefs, and personal values of a permanent nature.
6. Diversity and pluralism: there are leaders of all races, religions, genders, generations, and philosophies. A fruitful dialogue between them from different sectors can only be achieved if all of this diversity of leadership is known and accepted. (Fragueiro, 2020; Northouse, 2019)

The combination of two leadership styles as diverse as transformational and collaborative presents a great challenge: they do not usually occur naturally in the same person. However, in the face of such obvious signs from the context, we think that it is possible to achieve such a combination if leaders have a full understanding of the phenomenon, determination, and systemic intelligence. To achieve this, it is necessary to incorporate two key competencies into situational leadership, whose potential contribution is essential to highlight.

On the one hand, it is necessary for the leader to have "systemic intelligence": the leader needs to be able to appreciate the interconnections and interdependencies of the system as a whole and at all its levels, understanding "cause–effect" relationships or how changes in certain parts affect the whole.

Second, the new dynamics of relationship and network activity typical of a world of value-creation ecosystems require situational leadership "collaborative and transversal capacity," avoiding silos.

The Future of Business Schools: Understanding the New World

As we have seen, the fast pace of change has far-reaching implications. Business schools have to take advantage of the digital revolution to fulfill their mission: educate business leaders who understand the nature, relevance, and consequences of this revolution and, most important, its human impact. Leaders must have a new capacity to explore, reflect, and anticipate human needs and aspirations, based on data-driven and automated processes, to ignite human creativity and empathy. In this sense, it is crucial to understand the biggest shifts that are taking place in the leadership world:

1. From content-driven knowledge and skills to dynamic and ongoing learning with an open mindset
2. From a top-driven individual leadership approach to a horizontal team-building approach, which orchestrates competencies and the proper mindset
3. From vertical, silo-driven management dynamics to a data-driven, systemic, and collaborative intelligence
4. From an exclusive, short-term, and narrow focus of business success to an inclusive, medium- and long-term sustainable future
5. From a static, vertical, compartmental organizational structure with a short-term incentive system to an ecosystemic, diverse, flexible, and cooperative network of team projects.

Business Education in the New Era: Two Paths for Moving Forward

Over time, and particularly in the last decades, most top business schools have focused their core management education on providing value at three levels:

1. Knowledge (*"knowing"*)
2. Skills (*"doing"*)
3. Values (*"being"*)

Most programs are designed with that simple and effective framework, which still remains valuable but requires some reshaping, according to this new era of constant transformation.

Regarding *knowledge*, particularly related to digital technology, it deserves special attention, as was asserted before, to focus on the *logic behind* digitalization and the *tools* it provides, such as big data, AI, machine learning, robotics, the internet of things, autonomous vehicles, three-dimensional (3D) printing, nanotechnology, biotechnology, materials science, energy gathering, and quantum computing, among others.

Concerning *skills and competencies*, on the one hand, those related to human interaction with digital tools are key. Even more in the new era, new core competencies and skills are required, and it is of particular relevance to identify and focus on those that differentiate humans from machines; repetitive and systematic technology-related tasks, analytics, and automation, to mention a few, will not be core human activities at work anymore. On the contrary, human talents related to open reasoning, creativity, empathy, and collaboration, among others, will be core competencies to enhance human impact, leveraging the technological and scientific revolution.

As for *values*, the "being" of leaders' education becomes the compass for a deep understanding of people's dignity and for inclusive, sustainable development. In an era of acceleration and disruptive change, values serve to set a clear roadmap for human well-being and development.

In the words of one of the world's top business leaders in the industry of technology, Satya Nadella, CEO of Microsoft (2014–present), one of the most critical challenges is that "we want to build intelligence (AI) that augments human abilities and experiences. Rather than thinking in terms of human vs. machine, we want to focus on how human gifts such as creativity, empathy, emotion, judgement, ... can be mixed with powerful AI computation – ability to reason over large amounts of data and do pattern recognition more quickly – to help move society forward" (Nadella et al., 2017, p. 201).

A first and central path to move forward with business schools' value contribution, in an era of ongoing transformation, must focus on rethinking and delivering a new proposal of education to facilitate "lifelong learning" for business leaders in terms of knowledge, skills, and values. Because *learning* and *unlearning* have become two of the most critical competencies, to develop this ability and willingness will require a new mindset in the three stakeholders: business leaders, companies, and business schools. This new key competency could work in a dynamic interaction of co-creation among those three.

A second path – and critical challenge for business schools in this era – lies in an open mind regarding rethinking the approach to designing and deploying management education. As for many other industries, rethinking and redesigning the traditional education portfolio, in particular, long programs such as MBAs and executive MBAs, should be the next challenge. The need and will to prioritize an earlier entrepreneurial working experience, either in large or medium-sized corporations or even in a start-up, is a clear trend in young professionals.

In summary, as constant transformation and ongoing education throughout life become the new normal, continuing and close interaction with executives, individuals, and companies over time becomes a key central process in transforming business schools' model.

In conclusion, more than ever in history, perhaps, education has become central in respecting human dignity. As the world's dynamics change the way people learn and work, a new approach to education is the path to follow, and so for business schools, in educating leaders for a new world.

References

Fragueiro, F. (2020). Leading ever-changing companies. White Paper, Business Leadership 2030 Initiative, IAE Business School.

Friedman, T. H. (2018). *Thank you for being late*. Farrar, Straus and Giroux.

Harvard Business School. (n.d.). *About*. www.hbs.edu/about/Pages/default .aspx.

Hawkins, P. (2017). *Tomorrow's leadership and the necessary revolution in today's leadership development*. Henley Business School.

Herder-Wynne, F., Amato, R., and Uit de Weerd, F. (2017). *Leadership 4.0. A review of the thinking*. Oxford Leadership. www.oxfordleadership .com/leadership-4-0-review-thinking-report-2/.

Nadella, S., Shaw, G., Nichols, J. T., and Gates, B. (2017). *Hit refresh: The quest to rediscover Microsoft's soul and imagine a better future for everyone*. Harper Business.

Northouse, P. G. (2019). *Leadership: Theory and practice*. Sage.

Wharton. (n.d.). *About Wharton*. www.wharton.upenn.edu/about-wharton/.

World Economic Forum. (2018, September 17). *The future of jobs report 2018*. Centre for the New Economy and Society. www.weforum.org/ reports/the-future-of-jobs-report-2018.

5 Multi- and Interdisciplinary Research in a World of Crisis: A Responsible Research Solution

GERALD F. DAVIS, PETER MCKIERNAN,
AND ANNE S. TSUI

Introduction

The year 2020 will be remembered as a moment of omni-crisis at the intersection of public health, politics, and economics. A global pandemic on a scale not seen in a century struck tens of millions and left a wake of devastation. Governments around the world responded in divergent ways, from competent and well organized to chaotic and inept, with predictable consequences for their citizens. Their economies suffered the consequences as well, with many facing skyrocketing rates of unemployment and business failure. Those at the low end of the income spectrum fared the worst: in the United States, employment in the foodservice industry dropped from 12 million to 6 million in a single month, leaving the equivalent of the population of Denmark out of work.

A key lesson from the pandemic is that policy responses rooted in credible science yield better outcomes. Countries in which governments paid attention to scientific expertise and adjusted their actions in response to systematic evidence were much more effective in keeping their populations safe than those driven by whim or anecdote.

Like governments, businesses also stood to benefit from relevant expertise rooted in research. How should workplaces be organized to limit the spread of a virus? What are viable alternative sources of distribution if face-to-face contact is not possible? How can employees be kept engaged and connected when they are working from home? How can manufacturing facilities be rapidly reconfigured to make emergency medical equipment? Moreover, how can we build back better once the virus is vanquished?

In this situation, research in business and management could provide crucial guidance. Business schools hold a unique vantage point between academia and practice. Like an estuary, they stand between the fresh water and saltwater of the world of academia and business and policy. Given the wealth of expertise that resides in business schools, we might anticipate that executives would be making pilgrimages to seek out our counsel. However, with some key exceptions, business faculty members were not equipped in practical utility to help address this crisis. More to the point, many senior faculty members would have a hard time advising their untenured colleagues to take on this challenge because it would not contribute to the publications needed to achieve tenure. To be fair, over 80,000 COVID-19 related publications have emerged, but there has been a large number of retractions, even among top medical journals.[1] Relevance without rigor is also a poor bargain.

How is it possible that helping to save a business from collapse and saving workers from unemployment would be considered too risky for many faculty? Moreover, how strange is this state of affairs? In this chapter, we trace how business research evolved from anecdotes and war stories to highly rigorous social science with limited application in the real world. We then describe recent efforts to change the ecosystem surrounding research in business and management to be more responsible, producing work that is both rigorous and relevant.

Why We Do Not Live Up to the Promise

Those unfamiliar with business schools may be surprised to learn that they are at least as research intensive as the rest of the university. Business faculty routinely publish in top journals in economics, statistics, sociology, psychology, and political science, as well as field-based publications in accounting, finance, marketing, management, and operations, with rejection rates well above 90 percent. Moreover, the typical article in an academic business journal is at least as obscure and inaccessible to practitioners as work in other fields.

It was not always this way. Business schools spread across the United States in the early twentieth century to provide vocational

---

[1] See Primer (n.d.) for a running tally of articles on COVID-19. On retractions, see Rabin (2020).

training for managers to work in the new corporate economy, and research was decidedly secondary. According to the 1959 Gordon and Howell report "Higher Education for Business," funded by the Ford Foundation:

Much if not most research in the business schools attempts merely to describe current practice or, going a short step further, to develop normative rules which summarise what is considered to be the best of prevailing practice. The business literature is not, in general, characterised by challenging hypotheses, well developed conceptual frameworks, the use of sophisticated research techniques, penetrating analysis, the use of evidence drawn from the relevant underlying disciplines – or very significant conclusions. (Gordon and Howell, 1959, p. 379)

The authors urged business schools to recruit faculty trained in core social science disciplines to increase their rigor.

Business schools embraced this prescription with gusto over the next generation, creating a robust infrastructure for research and implementing evaluative criteria for faculty that favored research over teaching. Schools such as Stanford, Harvard, and Chicago hired scholars from top departments of economics, psychology, sociology, statistics, and elsewhere. Standards for tenure increasingly came to resemble those elsewhere in the university, with a strong emphasis on publication in scholarly journals. Applicability came to be increasingly detached from the evaluation of research.

Part of this detachment comes from how business research is both funded and evaluated. Business schools often rely primarily on internal funding sources for research and evaluate outputs based on publications and citations. Thus – ironically for a professional school aimed at improving practice – business schools are oriented almost entirely toward *internal* metrics of evaluation ("A" publications and Google Scholar citation counts), without the external accountability that comes from grant funding, as in other parts of the university.

Within the United States, business is perennially the most popular undergraduate major, year in and year out. Moreover, business education has spread around the globe and may count as one of the most successful American "exports." Along with the standard model of business, education has spread the standard model of research. "Management" journals indexed in the Web of Science tripled between 2003 (67) and 2019 (226), and the number of articles published each year increased from 2,730 to 11,668. There is an astounding amount of research, although its impact beyond academia remains in doubt.

The Responsibility Turn

Questionable science in business and management research and its perceived lack of relevance to an executive or policy audience has fashioned a global industry of critical publications. Ironically, writers have submitted these critiques to the very research audits that have helped fuel and shape the culture of "rush to research" at the root of the misguided behavior about which they speak. The malaise is widespread across the sciences and jeopardizes Merton's (1942) pillars of universalism, disinterestedness, communality, and organized skepticism, thus making the search for truth almost impossible. Ritchie (2020) speaks of

a deep corruption within science itself; a corruption that affects the very culture in which research is practised and published. Science, the discipline in which we should find the harshest scepticism, the most pin-sharp rationality and the hardest-headed empiricism, has become home to a dizzying array of incompetence, delusion, lies and self-deception. (Ritchie, 2020, pp. 6–7)

Science finds many cures, but it requires considerable "self-correction" if it is to find an urgent cure for itself. Riddled with the problems of fraud, bias, negligence, and hype (Ritchie, 2020), the recovery may be long and painful. A vaccine that focuses on the root causes rather than the symptoms is likely to have more remedial traction.

Sociological Patterning

Pressures from the three actors of rankings, ratings, and accreditation prescriptions led business schools to conform to common standards of research evaluation (Wilson and McKiernan, 2011). This conformity was made more successful since the early 1980s by the emergence of the "audit society" (Power, 1997). These pressures developed for different reasons (the sale of for-profit publications like the *Financial Times* and *The Economist*; the distribution of scarce research funding as in the UK Research Excellence Framework [REF]; and academic quality with the triple-badged Association of MBAs [AMBA],

EFMD Quality Improvement System [EQUIS], and Association to Advance Collegiate Schools of Business [AACSB]). They became the targets of both schools and individual academics, evoking Goodhart's (1975) law: "when a measure becomes the target, it ceases to be a good measure." More so, they took on a life-form of expectations, order, reactivity, and gaming, with hierarchy and legitimacy becoming dynamic forces that drove behavior patterns akin to what sociologist Donald MacKenzie might call "engines not cameras" (MacKenzie, 2006). At first, a stable and pragmatic sector experimented in *habituation*. Then, the preferred business model arose under *objectification*, where articles in top journals, their authors, and the related incentives became reified. The sector slid "naturally" into *sedimentation*, privileging elitism and accelerating the practice of scientific foibles as part of faculty survival and promotion. Inevitably, that sedimentation became path dependent for business schools, with strategy captured by both local institutional rules and regulations and those about the norms set by the three actors.

Such systems require shocks to stimulate new habituation or objectification. In broader science, the shocks were personal and came over several decades with the high-level exposure of the scientifically corrupt amid a perennial failure to replicate results. In business and management, the macro-eruption of the global financial crisis pierced theory, method, and the evidence base of both finance and economics while business and management, bereft of impactful research, had nothing to say (Starkey, 2015). The nadir reached, the existing sediment began to crack, and new habituation and objectification stages beckoned. Recalling the "communality" of Merton's (1942) pillars, scientists around the world gathered and called for change, creating organizational bonds of determined purpose and swearing allegiance to new principles of behavior to underpin them. The *responsibility turn* in science was underway.

The Emergence of the "Principles-Based" Responsibility Turn

The Principles for Responsible Management Education (PRME) of the United Nations influenced many enlightened institutions. The movement was established in 2007 to bring an appreciation of sustainability into business schools and help them produce leaders imbued with an innate concern and responsibility for the world around them. In 2020, it had attracted over 800 subscribers[2] claiming allegiance to its six principles. Principle 4 concerns research, and schools must promise to "engage in conceptual and empirical research that advances our understanding about the role, dynamics, and impact of corporations in the creation of sustainable social, environmental and economic value" (PRME, n.d., para. 1).

This sense of global social responsibility and multiple stakeholder alliances runs through the remainder of the PRME's principles. For many, the sentiments are real. However, for others, trapped in a cage of fast-produced research that satisfies personal promotion, ego, and monetary ambitions, they may remain hypothetical, with the PRME badge adorning school literature for marketing purposes only. To make it real, the ecosystem of business research into which PRME was born needed transformation.

Such significant change required attention to the root cause of academic publishing behavior. The latter has become driven by metrics, particularly citations of papers in top journals. In business schools, in particular, the perverse incentive structures that reward the production of such articles became the norm, and the costs of such production were huge.[3]

Previously, the assessment and measurement process for academic output was a human affair, where deans and others read the work themselves.[4] Nevertheless, with such explosions in growth, numeric ratios – often calculated for entirely different reasons – became a convenient alternative judgment.[5]

---

[2] Compared with the number of business schools in the world (over 10,000), however, this may seem a low percentage.

[3] The cost of each paper has been estimated at $400k (Terwiesch and Ulrich, 2014), assuming 50 percent of faculty time is committed to research and a calculated investment of $3.9 billion per year by the 780 AACSB-accredited schools (figures provided kindly by B. Glick of the Community for Responsible Research in Business and Management [cRRBM]; personal communication, 2018).

[4] In British universities, one of the senior academic posts was that of reader – usually seen as a cadetship for a full professorship. One of the roles of such readers was to read draft research papers from faculty members and act as a friendly critic before they entered the formal journal reviewing process. Many universities have abandoned the title now – and with it, the role.

[5] McKiernan and Tsui (2020) have argued for the possibility that the increasing metrification around research output may have concealed some of the scientific malpractice. Deans made tenure, promotion, and appointment decisions based more on such figures (e.g., Hirsch's *h*-index) than on human opinion.

However, these metrics were both poorly constructed and badly used. Moreover, their use had unintended consequences, such as extended reference lists to propel citations and reviewers requesting citations of their own work. Finally, many influential scientists said, "Enough is enough." Cell biologists meeting in San Francisco founded the Declaration on Research Assessment (DORA)[6] and began to focus on the elimination of single-metric-only judgments (e.g., the Journal Impact Factor) for articles, grant funding, recruitment, and promotion and advocacy for complementing any use of metrics with human opinion. DORA's formalization of the responsibility turn was followed quickly by other robust initiatives, such as the responsibility turn in psychology.

Experimental psychology was one of the first social science fields to grapple with its crisis of replication (Ritchie, 2020). In 2013, the Center for Open Science (COS) started at the University of Virginia with a mission to increase "openness, integrity and reproducibility of research" (COS, n.d.). COS members imagined a research future when every part of the research process was transparent and available to all. In particular, it championed preregistration, advocated the evaluation of scholars on the integrity of their scientific approach and not on where they published their output, and recommended the full and uninterrupted involvement of all stakeholders throughout the research cycle. Quickly, COS became well supported within the science community, with multiple significant donors. Reflecting the demand for such action, it amassed over 10,000 subscribers to its Open Science Framework (OSF) in good time. Although COS deals mostly with the natural sciences, its approach and principles were to inspire the cRRBM (see later discussion).

Europe's response to these scientific foibles was equally formidable. Following a position paper under the Science in Transition (SiT) banner – "Why Science Does Not Work as It Should and What to Do about It" (Dijstelbloem et al., 2013) – four academics from two Dutch universities inspired an impactful conference of researchers and policymakers in 2013. Their discussion sparked a 9-month national debate, whose many voices shifted the initial principles of the founders:

[6] See Munafò et al. (2017).

Science in Transition has designated seven related concerns about current science: the image of science; trust in science; quality; fraud and deceit; communication; education; and democracy and policy.... The bibliometric assessment of quality has to be replaced by alternative analyses, requiring pilots and experiments for each domain. Furthermore, scientists will have to involve their societal stakeholders in formulating the research agenda and must also define and seek out their public. (Dijstelbloem et al., 2013, p. 3)

By their admittance, SiT had joined a growing "worldwide chorus" (including DORA, COS, *The Economist*, Nobel Prize winners [e.g., Schekman], the *Lancet*, and others) to correct the self-inflicted wounds within the scientific community. They feared that science had become wrapped in a self-referential system that excluded the rest of society. Hence, stakeholder interaction became paramount and exported to other movements (e.g., see later discussion of cRRBM). In the SiT's immediate wake came the Leiden Manifesto[7] for research metrics that emphasized many DORA and COS principles but added the necessity for an analysis of the context for a better understanding of any judgments leading to rankings and ratings.

The responsibility turn spread internationally as it linked the ethical use of artificial intelligence (AI) in the research process with human behavior. As data sources become increasingly widespread on a labyrinthine internet, humans' ability to locate, decipher, and access the sources they cannot identify at speed becomes challenged. The FAIR Guiding Principles[8] (findability, accessibility, interoperability, and reuse) of digital assets informed researchers of best practice and helped to ensure replicability.

This series of scientific covenants has been complemented in business and management by the emergence of several global movements covering teaching, research, and practice, such as the Network for Sustainability Business (NBS), the Alliance for Research on Corporate Sustainability (ARCS), and the International Humanistic Management Association (IHMA). However, one is inspired to place responsibility firmly back with the researcher to ensure scientific prowess and societal utility – the cRRBM. This initiative prioritizes "challenge-centered impact" and focuses on knowledge creation, which is a

---

[7] Named after the University of Leiden, where the 2014 conference of the European network of indicator developers met (see Hicks et al., 2015).

[8] This work stems from workshops in Leiden in 2014 (see Wilkinson et al., 2016).

necessary precondition for responsible learning and education. Responsible research feeds credible and useful knowledge for responsible management learning and education (RMLE) (see Moosmeyer et al., 2020).[9]

The Community of Responsible Research in Business and Management

The threat to the credibility of science in the business disciplines is well documented (Bedeian et al., 2010; Schwab and Starbuck, 2017; Tsui, 2016). However, distinctive from the natural sciences, there also is a concern about the practical relevance of business research. Beginning in the early 1990s, many senior scholars, including the presidents of the Academy of Management (with almost 20,000 members, the largest management research association in the world), called for attention to improving the connection of our research to the world around us. Don Hambrick's presidential address in 1993, titled "What If the Academy Actually Mattered?," was considered the first to formally call for a critical examination of the relevance and meaning of our work. His description of our annual academic ritual was sobering:

Each August, we come to talk to each other [at the Academy of Management's annual meetings]; during the rest of the year, we read each other's papers in our journals and write our own papers so that we may, in turn, have an audience the following August: an incestuous, closed-loop. (Hambrick, 1994, p. 13)

Subsequent presidents, including Andy Van de Ven (2001), Denise Rousseau (2005), Angelo DeNisi (2009), James Walsh (2010), and Anne S. Tsui (2013), and more recently, Anita McGahan (2017) and Jackie Coyle-Shapiro (2020), have issued a similar call (e.g., Tsui, 2013). Their addresses emphasize the need for our research to focus on fundamental problems in our world, to improve the practical relevance of our studies, and more importantly, to have relevance for creating a better world. The president of the American Finance Association asked (and answered) the question, "Does finance benefit society?" during his presidential address in 2015 (Zingales, 2015).

---

[9] This handbook, published in 2020, evidences the rapid growth of RMLE, with 33 chapters by 65 leading international authors.

Editors of leading business journals (e.g., Davis, 2015; Reibstein et al., 2009; Tang, 2016) also joined the chorus by publishing an editorial on the same question of relevance. In essence, the business and management field faced both a "credibility crisis" and a "relevance crisis." These two crises were the impetus for the creation of the Responsible Research in Business and Management (RRBM) network.

The RRBM is a multidisciplinary network founded in 2015, representing the core disciplines of accounting, finance, management, marketing, and operations management in business schools. The founding team consisted of 24 highly accomplished senior scholars from 23 universities in 10 countries, along with four institutional partners, the European Foundation for Management Development (EFMD), the Association to Advance Collegiate Schools of Business (AACSB), the Principles for Responsible Management Education (PRME), and the Aspen Institute Business & Society (Aspen-BSP).

The 28 cofounders authored a position paper (RRBM, n.d.-a) that begins with a vision statement for business and management research. It notes that by 2030, business and management research will be used widely in business and nonbusiness organizations to improve the lives of people in our societies – that is, it notes that "executives [will] be making pilgrimages en masse to seek out our counsel." The RRBM's mission is to inspire, encourage, catalyze, and support credible and useful research in the business and management disciplines.

Responsible research is scientific work that produces credible knowledge that is also useful for practice. Achieving either alone does not qualify as responsible research. Responsible scientists work on fundamental problems for society and engage in rigorous research design to ensure the findings are reliable and replicable, along with careful estimates on the consequences of wrongful conclusions. The cofounders further formulated seven principles to guide research design, as described in the next section.[10]

Seven Principles of Responsible Research

The first principle, "Service to Society," is foundational (RRBM, n.d.-a). To bring benefits to all citizens (not only the privileged few)

---

[10] The RRBM position paper (RRBM, n.d.-a) provides detailed discussions of these seven principles.

and to avoid negative externalities on society are universal norms of the scientific community. Science in business schools should not enjoy an exception.

Principle 2 is "Valuing Both Basic and Applied Contributions" (RRBM, n.d.-a). Basic research provides understanding and sharpens prediction. Applied research aims to find reliable solutions to puzzles and thorny problems, with or without the benefits of robust theories. In-depth studies with new insights at a pre-theory stage are just as valuable as hypotheses-testing studies.

Principle 3, "Valuing Plurality and Multidisciplinary Collaboration" (RRBM, n.d.-a), refers to accepting different research themes, methods, forms of inquiry, interdisciplinary collaboration, and knowledge co-creation with practitioners. This approach recognizes that different realities may exist between the researcher and the researched, and truth may be a negotiated social construction. It also aims to encourage a focus on problems and investigations guided by the epistemology and ontology of the local context. For complex problems primarily, a multidisciplinary team and involvement of those who are living the problem may provide a contextualized understanding and comprehensive insight that may not be possible by applying a single disciplinary lens or by using the "outside-in" approach (Tsui, 2006).

Principle 4, "Sound Methodology" (RRBM, n.d.-a), applies to both theory-testing and theory-building studies using either quantitative or qualitative methods. Empirical research requires transparency in the data source, data manipulation and transformation, sample construction, and measurement, that is, open science practices. Rigor also applies to in-depth ethnographic field studies with qualitative data, although different criteria of rigor may apply.

Principle 5, "Stakeholder Involvement" (RRBM, n.d.-a), is about engaging relevant stakeholders in the research, from defining the research question to collecting data, interpreting the results, and checking agreement in the assumption of reality. Stakeholder involvement may be particularly important in studying ill-defined problems because even insiders may not be able to articulate or understand the problem with certainty. Similarly, diversity in regional differences becomes part of the consideration in defining the problem and identifying the underlying logic (e.g., indigenous theorization) for explanation and prediction. Research design should avoid influencing the research subjects' understanding of their realities or beliefs.

The "looping effect" should be avoided, and the "principle of charity" (subjects' reality takes precedence over the researcher's reality) has priority in the understanding of the phenomenon, especially in unfamiliar research contexts (Risjord, 2014, pp. 67–68).

Principle 6, "Impact on Stakeholders" (RRBM, n.d.-a), recognizes and rewards research studies that have a positive impact on diverse stakeholders and values knowledge that informs better business practices and better societies. Principle 7, "Broad Dissemination" (RRBM, n.d.-a), encourages the use of different forms of dissemination, taking advantage of internet technology or platforms, so that the research findings can reach diverse users in an easy-to-understand and timely manner.

In total, six of the seven principles (except principle 7 on dissemination) relate to the upstream side of the research process. This process supports the pursuit of problem-focused and solution-oriented research and research that has the potential to contribute to both basic knowledge and useful ideas for application, with sensitivity to regional differences. Principles 2 to 4 enhance the credibility of research findings. Principles 5 and 6 improve the relevance of the knowledge derived. The principles aim to solve the dual problems of rigor and relevance and avoid the homogenization of research practices, priorities, and valuation globally.

The RRBM emphasizes our responsibility as social scientists who are entrusted by society to contribute evidence-based solutions to solve society's problems of injustice and to realize the potential to create a world that respects human dignity and protects human rights. All institutions arose in the history of humanity to facilitate order, justice, and survival.

The RRBM is not the panacea to the problems in our research culture. It is a modest effort to encourage, stimulate, and catalyze the recognition of and actions toward research that aims to produce both credible and useful information for a better world.

Work in (Good) Progress

In the 5 years since its founding, the RRBM and its partners have made some modest yet encouraging progress. Many leading journals, such as the *Journal of International Business Studies* (*JIBS*), *Strategic Management Journal* (*SMJ*), and *Management and Organizational*

Review (*MOR*), have published editorials on increasing the transparency of research and preventing problems like p-hacking or HARKing (Schwab and Starbuck, 2017). Some journals have begun to join the open science initiative of the COS and to encourage authors to pre-register research designs and hypotheses before data collection and to share their data for verification or replication studies.[11]

Many journals have introduced special issues to encourage research on critical societal issues. For example, *JIBS* introduced a special issue: "The Global Scope of Corporate Sustainability: Multinational Firms, Supply Chains, and the Private Governance of Social and Environmental Issues." The *Academy of Management Journal*'s new special research forum "Joining Conversations in the Society on Management and Organisations" invites authors to join conversations that are taking place around the world (rather than conversations in the literature). This call for submissions suggests many new topics, such as analyzing the effects of caste systems on employment and discrimination in organizations; sexual harassment, diversity, and inclusion in the workplace; global health inequities; bribery; political influence; and personal politics. The *Journal of Marketing* has a special issue titled "Better Marketing for a Better World," and the journal of *Manufacturing & Service Operations Management* has an upcoming special issue titled "Responsible Research in Operations Management" (papers are under review as of the time of writing this chapter). As of early November 2020, there were at least nine special issues in leading journals with an active call for submissions.[12] These are the grand challenges of the twenty-first century, and the extant literature is silent on most of these topics.

The RRBM also inspired the creation of awards to recognize research that exemplifies the seven principles. One such award is the Manufacturing and Service Operations Management Society (MSOM) Society Award for Responsible Research in Operations Management;[13] this award is for research papers (published or presented). The Organizational Behavior (OB) division of the Academy of Management (AoM) inaugurated the Societal Impact Award, noting that "scholarly work with societal impact is both scientifically credible

---

[11] The *MOR* journal has a formal preregistration policy with preapproval of manuscripts (Lewin et al., 2016).

[12] The list of journal special issues is available from the RRBM (n.d.-b).

[13] RRBM (n.d.-c) provides information on the various awards.

and useful to society." These award-winning papers provide examples of how to engage in responsible research and hopefully inspire young scholars to follow their passion and be instruments of change for a better world. Further awards have been instigated by both the British and European Academies of Management.

Research in business schools is highly specialized. These award-winning research projects, although well-executed and on fundamental problems, are mainly single-discipline works. However, many of the grand challenges in the contemporary world (e.g., COVID-19 pandemic, poverty, inequality, injustice) are incredibly complex, evading the possibility of an accurate or complete understanding using any single disciplinary perspective. Understanding and solving some of these "wicked" problems will require multidisciplinary and multisector collaboration. Business research must emphasize, encourage, and reward inter- or multidisciplinary projects as a responsible participant in solving wicked problems. In the next section, we provide an example of a project that combined expertise in architecture, sociology, information technology, and management.

A Multidisciplinary Responsible Research Example

The significant challenges that confront societies today do not respect the tidy boundaries of academic disciplines. Consider the COVID-19 pandemic. For an individual who has caught the virus, it is a medical problem. For the broader community concerned about contagion, it is a public health problem. For governments at various levels (city, county, region, nation), it is a public policy problem. For those who run businesses and must balance the needs of customers, the safety and economic well-being of employees, and the demands of investors, it is a business problem. All these levels are interconnected, and durable solutions require insights that cross boundaries. Nevertheless, relevant experts often speak different scientific languages and apply different frameworks. ("Aerosol" means something very different to an epidemiologist and a marketing professor.)

We propose two things. First, interdisciplinary scholarship, rooted in the principles of responsible research highlighted previously, will be most effective in addressing societal challenges. Problems cross disciplines; thus, so must solutions. Second, we see business schools as being uniquely appropriate hubs for hosting such efforts. Earlier, we described business schools as an estuary between academia and the world of practice. At a fundamental level, business schools are about how to organize people and resources to get things done, and this is what all societal challenges require, from taking on pandemics and climate change to reducing inequalities across gender and race to ensuring access to food, education, and health care.

Consider an example. How does physical space shape social interactions, and how do these interactions, in turn, influence innovation in organizations? Answering this question implicates several different fields. Architecture scholars are skilled at measuring the attributes of the built environment and have developed quantitative methods to characterize the relations among different spaces as nodes in a network. Sociologists employ tools of social network analysis to quantify the relations among actors in a social system and how they change over time. Psychologists have theorized about the different properties of groups that influence creativity, such as the group's diversity. Strategic management scholars study the nature and production of innovation in organizations. Any of these fields has something useful to contribute to the question of space, interaction, and innovation. However, all of them together will likely yield far greater insights that can inform the production of innovative solutions.

This example is not entirely hypothetical. One of us (Davis) was a co-principal investigator on a study of precisely this question, along with colleagues in the College of Architecture and Urban Planning, the Sociology Department, and the School of Information (Wineman et al., 2014). The National Science Foundation in the United States funded the research, which unfolded over several years. Architects on the team used electronic charts of the floor plates of buildings to create heat maps based on which spaces were on the shortest paths between any given pair of rooms. Sociologists surveyed employees about the people they interacted with to analyze their social networks at work. Business scholars found ways to measure innovations as they developed from the gleam in the eye to a finished product. The study examined a diverse set of workplaces (involving software development, truck manufacturing, medical research, and engineering) to maximize the chances for generalizability and application. In the most intensive study setting, an entire floor of an office building was wired with location-tracking tools, and employee participants in the study carried location-tagged badges that allowed the team to track their interactions at work over several weeks. Participants also completed written surveys, and one of the researchers took up residence in the office for participant observation and one-on-one interviews. The result was a rich portrait of social networks at work and how they shaped the innovation process, demonstrating the different facets of "networks" observed using different methods. Moreover, one of the dissertations to emerge from this project created an entire suite of new dynamic network measures.

We now have a much richer understanding of how to organize space to create the kinds of social networks that yield innovation in organizations. However, we also have a strong sense of the points of maximum leverage for making a workplace safe in the event of a viral pandemic, which are – ironically – in opposition to those for creating innovation. Innovation thrives when the average geodesic (the shortest network path between any two people) is low, but this is also the prescription for maximizing viral spread. Sometimes even the researchers may not realize the ultimate applications of their work.

The potential audiences for work such as this are as diverse as the scholars who produced it. How should architects design buildings to promote human relationships? How should businesses organize spaces within buildings to encourage innovative networks? How should managers organize staffing engagements to yield the most productive and creative teams? Moreover, how can work be reorganized after the pandemic to balance needs for safety and innovation? Interdisciplinary work guided by principles of responsible research has rich potential to benefit society.

Conclusion

Effective multidisciplinary work, often embedded in practice, takes time, but that is time worth taking because the outcome is richer and more useful than operating with a single lens. Multi-lens work is becoming increasingly widespread. Indeed, some business schools (e.g., in the UK) that were doing little before the outbreak of the recent pandemic have responded to their government's calls for grant-aided research into the disease's impact on, for instance, manufacturing output, the homeless, care homes, and frontline workers. Much of this work involves combinations of academics from different disciplines, often in conjunction with medical scientists, spurred on by a national consciousness to pioneer solutions for the good of society. COVID-19 has triggered a portfolio of multidisciplinary activity that was not there before and may well continue after that. Practical relevance may have returned on a large scale, taking business and management research back to its roots.

In parallel, a whole swathe of global movements have kicked into action to counter the paucity of good science underpinning research and, most importantly, the credibility of the research results on which policy decisions depend. Among these, the RRBM has gained considerable traction in a short time because of the need for action recognized by many academics, especially junior ones with little influence over the system they had entered who have concerns about the practice inside it. Finding senior academics sponsoring a movement and taking actions that they dared not, or could not, take must have come as a blessing. Although it must also have seemed strange to them that the RRBM's birth came by way of the EFMD – an agency concerned with management development and recognized globally as an accreditation body (EQUIS) for business schools. Why would an accreditation agency be interested in quality and impactful research? Often, external eyes see things more clearly than internal ones – especially across the breadth of a sector. The EFMD's eye was broad because of the nature of its work. Its executives saw the need for action but also knew that the academics involved had to heal themselves. The EFMD's foresight in sponsoring the RRBM and its support throughout the years have been invaluable. The EFMD played its part in transforming the behavior of academics in the sector. We congratulate the EFMD on this achievement and upon its remarkable 50th milestone!

References

Bedeian, A. G., Taylor, S. G., and Miller, A. N. (2010). Management science on the credibility bubble: Cardinal sins and various misdemeanors. *Academy of Management Learning & Education*, 9(4), 715–725.

Center for Open Science. (n.d.). *Our mission is to promote openness, integrity and reproducibility of research*. www.cos.io/about/mission.

Davis, G. F. (2015). Editorial essay: What is organisational research for? *Administrative Science Quarterly*, 60(2), 179–188.

Dijstelbloem, H., Huisman, F., Miedema, F., and Mijnhardt, W. (2013, October 17). *Why science does not work as it should and what to do about it*. Science in Transition Position Paper. www.scienceintransition .nl/app/uploads/2013/10/Science-in-Transition-Position-Paper-final.pdf.

Goodhart, C. (1975). Problems of monetary management: The U.K. experience. In A. S. Courakis, ed., *Inflation, depression, and economic policy in the West*. Barnes and Noble Books, pp. 91–121.

Gordon, R. A., and Howell, J. E. (1959). *Higher education for business*. Columbia University Press.

Hambrick, D. C. (1994). 1993 presidential address: What if the Academy actually mattered? *The Academy of Management Review* 19(1), 11–16.

Hicks, D., Wouters, L., de Rijcke, S., and Rafols, I. (2015). Bibliometrics: The Leiden manifesto for research. *Nature*, 520(7548), 429–431.

Lewin, A. Y., Chiu, C. Y., Fey, C. F., Levine, S. S., McDermott, G., Murmann, J. P., and Tsang, E. (2016). The critique of empirical social science: New policies at management and organisation review. *Management and Organization Review*, 12(4), 649–658.

MacKenzie, D. (2006). *An engine, not a camera: How financial models shape markets*. MIT Press.

McKiernan, P., and Tsui, A. S. (2020). Responsible research in business and management: Transforming doctoral education. In D. C. Moosmeyer, O. Laasch, C. Parkes, and K. G. Brown, eds., *The Sage handbook of responsible management, learning and education*. Sage, pp. 485–501.

Merton, R. K. (1942). The normative structure of science. *The sociology of science: Theoretical and empirical investigations*. University of Chicago Press.

Moosmeyer, D. C., Laasch, O., Parkes, C., and Brown, K. G., eds. (2020). *The Sage handbook of responsible management, learning and education*. Sage.

Munafò, M. R., Nosek, B. A., Bishop, D. V., Button, K. S., Chambers, C. D., Du Sert, N. P., and Ioannidis, J. P. (2017). A manifesto for reproducible science. *Nature Human Behaviour*, 1(1), article 21.

Power, M. (1997). *Audit society: Rituals of verification*. Oxford University Press.

Primer. (n.d.). *COVID-19 primer*. https://covid19primer.com/dashboard.

Principles for Responsible Management Education. (n.d.). *What we do: Six principles*. www.unprme.org/what-we-do.

Rabin, R. C. (2020, June 14). The pandemic claims new victims: Prestigious medical journals. *New York Times*. www.nytimes.com/2020/06/14/health/virus-journals.html.

Reibstein, D. J., Day, G., and Wind, J. (2009). Guest editorial: Is marketing academia losing its way? *Journal of Marketing*, 73(4), 1–3.

Responsible Research in Business and Management. (n.d.-a). *Position paper*. www.rrbm.network/position-paper/.

    (n.d.-b). *A vision of responsible research in business and management*. www.rrbm.network/.

(n.d.-c). *Awards.* www.rrbm.network/taking-action/awards/.

Risjord, M. (2014). *Philosophy of social science: A contemporary introduction.* Routledge.

Ritchie, S. (2020). *Science fictions: Exposing fraud, bias, negligence and hype in science.* Bodley Head.

Schwab, A., and Starbuck, W. H. (2017). A call for openness in research reporting: How to turn covert practices into helpful tools. *Academy of Management Learning & Education,* 16(1), 125–141.

Starkey, K. (2015). The strange absence of management during the current financial crisis. *Academy of Management Review,* 40, 652–663.

Tang, C. S. (2016). O.M. forum – making O.M. research more relevant: "Why?" and "How?". *Manufacturing & Service Operations Management,* 18(2), 178–183.

Terwiesch, C., and Ulrich, K. T. (2014, July 16). *Will video kill the classroom star? The threat and opportunity of massively open on-line courses for full-time MBA programs.* https://ssrn.com/abstract= 2467557.

Tsui, A. (2016). Reflections on the so-called value-free ideal: A call for responsible science in the business schools. *Cross Cultural & Strategic Management,* 23(1), 4–28.

Tsui, A. S. (2006). Contextualisation in Chinese management research. *Management and Organization Review,* 2(1), 1–13.

(2013). 2012 presidential address. On compassion in scholarship: Why should we care? *Academy of Management Review,* 38(2), 167–180.

Wilkinson, M., Dumontier, M., Aalbersberg, I., Appleton, G., Axton, M., Baak, A., Blomberg, N., et al. (2016). The FAIR Guiding Principles for scientific data management and stewardship. *Scientific Data,* 3, article 160018.

Wilson, D., and McKiernan, P. (2011). Global mimicry: Putting strategic choice back on the business school agenda. *British Journal of Management,* 22(3), 457–469.

Wineman, J., Hwang, Y., Kabo, F., Owen-Smith, J., and Davis, G. F. (2014). Spatial layout, social structure and innovation in organisations. *Environment and Planning B: Planning and Design,* 41(6), 1100–1112.

Zingales, L. (2015). Presidential address: Does finance benefit society? *The Journal of Finance,* 70(4), 1327–1363.

Going Beyond Business

6 The Reshaping of Corporations and Their Governance by Climate Change and Other Global Forces – Implications for Leaders and Management Education

PETER LITTLE

Introduction

For business leaders in market economies, the sanctity of national law for setting their respective governance frameworks is diminishing. It is giving way to global forces and the activities of international institutions, alliances, and public opinion, spurred on by the laws of climate and nature. Previously, company leaders could have confidently said that they act in the interests of the company and its shareholders, that the company obeys applicable national laws that govern its activities, and that the company acts ethically and responsibly, but beyond that, they had wide discretion when carrying out their duties. Today, extra-territorial forces are redefining many aspects of corporate life and the agendas, roles, and responsibilities of corporations, their leaders, and governing boards.

An important illustration of this is the existential challenge for companies to transition from a focus on short-term profit to long-term sustainability and shareholder wealth creation. Likewise, there is a growing expectation that corporate leaders will take into account a wider range of stakeholders when exercising corporate powers. For CEOs, directors, and senior executives, new domains of responsibility are emerging with varying degrees of speed and certainty. They pose a challenge for leaders to keep pace with such fluidity and its implications for corporate governance. Some entities may carry on business in ignorance or defiance of the advancing forces, but the unstoppable march of those occupying the high moral ground who seek to advance matters of global moral concern, especially climate change, signals the inevitability of major change for most businesses and their leaders. And moreover, a company cannot rely on its nation's government to be the arbiter of which demands will be met and to what extent and within what timeframe.

Thus, even if a government declined to fully support the Paris Agreement (United Nations, 2015) targets or withdrew its support completely, it would not prevent global investors from withholding essential finance from a proposed project or forcing strategic change upon a corporation and its leaders. Nor would it prevent businesses from voluntarily acceding to international and national market forces that effectively oblige leaders to associate their brands with fast-evolving principles of good corporate citizenship. To this end, fluid extraterritorial powers, especially fueled by climate change and other environmental, social, and governance (ESG) considerations, are able to act ahead of and, when necessary, independently of national governments. Supranationality is an ever-increasing modern phenomenon, manifesting itself in global opinion and the reach and actions of non-state actors and movements, both challenging and supplementing the exclusivity of traditional principles of state-centered sovereignty.

Our era of fluid modernity provides a novel setting for issues of global concern to become deeply embedded into public discourses and ultimately flow into governance frameworks and corporate behavior. Modernity offers a translational efficiency never before experienced or available, probably outside of wars and pandemics, in relation to the regulation of business. Global agendas can now quite quickly filter down to influence governments, regulators, and national interest groups and, in consequence, change both local laws and business behavior. Influencers include global organizations, both public and private; global capital movements, such as institutional investors with unlimited reach; and social media, with its ubiquity and immediacy. Global and local standard setters also play an important role in this process of translation.

For the present purposes, four closely connected dimensions of these extraterritorial forces – namely, the laws of climate and nature, Climate Action 100+ (CA100+), the Task Force on Climate-Related Financial Disclosures (TCFD), and stakeholderism – will be considered in this chapter.[1] These are affecting the day-to-day settings of business

---

[1] Others of relevance include the wide-ranging and ever-expanding ESG movement, the increasing take-up of the Principles for Responsible Investment (PRI), and the increasing impact of the United Nations (UN) Sustainable Development Goals (SDGs; United Nations, n.d.).

life as global institutions and players have their agendas quickly translated into real action and real outcomes with impressive speed. For businesses and their leaders and those who educate them, this is the modern reality; a new era is unfolding.

Liquid Modernity

Liquid modernity (Bauman, 2012) describes contemporary global society in which many accepted elements are being uprooted or liquidized. Flexibility and immediacy are replacing established norms and practices. As a consequence, questions are being raised about the nature and purpose of modern corporations, how they should operate in the face of climate change and other concerns, the duties and accountabilities of their CEOs and boards, and the extent of their managerial power. Global power giveth and global power taketh away.

Power can move with the speed of the electronic signal – and so the time required for the movement of its essential ingredient has been reduced to instantaneity. For all practical purposes, power has become truly *extraterritorial*, no longer bound, not even slowed down, by the resistance of space. . . . This gives the power-holders a truly unprecedented opportunity: the awkward and irritating aspects of the Panoptical technique of power may be disposed of. Whatever else the present stage in the history of modernity is, it is also, perhaps above all, post-Panoptical. What mattered in Panopticon was that the people in charge were assumed always to be there, nearby, in the controlling tower. (Bauman, 2012, p. 10)

Now power can be amassed globally and brought to bear across borders with relative speed, with or without state sanction or participation and with both private and public outcomes. Today, transactions, information, and corporate power flow more fluidly than ever before, thereby allowing for global dominance over product and data markets and industries. Not even the great and feared trading behemoths of earlier centuries, such as the British East India Company, could have amassed dominance across the globe with equivalent speed and efficiency. As one commentator observes: "Imagine an economy without friction – a new world in which labor, information, and money move easily, cheaply, and almost instantly ... it's here" (Colvin, 2015, para. 2). For example, in 2017, 69 of the world's richest 100 entities by revenue, including countries, were corporations (Global

Justice Now, 2018), and incumbent enterprises are said to own 80 percent of the world's commercial data (Schumpeter, 2018).

Mark Zuckerberg, founder and chairman of Facebook, has said: "In a lot of ways Facebook is more like a government than a traditional company" (Farrell et al., 2018, para. 1). Its 28 billion users are far greater in number than the citizens in any one country, and its influence, market value, and revenues exceed those of many individual nations. This is but one example of the modern realities of supranational power that sits uneasily with traditional theories and limits of sovereignty.

Capitalism has become light in the process. "The passage from heavy to light capitalism, from solid to fluid modernity, may yet prove to be a departure more radical and seminal than the advent of capitalism and modernity themselves, previously seen as by far the most crucial milestones of human history at least since the neolithic revolution" (Bauman, 2012, pp. 125–126). But while light or fluid capitalism describes the transience of industrial production and the freely moving, profit-seeking global capital, it also facilitates the movement of socially focused, long-term aspirational investment and its demands. It is this phenomenon of liquid modernity that allows direct private action successfully to be taken in pursuance of globally agreed-on social and environmental goals. Social narratives around the world are themselves more fluid than they were 10 or 20 years ago.

Historically, those holding the power write the narratives, and as Bauman (2012) observes:

For at least two hundred years it was the managers of capitalist enterprises who dominated the world.... It was therefore their vision of the world, in conjunction with the world itself, shaped and reshaped in the likeness of that vision, that fed into and gave substance to the dominant discourse. (p. 55)

The dominant discourses, however, are beginning to change, as are those who shape and give effect to them. Now, international contributors such as the United Nations (UN), the World Economic Forum (WEF), PRI, CA100+, the TCFD, institutional investors, and powerful coalitions of interests united in beliefs and connected through modern media channels are exerting influence in time and reach way beyond what was possible or contemplated not so long ago. Speed, reach, and influence are now leveraged to shape policies, practices, products, and commitments while confronting corporations and their executives on issues of global and local community concern. Chief among them are climate change, protection of the environment, sustainability, ethical investment, human rights, and addressing inequality.

A feature of modernity has been a strong emphasis on short-term thinking and outcomes. "The 'long term', though still referred to by habit, is a hollow shell carrying no meaning; ... the 'short term' has replaced the 'long term' and made of instantaneity its ultimate ideal" (Bauman, 2012, p. 125). This is the environment in which corporations and their leaders have been operating, facing incessant market demands for short-term profits while battling to gain market support for initiatives and investments that could only be harvested in the long term. And all the while, they are being met with ever-expanding demands for good corporate citizenship, whose nature is also rapidly evolving. These are the realities of modernity that have substantially eliminated time and distance in the exercise of power. However, the global forces representing climate action are changing the short-term–long-term equation. Long-termism is making a spirited comeback to challenge the dominance of short-term thinking, planning, and investment.[2] Nevertheless, much remains to be played out in this contest between two "deep-pocketed" forces.

How Quickly Things Develop

It took many centuries for Christianity and Islam to evolve into global religions, at least 1,500 years in the case of Christianity. In contrast, the science and political movements associated with climate change have emerged in less than 60 years, and widespread acceptance by the public at large of climate change as an existential threat to communities has occurred in around 30 years (Weart, 2020) but with growing intensity over the last decade.[3] Black Lives Matter became a global movement in less than 7 years, and the MeToo movement became truly global in less than 3 years.

According to Thomas Friedman, the three largest forces on the planet, namely, technology, globalization, and climate change, are all accelerating at the same time (Friedman, 2016a, p. 120). As he says, even the pace of change is changing. In consequence, "so many aspects

---

[2] See page 131 for a discussion of the New Paradigm.
[3] See Fagan and Huang (2019).

of our societies, workplaces, and geopolitics are being re-shaped and need to be re-imagined" (Friedman, 2016a, pp. 3–4). To this list can be added corporations, their purpose, their regulation, and the expectations of those who lead and oversee them.

Friedman refers to 2007 as the moment when the globalization of thought, capital movement, and fluid power became turbo-charged. "The moment that Steve Jobs introduced the iPhone turns out to have been a pivotal junction in the history of technology – and the world" (Friedman, 2016b, p. 20). He describes how a whole group of new companies emerged in and around that year: "Together these new companies and innovations have reshaped how people and machines communicate, create, collaborate, and think" (Friedman, 2016b, p. 20). Friedman also points to the "Big Shift," which describes the knowledge *flows* that pass through countries and communities, creating opportunities and competitive advantages (Hagel et al., 2009b). As John Hagel observes of the globalization of flows: "We are living in a world where flow will prevail and topple any obstacles in its way."[4] Global opinion and capital pressure, now flowing in increasing harmony with that of nature and the climate, are becoming irresistible forces.

Climate Change – a Force of Nature, a Force for Change

Ascendancy of the Climate-Change Movement – toward Climate Sovereignty and the Sovereignty of Nature

International agreements, such as the United Nations Framework Convention on Climate Change (UNFCC) signed by 197 countries (United Nations, 1992) and the Paris Agreement signed by 186 of the UNFCC signatories, broadly frame the global movements on climate change and climate action. At the time of writing, the Paris Agreement has been ratified by 190 countries. Aided by the developing science generated by the Intergovernmental Panel on Climate Change (IPCC) and many scientists and scientific organizations around the world, a global belief, even global consciousness, has emerged.[5] Because of this

---

[4] An extract from Thomas Friedman interview with John Hagel, cited in Friedman (2016b, p. 128).
[5] See, for example, National Aeronautics and Space Administration (2020). Also, a recent survey showed that in 23 of 26 countries surveyed, climate change was

overwhelming scientific and public, albeit not universal, support for the notion that the climate change being witnessed in the world is human induced, businesses, their leaders, and their representative institutions have little choice but to respond accordingly. As a result, climate action now appears to be an unstoppable global force, with transitions to decarbonizing economies now backed by massive and growing investments,[6] perhaps meaning, in de Tocqueville terms, a revolution is underway as a result of rising expectations.

We are living in a state of anticipation, transnational in reach, where global warming and other issues "infuse a sense of looming time limits that generate urgency and anxiety about acting now to protect the future" (Adams et al., 2009, p. 248). Fear and hope are important factors, and we see these at work with climate change and climate action. "Anticipation is not just betting on the future; it is a moral economy in which the future sets the conditions of possibility for action in the present, in which the future is inhabited in the present" (Adams et al., 2009, p. 249). Thus, as climate-related disasters are seen as portents of future calamities, forces are amassing to take serious remedial action in the present.

This involves the participation of national governments, international governmental and nongovernmental organizations too numerous to list, private international capital, individual corporations, communities, individuals, and activist groups. Together, they comprise an international network of movements pursuing broadly common goals but often differentiated with respect to methodologies, timings, and impacts. Thus, globally engaged human thought is manifesting itself in a unique way – when else has this occurred so comprehensively and been so individually and institutionally embraced? And why does this groundswell of belief and support continue to gather strength and not waver? In large part, it seems, because the climate itself constantly catalyzes interest by delivering powerful and tangible reminders.

---

rated as a major threat to the respective nations by a majority (median score 68 percent) of those surveyed. See Fagan and Huang (2019).
[6] Bloomberg NEF research shows that more than $500 billion was invested in energy transitions in 2020, with a continuing upward trend. See Macdonald-Smith (2021, p. 17). Further, the value of sustainable investments globally is estimated to exceed $30 trillion (Statista, 2021). The adoption of formal climate action plans by individual companies is, however, still lagging global opinion. See also PricewaterhouseCoopers (2021) and Coppola et al. (2019).

Are we, accordingly, in this age of liquid modernity, moving toward the recognition of new forms of sovereignty arising from the impacts of climate and the responses of nature to human and corporate activity? Could it be said that climate sovereignty and the sovereignty of nature – a federation of sovereignties – are being claimed or reasserted by Mother Nature through the agency of, but not limited by, governing and institutional constituencies around the world and her foot soldiers paying respect and pledging loyalty and obedience to her needs and demands such as conservationists, climate activists, the public, and compliant capital? Mother Nature can be seen to be asserting control over her domain, rewriting social contracts globally and demanding compliance with the rules of her regime in new and more apparent ways. And her regime can be considered to be every bit as sovereign or even more so than limits of temporal and territorial power existing within nation-states and other sovereignties.

In modern international law, sovereignty is generally linked to territory and to the right of peoples to govern themselves, subject to some exceptions. Yet extraterritorial power and movements are increasingly influential in the affairs of nations and of humankind more broadly. Climate and environmental activism are cases in point, including the forces of direct private capital flowing seamlessly across the globe, largely unfettered by states or the conceptual limitations of territorial sovereignty in search of climate solutions and the protection of nature. They deserve more serious consideration and analysis in the sovereignty debates as to the nature and source of their power and authority. In a well-reasoned analysis, which has analogies for global climate action, it has been argued that the authority of the International Criminal Court derives not from state power but from the international community of citizens and their human rights. The author concludes:

A supranational *ius puniendi* can be inferred from a *combination of* the incipient stages of *supranationality* of a value-based world order and the concept of a world society composed of world citizens whose law – the *"world citizen law"* (*Weltbürgerrecht*) – is derived from universal, indivisible and interculturally recognized human rights predicated upon a Kantian concept of human dignity. . . . This community is the holder of the international *ius puniendi*. (Ambos, 2013, p. 314)[7]

---

[7] *Ius puniendi* means "the right to punish."

With climate action, by analogy, the right to "punish" or require obedience to long-standing norms ultimately derives not from territorial authority but from an even higher level of supranationality than "world citizen law," namely, climate sovereignty and the sovereignty of nature.

In the world prior to territoriality becoming the cornerstone of jurisdiction, other forms of sovereignty existed, based on, among other aspects, tribes, race, religion, or nationality (Kassan, 1935, p. 240). For example, consider papal sovereignty. "The Holy See is essentially international and has to deal with higher motives and interests than the political ascendency of any state or group of states" (von Redlich, 1932, p. 244). Further, "Rome looks on at the forward march of the course of events in this world, not only from an international standpoint, but from one still more exalted, seeing the course of human life and the life of nations and states '*sub specie aesternitatis*' – in the light of eternal truths and of the supernatural" (von Redlich, 1932, p. 244).

In Islam, sovereignty derives from Allah and is not associated with, or limited by, the notions of states or territorial jurisdiction. "Thus, real sovereignty belongs to Allah alone and it is spread from *arsh* to *farsh* (from the Throne of God to the floor of the earth)" (Ahmad, 1958, p. 249).[8] A recent analysis showed that some extra-legal and organic forms of sovereignty from premodern times continue to exist (Paris, 2020). These include, relevantly, the idea of an organic, civilizational, transnational Chinese nation – a form of transcendent universalism (Paris, 2020, pp. 472–473) not limited by China's territorial borders.

To recognize climate sovereignty and the sovereignty of nature as contemporary federated sovereignties is to acknowledge their organic and transcendent existence, possessing permanence, authority, and the capacity to exert power and influence over a global constituency. They confer the benefits of production and regeneration and impose limits within which sustainable life, natural assets, and ecosystems can flourish and endure. They command respect and obedience and can instill fear when their norms are seriously broken or threatened. This includes fear for the future of the planet, communities, and business and industry continuity; financial instability; the prospect of public shaming; loss of predictability or certainty in the lives of individuals

---

[8] See also Khir (1990).

or families; various forms of extinction; and the loss of safety and security. These sovereignties are potent forces.

In relation to corporations, which rely for their existence on natural capital,[9] these sovereignties are rewriting the rules of "citizenship." Oaths of allegiance are fast becoming mandatory. Being a good corporate citizen possessing moral legitimacy within these sovereignties has its onerous civic responsibilities, such as reducing greenhouse emissions and operating sustainably, but is accompanied by protected freedoms and benefits. Among others, there is freedom to continue in business and the benefits of a green reputation, together with supportive capital waiting to invest in and help transition and grow a business. And, some would say, the social license to operate is the ultimate concession, offering sovereign passports stamped with a visa for green-credentialed corporations to continue in business for the long term.

Conversely, industries and corporations not seen to be responding seriously to climate change and other social responsibilities are susceptible to having their social licenses to operate being canceled. This could arise, for example, through a government banning the extraction or processing of fossil fuels, as was highlighted by the newly elected US government's action to pause new oil and natural gas leases on public lands and in offshore waters.

Thomas Friedman (2016a) describes in an interesting way how Mother Nature controls her domain through a rigid and brutal rules-based regime: "Mother Nature also believes in bankruptcy. . . . She has no mercy for her mistakes, for the weak, or for those who can't adapt to get their seeds, their DNA, into the next generation. . . . What markets do with bankruptcy laws, Mother Nature does with forest fires" (p. 306). And also with other effects of climate change, it might be added. This is how Mother Nature's system of justice works. Friedman (2016a) suggests that "Mother Nature in her own way, appreciates the power of ownership" (p. 305). But in contrast to human systems, he notes, "Natural systems have no owners, no self-interested managers per se" (Friedman, 2016a, p. 305). Yet, green

---

[9] Natural capital is "the stock of ecosystems that yield a renewable flow of goods and services that underpin the economy and provide inputs and direct and indirect benefits to businesses and society"' (United Nations Environment Programme Finance Initiative, n.d., para. 2).

shoots are emerging where nature's ownership of its own capital is being recognized.

In New Zealand, personhood has been granted to the Wanganui River (Te Awa Tupua), from the mountains down to the sea, in a world first for river ownership (Chapron et al., 2019). No longer the property of the Crown, the river has its own identity and owns itself, with all the rights, powers, duties, and liabilities of a legal person. Similarly, personhood has been granted to what was formally a large national park (Te Urewera) containing lakes, forests, and mountains (Biggs et al., 2017, pp. 24–25). Personhood has also been conferred on the Ganges and Yumana Rivers in India, and rivers in Colombia possess rights to protection, conservation, maintenance, and restoration (Biggs et al., 2017, p. 27).

As well, Ecuador became the first country to enshrine rights of nature in its constitution, and under Bolivian national laws, the inherent rights of ecosystems are recognized (Biggs et al., 2017, p. 8). In the United States, the right of nature to exist and flourish has been recognized in a number of communities but with varying effects (West, 2020), and Ohio's Lake Erie was the first US example of an ecosystem to receive acknowledgment of its rights to exist, flourish, and naturally evolve (Community Environmental Local Defense Fund, 2020). Clearly, it is the early days in the process of fully recognizing the rights of nature; however, the movement's achievements are growing, and it has established the International Tribunal for the Rights of Nature, where cases are presented by an "Earth Defender" (Biggs et al., 2017, p. 36). Another example of natural capital emerging more clearly into the mainstream is the establishment of the Natural Capital Investment Alliance, which aims to invest $10 billion in natural capital investments by 2022. Falling under the banner of Prince Charles's Sustainable Market Initiative, it is seeking to monetize activities that protect natural capital. Its Terra Carta (Earth Charter) manifesto aims to broaden the notion of sustainability beyond net-zero emission targets to include nature, people, the planet, equality, and prosperity (Fernyhough, 2021).

Questions surrounding "standing" to act on behalf of nature, which can arise in formal legal proceedings (Miller, 2019), are avoided when direct action is taken by nature's champions and defenders. They can employ a variety of extra-legal measures, especially leveraging the power of institutional capital to achieve outcomes on behalf of nature and the planet.[10] As well, groundbreaking legal actions are emerging around the world (Setzer and Byrnes, 2020). Notably, actions are being brought against governments, corporations, and regulators at local, national, and international levels. Among a widely expanding range of plaintiffs are individuals, including children, as well as groups, corporations, nongovernmental organizations (NGOs), and local communities seeking enforcement of treaty obligations, national laws, policies and regulations, and corporate commitments. Furthermore, the bases for such claims are similarly expanding as plaintiffs seek to rely on established causes of action as well as asserting new foundations for claims to protect their interests, both personally and on behalf of their communities or the local or global environment. Claims extend to seeking protection against future harm by applying for injunctions or declarations or to receiving damages for present or future loss. Decisions have been handed down requiring governments to take affirmative action, and increasingly, actions are relying on human rights to found the claims (Setzer and Byrnes, 2020). New high-water marks are being set within countries and at the international level.

An extraordinary example involves the case *Lliuya v. RWE AG* (Global Climate Change Litigation Database, n.d.), in which the plaintiff, a Peruvian farmer, is suing a German utility company in a German court for the partial costs of remediation of threatened flooding in his home country due to the recent increase in volume in a glacial lake near his farm. This was allegedly caused by the impact of climate change upon a nearby glacier. Although the farmer was initially unsuccessful in his claim, on appeal, the case was accepted for hearing. The potential is for the company to be found liable for its relative contribution to global climate change as a result of its greenhouse gas (GHG) emissions and to contribute the same proportion to the costs of remediation (Germanwatch, n.d.). Many legal and scientific issues will be in contention, but the supranational dimension to this claim highlights the potential scope of climate-change liability as well as climate protection. In the age of liquid modernity and in light of the emerging consensus, it is hardly surprising that traditionally perceived limitations on the right to compel governments, regulators, and corporations to take action on climate change, either within or across jurisdictions, are succumbing to progressive judicial decision making.

[10] See, for example, the CA100+ discussion later in the chapter.

Reflecting the growing movement to protect nature's capital, the EU High-Level Expert Group on Sustainable Finance recommends making investor duties more explicit by including impacts and dependencies on natural capital and ecosystems and how these may be material to investors, companies, and insurers (EU High-Level Expert Group on Sustainable Finance, 2018). Another of its recommendations is to include consideration of natural capital among the good-faith duties of company directors (EU High-Level Expert Group on Sustainable Finance, 2018, p. 40). Corporations are now facing the formidable combined forces of climate and nature and those acting on their behalf, with far-reaching implications for all parties who are direct or indirect stakeholders in corporate life.

Climate Action 100+

An Overview of Private Politics and Financial Power

The climate-change phenomenon in raising global consciousness has spawned a multiplicity of organizations, both public and private, to vigorously campaign for radical changes to business practices and models. It is best described as a "regime complex for climate change" (Keohane and Victor, 2011, p. 7). It defines the "hodge-podge of loosely connected, decentralised institutional arrangements scattered around the globe that ... emerged in the absence of any unified, binding environmental policy regime" (McAdam, 2017, p. 190). This recognizes the elements that "are linked more or less closely to one another, sometimes conflicting, usually mutually reinforcing" (Keohane and Victor, 2011, p. 7).

Such regimes are loosely coupled sets of specific regimes, and in contemporary world politics, structural and interest diversity tend to generate a regime complex rather than a comprehensive, integrated regime (Keohane and Victor, 2011, p. 7). The former has two distinctive advantages, namely, flexibility across issues and adaptability across time (Keohane and Victor, 2011, p. 15). The regime complex for climate change emerged rather than having been comprehensively designed (Keohane and Victor, 2011, p. 19), reflecting the infeasibility of a comprehensive regime as a result of the complexity of issues, the multiplicity of power groupings in the international arena, and the fluidity of their respective interactions. The emergence of CA100+ is a prime example of this fluidity.

In the space available, CA100+, a powerful activist group, has been chosen to demonstrate the speed, reach, and outcomes that are occurring through the use of private politics (Baron, 2003)[11] – that is, using direct engagement to achieve change or resolve disputes without relying on the law or governments. CA100+ was established in 2017 to implement the first Global Investor Statement on Climate Change, which was published in the lead-up to the adoption of the Paris Agreement (Climate Action in Financial Institutions, 2019). As a senior executive at CalPERS[12] says: "Climate Action 100+ illustrates owners' ability to come together to solve the tragedy of the commons" (Rundell, 2020, para. 1). In this case, it's a coalition of 617 investor organizations of enormous financial scale, with combined assets exceeding $65 trillion (CA100+, 2020), which, remarkably, and presently surpasses the combined gross domestic product (GDP) of the United States, China, and Europe. Furthermore, these organizations represent vast numbers of grassroots members around the world who depend upon them for their long-term financial well-being. In the context of current global politics, both public and private, CA100+ possesses the legitimacy to succeed in its campaign: for it, "the time is right" (Sjöström, 2020, p. 9).

CA100+ signatories acknowledge the need for the world to transition to a lower-carbon economy consistently with the targets set by the Paris Agreement. Accordingly, three broad aims with potentially far-reaching governance consequences were specified in relation to 160 heavy emitters that are said to be responsible for up to 80 percent of industrial emissions.[13] CA100+ aims to secure commitments from each focus company to implement a strong governance framework that clearly articulates the board's accountability and oversight of climate-change risk and opportunities. Second, it wants reductions in GHG emissions across company value chains, consistent with the Paris Agreement's goal of limiting global average temperature increase to 1.5°C above preindustrial levels. And third, it is seeking enhanced corporate disclosure in line with the final recommendations of the TCFD. This includes disclosure of sector-specific expectations on climate change to enable investors to assess the robustness of companies'

---

[11] See also Reid and Toffel (2009).
[12] The California Public Employees' Retirement System.
[13] Representing $8.4 trillion in market capitalization in 32 countries (see CA100+, 2020).

business plans against a range of climate scenarios, including the Paris Agreement targets, and to improve investment decision making (CA100+, n.d.).

The expectation of companies is that they will have an ambition to achieve net-zero emissions by 2050, if not sooner, across their supply chains and a reduction in emissions of 45 percent by 2030 relative to 2010 levels. To this end, companies in collaboration with CA100+ are expected to develop and implement net-zero transition action plans for their value chains and sectors. This requires a resetting of corporate strategies over the short, medium, and long terms and may require companies to reinvent themselves and their operating models. The corporate thinking that is required, therefore, is not to view climate change as a corporate social responsibility issue but one that "is best addressed with the tools of the strategist, not the philanthropist" (Porter and Reinhardt, 2007, para. 1).

A useful analysis of the scope of these challenges is set out in a 36-page Royal Dutch Shell report (Royal Dutch Shell PLC, 2021). Another useful example of the sheer scale and ambition required to reimagine a major business lies in the proposal by Fortescue Metals Ltd, a global leader in the iron-ore industry, to become one of the world's largest energy providers by transitioning to becoming a global renewable resources company (Thompson, 2020) with a particular focus on green hydrogen. Beyond individual corporations, probably the most far-reaching transition proposed is that of the European Green Deal (European Commission, 2019).

A Net-Zero Company Benchmark launched by CA100+ in 2021 includes 30 indicators to provide a comprehensive analysis of which companies are leading the transition to net-zero emissions as well as providing indicators for investors to inform their investment and corporate-engagement strategies (Ceres, 2020a).[14] This initiative, accompanied by data tracking and analysis, sends strong messages to companies and their leaders that, increasingly, their climate data will be publicly available, with implications for their corporate reputations, brand health, and the ability to continue to attract investment. The intention is to hold companies accountable. As the CEO of Ceres, one of the five key stakeholders in CA100+, stated bluntly when referring to the proposed 2021 Net-Zero Company Benchmark: "We're going

[14] See CA100+ (2021) for details of the first report.

to hold them accountable. We'll assess their progress towards this call to action with the public benchmark next year" (Min, 2020, para. 4).

Ethical and moral considerations underpin the work of CA100+, but it is also motivated by self-interest because its signatories' investments are at risk of being devalued by climate change:

With our long-term investment horizon and multiple generations relying on us for pension security, establishing a thriving low-carbon global economy in which we can invest is vitally important to our ability to protect our members' assets and earn risk adjusted returns. Climate change is a systemic risk which needs to be managed and mitigated. For an intergenerational, universal owner like us, there is nowhere to hide. (CalPERS, 2019, p. 24)[15]

An advantage of private capital acting internationally is that it can cut through the intransigence and opposing political forces that inevitably appear when state-based reform is proposed. Nor is it forced to succumb to unacceptable compromises. It also avoids the impasse over the status of corporations under international law.[16] Importantly, it can escalate its use of financial power in cases when cooperation is not forthcoming. As will be seen, this is proving to be a successful strategy. Although CA100+ cannot achieve a green business revolution in the 5 years of the project, its success to date is, nevertheless, remarkable, with inevitable flow-on effects.

These impacts are shrinking timeframes between principle and practice. For example, TCFD disclosure is fast becoming the governing framework for climate-change governance, disclosures, and reporting well in advance of national legislation, except in rare instances.[17] Relying on the social movements' theory, Reid and Toffel (2009) affirm the effectiveness of private politics such as that exercised by CA100+. They found "that companies respond to private politics by

---

[15] For useful examples detailing the climate-change risk exposure of major institutional investors, see the analyses of two CA100+ signatories (CalPERS, 2020); see also AustralianSuper (2020).

[16] Other than in a few exceptional cases, corporations are not subject to direct duties under international law but wait for international obligations to be translated into national regulatory frameworks. The direct negotiation process taking place between large institutional investors and corporations bypasses this long-standing theoretical obstacle.

[17] See discussion on page 115 regarding mandatory reporting enacted by the New Zealand government.

adopting new practices that adhere to the underlying objective of the social activists" (Reid and Toffel, 2009, p. 1171). They also observe

that political context affects the success of a social movement in that firms under threat of regulation related to the social movement are more likely to agree to engage in practices consistent with the aims of the movement ..., as are firms that share an institutional field with firms under threat of regulation. (Reid and Toffel, 2009, p. 1171)

Presently around the world, national governments and regulatory bodies are moving at various speeds, generally slower than the private political forces[18] regarding, for example, reduction of carbon emissions, requiring climate risk reporting to improve financial market stability, and encouraging industry and corporate transitions. Evidence of this lies in the extent of commitments being undertaken by corporations around the world voluntarily, by agreement in response to market pressures or as a result of public and private politics, but nevertheless in advance of regulatory compulsion to do so.

Climate Action 100+ Disciple Model

With its highly committed action working groups deployed around the world, CA100+ has become a potent private force driving business transition in response to climate change.

Under the CA100+ model, signatories are entrusted as fiduciaries to engage with target companies in their respective jurisdictions, either alone or in partnership with other signatories, to achieve climate outcomes. There is a clarity of purpose that informs the discussions held with target companies.[19]

Although its main targets are the 160 identified major GHG emitters, the reach of CA100+ is now far more pervasive as its signatories, generally large institutional investors, use its goals to guide the other investment decisions they make. BlackRock, for example, is targeting 1,000 companies in 2021, reaching beyond direct heavy emitters to those who finance such companies (BlackRock, 2020b, p. 6). It should be noted that the signatories' shared unity of purpose may not always

[18] See, for example, Institutional Investors Group on Climate Change (IIGCC, 2020a), in which the IIGCC, a CA100+ member, urged the EU to set more aggressive 2030 targets in order to meet a 1.5°C Paris Agreement goal.
[19] See, for example, Boyd (2017).

prevent their own commercial interests from coming into conflict while they, themselves, are transitioning their portfolios.[20]

Engagement may take all or any of the following forms: holding one-on-one meetings with companies; holding group meetings with companies; conducting investor roundtables; making a statement at company annual general meetings (AGMs); supporting shareholder resolutions on climate change risk; voting for the removal of directors who have failed in their accountability of climate change risk; voting against reports, accounts, and company-led resolutions; and making joint statements with the company (CA100+, 2019). When necessary, the methods employed to achieve positive results can be scaled up according to the circumstances. CA100+ has firmly stated that it will approach unresponsive and poorly performing companies with targeted action strategies (Ceres, 2020a). A striking example of this approach is BlackRock's stated intention to increasingly use its voting power on shareholder resolutions where engagement is not providing sufficient outcomes or where its voting would accelerate progress in a particular company (BlackRock, 2020b, p. 7). This is a powerful business model at work.

CA100+ Achievements

As a stakeholder possessing power, legitimacy, and urgency (Mitchell et al., 1997, p. 878), CA100+ is achieving both tangible and precedential outcomes.[21] The first CA100+ Net-Zero Company Benchmark Report released in early 2021 contains a useful snapshot of areas in which significant progress is being made, as well as areas of continuing challenge for corporations. Thus, 52 percent of focus companies have made full or partial commitments to 2050 net-zero targets; 60 percent have made full or partial commitments to long-term (2036–2050) GHG emission reduction targets; and 67 percent have similarly

---

[20] See, for example, a recent occasion when BlackRock unsuccessfully voted for a resolution to bring forward closure of some Australian coal-fired power stations, which was opposed by some other signatories of CA100+ (Australian Centre for Corporate Responsibility, 2020).

[21] For a useful summary of climate-action outcomes analyzed in relation to the energy; materials and buildings; agriculture, food, and forestry; and transportation sectors, see CalPERS (2020).

committed to medium term (2026–2035) emission-reduction targets. Other areas in which major progress has been made, no doubt because these are the easiest and least complex to implement, are climate-policy engagement (63 percent), climate governance (89 percent), and commitment to TCFD disclosure (80 percent).[22]

In contrast, two areas that go to the heart of business operating models, strategy, and financing of transitions, namely, capital allocation alignment and decarbonization strategy, have achieved the least progress to date. Only six companies have made full or partial progress in aligning their capital allocation with their climate-action commitments, and only 40 percent of focus companies have achieved full or partial progress in developing and implementing a decarbonization strategy.

A few specific examples, however, highlight the progress being achieved. In 2018, Royal Dutch Shell PLC (Shell) announced its intention to reduce its carbon footprint by around half by 2050, to link its energy transition with long-term remuneration, and to disclose in line with the TCFD recommendations. Then, in April 2020, Shell announced a new ambition to become a carbon-neutral energy business by 2050 and to reduce scope 3 emissions by 65 percent by the same date (Royal Dutch Shell PLC, 2020). Importantly, the Shell CEO declared that its previous targets were not sufficient and that society had moved toward meeting the more ambitious Paris Agreement targets of 1.5°C (Royal Dutch Shell PLC, 2020).

Maersk, the world's largest shipping company, committed to net-zero emissions by 2050 (Maersk, 2019), and Glencore, the world's largest mining company by revenue, agreed to cap its coal production at current levels while prioritizing investment in commodities that support low-emission technologies, among other commitments (Glencore, 2020). Another notable success, following discussions with CA100+, was Total's announcement of its ambition to achieve 2050 net-zero emissions across its worldwide operations (IIGCC, 2020b). It further committed to assessing capital expenditure for its consistency with the Paris Agreement, together with annual reporting, and to

---

[22] See CA100+ (2021). This report also contains details of the progress of individual companies.

actively advocate for policies that support the achievement of net-zero emissions. The CA100+ 2020 Progress Report contains a full outline and analysis of corporate commitments and progress in key sectors (CA100+, 2020).

Lobbying commitments are another key feature of agreements reached between CA100+ and individual companies. This involves obtaining undertakings to ensure that lobbying by industry associations of which a focus company is a member is balanced and does not unduly emphasize the cost of taking action. Thus, significantly, BHP, the world's largest miner by market capitalization (Statista, 2020), worked with CA100+ and other key investors to establish its new Global Climate Policy Standards, which state that advocacy on climate policy should be balanced to avoid focusing on the cost of reducing emissions; fact-based, using the best available evidence and avoiding ambiguity; focused toward areas that present the greatest benefits to members and communities while avoiding advocacy that might unduly exacerbate policy tensions; and be technology and commodity neutral (BHP, n.d.).

Using the proxy system to propose shareholder resolution is another strategy being used to good effect by CA100+, more so in the United States than in Europe (Horster and Papadopoulus, 2019).[23] Importantly, the publicity associated with shareholder resolutions in major corporations also sends strong signals to others in the same industry: "firms are more likely to agree to engage in practices consistent with the aims of a social movement if they ... or other firms in their industry ... have already been targeted by a shareholder resolution on a related issue" (Reid and Toffel, 2009, p. 1171). Areas of focus for shareholder resolutions include director elections, climate strategies aligned with the Paris Agreement, board independence, alignment of executive remuneration with ESG metrics and Paris Agreement goals, and commitment to TCFD reporting.[24]

A truly remarkable example of CA100+ in action is its role in having a resolution passed by over 99 percent of the vote at the 2019 Annual

---

[23] See also Institutional Shareholder Services (2020); the coverage will extend to 3,700 companies globally across more than 20 capital market main indices and will be supported by a Custom Climate Voting service.
[24] See Lamanna and Berridge (2020). See also BlackRock (2020a).

General Meeting of BP (BP, 2019a). The resolution directed the company to include in its future Strategic Reports and other reports a description of its strategy, which the board believes to be consistent with the Paris Agreement goals. Further, the company was directed to state how future capital expenditure would be consistent with the Paris goals, together with climate-change metrics and targets over the short, medium, and long terms. Notably, it was supported by the BP board itself. Subsequently, BP set a 2050 net-zero target and announced that it would reinvent its business (BP, 2020). The company's detailed response to the direction is evident in the contents of its 2020 AGM Report (BP, 2019b).

Rarely, if ever, is a major corporation directed by its shareholders to undertake such far-reaching strategic steps;[25] however, it is a sign of the times when the legal niceties of traditional corporate-governance principles are giving way to global social realities and new ways of governing. Agreements freely entered into, such as those negotiated by CA100+ and the BP example, in particular, avoid issues of legal standing faced by shareholders or other stakeholders when trying to force changes to corporate policies and strategies.

Through a combination of direct actions and their flow-on effects, CA100+ is making a major impact on corporate responses to climate change in the countries in which it is active. Nevertheless, evidence of the sheer scale of the task confronting CA100+ lies in the findings of a recent global survey: it reveals that 60 percent of CEOs have not yet factored climate change into their strategic risk-management activities, and ironically, companies in countries with the highest exposure to natural hazards are least likely to have embedded climate change into their risk-management frameworks (PricewaterhouseCoopers, 2021). Likewise, a major European survey reveals that few companies have a governance and steering mechanism in place to develop and implement climate strategies (Coppola et al., 2019). Even so, CA100+ has achieved remarkable momentum in a short time, and with the commitment of its signatories and significant like-minded others, it is part of an impressive movement that is not only helping to transform corporate politics but also heralding the emergence of a new corporate governance paradigm.[26]

[25] At least in shareholder primacy jurisdictions.
[26] See discussion of the New Paradigm on page 131.

TCFD Reporting

One of the most significant reforms arising out of the climate-action movement is climate reporting (Reid and Toffel, 2009),[27] for which demand has been rising for several years. Of themselves, corporate disclosures may not achieve changes in corporate behavior or reductions in GHG emissions (Sjöström, 2020), but they are, nevertheless, crucial elements in the broader accountability framework that is emerging. They will assist in investment decision making; shaping corporations; and, coercively, enabling activists such as CA100+[28] to hold corporations to their stated climate actions.

It is now clear that the recommendations of the TCFD are gaining traction around the world as the preferred reporting framework (TCFD, 2020).[29] The TCFD was established by the Financial Stability Board (FSB) as an industry-supported initiative to consider the implications of climate-related issues for the financial sector, and it released its recommendations in 2017 (TCFD, 2017). TCFD recommendations are intended to be adoptable by all organizations and be included in financial filings, and they are designed to provide forward-looking information on the financial impacts of climate change to assist with decision making by users. There is a strong focus on risks and opportunities as organizations transition to a lower-carbon economy (TCFD, 2017, p. III). The core elements of TCFD reporting, governance, strategy, risk management, metrics, and targets (TCFD, 2017, pp. 14–16) require deep consideration, planning, and evaluation by companies. TCFD reporting is creating a new, multifaceted dimension for investment decision making and corporate governance more broadly.

The recent endorsement by the International Organisation of Securities Organisations (IOSCO) of a proposal from major international reporting standards organizations to align their respective frameworks with the TCFD recommendations in an endeavor to

---

[27] See also Thistlethwaite (2015). Here, the author explains how the Climate Disclosure Standards Board (CDSB) emerged from an international consortium exercising private environmental governance. And see also Ahmad (2017).

[28] See also the Children's Investment Fund Foundation and its disclosure-focused "Say on Climate" campaign directed at major international companies (van Leeuwen, 2021, p. 28).

[29] See also Demaria et al. (2019).

"deliver an integrated and consolidated set of disclosures that meets multiple stakeholders' needs" is a pivotal moment in climate-related disclosure (IOSCO, 2020, p. 3). The measures of TCFD's growing influence are contained in its 2020 Status Report, which reveals that it is supported by over 1,500 organizations globally, including financial institutions responsible for assets of $150 trillion (FSB, 2020). Nearly 60 percent of the world's 100 largest public companies either support the TCFD, report in line with the TCFD recommendations, or both. From 2020, TCFD reporting has become mandatory for PRI signatories totaling more than 3,000, with assets under management exceeding US$100 trillion (PRI, 2019).[30] And 42 percent of companies with a market capitalization greater than $10 billion disclosed at least some information in line with each individual TCFD recommendation in 2019 (FSB, 2020). As well, over 110 regulators, as well as governmental entities and governments around the world, now support the TCFD recommendations' framework (FSB, 2020, p. 71). This is amazing progress in a short period of years.

Recently, New Zealand (NZ) became the first country in the world to adopt mandatory climate-change reporting based on the TCFD framework. The NZ obligations apply to banks, asset managers, and insurers with assets exceeding $1 billion or premium income exceeding $250 million. The legislation is intended to help NZ meet its Paris Agreement targets and assist investors in valuing companies and realigning their portfolios to contribute to a lower-carbon world. At the same time, Australia, Canada, the UK, France, Japan, and the European Union are heading toward the requirement for companies to report climate risk (Fernyhough, 2020). The European Commission has also taken a major step forward by incorporating TCFD recommendations into its *Guidelines on Reporting Climate-Related Information* under the EU's reporting requirements to assist companies in making climate-related disclosures (FSB, 2020). CA100+, as already noted, regularly negotiates outcomes with companies that include a commitment to report climate matters in accordance with the TCFD voluntary-disclosure framework. From its very beginning, the pursuit of TCFD reporting was one of the three key objectives of CA100+ (Climate Action in Financial Institutions, 2019).

[30] See also PRI (2020).

Some of the most onerous of TCFD requirements are in setting and disclosing climate-related strategies. In particular, organizations are recommended to describe the climate-related risks and opportunities an organization has identified over the short, medium, and long terms (Climate Action in Financial Institutions, 2019, p. 14). These should have regard for the nature of the organization's assets and infrastructure and the fact that climate effects often manifest themselves over the medium and long terms (Climate Action in Financial Institutions, 2019, p. 20). There should also be a description of the specific climate-related risks for each of these terms that could have a material impact on the organization (Climate Action in Financial Institutions, 2019).

Significantly, organizations should disclose the resilience of their strategy, "taking into consideration different climate-related scenarios, including a 2°C or lower scenario" (TCFD, n.d., section C). This has been described as the most complex disclosure recommendation ever laid down because companies do not have historical data to compare with; commonly agreed-on climate scenarios; or consistency in methodologies for the assessment, quantification of, and reporting on climate impacts (KPMG Australia, 2020). The TCFD regards this form of scenario planning, although in its infancy, as one of its key recommendations because it allows information users to better understand the potential impacts of climate change on the organization over the coming decades. The TCFD (2020) status report demonstrates the difficulty corporations are having in complying with this onerous requirement (FSB, 2020, p. 2).

It follows that the more diverse are the business activities of a corporation, the more complex and challenging it will be to comply with the framework. For example, a major Australian international bank took 26 pages to set out its 2020 TCFD report to disclose the identification and management of its climate risks across its client base, which spans many industries (Macquarie, 2020). Nevertheless, with the support of major investors, regulators, and many major companies, the recommendations are becoming mainstream. And as TCFD reporting becomes more developed and uniform, its influence will surely grow. In particular, it can be expected to influence decision making by major investors, especially those with an ESG focus, and will more easily allow commitments made by corporations and their leaders to be tracked. In these ways, TCFD reporting is adding new and dynamic dimensions to corporate governance frameworks.

A Snapshot of CA100+ and TCFD Reporting in Australia

CA100+ in Australia

Australia has been chosen for the purpose of taking a single-country snapshot of the reach and impact of CA100+ and the TCFD recommendations for several compelling reasons. First, Australia is one of the world's leading mining countries, and as the largest exporter of coal and gas, it is a significant exporter of GHG emissions (Moss, 2020). Australian coal accounts for nearly 30 percent of the world's coal exports (Reserve Bank of Australia, 2019). Its contribution to the national GDP of 3.5 percent (Reserve Bank of Australia, 2019) makes the country heavily dependent on this revenue and underpins significant employment and community sustainability. And although domestic coal consumption has been declining, exports have been increasing (Reserve Bank of Australia, 2019). In the face of global climate action, there is, therefore, a vulnerability of mining companies to both price and global consumption trends as well as to the national economy as a whole.

Second, Australia hosts some of the world's largest mining companies, such as BHP and Rio Tinto, an Anglo-Australian company that is the second-largest metals and mining company in the world by market value (Statista, 2020). Of the 160 CA100+ focus companies, 13 are Australian. Further, nearly 10 percent of CA100+ signatories are Australasian, thereby implying the likelihood of a high degree of climate activism. Australia also has a high rate of climate-related litigation. According to a recent analysis (Setzer and Byrnes, 2020, p. 6), 98 such cases have been initiated, which is greater than the total of all European cases and 50 percent greater than those in the United Kingdom. Based on that analysis, Australia is second only to the United States for climate cases, but on a per capita basis, it is the most climate-litigious country in the world.

Finally, in the country's political setting, there is sharp disagreement between the main political parties on the setting of emission-reduction targets. Presently, the Australian government has not formally adopted the goals of the Paris Agreement, of which the country is a signatory, despite all Australian states having done so (Allens Linklaters, 2020b). Moreover, 56 percent of Australians consider climate change to be a serious and pressing problem requiring immediate action, and over

80 percent regard it as important for Australia to reduce its carbon emissions (Colvin and Jotzo, 2021). As we will see, ironically, while the national polity has been unable to establish a national consensus and action plan on climate change, CA100+, surely and steadily, assisted by the efforts of others, is achieving particularly significant successes. Some notable examples demonstrate the growing influence of CA100+ within Australia.

In consultation with CA100+, and in what has been described as a landmark shift for corporate Australia (Toscano, 2019), BHP agreed to develop targets for downstream emissions from its customers' use of its products (scope 3 emissions) and to act as a steward to its supply chain. It was the first major mining company to make such a commitment. This agreement complements the company's commitment to the Paris Agreement goals. Also, as noted earlier, BHP, in consultation with CA100+, published its Global Climate Policy, which committed to strict and progressive standards governing its public advocacy on climate change. Underpinned by global agreements, including the Paris Agreement and its temperature targets, the company states that climate policy should be constructive and targeted at emissions reductions, achievement of national targets at least cost, policies that support the development and deployment of low-emissions technologies, and policies that make a broader transition to a net-zero economy (BHP, n.d.).

Another prominent example of CA100+ in Australia is the commitment in February 2020 by Rio Tinto to reach net-zero emissions by 2050 and to spend $1 billion to achieve this target (Rio Tinto, 2020). Further, having committed to the TCFD reporting framework in 2018, it published its first TCFD report setting out the impacts of climate change and identified technological breakthroughs in materials that have a key role in low-carbon transition (Investor Group on Climate Change, 2019). While acknowledging these developments as progress, criticisms had been leveled about the pace of change, the absence of a comprehensive plan, and the commitment to all aspects of the CA100+ agenda.[31]

Australian Super, the largest retirement fund in Australia, is, together with other CA100+ signatories, targeting at least 12 other Australian companies to make CA100+ commitments following its successful negotiations with BHP. They are using their voting power

---

[31] See, for example, Market Forces (2020).

to help achieve these ends. A further useful example worth highlighting is the consultative engagement between CA100+ and Origin Energy, a major Australian company. The engagement was undertaken so that both parties could more fully understand and contribute to the company's alignment with the Paris Agreement, emissions reductions, increased disclosure, the alignment of climate action to executive remuneration, and its plans toward exiting coal-fired generation by 2032. It is regarded as a model for climate-action engagement with companies around the world (CA100+, 2019, p. 31).

A final example that signifies a serious change of pace in Australia is the release in June 2020 by the Minerals Council of Australia (MCA) of a Climate Action Statement that acknowledges the net-zero target, albeit without specifying a deadline for its achievement. The release of the statement followed public and investor pressure. Although open to criticism by some, the statement nevertheless shows that the combined global and local forces of climate action are reaching deeply into the control centers of carbon emission. The momentum that is currently at work will bring further and more specific outcomes. To this end, CA100+ influential member Australian Super has adopted an assertive stance in relation to the MCA announcement, warning that it was insufficient because it failed to specify how MCA members would contribute to the Paris Agreement goals. It vowed to maintain the pressure on all industry associations whose climate agendas did not match the stated goals of their members (Butler, 2019).

Through its gravitas and scale, CA100+ increased the velocity of climate-action forces in Australia, thereby accelerating the pace and depth of change. This is so not only in respect to a relatively small number of major emitters but also, through the ripple effects of its activities and especially its signature successes, in terms of the broader scope of climate action in Australia's corporate sector. In consequence, several powerful interest groups have been formed to pursue climate-action goals similar to those adopted by CA100+, including, notably, the Climate Leaders Coalition, an organization comprising 22 leading Australian corporations (Australian Climate Leaders Coalition, n.d.).

TCFD Reporting in Australia

Although there is as yet no mandatory climate-change reporting framework in Australia, the TCFD is rapidly gaining support for reporting generally or within or associated with a company's annual report (Deloitte, 2020).[32] Notably, the Australian government stated that TCFD reporting could be implemented by corporations without any law reform required for the recommendations to be implemented (Governance Institute of Australia, 2018). Further, the TCFD is gaining popularity with regulators, major investors, and major companies that are either committing to it or are now embedding it in their annual reports. Among the signatories to the PRI are 141 Australian investors who are committing to mandatory climate disclosure in accordance with TCFD recommendations (Governance Institute of Australia, 2020, p. 5).

In view of the necessity for such reporting, the Australian Securities & Investment Commission (ASIC) has recommended that publicly listed companies consider reporting their climate-change exposure and risk in accordance with TCFD recommendations (ASIC, 2018). Under ASIC Regulatory Guides, climate change is identified as a systemic risk that might affect a company's future financial prospects, and if it is a material business risk, a listed entity is required to disclose it (Allens Linklaters, 2020a). As a clear signal to the business world of the materiality of climate-related disclosure in corporate reporting, ASIC has undertaken deep-dive analyses and desktop audits in critical sectors such as energy and industrials (Ross, 2021). Similarly, the Australian Prudential Regulatory Authority (APRA) encourages Australia's large banking, insurance, and superannuation institutions to address the climate-data deficit through scenario analysis, stress testing, and disclosure of market-useful information, in accordance with TCFD recommendations (APRA, 2020).

Finally, the Australian Stock Exchange (ASX) recommends that a listed entity should disclose the existence of any material ESG risks and the management of such risks, and it further recommends that they be disclosed in accordance with the TCFD recommendations (ASX Corporate Governance Council, 2019, p. 27). Thus, TCFD reporting is gaining a major foothold in Australia, with implications for all corporations with climate-related risks as well as for their CEOs and governing boards.

---

[32] See also KPMG Australia (2020).

Stakeholderism and Corporate Purpose

Stakeholderism is the fourth global force to be considered in this chapter. In brief, stakeholder theory suggests that a corporation that is managed for the benefit of its whole body of stakeholders will produce better outcomes than those whose principal focus is profit making for shareholders. Although it is widely regarded that stakeholderism is an emerging form of responsible capitalism, others regard it more as a rebirth (Reich, 2014). It also enjoys public support, exemplified by the Edelman 2020 Trust Barometer, in which 87 percent of global respondents expressed a belief that stakeholders, not shareholders, are most important to the long-term success of companies (Edelman, 2020).

A stakeholder is "any group or individual who can affect or is affected by the achievement of an organization's purpose" (Freeman, 1984, p. 53). This is a wide and expanding group. It has been said to include "persons, groups, neighbourhoods, organisations, institutions, societies, and even the natural environment" (Mitchell et al., 1997, p. 853). In the current stakeholder and climate-action debates, investors, employees, suppliers, the community, nature,[33] and society are commonly referred to as stakeholders, not necessarily in that order. Furthermore, and due to the influence being exerted by them, CA100+, TCFD, and PRI (Majoch et al., 2017) could each be considered to be stakeholders in the corporations they affect.

Stakeholderism has been advanced as being the preferable central paradigm for the business and society field (Jones, 1995). "It focuses on the contracts (relationships) between the firm and its stakeholders and posits that trusting and cooperative relationships help solve problems related to opportunism" (Jones, 1995, p. 432). Further, "It implies that behavior that is trusting, trustworthy, and cooperative, not opportunistic, will give the firm a competitive advantage. In the process, it may help explain why certain 'irrational' or altruistic behaviors turn out to be productive and why firms that engage in these behaviors survive and often thrive" (Jones, 1995, p. 432).

Another explanation is that the capability to create close relationships with stakeholders represents a source of sustainable competitive advantage and that "the incremental benefits of a close relationship

[33] See, for example, WEF (2020).

capability can exceed the costs of a strategy used to develop and maintain it" (Jones et al., 2018, p. 388). Beyond issues of competitive advantage to corporations, stakeholder theory or stakeholderism is now taking on a significant public policy dimension, becoming as much a moral as an economic consideration. This is driven substantially by international public opinion as a means of tying corporations, their supply chains, and other stakeholders into the measures for addressing climate change and other major global concerns.

National laws typically define those to whom corporate boards and CEOs owe their duties when managing corporations and for defining the purposes of a corporation. In some places, shareholders are the primary focus (shareholder capitalism), whereas in others, it is a broader range of stakeholders (stakeholder capitalism).[34] However, stakeholderism is a global force gaining increasing traction in public discourses and consequent action. Strong support for it can be found in Europe, the UK, the United States, and many other countries. Although it lacks the cohesive support underpinning climate action across the globe, it is, potentially, a major disrupter of corporate theory and practice. If adopted in legislation as a mandatory obligation,[35] it will redefine the purpose of a corporation and substantially alter decision-making processes. In consequence, it would rewrite the rules and scope of discretionary business judgment. Although there are significant obstacles to its formal adoption in law,[36] its proponents have considerable momentum, nevertheless. Adoption of stakeholderism, accordingly, has significant implications not only for corporations, their leaders, and governing boards but also for shareholders, other stakeholders, regulators, and business schools and their accreditation bodies.

The Organisation for Economic Co-operation and Development (OECD) Principles of Corporate Governance incorporate a stakeholderism approach but without advocating that national corporate governance frameworks adopt a mandatory requirement to consider all stakeholders. It is recommended that a "corporate governance framework should recognise the rights of stakeholders ... and encourage active co-operation between corporations and stakeholders in creating

---

[34] For a useful comparison of two contrasting systems, see Georghiu (2015/2016).
[35] That is, if corporate leaders are not only authorized but compelled to consider all identified stakeholders when making decisions on behalf of a company.
[36] See further discussion on page 132.

wealth, jobs, and the sustainability of financially sound enterprises" (OECD, 2004, p. 21). And, further, where "stakeholder interests are protected by law, stakeholders should have the opportunity to obtain effective redress for violation of their rights" (OECD, 2004, p. 21). This might require a step-change for Enlightened Shareholder Value (ESV) jurisdictions in which corporate leaders are generally shielded from stakeholder actions seeking to challenge corporate decisions. The OECD Guidelines for Multinational Enterprises (OECD, 2011) similarly highlight the importance of stakeholders and recommend that their interests be taken into account but in a manner that is consistent with the ESV approach.

In Europe, the EU High-Level Expert Group on Sustainable Finance proposes to clarify the fiduciary duties of institutional investors and asset managers to incorporate ESG considerations into their decision making and to ensure that directors of investee companies are subject to sustainability duties (EU High-Level Expert Group on Sustainable Finance, 2018, pp. 20–23). It also proposed to adopt a mandatory form of stakeholderism. In particular, it proposes that director duties and corporate governance explicitly incorporate sustainability by requiring a director to act in good faith and in a way that is most likely to promote the success of the company for the benefit of its owners and other stakeholders. A director would be required to have regard for the following: the likely long-term consequences of any decision; the interests of the company's employees; fostering relationships with suppliers, customers, and others; the impact of the company's operations on the community and the environment; and saving the world's cultural and natural heritage (EU High-Level Expert Group on Sustainable Finance, 2018, p. 40).

A director would also have to exercise reasonable care, skill, and diligence and be aware of the direct and indirect impacts of the company's business model, production, and sales processes on stakeholders and the environment. As well, nonexecutive directors and supervisory boards would be required to develop a climate strategy aligned with climate goals and to describe the company's approach to the UN SDGs (EU High-Level Expert Group on Sustainable Finance, 2018, p. 41). These are far-reaching stakeholderism proposals that will face considerable implementation challenges but enjoy strong political support.

Further, in the EU Guidelines on nonfinancial reporting, the European Commission set out six guiding principles, including that reports should be stakeholder oriented (European Commission, 2017, p. 15) and that companies should report on their engagement with their stakeholders and how their information needs are taken into account. Under this model of reporting, shareholders are on an equal footing with all other identifiable stakeholders, a development that has been described as a significant step on the path toward stakeholderism in Europe (Howitt, 2020). It is also worth noting that the European Green Deal states that managing the transition to a sustainable Europe Investment Plan will lead to "significant structural changes in business models," impliedly incorporating stakeholder approaches (European Commission, 2019, p. 16).

The British Academy recently released the *Principles for Purposeful Business*, which are thoroughly researched and developed proposals to radically reform the underlying paradigm of corporate law and corporate governance (British Academy, 2019). If adopted, they would replace profit-making with corporate purpose, which would, inter alia, take into account social, political, and environmental issues. Profit would be an outcome of a company's purpose, not the central focus. The British Academy (2019) sets out eight principles for purposeful business (pp. 8–9):

1. Corporate law should place purpose at the heart of the corporation and require directors to state their purposes and demonstrate commitment to them.
2. Regulation should expect particularly high duties of engagement, loyalty, and care on the part of directors of companies to public interests where they perform important public functions.
3. Ownership should recognize the obligations of shareholders and engage them in supporting corporate purposes, as well as in their rights to derive financial benefit.
4. Corporate governance should align managerial interests with companies' purposes and establish accountability to a range of stakeholders through appropriate board structures. They should determine a set of values necessary to deliver purpose, embedded in their company culture.
5. Measurement should recognize impacts and investments by companies in their workers, societies, and natural assets both within and outside the firm.
6. Performance should be measured against the fulfillment of corporate purposes and profits, measured net of the costs of achieving them.

7. Corporate financing should recognize impacts and investment by companies in their workers, societies, and natural assets both within and outside the firm.
8. Corporate investment should be made in partnership with private, public, and not-for-profit organizations that contribute toward the fulfillment of corporate purposes.

These principles inextricably intertwine corporate purpose and stakeholderism and propose a new contract between business and society. Importantly, the British Academy (2019) cites four factors that highlight why change is needed now: the global nature of challenges facing society, such as climate change, especially, and the global nature of business itself; second, opportunities and challenges presented by new technologies; third, the increasingly intangible nature of companies and their assets; and fourth, the perception of business in wider society, noting that trust in business institutions is essential for social and economic progress (p. 12). In particular, the Academy asserts that companies must help to drive urgent change in response to "growing concerns around the external impacts of business regarding social inequality, the environment, competition, consumer protection, and privacy in digital markets" (British Academy, 2019, p. 12).

The proposals capture two underlying dimensions of corporate purpose, namely, the "positive benefit of producing profitable solutions to the problems of people and planet, and the avoidance of harm in not profiting from producing problems for people or planet" (British Academy, 2019, p. 20). A reformulated duty would make it mandatory for directors to state their companies' purposes, then act in ways they consider most likely to promote the fulfillment of the stated purposes and, importantly, be obliged to have regard for the consequences of any decision on the interests of shareholders and stakeholders in the company (British Academy, 2019, p. 20). In practice, therefore, corporate leaders would be empowered to pursue socially and financially advantageous outcomes for a business rather than having to put shareholder interests first. Accordingly, they could, in particular circumstances, prefer the interests of stakeholders other than shareholders so long as the corporate purpose is being fulfilled.

It would be a major corporate-law reform for shareholder-capitalism countries where directors presently enjoy greater freedom in decision making and would alter the balance between corporate and governmental responsibility for achieving social outcomes. A similar leap is suggested in a proposal regarding ownership, under which the traditional property-right view of the firm is turned on its head by suggesting that "ownership does not relate to the assets of a firm but to its purposes. Hence, with the rights of ownership come obligations and responsibilities to respect the interests of others affected by its purpose" (British Academy, 2019, p. 22). By developing these principles against the backdrop of the UN SDGs and the global movements for responsible and moral business,[37] the Academy's proposal significantly strengthens the forces for change. It is worth noting, in this context, the remarks of Larry Fink that "a strong sense of purpose and a commitment to stakeholders helps a company connect more deeply to its customers and adjust to the changing demands of society. Ultimately, purpose is the engine of long-term profitability" (Fink, n.d., section 3, para. 2).

Quite clearly, the views of the Academy and many other proponents of stakeholder capitalism are consonant with emerging global sentiments that expect business to be an engine for long-term wealth creation achieved in harmony with nature. A recent global survey shows that 56 percent of respondents believe capitalism does more harm than good; a minority of respondents trust business, in contrast to a strong majority of the informed public who do trust business; 73 percent desire change; a majority believe business serves the interests of only the few; and 87 percent believe that stakeholders, not shareholders, are most important to long-term company success.[38]

Under the Academy proposals, stakeholders, broadly defined, would be key participants in, and beneficiaries of, this form of business. What remains unclear is how competing claims upon corporate outcomes and any ensuing disputes can be resolved. The Academy states that "a purposeful business will also ensure that measures are in place to ensure accountability within the business for remaining faithful to its purpose and for ongoing monitoring and reporting of delivery of its purpose" (British Academy, 2019, p. 17). With responsible purposes clearly agreed upon, more stable ownership, inclusion of stakeholders in a company's governance structure, and better ongoing dialogue between a company and its stakeholders, it is implied, somewhat

---

[37] See also Harvard Business Review (2015).
[38] See Edelman (2020), involving 34,000 respondents in 28 countries.

hopefully, that less disputation will arise. However, perfect alignment of stakeholder interests even under these new arrangements cannot be assumed.

The respective interests of the corporation itself, management, capital, labor, suppliers, the community, and those acting on behalf of nature can be expected to fall out of alignment from time to time. And if a company strays from its stated purposes, especially if narrowly expressed, one or more stakeholders will want a mechanism for corrective action and one that is enforceable if all other attempts at resolution are unsuccessful. Ironically, many companies that are having to reimagine their businesses as a result of climate change might not have been able to do so if they were bound by narrow purpose statements.

A legal mechanism to consider such cases that are incapable of being resolved internally, through market forces, or through stakeholder pressure will need to be developed. Presently, in shareholder-primacy jurisdictions, the law favors wide discretionary decision making by corporate leaders, allowing them to determine, from time to time, what is in the best interests of a company, including in regard to stakeholder interests. To make such consideration mandatory would therefore require a major rewriting of corporate-governance principles and structures in those jurisdictions.

Interestingly, although the UK has traditionally followed the shareholder-primacy model, it has incorporated stakeholders into legislation in two explicit ways. First, Section 172(1) of the UK Companies Act, which enshrines the principle of ESV (Williams, 2012, p. 360),[39] requires that the directors of a company must act in a way they consider, in good faith, would be most likely to promote the success of the company for the benefit of its members as a whole and, in doing so, have regard for, among other matters, the likely consequences of any decision in the long term and the interests of other stakeholders – employees, suppliers, customers and others, the community, and the environment. However, it has been argued that, notwithstanding the references to stakeholders, the section introduced in 2006 makes little difference to the preexisting law (Williams, 2012, p. 362). In other words, there is little difference between the ESV

---

[39] See also Keay (2007).

approach adopted in the UK and that of the traditional shareholder-value approach that exists in other places.[40]

Section 172(2) of the UK Companies Act, however, expressly allows the directors of a company whose purposes consist of or include purposes other than the benefits of its members to give effect to those nonmember stakeholder interests. In most cases, however, corporations have wide discretion over the purposes for which business can be carried on. B Corporations, which balance purpose and profit, are notable exceptions.[41]

A second stakeholder requirement under English company law is that specified large companies are required to publish in their annual reports how the directors have regarded the stakeholder matters set out in Section 172(1) of the UK Companies Act. In particular, they must specify how they have engaged with employees, showed regard for their interests, and considered the effect of that regard on the principal decisions taken by the company during the financial year. Similar disclosures are required regarding other stakeholders, such as suppliers and customers.[42] Because these reports are only starting to be filed, it is too early to tell whether such ex post facto requirements will have any significant bearing upon the extent to which directors take account of and prioritize respective stakeholder interests when making major decisions.

Also, to be noted is that the 2018 UK Corporate Governance Code issued by the UK Financial Reporting Council embraces purpose as the central principle (Financial Reporting Council, 2018). Finally, in 2019, the Institute of Directors issued a 10-point manifesto that was designed to achieve three broad objectives, the first of which was to "increase the accountability of the UK corporate governance system to stakeholders and wider society" (Institute of Directors, 2019, p. 3).

In America, the US Business Roundtable 2019 "Statement on the Purpose of a Corporation," signed by 181 CEOs (Business Roundtable, 2019) representing $13 trillion of market value, was widely regarded as a watershed occurrence and elevated the intensity of global debate concerning corporate purpose and stakeholderism.

---

[40] In the United States and Australia, for example.
[41] Nee (2020) refers to the growing number of B Corporations across the world, including increasing numbers of large established corporations.
[42] See Section 414CZA(1) of the UK Companies Act. See also PricewaterhouseCoopers (2020).

Whether it becomes a pivotal moment in a fuller adoption of stakeholderism remains to be determined because the signatories were not calling for and did not support radical changes to corporate governance structures, which could have serious unintended consequences (McMillon and Bolten, 2020). They also believed that prescriptive government control over business would hurt many stakeholders who are in need of help (McMillon and Bolten, 2020).

While acknowledging that each participating company has its own corporate purpose, the signatories expressed a fundamental commitment to stakeholders to delivering value to their customers; investing in their employees; dealing fairly and ethically with their suppliers; supporting the communities in which they operate and protecting the environment by embracing sustainable practices across their businesses; and generating long-term value for shareholders, who provide the capital that allows companies to invest, grow, and innovate.[43]

As widely welcomed as this statement was, it has generated considerable controversy around what it means and how it will be implemented. Professors Bebchuk and Tallarita (2020, p. 133) conclude that, in effect, the Business Roundtable statement does not move away from ESV and was not intended to shift the corporate-governance requirements of the signatories or others. They noted that there was little evidence to show that the signatories had adjusted their corporate-governance settings following the statement and that most were already meeting the principles set out in the statement. They regarded it largely as a public relations exercise (Bebchuk and Tallarita, 2020, p. 98).[44] At the very least, however, it may be regarded as an influential statement of good contemporary corporate citizenship against which the signatories are prepared to be publicly judged, expressed in the hope that others will follow suit. Furthermore, the statement adds significant weight to the global forces advocating action on climate and long-term business sustainability and is widely cited in literature and debates concerning the future of stakeholderism. Notably, stakeholderism is likely to receive a boost as a result of the US elections, due to the opinion of the new president that corporations

---

[43] For the full statement, see Business Roundtable (2019).
[44] See also Winston (2019), who argues that it is merely the start of a long-term journey.

have responsibilities to workers, the community, and the country as well as to shareholders and that the era of shareholder capitalism should be brought to an end (Hinks, 2020).[45]

Subsequent to the Business Roundtable statement, the WEF issued a bold stakeholder manifesto (Schwab, 2019) in 2020, stating:

> The purpose of a company is to engage all its stakeholders in shared and sustained value creation. In creating such value, a company serves not only its shareholders, but all its stakeholders – employees, customers, suppliers, local communities, and society at large. The best way to understand and harmonize the divergent interests of all stakeholders is through a shared commitment to policies and decisions that strengthen the long-term prosperity of a company. (Schwab, 2019, part A)

In asserting that a company is more than a wealth-generating economic unit and that it fulfills human and societal aspirations as part of the broader social system, the manifesto suggests that performance must be measured by how a company achieves environmental, social, and good-governance objectives as well as by the return to shareholders (Schwab, 2019, part B). Furthermore, a company that is multinational in scope is to be regarded as a stakeholder, "together with governments and civil society – of our global future" (Schwab, 2019, part C). These conceptions go much further than merely displacing shareholder capitalism as they seek to hold companies that trade internationally, and their controllers, globally accountable for improving the world.

Contributing to the 2020 WEF, Professor Mayer asserts that corporate purpose is "rapidly becoming a global phenomenon" (Mayer, 2020, para. 2) and that once a clear, all-encompassing understanding of corporate purpose is achieved, everything else will follow from that (Mayer, 2020). Citing the British Academy *Principles for Purposeful Business*, he argues that it's "no longer a question of whether and why to change, but what and how to do it" (Mayer, 2020, para. 6). Resolving the "how" question cannot be underestimated; however, while this receives attention, an alternative and stakeholder-friendly form of negotiated corporate governance is emerging.

---

[45] See also the Accountable Capitalism Act proposed by Senator Elizabeth Warren that would mandate stakeholderism for all US corporations with annual revenue exceeding $1 billion (Accountable Capitalism Act, n.d.).

The New Paradigm – Negotiated Stakeholderism

The New Paradigm (Lipton, 2016), in which large companies and large investor funds deeply collaborate to implement shared long-term financial, social, environmental, and sustainability goals, has emerged as a negotiated form of stakeholderism. It rests on the propositions that "private ordering through the New Paradigm by corporations and investors who best know their respective concerns and needs is more likely to result in balanced solutions than government interventions" (Lipton, 2017, section 4, para. 3) and that stakeholder governance and ESG are in the best interests of shareholders. It further maintains that the "board can exercise business judgement to implement the company's objectives and the company and its shareholders engage on a regular basis to achieve mutual understanding and agreement as to corporate purpose, societal purpose and performance. Ultimately, the shareholders' power to elect the directors determines how any conflicts are resolved if they are not resolved by engagement" (Lipton, 2019, section 3, para. 1). Thus, in being implemented without any need for governments to rewrite corporate-governance legal frameworks, the New Paradigm is less reliant on corporate law for guiding principles and dispute resolution.[46] As a consequence, negotiated stakeholderism coexists as an alternate and sometimes overlapping system of corporate governance even in shareholder-primacy jurisdictions.

Through direct action such as that employed by CA100+, goals for the climate and other important issues can be more quickly put in place. In the process, particular stakeholders, such as the environment, may be accorded preferential treatment or are, at least by agreement, considered in new ways or with increased levels of urgency. The New Paradigm, accordingly, responds to incessant modernity demands to redefine the purpose of corporations, protect the environment, and create long-term sustainable businesses.

Even though New Paradigm agreements are less reliant on corporate law, it does not mean that this domain is or will be free from conflicts requiring resolution. Even where, for instance, CA100+ signatories are active, including where agreements have been struck, proxy campaigns are continuing in many cases to increase or accelerate the corporate commitments. And as the ongoing costs and complexities of

---

[46] See Goshen and Hannes (2019).

transitioning to new business models emerge, tensions between aspiration and reality may well give rise to formal disputes. Because the New Paradigm is voluntary, it is still possible that major and influential shareholders may change their views on a particular issue or the directions and purpose of a company more generally.

Nevertheless, as climate action, PRI, and UN SDGs gain even wider acceptance, negotiated governance solutions are likely to increase. The New Paradigm, however, is not a comprehensive system. For those outside of the negotiation or collaborative system, such as smaller companies, those that don't attract institutional capital, and those that have not received or have not acceded to approaches from such investors, corporate law retains its traditional role. Shareholders in these types of situations who wish to advance ESG objectives in jurisdictions that enshrine the shareholder-primacy approach cannot, without board support, force companies to adopt such agendas. A recent attempt at the Woodside Petroleum Ltd (a leading Australian company) 2020 AGM highlights the obstacles faced by shareholders wishing to influence the company's climate policies.

There, a resolution was unsuccessfully proposed to alter the company's constitution to allow for shareholders to pass advisory resolutions that would not bind the board. Shareholders, according to local law, could not compel the directors to act in particular ways, but with a constitutional amendment, they could pass advisory resolutions as indications of climate-related actions shareholders wanted the company to take. Notwithstanding the failure of the resolution to pass, a majority of votes cast in favor of Paris Agreement goals and targets prior to the meeting sent the board a clear message expressing the opinion of the majority. In a shareholder-primacy jurisdiction such as Australia, these are substantial hurdles to be faced by those wanting to influence the company's direction and strategies in the absence of being able to negotiate a New Paradigm type of agreement or replace the board.

Challenges to Implementing Pluralistic Stakeholderism

In a well-considered analysis of the obstacles to implementing stakeholderism, Bebchuk and Tallarita (2020) distinguish between two types of corporate governance, namely, ESV and pluralistic stakeholderism, the latter of which they conclude faces insurmountable hurdles to its adoption.[47] The former, they argue, is little different from share-holder value, which has deep roots in corporate-law history and gives effect to shareholder primacy. ESV, such as exists under English company law and in many other jurisdictions, recognizes that in the course of advancing shareholder interests, corporate leaders may take into account the interests of other stakeholders, as they often do, but without being compelled to do so.[48]

Pluralistic stakeholderism, in contrast, "treats stakeholder welfare as an end in itself" where "the welfare of each group of stakeholders is relevant and valuable independently of its effect on the welfare of shareholders" (Bebchuk and Tallarita, 2020, p. 114). Directors are faced with independent constituencies, thereby requiring them to "weigh and balance a plurality of autonomous ends" (Bebchuk and Tallarita, 2020, p. 114). The authors outline a number of problems with implementing this form of stakeholderism. Whether it can be practiced and enforced when there are divergent needs and priorities among the stakeholders is a fundamental challenge to its successful operation as a system, with the serious possibility that substantial new costs may be imposed on stakeholders, society, and shareholders (Bebchuk and Tallarita, 2020, p. 176). How corporate leaders would decide what is in the interests of a community or society more broadly is a vexed question that will not always be easily determined or necessarily acceptable to respective stakeholders affected by such a judgment.

The nonalignment of incentives also has to be considered. Traditionally, corporate leaders are not incentivized to pursue stake-holder interests in exercising their discretions (Bebchuk and Tallarita, 2020, p. 139). There are, however, significant examples emerging where, through direct negotiation by major investors individually and collectively, such as through CA100+, nonfinancial incentives are being introduced. For instance, meeting climate-related benchmarks can be an incentive to retain the support of key employees or an investor or to keep the investor from taking other action against the

---

[47] For a rebuttal, see Mayer (2021).

[48] For example, in the interests of the corporation's reputation and to retain the loyalty of employees and their financiers, it may be decided, legitimately, not to pursue a profitable opportunity that could be damaging to the environment or result in an increase of GHG emissions.

board or the CEO. But at present, these occurrences are still exceptions to the rule, albeit growing in number and impact.

It is also argued that pluralistic stakeholderism might insulate corporate leaders from accountability and further entrench managerialism (Bebchuk and Tallarita, 2020, p. 165). Accountability to all may lead to accountability to no one (Council of Institutional Investors, 2019). It might also raise illusory hopes that corporate leaders will protect the interests of stakeholders (Bebchuk and Tallarita, 2020, p. 101), whereas legislators and regulators might be deflected from acting to protect stakeholder interests where such intervention is necessary (Bebchuk and Tallarita, 2020, p. 172). Overall, the authors conclude that pluralistic stakeholderism would not make stakeholders better off. In relation to those wanting action on climate change, they say it is time "to abandon the illusory hope offered by stakeholderism" and "devote all efforts and resources to advancing laws, regulations, and policies that address the catastrophic threat of climate change and to educating the public about the urgency of adopting such measures" (Bebchuk and Tallarita, 2020, p. 175). Even so, there are growing instances of significant climate outcomes being achieved through private negotiations and actions that are supplementing government measures.

Another matter to consider is that pluralistic stakeholderism and mandatory purpose statements open up various possibilities for legal action to be initiated by disaffected stakeholders. First, for the objectives of pluralistic stakeholderism to be fully achieved, corporate leaders will need to have a duty, rather than a discretion, to consider and weigh up the respective interests of identified stakeholders. From the perspective of stakeholders, this system could only be fully effective if the law is adapted to provide the means for subjecting corporate decisions to judicial scrutiny on behalf of stakeholders who believe that their interests have not been considered appropriately or at all.

Who would have the standing to mount challenges and what threshold tests they would have to satisfy in these circumstances would also need to be determined. It would require, therefore, a radical departure from the present system of corporate governance in shareholder-primacy jurisdictions for fully enforceable pluralistic stakeholderism to be introduced. In such circumstances, a legal quagmire could well ensue as stakeholders with heightened expectations, motivated by varying degrees of self-interest and altruism, seek to advance or protect their particular interests. At the same time, corporate decision makers would be able to cite a wider range of issues they considered in order to justify their decisions, with the potential to diminish their accountability.

Finding a practical solution to this will not be easy. Nevertheless, a modern and reformed corporate-governance system that reflects global realities is likely to need to incorporate enforceable rights for stakeholders, fairly apportioned between them *inter se*. Such a system faces the challenge of establishing the rights' regime so that it does not unduly impede legitimate business activity or the courts that will have to mediate between the claims of various stakeholder interests that have to be appropriately weighed and prioritized. In the meantime, market forces and New Paradigm types of agreements are playing an increasing role in ensuring that certain stakeholder interests are considered, especially when climate change and ESG issues are involved.

Despite the implementation challenges it brings, the adoption of pluralistic stakeholderism cannot be ruled out. As difficult as it may be to rewrite the foundations of corporate governance, at least in those countries where shareholder primacy prevails, in the age of liquid modernity, anything seems possible. Momentum is a transformative force today. To this end, it is reasonable to ask whether traditional corporate-governance models can remain immune to change, even radical change, when the world of business is dramatically changing. Global opinion and public politics are being transformed by concerns for the planet, issues of sustainability more broadly, human rights, and issues relating to inequality. Who could have imagined, just a few years ago, large corporations agreeing to reinvent their business models in order to protect the planet? Now the momentum is growing for corporations to govern for long-term wealth creation, be good corporate citizens, demonstrate their care for the environment, and explicitly take into account their stakeholders in operating their businesses. In the Western world especially, corporations and their leaders can no longer separate their business responsibilities from global moral imperatives.

Thus, bolstered by the groundswell of support for stakeholderism in one form or another, the next few years may determine whether and how it will be formally adopted and how the implementation issues will be addressed. As climate sovereignty and the sovereignty of nature, together with other compatible ESG forces, are in the ascendency, they may well answer each of the unresolved questions.

In the meantime, a changing landscape is confronting all stakeholders, including corporations, their leaders, investors, and interest groups – including business schools. All need to respond to how corporate governance is evolving through negotiated agreements, market pressures, global opinion, and serious proposals for law reform. The tectonic plates are shifting.

Global Forces and Some Implications for Business Schools and Their Accreditation

When stepping back and reflecting on the mighty forces confronting our world, we are compelled to ask how business schools and accreditation bodies will respond to what is unfolding. Consider the combined effects of climate change and climate action, CA100+, the TCFD reporting framework, PRI, ESG, and calls for corporate leaders to operate their businesses for all identifiable stakeholders. As a result, managerial discretion is shrinking under the weight of global expectations, capital activism, and public politics. Separation of ownership and control must now be interpreted in the light of these modern developments. And then there are the seismic impacts of digital disruption and disruptive innovation on businesses and business models. Together, these are transforming business practices and governance before our very eyes. Business schools are challenged to keep pace. Their mission statements, which not uncommonly proclaim the intention to prepare students for thriving careers in a fast-changing world, will be meaningless if the forces of change are ignored.

Consider the knowledge and skills required of a corporate CEO whose business is affected by climate change and who will need to make more scientifically based operational, strategic, financial, and reporting judgments for which the CEO will be accountable. Boards are facing the same issues. Responding to climate change may require a corporation to completely revise its business model, thereby needing expert leadership and courage to implement the transition. Just as companies, in response to the global winds of change, are having to undertake onerous transitions, so too, by analogy, will business schools. Theirs won't be driven by green energy and the like but by how to transition to program portfolios built on theories, both traditional and emerging, that are relevant for explaining and understanding contemporary business in its modern setting.

If, for example, an MBA program specializes in strategic management and leadership and does not incorporate the effects of the global
forces that are reshaping business models, spawning new finance
models (Fink, n.d.),[49] and transforming key aspects of corporate governance, how will it advance the knowledge and practices of those
undertaking the course? Will management of strategic transitions
become a key focus? And how do you prepare graduates or executives
to redesign a business model, create new strategies, and link these to
capital allocations that, according to the CA100+ Net-Zero
Benchmark, are proving to be most challenging?[50] Because these touch
every part of the business, does this mean that systems thinking must
become a key component of management education?

Consider the professional input that is required to model, manage,
report on, value, and audit climate-change risks and manage the associated communication and public relations. Think of the skill base and
judgment required by a climate-reporting auditor to certify that a
company's disclosure meets the legal requirements of materiality and
the broader demands of TCFD reporting. As well, recruitment and
human-resource-management practices and the teaching of them will
all be affected by these fast-unfolding realities. Ensuring that those who
are recruited have values that align with those of the company and its
purposes will become even more important in the future. Similar
observations can be made in relation to every major taught or domain
covered in business school programs. What will be the value of any
major if it fails to adapt to the forces of change?

The mindsets needed to lead, to manage, or even to have sustainable
professional careers will be even more closely scrutinized as time goes
by. Successful business professionals will need to have, at least, the five
minds identified by Howard Gardner (2008): the disciplined mind, the
synthesizing mind, the creating mind, the respectful mind, and the
ethical mind. The synthesizing and ethical minds will assume greater
importance than ever before in the face of morally based global changes.

To the foregoing list can be added the curious mind,[51] which will
need to constantly follow the knowledge flows in order for leaders and
business professionals to be transformed by the renewing of their

---

[49] See also "Sustainable Finance" in EU High-Level Expert Group on Sustainable
Finance (2018).
[50] See CA100+ (2021).
[51] See, for example, Ready (2019) and also Gino (2018).

minds. "Those who master the ability to learn faster will achieve much higher impact in a rapidly changing world" (Hagel, 2020, section 3, para. 2). Business schools have a challenging but exciting task to adapt to modernity and fully participate in the slipstream of disruption that is unfolding in our world. So, it might be time to introduce a modernity test for all programs they offer.

As Hagel et al. (2009a) explain, value is shifting from knowledge stocks to knowledge flows. "As the world speeds up, stocks of knowledge depreciate at a faster rate..... In more stable times, we could sit back and relax once we had learned something valuable, secure that we could generate value from that knowledge for an indefinite period. Not anymore. To succeed now, we have to continuously refresh our stocks of knowledge by participating in relevant flows of new knowledge" (Hagel et al., 2009a, para. 5). Corporations, therefore, face the challenge of scaling their knowledge accordingly (Hagel and Brown, 2017). Similarly, a challenge for business schools is to be sufficiently entrepreneurial and agile to participate as genuine stakeholders in these knowledge flows and in the process of lifelong learning and continuing self-development.[52]

Microcredentials, small-bite learning, and nondegree learning will play an even greater role in the future of management education. For many business schools to participate meaningfully in these markets, substantial barriers to entry, both internal and external, will have to be overcome. It is also likely that live paid subscription streaming services will develop as an important contemporary form of flows. They will provide research-based, cutting-edge insights to knowledge-hungry professionals who want to incorporate and leverage the latest thinking into their professional practices and decision making through instantaneity.

Proactive leadership, speed of action, and reputation will most likely define the winners here – those who can successfully connect with global audiences on issues of global significance, in real time. For those in the workplace, it will not be sufficient to change the speed of their learning – they must learn at the speed of change. As the chair of Shell says, "Over the course of the coming decades, as the world moves increasingly towards lower-carbon energy, we will have to learn new skills at Shell. The ways we work will have to evolve" (Royal Dutch

---

[52] See Friedman (2016b).

Shell PLC, 2021, p. 5), and if modern workplaces have to be reimagined (Friedman, 2016b), business schools have a major role to play in the process.

Presently, many of the orthodoxies on which business schools base their programs are being called into question by developments in global thinking and practice, but are schools keeping pace? So often, curriculum design and delivery lag too far behind what is happening in the real world. Most accredited schools, for example, are able to point to aspects of ethics, responsibility, and sustainability (ERS), but often, they are not systematically enshrined in the content and framing of the courses or in research strategies and outputs. This occurs notwithstanding the well-designed elements of the EFMD Quality Improvement System (EQUIS) standards relating to ERS, which permeate most chapters of the standards. Maybe the accreditation process should be used as an even greater lever to bring about a more holistic approach to teaching and researching ERS issues and climate-change transitions.

A recently released report (Ceres, 2020b) sets out what is required to become a just and sustainable company by 2030, within the context of the UN SDGs, themselves increasingly becoming framing concepts. For European schools, the proposed European Green Deal, which sets out comprehensive requirements for transitioning to a Sustainable Europe, will have an impact on business programs. Key issues include fighting climate change; measures to manage the transition, including green finance; sustainable investment; and the role of the private sector (European Commission, 2019, 2.2.1, pp. 15–17). Tax reforms will also play a key role in facilitating sustainable behavior (European Commission, 2019, 2.2.2, p. 17). "New technologies, sustainable solutions and disruptive innovation are critical to achieve the objectives of the European Green Deal" (European Commission, 2019, 2.2.3, p. 18). Universities are expected to play a role in developing competencies, skills, and attitudes on climate change and sustainable development (European Commission, 2019, 2.2.4, p. 19).

Further, Article 12 of the Paris Agreement requires countries to cooperate in taking measures, among others, to enhance climate-change education and training. In consequence, lessons in climate-change activism may soon become mandatory in schools of signatory nations (Lloyd, 2021) and have been incorporated into the New Zealand curriculum (Graham-McLay, 2020). It's entirely foreseeable, therefore, that business courses and accreditation standards may soon, too, give effect to Article 12.

Other developments also have implications for business schools. As institutional capital and large businesses grow the number and significance of their "New Paradigm"[53] agreements, corporate theories are being reshaped. And when principles of capital are taught in future, it will only be right and proper to consider natural capital as part of the curriculum. It is gaining traction as an element of corporate governance, risk management, finance, and investment and is a key consideration in climate action and sustainable business. Under the European Green Deal, the Commission will support "businesses and other stakeholders in developing standardised natural capital accounting practices within the EU and internationally" (European Commission, 2019, p. 17). Further, globalization is taking on a new and expanded meaning. As Thomas Friedman observes, the global flows of knowledge and information "are exploding and they are the new globalisation" (Friedman, 2016b, n.p.).

Stakeholderism in its various guises must also be on the radar of business schools and may become the guiding principle of enlightened corporate governance and good corporate citizenship, whether backed by legally enforceable stakeholder rights or otherwise. These important and developing forces invoke serious questions about the design and accreditation of fit-for-purpose business programs in the modern liquid world. If pluralistic stakeholderism is adopted, it may require corresponding amendments to the EQUIS standards and also to the way in which accreditation visits are structured. Presently, a school's corporate links are an essential element in gaining and retaining accreditation, and peer-review teams (PRTs) meet with corporate partners during an accreditation visit. But if pluralistic stakeholderism is institutionalized, the standards may need to reflect not only that there are corporate links but also that the school and its corporate partners are making positive contributions to meeting stakeholder outcomes. At the very least, the nature of the corporate connections' conversation during a PRT visit will become more multilayered.

Successful business school leaders are likely, therefore, to be those who, through productive paranoia (Collins, 2011, pp. 27–30), are best able to anticipate and embrace the forces of change and the new

---

[53] See earlier discussion on page 131.

realities they bring with them. As Juan Goytisolo says: "If one lives only in the present, one risks disappearing together with the present."[54] Or, in the words of Søren Kierkegaard, "Life can only be understood backwards but it must be lived forwards" (Kierkegaard, 1843). Presenting the past as a guide or model for the future may have been sufficient in the past but not in our increasingly liquid world.

For life to be lived forward requires new forms of leadership thinking and action. However daunting this may appear to be, many lessons can be learned from the COVID-19 pandemic. First, it required all institutions to respond rapidly to new global realities. Organizations, including business schools, were forced to pivot; this often meant radical leadership decisions had to be made and implemented, including quickly providing their products and services in alternative ways and deploying their workforces from home. For many, such actions secured their survival; others, unfortunately, fell by the wayside, and remarkably, a good number thrived. Leadership thinking and action, both prepandemic and during the pandemic, no doubt contributed to the outcomes for individual organizations. For example, those with entrenched digital strategies and systems benefitted greatly from the e-commerce and online-delivery booms. Their leaders had them well placed to thrive, notwithstanding severe disruptions, even black swan events. And for those that survived by adapting quickly by going beyond the methodologies to which they were firmly committed, such as business schools with no digital strategy or commitment to online teaching and learning, potentially transformative lessons have been learned for the future.

With the global forces at work, COVID-19 has shown us the dangers of limited thinking. A recent publication highlighted how limited forms of thinking led to mistakes in dealing with the pandemic (Martin et al., 2020). In the early stages, it was regarded as a scientific problem when it was, in reality, "a sprawling, complex system of a challenge that would also call on holistic thinking and values-balancing decisions" (Martin et al., 2020, para. 11). Paralysis, they argue, follows from limited thinking. COVID-19 has demonstrated that new global realities can and must be responded to even when it requires loosening one's attachment to deeply held orthodoxies. When existential threats such as a pandemic or the creeping effects of climate

[54] Cited by Bauman (2012, p. 205).

change confront the world, leaders of business schools and other leaders can't bargain with or ignore the hard realities of liquid modernity.

A searching accreditation test for a business school might well become, therefore, "How is the school responding to modern global forces, and how is it preparing professionals, managers, and leaders for 2030 and beyond to 2050?"

References

Accountable Capitalism Act. (n.d.). www.warren.senate.gov/imo/media/doc/ Accountable%20Capitalism%20Act%20One-Pager.pdf.

Adams, V., Murphy, M., and Clarke, A. E. (2009, September). Anticipation: Technoscience, life, affect, temporarily. *Subjectivity*, 28(1), 246–265.

Ahmad, F. M. (2017, September). *Beyond the horizon: Corporate reporting on climate change*. Centre for Climate and Energy Solutions.

Ahmad, I. (1958, December). Sovereignty in Islam. *Pakistan Horizon*, II(4), 244–257.

Allens Linklaters. (2020a, May). *Targeting net-zero: A climate change guide for legal and compliance teams in Australia*. www.allens.com.au/globa lassets/pdfs/campaigns/targeting_net_zero_climate_change_guide_may_ 2020.pdf.

(2020b, May 26). *The big picture: Australia's commitments under the Paris Agreement*. www.allens.com.au/insights-news/insights/2020/05/ climate-change-guide/the-big-picture-australias-commitments-under- the-paris-agreement/.

Ambos, K. (2013, March 12). Punishment without a sovereign? The *Ius puniendi* issue of international criminal law: A first contribution towards a consistent theory of international criminal law. *Oxford Journal of Legal Studies*, 33(2), 293–315.

ASX Corporate Governance Council. (2019, February). *Corporate govern- ance principles and recommendations*, 4th ed. www.asx.com.au/docu ments/asx-compliance/cgc-principles-and-recommendations-fourth-edn .pdf.

Australian Centre for Corporate Responsibility. (2020, October 7). *AGL AGM: BlackRock support demonstrates Australian investors lag for- eign peers*. https://accr.org.au/news/agl-agm-blackrock-support-demon strates-australian-investors-lag-foreign-peers/.

Australian Climate Leaders Coalition. (n.d.). *Home page*. www .climateleaders.org.au/.

Australian Prudential Regulation Authority. (2020, February 24). *Understanding and managing the financial risks of climate change*.

www.apra.gov.au/understanding-and-managing-financial-risks-of-cli
mate-change.

Australian Securities & Investment Commission. (2018, September). *Climate risk disclosure by Australia's listed companies.* https://download.asic
.gov.au/media/4871341/rep593-published-20-september-2018.pdf.

AustralianSuper. (2020, May). *Climate change report: Managing the transition to a low carbon economy.* www.australiansuper.com/-/media/aus
tralian-super/files/investments/how-we-invest/climate-change/climate-
change-report.pdf.

Baron, D. P. (2003). Private politics. *Journal of Economics & Management Strategy*, 12(1), 31–66.

Bauman, Z. (2012). *Liquid modernity.* Polity Press.

Bebchuk, L. A., and Tallarita, R. (2020, December). The illusory promise of stakeholder governance. *Cornell Law Review*, 106, 91–178.

BHP. (n.d.). *Global climate policy standards.* www.bhp.com/-/media/docu
ments/ourapproach/operatingwithintegrity/industryassociations/200814_
globalclimatepolicystandards—aug20.pdf?la=en.

Biggs, S., Lake, O. O., and Goldtooth, T. B. K. (2017). Rights of nature & mother earth, rights-based law for systemic change. Movement Rights, Women's Earth & Climate Action Network, Indigenous Environmental Network. www.ienearth.org/wp-content/uploads/2017/11/RONME-
RightsBasedLaw-final-1.pdf.

BlackRock. (2020a, September). *Investment stewardship annual report.* www.blackrock.com/corporate/literature/publication/blk-annual-stew
ardship-report-2020.pdf.

(2020b, December). *Our 2021 stewardship expectations – global principles and market-level voting guidelines.* www.blackrock.com/corpor
ate/literature/publication/our-2021-stewardship-expectations.pdf.

Boyd, T. (2017, November 1). Larry Fink says BlackRock will take activism to a "whole new level." *Australian Financial Review.* www.afr.com/
companies/larry-fink-says-blackrock-will-take-activism-to-a-whole-new-
level-20171031-gzc2lt.

BP. (2019a, May 21). *Notice of BP Annual General Meeting 2019.* www.bp
.com/content/dam/bp/business-sites/en/global/corporate/pdfs/investors/
bp-agm-notice-of-meeting-2019.pdf.

(2019b). *Energy with purpose, BP annual report and form 20-F 2019.* www.bp.com/content/dam/bp/business-sites/en/global/corporate/pdfs/
investors/bp-annual-report-and-form-20f-2019.pdf.

(2020, February 12). *BP sets ambition for net-zero by 2050, fundamentally changing organisation to deliver.* www.bp.com/en/global/corpor
ate/news-and-insights/press-releases/bernard-looney-announces-new-
ambition-for-bp.html.

British Academy. (2019, November). *Future of the corporation, principles for purposeful business*. www.thebritishacademy.ac.uk/documents/224/future-of-the-corporation-principles-purposeful-business.pdf.

Business Roundtable. (2019, August 19). *Statement on the purpose of a corporation*. https://s3.amazonaws.com/brt.org/BRT-StatementonthePurposeofaCorporationOctober2020.pdf.

Butler, B. (2019, October 2). AustralianSuper tells Minerals Council its climate policy is "not strong enough." *The Guardian*. www.theguardian.com/australia-news/2019/oct/02/australiansuper-tells-minerals-council-its-climate-policy-is-not-strong-enough.

CalPERS. (2019, December). *Climate change risk – CalPERS' first response to Senate Bill 964*. www.calpers.ca.gov/docs/forms-publications/addressing-climate-change-risk.pdf.

(2020, June). *CalPERS' investment strategy on climate change, first report in response to the taskforce on climate-related financial disclosure*. www.calpers.ca.gov/docs/board-agendas/202006/invest/item08c-01_a.pdf.

Ceres. (2020a, September 14). *Climate Action 100+ calls for net-zero business strategies & sets out benchmark of largest corporate emitters*. www.ceres.org/news-center/press-releases/climate-action-100-calls-net-zero-business-strategies-sets-out-benchmark.

(2020b, October 7). *Ceres introduces the Ceres Roadmap 2030: A 10-year action plan for sustainable business leadership*. www.ceres.org/news-center/press-releases/ceres-introduces-ceres-roadmap-2030-10-year-action-plan-sustainable.

Chapron, G., Epstein, Y., and López-Bao, J. V. (2019, March 29). A rights revolution for nature. *Science, 363*(6434), 1392–1393.

Climate Action 100+. (n.d.). *Investor signatories*. www.climateaction100.org/investors.

(2019) *Progress report*. www.climateaction100.wpcomstaging.com/wp-content/uploads/2019/10/progressreport2019.pdf.

(2020) *Progress report*. www.climateaction100.org/wp-content/uploads/2020/12/Climate-Action-100-2020-Progress-Report_Final.pdf.

(2021, March 22). *Climate Action 100+ issues its first-ever net zero company benchmark of the world's largest corporate emitters*. www.climateaction100.org/news/climate-action-100-issues-its-first-ever-net-zero-company-benchmark-of-the-worlds-largest-corporate-emitters/.

Climate Action in Financial Institutions. (2019, June). *Climate Action 100+*. www.mainstreamingclimate.org/climate-action-100/.

Collins, J. (2011). *Great by choice*. Random House Business Books.

Colvin, G. (2015, October 22). Why every aspect of your business is about to change. *Fortune*. https://fortune.com/2015/10/22/the-21st-century-corporation-new-business-models/.

Colvin, R. M., and Jotzo, F. (2021, March 24). Australian voters' attitudes to climate action and their social-political determinants. *Plos ONE.* https://journals.plos.org/plosone/article?id=10.1371/journal.pone.0248268.

Community Environmental Local Defense Fund. (2020, September 16). *Rights of nature.* https://celdf.org/advancing-community-rights/rights-of-nature/.

Companies Act. (2006). www.legislation.gov.uk/ukpga/2006/46/contents.

Coppola, M., Krick, T., and Blohmke, J. (2019, December 12). *Feeling the heat? Companies are under pressure on climate change and need to do more.* Deloitte. www2.deloitte.com/us/en/insights/topics/strategy/impact-and-opportunities-of-climate-change-on-business.html.

Council of Institutional Investors. (2019, August 19). *Council of Institutional Investors responds to business roundtable statement on corporate purpose.* www.cii.org/aug19_brt_response.

Deloitte. (2020, February). *Clarity in financial reporting: Disclosure of climate-related risks.* www2.deloitte.com/content/dam/Deloitte/au/Documents/audit/deloitte-au-audit-clarity-disclosure-climate-related-risks-070220.pdf.

Demaria, S., Rigot, S., and Borie, S. (2019, May). *A new measure of environmental reporting practice based on the recommendations of the Task Force on Climate-Related Financial Disclosures.* https://halshs.archives-ouvertes.fr/halshs-02407136.

Edelman. (2020). *Edelman trust barometer 2020.* https://cdn2.hubspot.net/hubfs/440941/Trust%20Barometer%202020/2020%20Edelman%20Trust%20Barometer%20Global%20Report.pdf?utm_campaign=Global:%20Trust%20Barometer%202020&utm_source=Website.

EU High-Level Expert Group on Sustainable Finance. (2018). *Financing a sustainable European economy.* https://ec.europa.eu/info/sites/info/files/180131-sustainable-finance-final-report_en.pdf.

European Commission. (2017, June 26). *Communication from the Commission, guidelines on non-financial reporting (methodology for reporting non-financial information). Principle 3.5.* https://ec.europa.eu/transparency/regdoc/rep/3/2017/EN/C-2017-4234-F1-EN-MAIN-PART-1.PDF.

(2019, December 11). *Communication from the Commission to the European Parliament, the European Council, the Council, the European Economic and Social Committee and the Committee of Regions, the European Green Deal.* https://eur-lex.europa.eu/resource.html?uri=cellar:b828d165–1c22–11ea-8c1f-01aa75ed71a1.0002.02/DOC_1&format=PDF.

Fagan, M., and Huang, C. (2019, April 18). *A look at how people around the world view climate change.* Pew Research Center. www

.pewresearch.org/fact-tank/2019/04/18/a-look-at-how-people-around-the-world-view-climate-change/.

Farrell, H., Levi, M., and O'Reilly, T. (2018, April 10). *Mark Zuckerberg runs a nation-state, and he's the king.* Vox. www.vox.com/the-big-idea/2018/4/9/17214752/zuckerberg-facebook-power-regulation-data-priv acy-control-political-theory-data-breach-king.

Fernyhough, J. (2020, September 15). New Zealand makes climate reporting compulsory. *Australian Financial Review.* www.afr.com/companies/financial-services/new-zealand-makes-climate-reporting-compulsory-20200915-p55vno.

(2021, January 12). Prince Charles transcends carbon in new green alliance. *Australian Financial Review.* www.afr.com/companies/financial-ser vices/prince-charles-transcends-carbon-in-new-green-alliance-20210111-p5 6t9v.

Financial Reporting Council. (2018, July). *The UK Corporate Governance Code.* www.frc.org.uk/getattachment/88bd8c45-50ea-4841-95b0-d2f4f48069a2/2018-UK-Corporate-Governance-Code-FINAL.pdf.

Financial Stability Board. (2020, October 29). *2020 Status report: Task force on climate-related financial disclosures.* www.fsb.org/2020/10/2020-status-report-task-force-on-climate-related-financial-disclosures/.

Fink, L. (n.d.). *A fundamental reshaping of finance.* BlackRock. www .blackrock.com/us/individual/larry-fink-ceo-letter.

Freeman, R. E. (1984). *Strategic management: A stakeholder approach.* Pitman.

Friedman, T. L. (2016a). *Thank you for being late, an optimist's guide to thriving in the age of accelerations.* Farrar, Straus and Giroux.

(2016b, October 14). *Thomas Friedman's keynote address at the UN.* www.un.org/en/desa/thomas-friedmans-keynote-address-united-nations.

Gardner, H. (2008). *Five minds for the future.* Harvard Business Press.

Georghiu, E. C. (2015/2016). The diversity of corporate governance models in Europe: An analysis of the UK shareholder model and the German stakeholder model and their current significance. Unpublished PhD thesis, Leiden University Faculty of Law. www.academia.edu/34566580/The_diversity_of_Corporate_Governance_Models_in_Europe_An_analysis_of_the_UK_shareholder_model_and_the_German_stakehold er_model_and_their_current_significance.

Germanwatch. (n.d.). *Saúl versus RWE – the Huaraz case.* https://germanwatch.org/en/huaraz.

Gino, F. (2018, September–October). The business case for curiosity. *Harvard Business Review.* https://hbr.org/2018/09/the-business-case-for-curiosity.

Glencore. (2020, December 4). *Climate Report 2020: Pathway to net zero.* www.glencore.com/media-and-insights/news/Climate-Report-2020–Pathway-to-Net-Zero.

Global Climate Change Litigation Database. (n.d.). *Luciano Lliuya v. RWE AG.* http://climatecasechart.com/climate-change-litigation/non-us-case/lliuya-v-rwe-ag/

Global Justice Now. (2018, October 17). *69 of the richest 100 entities on the planet are corporations, not governments, figures show.* www .globaljustice.org.uk/news/2018/oct/17/69-richest-100-entities-planet-are-corporations-not-governments-figures-show.

Goshen, Z., and Hannes, S. (2019, May). The death of corporate law. *NYU Law Review*, 94(2), 263–314.

Governance Institute of Australia. (2018, April 4). *Australians free to adopt TCFD reporting on climate risk.* www.governanceinstitute.com.au/news-media/news/2018/apr/australians-free-to-adopt-tcfd-reporting-on-climate-risk/.

(2020, February). *A practical guide to reporting against ASX Corporate Governance Council's corporate governance principles and recommendations.* www.governanceinstitute.com.au/advocacy/thought-leadership/climate-change-risk-disclosure/.

Graham-McLay, C. (2020, January 13). New Zealand schools to teach students about climate crisis, activism and "eco anxiety." *The Guardian.* www.theguardian.com/world/2020/jan/13/new-zealand-schools-to-teach-students-about-climate-crisis-activism-and-eco-anxiety.

Hagel, J. (2020, July). *From the gig economy to the guild economy.* www .johnhagel.com/category/flow/.

Hagel, J., and Brown, J. S. (2017, June 7). Great businesses scale their learning, not just their operations. *Harvard Business Review.* https://hbr.org/2017/06/great-businesses-scale-their-learning-not-just-their-operations.

Hagel, J., III, Brown, J. S., and Davison, L. (2009a, January 27). Abandon stocks, embrace flows. *Harvard Business Review.* https://hbr.org/2009/01/abandon-stocks-embrace-flows.

(2009b, July–August). The big shift: Measuring the forces of change. *Harvard Business Review*, 87(7–8), 86–89.

Harvard Business Review. (2015). *The business case for purpose.* https://hbr .org/resources/pdfs/comm/ey/19392HBRReportEY.pdf.

Hinks, G. (2020, November 9). Biden presidency set to bring corporate governance shift. Board Agenda. https://boardagenda.com/2020/11/09/biden-presidency-set-to-bring-corporate-governance-shift/.

Horster, M., and Papadopoulus, K. (2019, January 7). Climate change and proxy voting in the U.S. and Europe. https://corpgov.law.harvard.edu/2019/01/07/climate-change-and-proxy-voting-in-the-u-s-and-europe/.

Howitt, R. (2020, August 4). Companies should embrace Europe's roadmap to stakeholder capitalism. Board Agenda. https://boardagenda.com/2020/08/04/companies-should-embrace-europes-roadmap-to-stakeholder-capitalism/.

Institute of Directors. (2019). *IoD manifesto: Corporate governance.* www.iod.com/Portals/0/PDFs/Campaigns%20and%20Reports/Corporate%20Governance/IoD%20Manifesto%20-%20Corporate%20Governance.pdf?ver=2019-11-19-082215-783.

Institutional Investors Group on Climate Change. (2020a). *IIGCC report: Ambitious EU 2030 action essential for achieving net zero emissions.* www.iigcc.org/download/iigcc-report-ambitious-eu-2030-action-essential-for-achieving-net-zero-emissions/?wpdmdl=3844&masterkey=5f58a06689ae3.

(2020b, May 5). *Total commits to net-zero emissions through Climate Action 100+ investor engagement* [Press Release]. www.iigcc.org/news/total-commits-to-net-zero-emissions/.

Institutional Shareholder Services. (2020, March 9). *ISS climate voting policy.* www.issgovernance.com.

International Organization of Securities Organisations. (2020, October 28). *Open response to the open letter from CDP, Climate Disclosure Standards Board (CDSB), Global Reporting Initiative (GRI), International Integrated Reporting Council and Sustainability Accounting Standards Board (SASB) proposing avenues for working together to meet the needs of capital markets.* www.iosco.org/library/speeches/pdf/20201029-Erik-Thed%C3%A9en.pdf.

Investor Group on Climate Change. (2019, February 27). *Global investors welcome climate change report from Rio Tinto.* https://igcc.org.au/global-investors-welcome-climate-change-report-from-rio-tinto/.

Jones, T. M. (1995). Instrumental stakeholder theory: A synthesis of ethics and economics. *Academy of Management Review*, 20(2), 404–437.

Jones, T. M., Harrison J. S., and Felps W. (2018). How applying instrumental stakeholder theory can provide sustainable competitive advantage. *Academy of Management Review*, 43(3), 371–391.

Kassan, S. (1935, April). Extra territorial jurisdiction in the ancient world. *The American Journal of International Law*, 29(2), 237–247.

Keay, A. (2007, December). Tackling the issue of the corporate objective: An analysis of the United Kingdom's "enlightened shareholder value approach." *Sydney Law Review*, 29(4), 577–692.

Keohane, R. O., and Victor, D. G. (2011, March). The regime complex for climate change. *Perspectives on Politics*, 9(1), 7–23.

Khir, B. M. (1990). The Islamic concept of sovereignty. Unpublished PhD thesis, University of Edinburgh.

Kierkegaard, S. (1843). *Journals IV A 164.* P.G. Philipsen.

KPMG Australia. (2020, May 26). *Preparing for climate-related disclosures: How the TCFD recommendations are impacting insurers and the challenges ahead.* https://home.kpmg/au/en/home/insights/2020/05/prepar ing-for-climate-related-disclosures.html.

Lamanna, M., and Berridge, R. (2020, March 17). *Climate Action 100+ targets the 100 largest corporate GHG emitters.* www.proxypreview .org.

Lipton, M. (2016, September 2). The new paradigm: A roadmap for an implicit corporate governance partnership between corporations and investors to achieve sustainable long-term investment and growth. World Economic Forum. https://www.wlrk.com/webdocs/wlrknew/ AttorneyPubs/WLRK.25960.16.pdf

(2017, January 11). Corporate governance: The new paradigm. Harvard Law School Forum on Corporate Governance. https://corpgov.law .harvard.edu/2017/01/11/corporate-governance-the-new-paradigm/.

(2019, February 11). *It's time to adopt the new paradigm.* Harvard Law School Forum on Corporate Governance. https://corpgov.law.harvard .edu/2019/02/11/its-time-to-adopt-the-new-paradigm/

Lloyd, G. (2021, January 20). Green activism mandate in schools. *The Australian.* www.theaustralian.com.au/nation/politics/green-activism-mandate-in-schools/news-story/9ae6bdadd9235b999aa1cde5278da4ff.

Macdonald-Smith, A. (2021, January 21). Decarbonisation spend tops $US500 b. *Australian Financial Review.* www.afr.com/companies/ energy/decarbonisation-spend-tops-us500b-20210120-p56vgo.

Macquarie. (2020, July). *Macquarie and climate change, TCFD implementation progress and scenario analysis.* www.macquarie.com/assets/ macq/impact/esg/policies/tcfd-implementation-progress-and-scenario-analysis-fy20.pdf

Maersk. (2019, June 26). *Towards a zero-carbon future.* www.maersk.com/ news/articles/2019/06/26/towards-a-zero-carbon-future.

Majoch, A. A. A., Hoepner, A. G. F., and Hebb, T. (2017). Sources of stakeholder salience in the responsible investment movement: Why do investors sign the principles for responsible investment? *Journal of Business Ethics*, 140, 723–741.

Market Forces. (2020, May 7). *Huge gains in investor support for real climate action at Rio Tinto.* www.marketforces.org.au/huge-gains-in-investor-support-for-real-climate-action-at-rio-tinto/.

Martin, R. L., Straub, R., and Kirby, J. (2020, October 2). Leaders need to harness Aristotle's 3 types of knowledge. *Harvard Business Review.* https://hbr.org/2020/10/leaders-need-to-harness-aristotles-3-types-of-knowledge.

Mayer, C. (2020, January 7). It's time to redefine the purpose of business. Here's a roadmap. World Economic Forum. www.weforum.org/agenda/2020/01/its-time-for-a-radical-rethink-of-corporate-purpose/.

(2021, February 17). Shareholderism versus stakeholderism – a misconceived contradiction: A comment on "The Illusory Promise of Stakeholder Governance" by Lucian Bebchuk and Roberto Tallarita. Harvard Law School Forum on Corporate Governance. https://corpgov .law.harvard.edu/2021/02/17/shareholderism-versus-stakeholderism-a-misconceived-contradiction-a-comment-on-the-illusory-promise-of-stakeholder-governance-by-lucian-bebchuk-and-roberto-tallarita/.

McAdam, D. (2017). Social movement theory and the prospects for climate change activism in the United States. *Annual Review of Political Science*, 20(1), 189–208.

McMillon, D., and Bolten, J. (2020, October 2). Letter to the honorable Elizabeth Warren, United States Senate. Business Roundtable. www .businessroundtable.org/business-roundtable-letter-to-us-senator-eliza beth-warren-2.

Miller, M. (2019). Environmental personhood and standing for nature: Examining the Colorado River case. *University of New Hampshire Law Review*, 17(2), 13. https://scholars.unh.edu/cgi/viewcontent.cgi?art icle=1341&context=unh_lr

Min, S. (2020, September 16). Investor-led CA100+ to judge companies on sustainable benchmark. www.ai-cio.com/news/investor-led-climate-action-100-judge-companies-sustainable-benchmark/.

Mitchell, R., Agle, B., and Wood, D. J. (1997, October). Toward a theory of stakeholder identification and salience: defining the principle of who and what really counts. *Academy of Management Review*, 22(4), 853–886.

Moss, J. (2020). Climate transition series, Australia: An emission super-power. UNSW Sydney. https://climatejustice.co/wp-content/uploads/2020/07/Australia-_-an-emissions-super-power.pdf.

National Aeronautics and Space Administration. (2020). *Scientific consensus: Earth's climate is warming*. https://climate.nasa.gov/scientific-con sensus/.

Nee, E. (2020, fall). B Corps grow up. *Stanford Social Innovation Review*. https://ssir.org/articles/entry/b_corps_grow_up.

Organisation for Economic Co-operation and Development. (2004). *OECD Principles of corporate governance*. www.oecd.org/corporate/ca/corpor ategovernanceprinciples/31557724.pdf.

(2011). *OECD guidelines for multinational enterprises*. www.oecd.org/daf/inv/mne/48004323.pdf.

Paris, R. (2020, summer). The right to dominate: how old ideas about sovereignty pose new challenges for world order. *International Organization*, 74(3), 453–489.

Porter, M. E., and Reinhardt, F. L. (2007, October). Grist: A strategic approach to climate. *Harvard Business Review*. https://hbr.org/2007/10/climate-business-_-business-climate.

PricewaterhouseCoopers. (2020, July). *Governance reform and the impact on corporate reporting*. www.pwc.co.uk/audit-assurance/assets/pdf/governance-reform-and-impact-on-corporate-reporting.pdf.

(2021). *PwC 24th annual global CEO survey*. www.pwc.com/gx/en/ceo-agenda/ceosurvey/2021.html.

Principles for Responsible Investment. (2019, February 19). *TCFD-based reporting to become mandatory for PRI signatories in 2020*. www.unpri.org/news-and-press/tcfd-based-reporting-to-become-mandatory-for-pri-signatories-in-2020/4116.article.

Principles for Responsible Investment. (2020). *PRI signatory growth*. https://dwtyzx6upklss.cloudfront.net/Uploads/g/p/y/globalaumandaoaumexternaluse_110617.xlsx.

Ready, D. A. (2019, July 18). In praise of the incurably curious leader. *MIT Sloan Management Review*. https://sloanreview.mit.edu/article/in-praise-of-the-incurably-curious-leader/.

Reich, R. (2014, August 12). *The rebirth of stakeholder capitalism?* Social Europe. www.socialeurope.eu/stakeholder-capitalism.

Reid, E. M., and Toffel, M. W. (2009). Responding to public and private politics: Corporate disclosure of climate change strategies. *Strategic Management Journal*, 30(11), 1157–1178.

Reserve Bank of Australia. (2019, September 19). *The changing global market for Australian coal*. www.rba.gov.au/publications/bulletin/2019/sep/the-changing-global-market-for-australian-coal.html.

Rio Tinto. (2020, February 26). *Rio Tinto to invest $1 billion to help meet new climate change targets*. www.riotinto.com/en/news/releases/2020/Rio-Tinto-to-invest-1-billion-to-help-meet-new-climate-change-targets.

Ross, D. (2021, January 16). Corporate watch dog puts climate change warnings into action. *The Australian*. www.theaustralian.com.au/business/corporate-watchdog-puts-climate-change-warnings-into-action/news-story/74a69dd7f694d1967820d3511b721db9.

Royal Dutch Shell PLC. (2020, April 16). *Responsible investment annual briefing 2020*. www.shell.com/investors/investor-presentations/2020-investor-presentations/responsible-investment-annual-briefing-april-16-2020.html#vanity-aHR0cHM6Ly93d3cuc2hlbGwuY29tL2ludmVzdG9ycy9uZXdzLWFuZC1tZWRpYS1yZWxlYXNlcy9pbnZlc3Rvci1wcmVzZW50YXRpb25zLzIwMjAtaW5Cb3RtcHJlc2VudG

F0aW9ucy9yZXNwb25zaWBJsZS1pbnZlc3RtZW50LWFubnVhbC1icmll
ZmluZy1hcHJpbC0xNi0yMDIwLmh0bWVWww

Royal Dutch Shell PLC. (2021). *Shell energy transition strategy.* www.shell
.com/promos/energy-and-innovation/shell-energy-transition-strategy/_
jcr_content.stream/1618407326759/7c3d5b317351891d2383b3e9f1
e511997e516639/shell-energy-transition-strategy-2021.pdf.

Rundell, S. (2020, September 11). *CalPERS' Simpson on Climate Action 100
+.* Top 1000 Funds. www.top1000funds.com/2020/09/calpers-simp
son-on-climate-action-100/.

Schumpeter. (2018, January 3). 2018 will be the year that big, incumbent
companies take on big tech. *The Economist.* www.economist.com/busi
ness/2018/01/03/2018-will-be-the-year-that-big-incumbent-companies-
take-on-big-tech.

Schwab, K. (2019, December 2). Davos manifesto 2020: The universal
purpose of a company in the fourth industrial revolution. World
Economic Forum. www.weforum.org/agenda/2019/12/davos-mani
festo-2020-the-universal-purpose-of-a-company-in-the-fourth-indus
trial-revolution/.

Setzer, J., and Byrnes, R. (2020, July). *Global trends in climate change
litigation: 2020 snapshot.* www.lse.ac.uk/granthaminstitute/wp-con
tent/uploads/2020/07/Global-trends-in-climate-change-litigation_2020-
snapshot.pdf.

Sjöström, E. (2020). *Active ownership on environmental and social issues:
What works? A summary of the recent academic literature.* www.ap7
.se/app/uploads/2020/03/active-ownership-on-environmental-and-social-
issues.pdf.

Statista. (2020, April 28). *Leading mining companies worldwide based on
market value.* www.statista.com/statistics/272706/top-10-mining-com
panies-worldwide-based-on-market-value/.

(2021, August 4). *Value of sustainable investment assets worldwide
2014–2020, by region.* www.statista.com/statistics/742097/sri-assets-
value-by-region/.

Task Force on Climate-Related Financial Disclosures. (n.d.). *Recommended
disclosures, strategy.* www.tcfdhub.org/strategy/.

(2017, June). *Final report: Recommendations of the task force on climate-
related financial disclosures.* www.fsb-tcfd.org/wp-content/uploads/
2017/06/FINAL-2017-TCFD-Report-11052018.pdf.

(2020, March). *Task force on climate-related financial disclosures.* www
.fsb-tcfd.org/wp-content/uploads/2020/03/TCFD_Booklet_FNL_Digital_
March-2020.pdf.

Thistlethwaite, J. (2015). The politics of experimentation in climate change
risk reporting: The emergence of the Climate Disclosure Standards
Board (CDSB). *Environmental Politics*, 24(6), 970–990.

Thompson, B. (2020, November 11). Forrest unveils staggering vision for Fortescue in renewables. *Australian Financial Review*. www.afr.com/companies/mining/forrest-unveils-staggering-vision-for-fortescue-in-renewables-20201110-p56d3h.

Toscano, N. (2019, July23). BHP sets emission cuts for customers in major carbon push. *Sydney Morning Herald*. www.smh.com.au/business/companies/bhp-sets-emissions-cuts-for-customers-in-major-carbon-push-20190723-p529wk.html.

United Nations. (n.d.). *The 17 goals*. https://sdgs.un.org/goals.

(1992). *What is the United Nations Framework Convention on Climate Change?* https://unfccc.int/files/essential_background/background_publications_htmlpdf/application/pdf/conveng.pdf.

(2015). *The Paris Agreement*. https://unfccc.int/process-and-meetings/the-paris-agreement/the-paris-agreement.

United Nations Environment Programme Finance Initiative. (n.d.). *Natural capital finance alliance*. www.unepfi.org/ecosystems/ncfa/.

van Leeuwen, H. (2021, March 20–21). Climate activist has big banks in his sights. *Australian Financial Review*, p. 28.

von Redlich, M. D. R. (1932, July). Papal sovereignty. *Social Science*, 7(3), 237–245.

Weart, S. R. (2020, February). *The discovery of global warming*. American Institute of Physics. https://history.aip.org/climate/index.htm

West, E. (2020, February 4). *Could the Ohio River have rights? A movement to grant rights to the environment tests the power of local control*. Environmental Health News. www.ehn.org/ohio-river-nature-rights-2645014867.html.

Williams, R. (2012). Enlightened shareholder value in UK company law. *UNSW Law Journal*, 35(1), 360–377.

Winston, A. (2019, August 30). Is the Business Roundtable Statement just empty rhetoric? *Harvard Business Review*. https://hbr.org/2019/08/is-the-business-roundtable-statement-just-empty-rhetoric.

World Economic Forum. (2020, January 8). Why nature is the most important stakeholder of the coming decade. *European Sting*. https://europeansting.com/2020/01/08/why-nature-is-the-most-important-stakeholder-of-the-coming-decade/

7 | Transforming Business Schools into Lighthouses of Hope for a Sustainable Future

DANIEL TRAÇA

I. Introduction

As the European Foundation for Management Development (EFMD) celebrates 50, the world undergoes a state of deep existential crisis. Events unfold in front of our eyes that are impossible to understand for anyone born around the same time as EFMD. This state of affairs predates the current pandemic, when climate change, aging populations, data privacy, and exploding inequality, to cite a few, were already pushing institutions to the brink.

We have lived through many bad and good times in the last century. But in all those times, we had theories that allowed us to understand world events and make valid predictions about how they would evolve. Even the most dramatic event of the last half century, the fall of communism, had a narrative that all could share and understand.

In that context of predictability and epistemological security, business schools grew in scope and influence, boosted by the push for quality and innovation of accreditation agencies. This expansion coincided with the spread of neoliberalism, and many argue that business schools were its evangelists, as graduates educated in its theories set off to positions of influence. By the turn of the century, neoliberalism showed signs that it was unfit to sustain stable and shared growth as inequality grew and financial crises emerged worldwide. The situation reached its nadir in 2008 as the world lived through one of its most significant financial troubles. The trials of neoliberal ideas, and the crisis that outlined them, have created a severe legitimacy crisis for business schools. The current pandemic will only heighten the challenge as society looks to universities for intellectual leadership.

The first part of this chapter argues that the triad of globalization, technology, and sustainability has disrupted human societies' underlying economic context worldwide. The underlying economic context sets the stage for the institutions that organize communities and is

154

defined by the dominant technological, mental, natural, and geostrategic forces and pressures. Given this disruption, most theories and all ideologies imagined in the twentieth century (and before), including neoliberalism, are unfit to shape economic and political systems that ensure peace and prosperity. The existential crisis mentioned at the onset of this chapter is, therefore, an epistemological crisis. The new underlying context requires new institutions, knowledge, and skills to restore stability, predictability, inclusivity, and above all, hope.

A courageous agenda and purposeful leadership at business schools must be part of the solution to redesigning the fit-for-purpose institutions, knowledge, and skills for this century. On the one hand, we need a shift in the management and governance of businesses, which has been the business of business schools. On the other hand, we must have equally essential changes in other institutions, such as governments and nonprofits, which should also become the business of business schools.

As breeding grounds for the knowledge and the leaders of tomorrow, business schools must live up to their reason for existence. Their response will define their public value and legitimacy for the coming decades. It will also outline the world our students will inherit and the historical legacy of our generation.

The second part of this chapter argues that business schools need to enhance their commitment to sustainable innovation to fulfill this role. Thus, they must make central to their strategies and cultures the principles of and the accountability for sustainable impact. They must also develop a more open and deeper engagement with a broader group of stakeholders, including extending beyond business to nonprofits and the public sector and reaching out beyond finance and economics to politics, law, international relations, history, technology, and science – in other words, building a cross-stakeholder and interdisciplinary agenda that develops leaders mindful of the human experience. This interdisciplinarity must create new knowledge of relevance to address the challenges of the present and the future. The chapter concludes by discussing the impediments to reform borne by business schools' current business and governance models and assessing the lessons of the COVID-19 crisis for their digital transformation.

This chapter's main contribution is to focus the discussions taking place in the literature in the context of the future instead of the past. The fundamental changes in the underlying context imply that looking at the role of business schools and neoliberalism in the twentieth century is an academic endeavor with limited relevance to our shared future. The focus should be on imagining solutions that work in the new context that we are only now beginning to discover. Given the dramatic challenges ahead and the vertiginous speed at which they unfold, the call for action should leave no business school dean unmindful. As we attract many thousands of students every year, our first order of accountability should be to them and their future.

II. The Rise and Fall of Neoliberalism and the Legitimacy of Business Schools

Fifty years of EFMD fostered the rise in business schools' influence and scope worldwide. As EFMD learned to walk, the world was reimagining the postwar success after a decade of crisis in the 1970s. The neoliberal prophecy transformed John Stuart Mill's promotion of individual freedom and agency into the empire of the markets and promised a chimera of growth by restraining government and regulations. Its prophets supported a nonnuanced worldview. Milton Friedman proposed the pursuit of profit as the sole responsibility of business. Thatcher preached that "the government of business is not the business of government." Fama proclaimed that "financial markets are perfect." And Fukuyama predicted "The End of History," when all the earth's peoples would assemble under a neoliberal worldview and rules.

Neoliberalism was the epilogue to the underlying economic context that emerged in the West and spread to the developing world after World War II. The underlying economic context refers to the stage that frames the development of economic, social, and political institutions that organize communities. It is set by the prevailing technological, mental, natural, and geostrategic forces and pressures. The Enlightenment, World War II, and the steam engine are examples of past changes to the underlying economic context that have required institutional transformations to ensure a stable and predictable framework for societal dynamics.

The underlying economic context of the second half of the twentieth century was a goldilocks environment that ensured peace, prosperity, and harmony – after decades of hopelessness that had taken humanity to the brink in the first half of the century. Innovations in technology and management churned never-before-seen productivity growth rates, raised living standards, and improved material quality of life. Global trade and investment benefited from the peace that memories of World War II and the strategy of mutually assured destruction secured. International institutions supported by the Pax Americana assured stable global governance. European unification showed the power of enlightened leadership to overcome the shortcomings of humanity's nationalistic instincts. Cross-boundary media, communications, and transport fostered the convergence of human cultures and values. Global firms became increasingly efficient and a staple of development strategies. Central banks mastered the volatile effects of inflation, which had eroded many social and political orders before World War II. And increased access to education, active social policies, and semiskilled-biased technological change in services and the factory floor nurtured middle-class prosperity.

By the turn of the twentieth century, the signs of discredit in neoliberalism were emerging. The gap between rich and poor skyrocketed. Recent estimates show that the top 1 percent of the global income distribution captured 27 percent of the rise in income between 1980 and 2016, whereas the bottom 50 percent captured only 12 percent (Alvaredo et al., 2018). A disturbing element is the squeeze of the middle class in industrialized economies. The climate crisis also showed little sign of abating. The Kyoto Climate Protocol, which relied on market-driven approaches to fight global warming, entered into force in 2005 and failed to produce the expected results. By 2008, the financial crisis brought the global economy to its knees. It sparked severe austerity policies worldwide, damaging the financial industry's legitimacy and reputation and relaunching old debates between pro-government and pro-market doctrines that had pitted left against right throughout the twentieth century.

In the wake of the inequality, climate, and financial crises, the legitimacy of neoliberalism and its institutions and stakeholders have fallen deep into disarray. Raworth (2017) and Collier (2018) were among the many who departed from the mainstream to offer a critical view of how neoliberalism and the academic body sustaining it had evolved and suggested roads for improving it. Peter Bakker, president of the World Business Council for Sustainable Development, cited in Dyllick (2015), summarizes the ongoing malaise: "The conventional model for capitalism is found wanting in terms of the benefits to the majority of society, the impact on the planet, and even in terms of continued economic prosperity. The call for change rings loud – capitalism requires a new operating system and needs a reboot if we are to avoid the ultimate recession or worse total collapse" (p. 17).

As individuals, organizations, and nations worldwide adopted neo-liberal ideologies in the 1980s, business schools became the order's temples and prospered. They received tribute and paid back hefty returns to graduates, their employers, and supportive academics. Cornuel (2005) argued that these returns assured that "in the future, the legitimacy of business schools will no longer be questioned" (p. 819).

On the other end, when the neoliberal order began to unravel, business schools were under siege, and their legitimacy was challenged. Mintzberg's (2004) contribution was clairvoyant when he argued against the narrow and academic focus of business school curricula, which ignored the role of professional managerial skills that had to be learned from experience. Goshal (2005) claimed that business schools had been teaching amoral theories that undermined sound management. They were accused of promoting selfish behavior and biasing minds against social responsibility. Khurana (2007) argued that business schools sold their soul to corporate interests. More recently, as Parker (2018) contended that "the business school acts as an apologist, selling ideology as if it were science as part of the longest public relations campaign in history" (p. ix), the challenge to their legitimacy reached its zenith.

The debate rages on, but it remains too fixated on the past: on the allegiance of business schools to corporate capitalism and the frailties of neoliberal thinking, paying insufficient attention to the disruptions that occurred in the underlying economic context in the last 15 years. It is possible that neoliberalism would have collapsed from within, even in an unchanged underlying context, like communism had done four decades before. However, the critical challenge now is to address the changes in the underlying economic context that are making the theories and institutions developed in the twentieth century unfit for purpose. They must be rehabilitated with extreme urgency.

III. Builders of Sustainability, Inclusivity, and Meaning in a Disrupted World

A. *Globalization, Technology, and Sustainability as Disruptors of the Underlying Economic Context*

The economic and political trends that tore apart the early-twenty-first-century environment are associated with three central forces: globalization, technology, and sustainability. Globalization captures the incredible rise in the flows of people, goods, services, and capital across immensely separate regions, not only in physical distance but also in culture, political systems, and history. Globalization is the destiny of humanity and the safest road to peace. Since the 1980s, it has had and will continue to have dramatic effects on income distribution and job insecurity and on the state's power against global corporations. It has widened the pit between a thriving elite of globetrotters and the masses of the low-skilled, low-mobility, low-adaptability workforce (Saval, 2017).

The recent years have increased the complexity of globalization. Now, we trade in a highly intertwined multipolar global economy comprising regions with widely diverse cultures and antithetical economic systems in deep rivalry for dominance, stressing international relations and risking an atavistic resurgence of protectionism and nationalism. For business schools, this demands insights into cross-cultural management, international economics, and international business that encompass the political, geostrategic, and historical dimensions of management. Starkey and Thomas (2019) argue that business schools in China are already making their difference in teaching a very contextually influenced approach to management theories while competing in rankings against leading US and European schools.

Technology is the second force. The disruption of digital technology and artificial intelligence has challenged the convergent socioeconomic frameworks of the twentieth century, which nurtured the middle class that ensures social stability. The automation these technologies bring about will swipe through labor markets, creating unemployment, inequality, and social upheaval (Ford, 2016; Manyika et al., 2017). Digital companies have reached gigantic size through platform models that exploit their users' data and engage in very aggressive anticompetitive practices and tax arbitrage (Daub, 2020). Their business models pervert traditional economic theory on pricing and competition policy and challenge regulation's ethical and legal aspects (Rifkin, 2015). The theories that have underpinned the practice of management and policy-making during the twentieth century frequently seem inapt for the realities of unbounded increasing returns and intangible capital (Haskel and Westlake, 2017). It is urgent to reassess these theories; to unlearn the old; and to rebuild institutions, knowledge, and skills on the new. For business schools, the proximity with engineering and technology must be an integral part of the new mission. The most dramatic gap in today's labor force is the analytical translators that bridge business and technology (Henke et al., 2018).

Throughout the last two centuries, technology and globalization, accelerated by the neoliberal agenda of free trade and free enterprise, have contributed to improvements in wealth and living conditions in developed and developing countries. Technologies under development hold tremendous promise to address humanity's biggest challenges. However, both can have extreme distributional effects that leave large swaths of the population worse off and expand inequality within societies, with distressing political consequences. Therefore, their societal implications depend on the capabilities (institutions, knowledge, and skills) of political and economic systems to minimize those adverse effects and compensate the losers.

Sustainability, the third force, is a normative principle that has gained relevance with the exploding climate crisis and the rising political fragility of capitalism. Sustainability is still a young and general concept, used in very different ways and evolving rapidly (Muff et al., 2017). Overcoming the climate crisis must remain the priority of our time and our promise to the next generation. But the term encompasses a social dimension beyond the environmental aspect and balances these two dimensions with the economic viewpoint, promoting a triple-bottom-line balance of people, planet, and prosperity.

The relevance of business for sustainable development led, by the late twentieth century, to a corporate social responsibility engagement that failed to go beyond greenwashing and marketing. The call for business leaders to work with the UN to "initiate a global compact of shared values and principles" led to the UN Global Compact in 2000. Beginning with an initial group of 44 firms, the UN Global Compact has grown to more than 12,600 companies and civil society organizations in 160 countries. Along with forums such as the World Business Council for Sustainable Development and the Global Reporting Initiative, it complements top-down regulation, highlighting the need for change in business practice to become an active partner for sustainable development, at the risk of complete delegitimization in society.

In 2015, the UN adopted an agenda for 2030, focused on progress in 17 Sustainable Development Goals (SDGs), stressing the economic, social, and environmental dimensions of progress. The goals set up an essential frame for reestablishing business legitimacy as they build globally espoused targets and an international language to report them. Muff and colleagues (2017) argue that the emerging typology of sustainability has shifted perspective from an inside-out to an outside-in approach, which allows business and civil society to apply the goals to their institutional context. Weybrecht (2017) contends that for companies, successful implementation of the SDGs will strengthen the enabling environment for doing business, minimizing risks while also providing a myriad of new opportunities.

The challenge remains how. In a recent op-ed, Bill Gates argues that very frequently, the chief executive wants to know: "What can my company do that will make a difference?" (Gates, 2021, para. 2). He proposes a plan for business leaders focused on mobilizing capital, procurement, research and innovation, and dialogue with the public sector. The main point here is that the world yearns for insights that make business a credible and legitimate partner for a sustainability agenda benefiting our planet and our species.

B. *Reflections for the Redesign of Capitalism at Business Schools*

The disruption of globalization, technology, and sustainability render most, if not all, the major theories and ideologies of the twentieth century unfit for today. The political and social tensions of the last 15 years, unimaginable only 30 years ago, are a sign that we are approaching a breaking point. We need new international institutions, new managerial practices, new skills, new corporate governance, new policies, and new political systems that are fit for purpose in the underlying context.

This existential and epistemological challenge of redesigning human societies opens the opportunity for the renovation of the "public value" of business schools toward a new legitimacy. Next, I highlight four areas for reform that would have important implications in the mission and scope of business schools: redefining the corporation's purpose, enhancing the managerial effectiveness of government, blurring the boundaries between corporates and nonprofits, and delivering the skills for the future.

The Purpose and Governance of Business
In August 2019, 200 leaders of the top US corporations at the Business Roundtable updated the "Statement on the Purpose of a Company" to

focus on the value created for a plurality of stakeholders. It was a symbolic departure from shareholder value, which the Roundtable espoused since its creation. After the crises and scandals, it was evident that the stock market's discipline did not ensure the focus on long-term returns and public value. Visionary leaders, such as Paul Polman at Unilever (Skapinker and Scheherazade, 2016), have introduced new paradigms of business purpose that build on "shared value" (Porter and Kramer, 2011). They are the exception that must become the rule.

The development of corporate impact metrics and the reorganization of purpose and governance around them remain first-order priorities for knowledge and talent development at business schools. The SDGs open the door to a new definition of purpose for the corporation toward an impact-driven agenda. Lacy and colleagues (2012) find that CEOs see sustainability as more important than ever: growing in strategic importance, driving new business models, and essential for long-term success. They also find that CEOs see education as the most critical development issue for the future success of their business and see developing new skills, knowledge, and mindsets for the next generation of business leaders as a vital enabling condition to accelerate a tipping point in the integration of sustainability into the core.

The Managerial Effectiveness of Government

By the end of the twentieth century, with the state's role in decline, business schools moved away from the management of public entities (government, municipalities) and public policy. However, the crisis of recent years, the successful models in East Asia, and more recently, the COVID-19 crisis have placed government effectiveness and the quality of public-sector management back at the center of progress.

The underlying context of the twenty-first century and its potential for divergence and social upheaval described previously will reignite the state's role as a societal moderator. Therefore, societies must develop well-managed state institutions that effectively protect their citizens, provide public services, manage public policy, and cooperate internationally. For this, many will need the same managerial capabilities that corporations have developed and that business schools have become effective at delivering – to name a few: innovation, leadership, customer centricity, operational excellence, accountability to stakeholders, and cross-cultural management. Hence, a substantial contribution of business schools in developing the talent and insights for more effective government would go a long way in building more resilient societies.

Moreover, progress will also demand deep and trustful partnerships between the public and the private sector. Since the late twentieth century, many efforts have failed because the corporate and public staff members speak different languages and have not learned to collaborate. Their joint education would go a long way toward fostering the success of these partnerships.

Blurring Boundaries of Corporates and Nonprofits

While the state receded, a new family of stakeholders, classified under the placeholder nongovernmental organizations or nonprofits, exploded worldwide to address societal challenges. Nonprofits are a vast and diverse class, mostly financed through philanthropy. Their primary purpose is to create an impact in society, for which they need efficient management to keep costs low and outreach high. Their relevance will increase with the challenges ahead, given their capabilities in grassroots innovation and proximity to communities.

In many cases, nonprofits have leveraged these capabilities to build deep partnerships with the corporate and public sectors, addressing public-service challenges or delivering commercial products to the bottom of the pyramid. These partnerships are never easy and often fail because the parties do not share a common language and have a deep mistrust. Moreover, as corporate purpose and governance increasingly acknowledge the relevance of impact, and nonprofits look to become more efficient at managing their resources, the boundary between these organizations will fade, and their governance will converge, such as proposed by the B-Corp certification (Wilburn and Wilburn, 2015).

This suggests a convergence of their educational journeys to forge mutual understanding and a shared language and facilitate cross-stakeholder partnerships. Unfortunately, the development of talent and knowledge for nonprofits remains a side priority for business schools. Although there is an increasing demand by young professionals, business schools have not addressed their needs. Tuition structures, for example, fail to recognize their lower expected salary and high expected impact.

Skills for the Future

With the revolutions in digital and data technology, the skill set of managers is changing rapidly. Although the demand for managers with data-handling skills is on the rise, these are likely to become commodities as interfaces become user-friendly, similar to what happened with spreadsheet skills. However, understanding technology and, above all, dialogue and collaboration with technologists have become pivotal.

Soft skills are likely to be the only future-proof skills at a time of high-speed technological development. Looking at the impact of information communication technology (ICT) on demand for skills through a meta-analysis of the literature, van Laar and colleagues (2017) highlight the seven core skills of technical, information management, communication, collaboration, creativity, critical thinking, and problem solving and the five contextual skills of ethical awareness, cultural awareness, flexibility, self-direction, and lifelong learning.

Moreover, as mentioned before, globalization's rising complexity implies a historical, political, and geostrategic understanding of cross-country relationships. Many authors have also argued for a revision of the learning goals of business schools that moves away from narrow functional knowledge, relying heavily on finance and economics, and toward a stronger focus on applying (doing) and reflecting on values, attitudes, and purpose (sensing) (Dyllick, 2015).

All these dimensions are highly challenging for business schools. They require a strong partnership with science and technology and the humanities, which have a deep cultural distrust of business schools. Besides, they force a complete reinvention of delivery and assessment methods. How to teach and evaluate creativity, collaboration, purpose, or empathy in a classroom and evaluate learning through exams, especially in an economic context that demands a large class size to be financially sustainable? The challenge is more substantial for learners already in the workforce, who must reskill for the future, with the extra hardship of unlearning the old to learn the new.

Recent developments have stressed the importance of project-based learning and the co-creation of learning opportunities with external stakeholders, either from governments, nonprofits, or businesses. Entrepreneurship is also a critical tool to develop these skills. Several schools have committed heavy resources to the development of entrepreneurship hubs, looking to foster start-ups and innovation. However, entrepreneurship's potential in developing skills for the future dwarfs the effects on creating new ventures (Ulvenblad et al., 2013).

IV. Business Schools as Lighthouses of Hope

The previous section has argued that the triad of globalization, technology, and sustainability has disrupted the underlying economic context and that capitalism is open to a redesign of institutions, knowledge, and skills. Some clues that hold promise for business schools have also been provided.

This section proposes that business schools have a fundamental role in developing the institutions, knowledge, and skills needed to reboot capitalism in the twenty-first century. Their knowledge capabilities and their license to educate the youth mean that it is their responsibility to lead toward the future – that is, to spark the ideas, nurture the solutions, and breed the talent that will help transform our economic and political system into a beacon of resilient hope and shared prosperity. Throughout history, universities have been at the forefront of the creative intellectual energy that moves societies toward their future. The intellectual freedom, critical thinking, and creative rigor that they embody have always been the lighthouses of humanity's progress, away from the darkness of insecurity and fear. Business schools must step up to this challenge in partnership with businesses and society as a whole. They are responsible for the kind of leaders they send out into the world.

This call to action opens the space for a renaissance of business schools – different, more open, more impactful. Their future mission must be to envision the institutions, organizations, knowledge, and skills for post-neoliberalism and the effective ways of managing them. The redesign of business schools to reimagine the purpose of the corporation, broaden its scope to the management of nonprofits and government, and build the skills of the future represents an opportunity to enhance the "public value" of business schools, as proposed by Wallace Donham, the second dean of Harvard Business School almost a century ago (Starkey and Thomas, 2019), and to reestablish their legitimacy in the process.

To be clear, I am not espousing that the challenges facing capitalism and our cultural environment result from the actions, intended or unintended, of business schools. Neither am I claiming that business schools do not share part of the blame for some hyperbolic interpretations of neoliberalism. The urgency of the situation we live in should focus us on the future, not the past, especially when the context is changing so much and so fast. This said, it remains true that business schools were torchbearers of late-twentieth-century neoliberalism, and as such, they have the responsibility to lead the agenda for its redesign. With great power comes great responsibility. Who will take on this responsibility if business schools do not stand up to the task?

A mission of forward-looking innovation in institutions, knowledge, and skills for the new underlying context poses challenges for the internal organization of business schools. First and foremost, it requires an internal culture of innovation grounded on a set of values for sustainable impact. Business schools have outpaced other departments of universities in fostering spaces and incentives for innovation, and herein lies their advantage, but the demands of the future we face need more.

For the remainder of this section, I will discuss how business schools must transform internally to respond effectively and in a timely manner to this innovation challenge. The first element is to create a culture of accountable impact, focused on the SDGs. The second is to open up by strengthening engagement, broadening the core stakeholder list, and widening interdisciplinarity. This implies a reversion of the trend to isolation and lack of accountability that characterized their 100-year history and, therefore, will face dramatic resistance. Leadership will be critical to overcome that resistance, but so will collective action.

A. Reversing the Isolation of the Business School

At the onset of their rise to stardom, business schools brought universities closer to reality and impact, leveraging their origin as professional schools designed to develop managerial capabilities (Starkey and Thomas, 2019). This openness quickly narrowed to the corporate world, at the cost of estrangement from other managerial competence seekers, including government, foundations, and nonprofits. A wider approach to management would have had a significant impact on Western societies by strengthening the effectiveness of these stakeholders and creating a shared language for collaboration and co-creation. But it was not to be.

In time, the estrangement grew even to the corporate entities that had created and nurtured them at the onset. Under US schools' influence and the search for academic respectability, the theoretical model, focusing on abstract research, the scientific method, and peer-based evaluations, spread to business schools. The increased rigor provided a more solid footing for many of the research contributions; attracted highly talented academics to the field; and permitted a fruitful collaboration with other academic areas, such as economics, psychology, and sociology. In this process, adjunct faculty with insights from practice and the ability to bridge into academia gave way to core faculty, tenure systems, and doctoral degrees. This was a welcome move, to the extent that it created academic excellence and a body of committed faculties that helped grow business schools. But it slowly isolated business schools.

What drove this movement is beside the point. But the wedge it created between business schools and their external stakeholders and the damage done to their "public value" and their legitimacy are clear. Participating in a dean's conference by the Association to Advance Collegiate Schools of Business (AACSB) or the EFMD Quality Improvement System (EQUIS) or reading the journals or the press is an exercise of constant self-doubt. Dyllick (2015) argues that the efforts to pursue "scientific rigor and gain academic legitimacy have been taken to an extreme, resulting in an increasingly self-centered community of business schools, isolated from business practice and society" (p. 16). Podolny (2009) argues that most business school academics are not curious about what goes on inside organizations (Wilson and Thomas, 2012). Writing in the *Financial Times*, Michael Skapinker (2011) reports that, in response to a column published in 2008 on "why business ignores the business schools," where he highlighted the gap between researchers and practitioners, he received extensive comments from business school academics, overwhelmingly agreeing that managers generally ignored them.

The estrangement from stakeholders must be addressed to retrieve the legitimacy of business schools and their capability to play their role in reframing our institutions, skills, and knowledge in the context of the century's turbulence ahead. For this, business schools will have to reform and transform in multiple dimensions of their ethos.

B. Transforming the Business School – Part I: Impact

The first dimension of the transformation is the unwavering commitment to impact. In recent years, impact has gained relevance as a result of its inclusion in the criteria of accreditation agencies. EFMD has begun a Business School Impact System (BSIS) that provides an impact accounting framework to identify, measure, and assess impact in seven categories: financial, educational, business development, intellectual, regional, and societal. According to Shenton and Kalika (2017), following their engagement with BSIS, schools tend to revisit their "fundamental purpose," raising questions of identity and historical roots. In time, this pushed them toward more engagement with external stakeholders and toward regaining legitimacy with their regional corporate community. It also had implications at the pedagogical level and, albeit to a lesser extent, for their research. Kalika and Shenton (2020) suggest that all organizations can apply BSIS, whatever their mission.

Research has been a highly controversial aspect of business school impact. The professional literature and many deans' conferences have discussed at length the distance between researchers and the modern organization and its managers. Wilson and Thomas (2012) and Dyllick (2015) are part of a large body of literature highly critical of the low-value-added contribution by business school research published in top journals. However, O'Brien and colleagues (2010) show that business schools with stronger research output add economic value to their students in the form of higher wages and faster wage progression, although they find that there are decreasing returns that become negative in what they address as "excessive research."

To enhance its impact and contribute to the redesign of capitalism, research must balance the search for truth and methodological rigor with the solutions it generates for society's challenges. Kalika and Shenton (2020) argue that BSIS encourages the tracking of impactful research and, in some cases, a strategic alignment of the research agenda. However, with career progress for academics mainly a function of publication in four-star or A-rated journals and driven by opportunities for mobility, the scope for a school-determined research agenda is limited (Wilson and Thomas, 2012).

Measuring impact as a by-product is not enough. In the core dimensions of learning and knowledge, but also in its engagement and operations, impact must move to the core of the business school's mission and strategy. This means going beyond the BSIS approach of assessing impact to outlining an impact model. This model should highlight the dimensions of impact that the school is accountable for in its activities, the impact targets it commits to, a strategy that allows the school to potentiate its community to reach those targets, and resources available. The closer the impact strategy is to the business strategy, working from a shared value framework (Porter and Kramer, 2011), the larger the resources available and the stronger its reach will be. The final impact must be assessed and measured, using metrics of outputs and outcomes that capture the activities and their end outcomes, including direct measurement and surveys of the stakeholders and their perceptions. Finally, business schools must be accountable for their impact on stakeholders and the public by reporting clearly and transparently.

Sustainability must be at the center of any impact model. As was highlighted before, it is the new metric of progress for human societies. Weybrecht (2017) argues that "sustainability provides a unique opportunity for management education, and should be seen as such," but that "business schools are still, to a certain degree hiding undisturbed behind closed doors and, despite being crucial in the implementation of the SDGs, have not yet been as engaged as they could, and need to be" (p. 85). She continues that "business schools have a responsibility to translate this important global plan into something that resonates with their community. This can then be used to mobilize support internally, to coordinate curriculum, research, and operations on campus. ... The opportunity is there for business schools to use these terms to bring people, ideas, and research together, not to separate them. But beyond having a positive impact through teaching and research, the SDGs provide another opportunity for business schools who are able and willing to engage; that of being a true driver and enabler of change" (p. 85).

The Principles for Responsible Management Education (PRME) initiative provides an important community for business school engagement with responsible management. In 2007, the UN Global Compact launched the PRME, an initiative to ready tomorrow's business leaders in the quest for sustainable business. PRME engages business schools as signatories, promotes collaborative activities, and emphasizes reporting through the Sharing in Progress reports (Haertle et al., 2017). Perry and Win (2013) report that the initiative is perceived as having a limited impact within the partner schools and "is gaining support based on activity that is already occurring and because it supports the school's accreditation" (p. 58). In 2015, PRME espoused the SDGs, and in 2019, PRME launched the SDGs Dashboard, a data-reporting platform noting business schools' contributions to the goals.

One challenge to the use of PRME as an impact framework is that it ignores two crucial elements of the business school as an organization. First, school policies are an essential element of their contribution to the SDGs. Diversity and inclusion in human resources and faculty policies and, more importantly, in admissions are critical elements of the SDGs. Second, business schools must also be accountable for the environmental impact of their operations. Hence, an extended PRME framework provides an exciting roadmap for defining a business school's impact model.

C. *Transforming the Business School – Part II: Opening Up*

Although business schools have been apt at opening among themselves, with a multitude of collaboration in joint degrees, international networks, and exchange agreements, opening to external stakeholders has proven more challenging. Hawawini (2005) proposed a change in business schools' governance to include alumni and corporate sponsors in the search to attract additional funding through fundraising campaigns. We must open beyond this.

The future of business schools is to become platforms of community engagement, where alumni, corporate partners, and other stakeholders in civil society committed to a sustainable future join the work of developing the leaders for that future. In the era of crowdfunding and digital platforms, business schools can attract the human energy and financial resources that share that common purpose. This would be the ultimate test of their legitimacy.

Engagement is critical to business school innovation. Shenton and Kalika (2017) argue that business schools committed to impact quickly understand these partnerships' importance. Cross-stakeholder partnerships will enable business schools to take advantage of external partners' experience and insight to co-create and co-deliver skills and understanding. It takes a cross-fertilizing effort to develop knowledge and talent that are impactful, as the analytical might of academia meets the experience and case studies of those on the front line of action. These partnerships will also provide resources that many business schools desperately need, as a result of being chronically underfunded by state budget constraints and growing social inequality, as suggested by Hawawini (2005).

Another dimension of openness involves expanding the traditional list of stakeholders. As discussed before, the focus on business instead of management has drawn business schools away from governments and nonprofits. The upshot is that in many nations, the managerial capabilities of these two institutions have not caught up. Yet, nonprofits and governments are a fundamental element of twenty-first-century capitalism. Social innovation has endowed nonprofits with an uncanny ability to understand new markets' challenges and opportunities. Partnerships with nonprofits are a pivotal part of the SDGs, but they are fraught with communication challenges and mistrust. Sharing an educational journey would go a long way in facilitating an exploration of the complementarities among these stakeholders, as suggested by Gates (2021).

Finally, the third dimension of openness is interdisciplinarity. One of the harmful effects of the development of science was the specialization into silos of knowledge that ignore adjacent scientific areas. It is clear today that such specialization is counterproductive and that responding to our century's challenges requires collaboration between different knowledge areas. As mentioned before, delivering the skills of the future requires convergence with science and technology, on the one hand, and international relations, politics, and history, on the other hand. Interdisciplinarity is a challenging exercise in collaboration because it requires learning a new language and humbly accepting different versions of the truth. It requires unlearning many established paradigms to relearn new ones. Such an attitude is uncanny to academics' mindset. Some of this effort will require leadership to foster interdisciplinary centers.

D. Resistance to Change

The pressure to open up has been on the agenda for nearly a decade now. Accreditation agencies, such as EFMD and AACSB, have been at the forefront, adjusting standards and spreading best practices. Stiff resistance comes from two sources: the governance model and the business model.

The first source of resistance is the collegial governance model and the career-management system of faculty. Academic freedom, job security, and collegiality emerged to promote boldness and freedom of thought and are the hallmark of university governance. However, they have become barriers to change because incumbent faculty's intrinsic biases and self-interest can block change. Given that the peer-review and editorial system in research journals is in a close loop with faculty, the system becomes impenetrable. Moreover, because mobility and outside options matter more for faculty careers than internal recognition and rewards, especially for untenured faculty, any behavior change must come from collective action among the leading schools in the system.

The second source of resistance is the market-driven business model, where students' tuition covers costs. Government funding has declined in most countries, and tuition levels have skyrocketed, threatening the returns from a business degree in many regions of the world (Wilson and Thomas, 2012). This has undermined the contribution of business schools to social mobility. One drawback is the transfer of rents from students to faculty as schools use the escalating tuition costs to compete for faculty, raising wages and, therefore, their cost structure.

More importantly, this business model slows innovation and change. Cornuel and Hommel (2015) identify five potential barriers to responsible management education (RME): student preferences, the challenge of delivering it online, the intellectual fuzziness of the concept, the standardization of teaching models, and the pressure from rankings. According to Dyllick (2015), business students are more focused on an attractive, well-paid future career than those in other majors. He also reports that business majors are less likely to discuss ideas outside class or read books, according to the National Survey of Student Engagement. Hence, business school rankings focused on salary progression have become the centerpiece of student recruitment and a barrier to change and innovation because innovations that risk rankings, standardization, or employability threaten survival (Khurana, 2007; Wilson and Thomas, 2012). Cornuel and Hommel (2015) conclude that unless companies change their business and recruitment strategies and the intellectual underpinnings of modern management adjust, business schools will continue to focus on graduates' short-term returns.

However, Generation Z, which will sustain business schools in the coming decade, shows a much stronger commitment to sustainability. In a survey of the incoming class of master's students at Nova School of Business and Economics (SBE) in 2019, 87 percent wanted their studies to help them learn how they could positively affect the world, and 90 percent agreed that universities should actively incorporate and promote learning for sustainable development. The times seem to be changing.

In the end, business schools will have to answer to society, and competition will demand change. The experience of Nova SBE serves to illustrate. The fundamental motivation for our openness to civil society entities and the focus of our mission on impact comes from international competitive pressure. Our openness and commitment to impact attract students who join us from all corners of the world. They are our mission of sustainable impact and our livelihood in a shared-value approach. In this sense, greater competition on openness and impact criteria will be a relentless force for transformation. For example, the Research Excellence Framework and the Teaching Excellence Framework in the UK impose a demonstration of impact on universities' public funding.

E. A Not-So-Digital Future

The drive for more openness, innovation, and impact to live up to the responsibility to develop institutions, knowledge, and skills for a sustainable future coincides with the effects of technology and globalization on our sector. These effects have been felt for a couple of decades now. The international flow of students and faculty and the threat from nimble digital players enhanced the competitive stress. As we reform for collective legitimacy, we must adjust for individual survival.

Fortunately (or unfortunately), business schools have proven more apt to respond to the competitive challenge than to the legitimacy challenge. They answered incredibly well to the challenge of internationalization. Student exchange and faculty mobility skyrocketed early in the century, promoted by European Union financing, the globalization of business and trade, and the swift adherence to English as a shared language. Here, business schools were quickly ahead of the rest of their host universities.

Meanwhile, the much-feared disruption by digital entrants proved elusive. Students continued to prefer to travel to facilities where they would share an enriching exchange of body warmth and nonverbal communication, at the same time that they shared ideas. In 2020, the COVID-19 pandemic forced billions to learn from home and might be a turning point. However, an early indication is that students are yearning to head back to campuses, even if they acknowledge the value of using asynchronous, video-based learning for parts of the learning process. In surveys of students at Nova SBE during the COVID-19 pandemic, 50 percent of students preferred a fully presential model, 45 percent favored a blended model, and less than 5 percent selected a fully online model, even if the pandemic created health risks from attending presential classes. Moreover, the ineffectiveness of monitoring technologies has undermined online evaluation's credibility, challenging the move to online degrees. In our surveys, only 34 percent of students considered online assessment to be honest and fair, and only 38 percent believed that it effectively evaluates learning.

The upshot will be the generalization of blended-learning, flipped-classroom models, where digital will complement but not replace the warmth of campus life. The Netflix moment never came. Business schools will not hollow out like movie theaters and bookstores did. This is good news for business schools that have invested heavily in first-rate facilities, which will remain a source of competitive strength instead of a legacy burden in the digital age's competitive struggle.

The digital transformation will nevertheless change business schools in alternative ways. Artificial intelligence and the data revolution of this decade, which is rippling across sectors, will, from my perspective, have more dramatic effects than the digital, internet-based revolution of the first two decades of the century. Klutka and colleagues (2018) argue that artificial intelligence will affect student acquisition and student affairs, help instructors grade, and supply struggling students with the resources they need to succeed. In the future, this could free up faculty members to oversee large classes while still engaging with students on a deeper level.

V. Conclusion

By 2005, Cornuel (2005) and Hawawini (2005) confirmed the legitimacy of business schools for the value they were creating for their stakeholders and painted an optimistic scenario for their future. Yet, more than 15 years later, as EFMD celebrates 50, business schools' legitimacy is a matter of heated debate. For some, they are irrelevant. For others, they are villains for their role in the expansion of neoliberalism after the 1980s. For most, they have expanded the corporate world's managerial talent, although they should adjust some of their insights.

I have argued that business schools should focus on the future as they seek to reestablish their legitimacy. The underlying economic context has changed much over the last 15 years as a result of the accelerated changes brought about by globalization, technology, and sustainability. We must redesign our institutions, knowledge, and skills to restore society to a path of shared and stable prosperity. Engaging in this redesign is an opportunity and a responsibility for business schools. It is a crucial element of their license to operate and their accountability to their students.

However, before we redesign the institutions, knowledge, and skills that frame our society, business schools must redesign themselves. An unwavering commitment to bringing sustainable impact to the core of the mission, strategy, and accountability is a priority. The other is opening to deep engagement with external stakeholders, including business, nonprofits, and government, and an interdisciplinary approach that bridges politics, science, law, technology, history, and international relations to the core finance and economics areas. Such internal redesign is not an easy task for business school deans, who often face business and governance models highly resistant to change. The art of change management has been studied at length and depends essentially on leadership. The urgency of the change ahead of us should inspire the deans of the future.

The good news is that the COVID-19 crisis has clarified that the digital transition will not hollow out business schools like it emptied movie theaters and record stores before, soothing fears of disruption. This realization heeds the vital lesson that our schools' essence is the knowledge sharing, social experience, and shared purpose students find on our campuses. That is the same human essence that sustains communities and provides purpose to human beings in the perennial tension between the individual and the group (Collier, 2018). The preservation of our communities' human essence should be the inspiration for what we teach and research for the sake of our future.

References

Alvaredo, F., Chancel, L., Piketty, T., Saez, E., and Zucman, G. (2018). *World inequality report*. World Inequality Lab.

Collier, P. (2018). *The future of capitalism: Facing the new anxieties*. Harper.

Cornuel, E. (2005). The role of business schools in society. *Journal of Management Development*, 24(9), 819–829.

Cornuel, E., and Hommel, U. (2015). Moving beyond the rhetoric of responsible management education. *Journal of Management Development*, 34 (1), 2–15.

Daub, A. (2020, September 24). The disruption con: Why big tech's favourite buzzword is nonsense. *The Guardian*. www.theguardian.com/news/2020/sep/24/disruption-big-tech-buzzword-silicon-valley-power.

Dyllick, T. (2015). Responsible management education for a sustainable world: The challenges for business schools. *Journal of Management Development*, 34(1), 16–33.

Ford, M. (2016). *The rise of the robots: Technology and the threat of mass unemployment*. One World Publications.

Gates, B. (2021, February 19). My green manifesto. *Financial Times*. www.ft.com/content/c11bb885-1274-4677-ba05-fcbac67dc808.

Goshal, S. (2005). Bad management theories are destroying good management practices. *Academy of Management Learning & Education*, 4(1), 75–91.

Haertle, J., Parkes, C., Murray, A., and Hayes, R. (2017). PRME: Building a global movement on responsible management education. *The International Journal of Management Education*, 15(2-B), 66–72.

Haskel, J., and Westlake, S. (2017). *Capitalism without capital: Rise of intangible economy*. Princeton University Press.

Hawawini, G. (2005). The future of business schools. *Journal of Management Development*, 24(9), 770–782.

Henke, N., Levine, J., and McInerney, P. (2018). You don't have to be data scientist to fill this must-have analytics role. *Harvard Business Review*. https://hbr.org/2018/02/you-dont-have-to-be-a-data-scientist-to-fill-this-must-have-analytics-role.

Kalika, M., and Shenton, G. (2020). Measuring business impact: The lessons from the business schools. *Corporate Governance*, 21(2), 268–278.

Khurana, R. (2007). *From higher aims to hired hands*. Princeton University Press.

Klutka, J., Ackerly, N., and Magda, A. (2018). Research report: Artificial intelligence in higher education: Current uses and future applications. Learning House/Wiley Education Services. https://edservices.wiley.com/ai-in-higher-ed/.

Lacy, P., Haines, A., and Hayward, R. (2012). Developing strategies and leaders to succeed in a new era of sustainability: Findings and insights from the United Nations Global Compact-Accenture CEO Study. *Journal of Management Development*, 31(4), 346–357.

Manyika, J., Lund, S., Chui, M., Bughin, J., Woetzel, J., Batra, P., Ko, R., and Sanghvi, S. (2017). *Jobs lost, jobs gained: Workforce transitions in a time of automation*. McKinsey Global Institute.

Mintzberg, H. (2004). *Managers not MBAs: A hard look at the soft practice of managing and management development.* Berrett Koehler.

Muff, K., Kapalka, A., and Dyllick, T. (2017). The gap frame – translating the SDGs into relevant national grand challenges for strategic business opportunities. *International Journal of Management Education*, 15(2-B), 363–383.

O'Brien, J. P., Drnewich, P. L., Crook, T. R., and Armstrong, C. E. (2010). Does business school research add economic value for students? *Academy of Management Learning and Education*, 9(4), 638–651.

Parker, M. (2018). *Shut down the business school: What's wrong with management education.* Pluto Press.

Perry, M., and Win, S. (2013). An evaluation of PRME's contribution to responsibility in higher education. *Journal of Corporate Citizenship*, 2013(49), 48–70.

Podolny, J. (2009). The buck stops (and starts) at business school. *Harvard Business Review*, 87(6), 62–67.

Porter, M., and Kramer, M. (2011). Creating shared value. *Harvard Business Review*, 89(1/2), 62–77.

Raworth, K. (2017). *Doughnut economics: Seven ways to think like a 21st-century economist.* Chelsea Green Publishing.

Rifkin, J. (2015). *Zero marginal cost society.* Griffin.

Saval, N. (2017, July 14). Globalisation: The rise and fall of an idea that swept the world. *The Guardian.* www.theguardian.com/world/2017/jul/14/globalisation-the-rise-and-fall-of-an-idea-that-swept-the-world.

Shenton, G., and Kalika, M. (2017). The impact of BSIS. *Global Focus – the EFMD Business Magazine*, 11(1), 44–47.

Skapinker, M. (2011, January 24). Why business still ignores business schools. *Financial Times.* www.ft.com/content/2198d908-280f-11e0-8abc-00144feab49a.

Skapinker, M., and Scheherazade, D. (2016, September 29). Can Unilever's Paul Polman change the way we do business? *Financial Times.* www.ft.com/content/e6696b4a-8505-11e6-8897-2359a58ac7a5.

Starkey, K., and Thomas, H. (2019). The future of business schools: Shut them down or broaden our horizons? *Global Focus – the EFMD Business Magazine*, 13(2), 44–49.

Ulvenblad, P., Berggren, E., and Winborg, J. (2013). The role of entrepreneurship education and start-up experience for handling communication and liability of newness. *International Journal of Entrepreneurial Behaviour & Research*, 19(2), 187–209.

van Laar, E., van Deursen, A., van Dijk, J., and de Haan, J. (2017). The relation between 21st-century skills and digital skills: A systematic literature review. *Computers in Human Behavior*, 72, 577–588.

Weybrecht, G. (2017). From challenge to opportunity – management education's crucial role in sustainability and the Sustainable Development Goals – an overview and framework. *International Journal of Management Education*, 15, 84–92.

Wilburn, K., and Wilburn, R. (2015). Evaluating CSR accomplishments of founding certified B Corps. *Journal of Global Responsibility*, 6(2), 262–280.

Wilson, D., and Thomas, H. (2012). The legitimacy of the business of business schools: What's the future? *Journal of Management Development*, 31(4), 368–376.

8 | Rethinking Management Education in Dynamic and Uncertain Markets: Educating Future Leaders for Resilience and Agility

RAJENDRA SRIVASTAVA

On March 24, 2020, at 8:00 p.m., when Indian prime minister Narendra Modi announced a nationwide lockdown following the outbreak of the global pandemic, the entire Indian School of Business (ISB) community responded with alacrity. The pressing requirement and biggest challenge was to vacate around 800 students from ISB's two campuses in two different states of India distanced by 1,800 kilometers within 24 hours, which was completed safely with a sense of esprit de corps. Like everyone else, even though we were not prepared for such an eventuality, ISB was at its agile best.

Since then, in the last 9 months (I am writing this in December 2020), although the early days were very challenging, slowly but surely, the school returned to near normalcy. After evacuating the students in March, we sanitized the two campuses, one of 90 acres (Mohali) and the other of 250 acres (Hyderabad); completed the existing classes for the Post Graduate Programme (PGP; which is equivalent to, and will hitherto be used interchangeably with, an MBA) and the modular programs online; achieved near 100 percent placements; continued and completed the admissions process for the new MBA cohort; had the virtual graduation program for the previous batch; started online classes for the new batch; and finally, brought in the MBA class of 2021 physically to the two campuses. This was made possible because of our financial stability; complete passion, dedication, and hard work from all the stakeholders involved; regular meetings with the full Board of Directors as well as smaller task forces; scaling up of infrastructure needs like information technology; and teamwork, frequent and transparent communication, and a deep sense of mission. All the above subsets broadly make up what can be termed *organizational and individual resilience.*

This chapter provides two perspectives: (1) what we did at ISB to attend to the immediate challenges imposed by COVID-19, that is, to maintain business continuity, and (2) what we, as management institutions, need to do to

179

reshape educational offerings so that graduates are better prepared to handle the new normal that has emerged.

The first challenge, maintaining business continuity, has so far involved adopting hybrid/blended learning processes, combining online synchronous and asynchronous online delivery, and preserving interactive dialogue and the peer-to-peer learning that is the hallmark of teaching at ISB. This has had a differential impact on full-time versus modular programs as well as nondegree executive education. The faculty had been debating the adoption of blended learning for a few years and had implemented it in part in only one out of our four programs (the weekend program for working professionals was delivered about 20 percent online), but the sudden arrival of COVID-19 cut short the debates. We rolled up our sleeves and got going. This chapter catalogues the creative approaches we adopted to overcome some challenges – while others persist.

The second challenge requires rethinking the program content and learning mechanisms. This will require a change in our own – that is, the educators' – mindset. The increase in uncertainty – and its cousin, ambiguity – will mean that our foci in management education will have to shift from operational excellence and efficiency to resilience, from process optimization to flexibility in dynamic markets, from annual budgets to quarterly or even monthly ones, from core competence to multiprocess excellence and multiple business models to accommodate variance in challenges across product markets. This will not be an easy task. While we profess the value of multidisciplinary thinking and the importance of process over function, most management faculties are organized by function (finance, marketing, accounting), with incentives organized by depth within narrowly defined research issues rather than collaboration across disciplines. Much of the time in academic committees can be spent on guarding the turf rather than embracing the benefits of diversity in thinking, making structural changes in academia slower than in most organizations, with the plausible exception of the church.

There is an old saying: practice what you preach (and teach). In retrospect, perhaps we never thought that we ourselves would be called upon to actualize this. This is not the first time that crises have adversely affected management education in recent years. The global financial crisis of 2008 and the 9/11 World Trade Towers destruction at global levels, natural disasters and tsunamis at regional levels, and past pandemics like severe acute respiratory syndrome (SARS) and Ebola have all upended businesses and economies. But the 2020 COVID-19 pandemic stands out for its magnitude and duration. While affecting global and national economies in fundamental ways, the pandemic has consequently affected business schools and management education in deep and long-term ways. It has made academic leaders, scholars, policymakers, and the higher education community rethink their own position and future existence. ISB is no exception.

Impact on Business Schools: A Case Example of ISB

Business schools have been affected both adversely and positively by COVID-19. An immediate effect was the response to the psychological and intangible impact on the diverse stakeholder community. As a private and global business school, our stakeholders consist of students, faculty (both visiting and residential), parents, nonteaching staff of various departments, the state and the central governments, and the Board of Directors – to name just a few. In the early days, the fear of the pandemic was an overriding concern, and naturally, the health, safety, and security of all our people were uppermost priorities. We were also not sure how long the closure of the campuses would last. Although safety protocols were and are in place, this crisis was the first of its kind, and therefore we had to learn and improvise solutions as we went along. A major challenge was that with the students having reached their destinations and homes safe and sound, the examination results needed to be announced after their computation. Additionally, we had to ensure that the graduating students were placed and that any job offers that were reneged were offset by new opportunities. That was put on a priority basis even as the admission process for the new MBA batch of 2021 was in full force. Additionally, amid this turmoil, ISB became the first school in India to host an online graduation ceremony.

Obviously, as in all other institutions of higher education, students and parents were having second thoughts on joining the current batch. With a combination of dexterity and transparency, the admissions team set about reaching its target of approximately 880 students for the MBA class. That was not easy because many of them deferred their admissions; some had problems with getting their student loans; and others were not sure that if they quit their jobs and joined the class, renewed placements would be easy and salaries would be as per past track record in pandemic-hit global and national economies. That was when teamwork, hard work, persuasion, and creativity all came together to ensure that the final admission numbers were not way below those of previous years but much better than expected and far better than those of other competitive business schools. Our *rapid response team*, comprising faculty, admissions and delivery staff, information technology, and campus operations, rose to meet challenges, sharing information and perspectives twice a week.

We were acutely conscious, at the same time, of preserving our hard-won institutional reputation by sending clear communications and responses to traditional media and social media; making decisions in the best interests of the institution while considering diverse views and discussions; interacting with and responding to governments at multiple levels; and keeping channels of conversation open with competitors and partners in India and overseas to understand how others were coping and address and answer collectively and individually the concerns of students, alumni, parents, and potential students. Importantly, we decided to engage with and listen to students on a continuous basis to build our own solutions to the overriding fear that the unique campus experience and interactive classes managed by a global faculty would be diluted by online courses. That is, our brand was based on an intense classroom and extracurricular experience, quite at odds with post–COVID-19 online regimen.

The third significant hurdle was to get the PGP class of 2021 up and running as fast as possible – in a completely new format: digital classes. While many of the leading business schools across the world took a long-term view right at the start that the entire academic year would be online, at ISB, we decided that we would take a more difficult but preferred route of going online only until needed, and when possible and permitted by the government to open the campuses, we would welcome the students. In effect, it would be a hybrid model. We did have some teething problems in creating the right technology platform, setting up three-camera studios, and developing technology support staff. But once that was taken care of, things went relatively smoothly. However, it was not a perfect ecosystem because teacher training was necessary, and several faculty members are still learning how to use relevant features (e.g., virtual breakout rooms); also, given that the students were in various parts of the country, with a few of them overseas, too, they did have internet-bandwidth issues.

The fourth set of issues involved managing business continuity and maintaining our reputation and brand across our product (program) portfolio. Although we did fall short on revenues from the MBA admissions because of lower admission numbers, there was also, at the same time, an increase in our costs for the information technology infrastructure, maintenance, and training, to name a few expenditure heads. At the same time, because of the lockdown and plummeting corporate revenues, the share of revenue from executive education came down sharply. This was because of a weakness in the executive education revenue model, which depended almost wholly on nondigital classes. The management also made a conscious decision not to cut the salaries of the 600-odd staff and the 70-odd faculty despite some financial pressures. This was contrary to what many business schools in India and overseas did. We did this because of our strong conviction that the heart quotient (empathy) of our school is quite high, and the well-being of our people is uppermost. Although the challenges just described were particular to ISB, they are also emblematic of the problems faced by most of the leading business schools and universities in India and overseas.

At another level, although ISB is a world-class business school on every count, we are still not as "global" as we would like to be. That means that although we have a reasonably good share of international visiting faculty, our share of international students is not high. However, that is not the case with many higher education institutions in the United States, the UK, Canada, and Australia. All of them depend a lot on international students, and in recent years, despite the respective country restrictions on student visas and the high cost of education, students from countries like China and India thronged institutions in these countries. All this means that the financial position of business schools and other universities in these countries has been under greater pressure while ISB has held steady and is now headed into the positive zone for two reasons. First, the demand for our modular programs (e.g., executive MBA [EMBA] that meets for a week approximately every 6 weeks; MBA for working professionals that meets every other week) has increased significantly because these programs enable participants to ride out uncertainty related to reemployment after course completion. Second, travel restrictions have perhaps shifted Indian demand for foreign universities to better domestic options.

Although many of the top American universities are financially comfortable, perhaps with large endowments, that is not the case for most business schools. In India, of the roughly 6,000 business schools scattered across the length and breadth of the country, only the top-ranked ones are run on a financially viable business model (Taxila Business School, n.d.). That is because the main revenue model of the private schools consists of tuition and boarding fees, and government-promoted ones like the Indian Institutes of Management (IIMs) and Indian Institutes of Technology (IITs) have a regulatory bar on raising student fees, along with many other such restrictions.

Response of Business Schools: Creating Resilient and Agile Structures

For 30 years, I was involved in the management of the Austin Technology Incubator at the University of Texas. There, we talked about how entrepreneurs must build an airplane while flying it. The task we faced at ISB in managing the consequences of COVID-19 was a tad more difficult – *rebuilding an airplane as you try to land it in turbulent weather.*

Given the previously described landscape of problems and challenges that arose because of the pandemic and the resultant lockdown, as some of the classic management lessons teach about responding to crises, the first move at ISB was to form a multidisciplinary COVID-19 task force. With representatives from each department, this group met on a daily and more frequent basis virtually and sometimes even offline, putting their own safety at risk. The discussions from these meetings formed the basis of the action plan on sanitization, infrastructure maintenance, the safety of the faculty on the two campuses, and interacting with the local government while at the same time quickly laying the foundation for the new batch of online classes. We realized that greater collaboration and teamwork would be needed in the new normal. For example, while we are all heartened by the very promising start to Round 1 of the admissions process for the PGP 2021 cohort, we are now looking at how there can be greater support from the Alumni and the Career Advancement Services teams to ensure the same success in Rounds 2 and 3.

As the lockdown and the march of COVID-19 progressed, it soon became clear that the pandemic and the abnormalities of life would continue and have an impact for a year or two – not just a few months as many thought initially. In such a possible scenario, we needed to review our short- and long-term goals and path ahead and see where course corrections were needed.

Although initially the students adjusted and were happy with online classes, they experienced problems with bandwidth and other related issues. Whereas many reputable higher educational institutions in India and overseas decided to go online for the entire academic year, we believed that a superior hybrid model of offline and online combined with "value additions" was what the students would look forward to. Value for money (fees) also emerged in the minds of the students and their families. We realized that we had to respond to this new state of mind. The answer lay in enhancing our value-added benefits through new features such as the Digital Headstart Module (DHM), which helps students join and navigate the digital format and learning management system (LMS); an additional term of new content (e.g., modular courses such as crisis management, using blockchains in management processes, digital transformation); truly interactive classes; extra experiential modules such as JumpStartIndia@ISB (JSI@ISB) (ISB, 2021); and subsidized executive programs as part of lifelong learning at ISB. We also developed a "wellness fund" to support students impacted by the pandemic during the program.

JSI@ISB, an innovative initiative where the students work with faculty and nonprofit organizations on ventures that will be useful to the nation in the COVID-19 era, was conceptualized and implemented with great success. We realized that the students wanted to add to their experience in current circumstances beyond academic pursuits. The goal is to support the government's informed decisions during the crisis and build a vibrant, healthier, and more robust India. The initiative was launched in mid-May and began with eight overarching topics that focused on key primary areas of recovery. In a span of 6 months, there have been around 40 projects, with the close involvement of 250 students and several faculty members. The key topics under this initiative include areas such as food and agriculture; informal (gig) economy; boosting the economy; monitoring the recovery; transportation, logistics, and mobility; health care; institutionalizing remote work; and corporate health tracking.

One of the key objectives of this initiative is to work closely with the government of India. To date, we have already signed memorandums of understanding (MOUs) or started engagements with various state governments and central ministries. ISB has built good relationships with all the growing government engagements over the period of the last 6 months. As a part of this initiative, several sessions and panel discussions were organized to bring together the different perspectives of key stakeholders and government. These sessions were very well received and attended by interested students as well. Additionally, to gauge the progress of the projects and help foster coordination and cooperation among students and mentors, a Preliminary Project Presentation was organized in mid-July. During this 2-day period, the students presented their project objectives, progress, and future road maps and got the opportunity to address audience questions. Another round of presentations is planned to present and discuss the outcomes of various projects under the JSI@ISB initiative.

Digital learning is only the tip of the far-reaching changes that technology will usher in over the coming years. Not only do students and faculty need to be more tech-savvy, but even the staff, processes, and infrastructure need to move with the times. This, we believe, will usher in the transformation to ISB Digital. Our cybersecurity and information technology (IT) security will have to be strengthened. In moving toward ISB Digital, the school has set up a high-powered working group of Board members to suggest a strategy and roadmap. We must develop our brand in this space and cannot simply have "online" digitally recorded versions of our programs. This will not differentiate us from other platforms, such as Coursera. The faculty members must hone their skills and use up-to-date studios to develop interactive learning processes. The medium-term objective: our delivery should not be seen as merely ISB Online but should be recognized as "ISB Digital Interactive." All this has not been easy because our programs span five locations (Hyderabad, Mohali, Gurgaon, Mumbai, and Bengaluru), including two major campuses (Hyderabad and Mohali). We also realized that we needed to "remodel" our business model. The main revenue stream for our school has traditionally been the 1-year MBA PGP program, which absorbs about 900 students every year. Although we held ground on this immediately in our admissions, we realized that going forward, we needed to strengthen our PGP modular programs, the advanced management programs, and the executive education programs. We needed to rethink these. At the same time, there were cost pressures as a result of increased expenditures on COVID-19 preparedness and well-advanced digital platforms. All these and more pioneering work will also involve a new look at our financial plans and long-term financial viability and robustness because of fresh investments, increased competition, global financial metrics, and governance structures and mechanisms.

The importance of being in constant touch with all our major stakeholders was not lost on us. The school has been in regular contact with the governments both in the center and in the two states where we have campuses to understand their latest thinking and the proactive steps that we should take to onboard students when the governments give the go-ahead. We are also in touch with other leading business schools, both within the country and overseas, to understand how they have progressed and what plans they are making for the future. We also keep in touch with our three partner business schools: Kellogg, Wharton, and London Business School.

The Governing Board of ISB, comprising leading overseas and domestic business and academic leaders, played a critical role in advising and supporting the management and leadership of the school. Apart from the quarterly Board meetings, it also formed smaller task forces when and where needed to give expert guidance as we went along this journey in a pandemic-induced regime. At the same time, we were constantly reminded that every step and decision of the school leadership should uphold ISB's hard-earned global status and reputation built over the last two decades.

New Normal: Learning from and Planning for the Future

Although challenging, 2020 has not exactly been a bad year for ISB. Poets & Quants gave ISB an integrated ranking of 16 worldwide across *Financial Times, Forbes, Bloomberg Businessweek,* and *The Economist.* The resident faculty is ranked in the top 25 globally in terms of per capita research productivity in the leading global management (UT-Dallas 24) journals. ISB had the honor of receiving global visibility with accreditations from the Association of MBAs (AMBA), the EFMD Quality Improvement System (EQUIS), and the Association to Advance Collegiate Schools of Business (AACSB). We gained the unique distinction of becoming the 100th and the youngest business school in the world to achieve the coveted "Triple Crown" accredit-ations. And we are certainly poised to not only recover but also flourish if we make the right investments in faculty, the technology infrastructure, and enhancing the quality of learning.

Ironically, just 3 weeks before the lockdown, we had a "Board Strategy Day" to lay down ISB's roadmap for the future. It included three components: digital transformation in terms of both content (e.g., financial technology [FinTech]) and delivery formats (e.g., blended learning), global presence, and corporate/government engage-ment. All three thrusts have been facilitated – or at least forced upon us – by pandemic-instigated challenges. *Perhaps, as Truman mused, we should never waste a good crisis.*

Even as the pandemic and the economic recession will usher in an era of shake-up and consolidation in the Indian higher education segment, our long-term survival will also depend on how we respond to the macro-policy environment, the new National Education Policy (NEP) that was announced by the Union government a few weeks back during the pandemic (Chattopadhyay, 2021). We had to be dynamic and resilient as well. The NEP will bring the global universities like Harvard and Yale to our backyard and increase competition. Although ISB is a world-class institution, we needed to go global and reinvent ourselves on many other fronts. We realized that we needed to embark on a journey of ISB Global and ISB 2.0.

In ISB's fascinating journey of only 20 years, we have created a formidable and influential alumni base of about 11,700 business leaders, growing at roughly 1,200 per year. On this count, we are perhaps among the fastest-growing business schools in the world. Although the role and relevance of alumni have long been recognized by global institutions of higher education, the pandemic era reaffirmed our faith and recognition of this important stakeholder group. Alumni helped us in our placements, funding, knowledge, and net-work. We became closer as a community. This was another positive outcome in this era.

As an organization, we will have to adjust to a "new normal." To manage uncertainty, we will have to be more agile and flexible to adjust to changes in our competitive environment, the preferences of our students, and constraints imposed by regulators. Although the market for education is tighter, new competitors are pouring in from UCLA's Post Graduate Programme in Management for Executives

(PGPX) India program to the Washington University–IIT Bombay EMBA. Even after the pandemic subsides and vaccines are available, we believe that the virtual environment is here to stay for a while in some form or another.

Clearly, 2020 has been a year of inflection for us at ISB. The renewed continuance of our journey of ISB 2.0 has indeed been with a clear redirection toward going digital, going global, and promoting greater societal and nation-building. Now, more than ever, we need to be creative, adaptive, and resilient. Digital transformation has enabled us, at least in executive education, to expand our wings internationally and within custom-designed programs for Indian multinational corporations (MNCs). And JSI@ISB has expanded our corporate and government connection. As we look toward the future, our program and research portfolio will surely embrace the online MBA (iMBA), lifelong learning contracts, and specialized master's programs (e.g., science, technology, engineering, and mathematics [STEM], FinTech, and digitally focused concentrations). Another opportunity is for ISB to embrace the demand for local content – case studies and theoretical frameworks that address challenges faced by small but growth-oriented companies going up the performance ladder globally. Tech research is performed in Bengaluru and patented in Silicon Valley. Garments are manufactured in Punjab but branded in Oregon. These organizations must learn how to enhance both value creation and value appropriation.

Implications for Business: The Paradox of Uncertainty and Dynamism

As we have seen from the foregoing discussion, COVID-19 has induced business schools to reinvent themselves through a judicious mix of resilience, agility, and adaptive structures. The case example and references to ISB are only indicative; equally importantly, this is how successful and progressive schools managed in the year 2020. If this has been the experience of business schools, what has been that of businesses?

The pandemic upended the world in ways unimagined in recent memory. Its impact has been felt on economies, societies, lives, livelihoods, health care, global institutions, businesses, educational institutions, and virtually every aspect of life across almost all nations of the world.

In normal times, organizations face many challenges, and the progressive ones equip themselves to deal with them. But COVID-19 has brought about issues and challenges beyond those in normal times that have drawn up questions about their very survival. Although this is not the first time that a crisis of global scale has spiked companies, what is different this time is its duration and magnitude. Leaders and managers found that their best-equipped strategies and experiences were often not enough to keep them above the water. One important reason is that, surprisingly, this has been a period of both uncertainty and dynamism – paradoxical and more complex in many ways.

This dichotomy and paradox of uncertainty amid dynamism is what has given us hope amid despair. Although the immediate and short-term impacts have been devastating for the majority, we have seen that some nations have been more resilient than most others. While some economies, sectors, and companies have done well, many others have fallen by the wayside. We have also seen that some countries have been able to respond much faster than others. This is also true in the smaller case of businesses and other institutions.

What has differentiated these more successful countries and corporations is resilience and agility. However, those in this group are the minority, and it will be useful to learn lessons from them in survival and existence. Consider some instances of the paradox of uncertainty and dynamism.

At the macroeconomic level, the latest International Monetary Fund (IMF) data show that the Indian economy was expected to contract by 10.3 percent in 2020 but could rebound very gradually in 2021 (Suneja, 2021). The UN's International Labour Organization projected that COVID-19 pushed an additional 400 million people into poverty in the last few weeks of 2021, even as the richest of the rich, such as Mukesh Ambani and other billionaires like Jeff Bezos, have grown richer still ("About 400 Million Workers in India," 2021). Similarly, whereas sectors like commercial real estate and automobiles have crashed, others, such as health care, e-commerce, and digital, have moved up the ladder.

When companies were able to pull themselves up after the first round of lockdowns was lifted in many countries, one of the first pandemic-induced changes was the way in which employees worked. In the formal sector, the norm of work changed overnight from working in the office to working from home. But after many months of the pandemic and many months of lockdown, while many companies have shut down – permanently or for the medium term – their physical commercial spaces, work from home has gathered momentum. This also means that managers and business leaders will have to restructure their home-office spaces. For example, managers from the large metropolises working in, say, software companies in Bengaluru will move back to their smaller hometowns and villages. These managers will have to reorient themselves from working in swanky offices to the confines of their smaller homes, with all their limitations. Experts also say that after vaccine availability, hybrid ways of working will also come into play, such as working part of the week at the office and part of the week from home.

If one looks hard enough, there are always silver linings to dark clouds. For example, India's truck manufacturing industry was hit hard at first as a result of the imposition of the pan-India Goods and Services Tax (GST), which reduced friction for transportation across states, leading to higher utilization and therefore lower short-term demand for vehicles. Then, technology hit home, and shipping companies started using scheduling algorithms to further enhance the daily utilization of vehicles. Although this has temporarily reduced the demand for vehicles, the demand for services related to transportation has increased dramatically. In another context, Amazon India has successfully leveraged the small *kirana* (mom-and-pop) stores to close the last-mile delivery. These models (order online and pick up at a convenience store, which, by the way, will also deliver) have been exported to Brazil and Mexico. These case studies represent what the West can learn from the East and therefore provide content for global management schools. ISB's investment in the Centre for Learning and Management Practice (CLMP) and ISB-Studios will help facilitate ideas from the East for the West (and the East).

COVID-19 and related developments have also had an impact on the business models and operating models of companies. With the public transportation sector having shrunk dramatically, companies like Uber have shifted their focus on urban ride shares to home delivery, with the spotlight on Uber Eats. At operating levels, if quarterly and annual budgets were the norm, today, companies are looking at shorter planning cycles. Revenue assumptions that finance managers had planned for 2020 are no longer valid after the dramatic economic contraction. Offline retail and malls have moved into the online and e-commerce space. Giant trade fairs, exhibitions, and conferences, which used to get large sponsorships, have moved to the virtual world. There has been a perceptible growth of educational technology (EdTech), FinTech, and online pharmacy (e-pharma) companies.

The global pandemic has also reoriented international relations and geopolitics. With the American economy contracting, the Trump administration took measures that would adversely affect Indian software companies. With the Chinese economy hit, global trade took a phenomenal blow. European countries like the UK, France, and Spain have seen large-scale unemployment, with the result that it has affected Indian workers in those countries. Similarly, with the Middle East economy being affected, large numbers of Indian migrant workers have returned to their home countries. Likewise, in India, with urban factories and manufacturing taking a toll, migrant workers have returned to their villages in their home states. All of these have affected the growth of Indian manufacturing.

In the light of the dichotomy, McKinsey analyzed 25 companies that had recently undergone agile transformations in some of their businesses (Handscomb et al., 2020). These companies' agile units responded better to COVID-19 shocks than nonagile units based on parameters like customer satisfaction, employee engagement, and operational performance. The examples can go on, but the main point is that economies and companies have seen a period of simultaneous dynamism and uncertainty that signals an acute and urgent need for resilient and agile managers and leaders.

Educating Future Leaders for Resilience and Agility

From the foregoing discussion, we have seen how business schools and businesses that have succeeded and perhaps even thrived in the pandemic are those that are resilient and agile. If successful institutions need such characteristics, can they be managed and led without leaders who amplify those traits? Indeed, both of these ideas are not new in the management education field. But in the context of going forward, beyond the pandemic, we increasingly need more of such leaders.

Resilience and agility involve a mix of leadership, psychological, and personality traits. Can they be taught in classrooms? Can they be acquired in short periods in either MBA, executive education, or advanced management programs? In another context, it has now been established that both leaders and entrepreneurs are not just born with those abilities, but they can be molded to learn and embody those competencies through teaching and experiences. Similarly, resilience and agility, the needs of the hour, can also be acquired.

Resilience and agility, however, must be at the system level. Agile private companies can be and are thwarted by public policy structures and administrators. Here, COVID-19 has provided two opportunities. JSI@ISB represents the first baby steps toward bringing management principles to public administration, hopefully culminating in initial programs for public management. Public administrators are trained to administer. They need to learn management. ISB has a unique opportunity to be a platform for dialogues between corporate managers and public policy decision makers and administrators, thereby complementing management literature from the West.

Academic research into resilience started about 40 years ago with pioneering studies by Professor Norman Garmezy (1918–2009), a psychologist who was known as the "grandfather of resilience studies." Since then, there have been many resilience-related theories, but one of the most studied circumstances around resilience is that of people surviving the Holocaust. In his bestselling book *Man's Search for Meaning*, Viktor Frankl inspired millions of ordinary people and management leaders toward resilience (Frankl, 1985). In more recent times, Jim Collins, with his book *Good to Great*, gave it a contemporary context (Collins, 2001). And Srivastava and colleagues (1998) propose business innovations that balance short-term efficiency with growth and risk (resilience) management by leveraging multiprocess excellence in product-market ecosystems.

All these perspectives together are being brought forward to the concept and practice of resilience in a postpandemic world. Therefore, tomorrow's resilient managers will be able to accept reality quickly – finding meaning and purpose in a world that may be uncertain and dynamic – and work for the greater good of the institution, society, and the world. These principles can themselves be applied to the education industry. Academic institutions can embrace the concept of customer lifetime value by developing lifelong learning contracts with periodic new-content boot camps, career-transition services via alumni networking and job portals, and leadership coaching when their graduates want to switch jobs down the line.

Academic institutions must not only collaborate among themselves but also with corporate and government communities. In many areas, such as FinTech, the artificial intelligence/machine learning (AI/ML) industries are ahead of academia because they have access to more resources and data. Consequently, academic institutions must share ideas and programs – and people. As an example, in developing programs on artificial intelligence for senior executives, ISB has partnered with Microsoft. Such academic–business learning alliances can bring unique perspectives to both sides because industry often does not have the luxury of time to examine issues in depth, and academic partners can unearth new perspectives. Indeed, based on a government-sponsored online conference titled "Vaishwik Bharatiya Vaigyanik (VAIBHAV) 2020," ISB has come up with a framework to justify industry–government–academic cluster-based research parks and special education zones.

Agile managers who lead agile corporations, on the other hand, are those who can collaborate and cooperate in a world of volatility, uncertainty, complexity, and ambiguity (VUCA); can transform themselves and their competencies quickly to adapt to changing circumstances; and crucially, can solve wicked and complex problems that arise out of extraordinary situations. For example, it is unprecedented to have a large cohort of people, all over the world, starting to work remotely at once. But the last year of COVID-19 has shown that these managers can adapt to the changing environment.

In fact, COVID-19 is a classic example of how one can find opportunities in challenges. The future of work is being recrafted. Global supply chains are taking new shapes. Factories are getting leaner and more flexible. Artificial intelligence and the internet of things (IoT) are emerging as new frontiers. Entire industries, such as media and entertainment, are being reinvented.

A World Economic Forum report (Kretchmer, 2021) cites that during the pandemic, female political leaders in Denmark, Finland, Germany, Iceland, New Zealand, and Norway were managing the crisis better than their male counterparts. Resilience, pragmatism, benevolence, trust in collective common sense, mutual aid, and humility are mentioned as common traits of the success of these female leaders.

COVID-19 is forcing a change in behaviors, values, and mindsets. Reskilling and upskilling will increasingly become the needs of the hour. If we do not reskill, there will be talent shortages. Even as job losses and unemployment have been rampant in the COVID-19 era, there is a mismatch between demand and supply. There is also a shortage of high-quality trainers. All of these will be the megatrends in business in 2021. Business and business leaders will never be the same.

New Pathways: Beyond 50 Years of EFMD and 20 Years of ISB

In 2021, EFMD Global celebrated 50 years of its establishment and growth since 1971, with a mission to create socially responsible managers. ISB commemorated 20 years of service, being set up as a pioneering private-sector Indian management education institution with a world-class focus. In the intervening years of both organizations, they have been trailblazers. But their future responsibilities will be dramatically different from those of their past. The reason is 2020 – the year of the global COVID-19 pandemic, in many ways, is a year between the past and tomorrow. Those of us in the global management education space have a new calling to respond to the emerging trends from the pandemic or those that have been catalyzed by it. Here is my attempt to summarize 10 key trends that I foresee:

- In the wake of online universities and digital classes, group learning, and teamwork will be critical.
- Shorter MBAs, such as 1-year programs, will gain popularity among students.
- Management education could be repackaged with part classroom learning and part employment.
- Globalization is not going away (value migration will be the way of the future), although we will have more localized content.
- Indian business schools will need to increasingly equip themselves to be world-class global institutions.
- While companies will increasingly use artificial intelligence and other technologies, augmented intelligence in companies will necessitate refreshed course curriculum and pedagogy.
- Lifelong learning and executive education will gather steam.
- Corporate–academia partnerships will see higher levels of acceptance.
- In India, there will be greater pushback by the government to have a greater say in higher education.

- But regulation is not the answer; natural and volunteer programs for nation-building, like ISB's Jumpstart India, will give world-class management education greater acceptability.

In closing, academic institutions must manage and learn from their ecosystems, which include not only academic partners but also the corporate community, government, civil society, and of course, alumni.

References

About 400 million workers in India may sink into poverty: UN report. (2020, April 8). *Economic Times.* https://economictimes.indiatimes .com/news/economy/indicators/about-400-million-workers-in-india-may-sink-into-poverty-un-report/articleshow/75041922.cms?from=mdr

Chattopadhyay, S. (2021). National Education Policy, 2020. *Economic & Political Weekly*, 55(46). www.epw.in/journal/2020/46/commentary/ national-education-policy-2020.html.

Collins, J. (2001). *Good to great: Why some companies make the leap ... and others don't.* Harper Business.

Frankl, V. E. (1985). *Man's search for meaning.* Simon and Schuster.

Handscomb, C., Mahadevan, D., Schor, L., Sieberer, M., Naidoo, E., and Srinivasan, S. (2020). *An operating model for the next normal: Lessons from agile organizations in the crisis.* McKinsey & Company. www .mckinsey.com/business-functions/organization/our-insights/an-operating-model-for-the-next-normal-lessons-from-agile-organizations-in-the-crisis.

Indian School of Business. (2021). *JumpStartIndia@ISB.* www.isb.edu/en/ research-thought-leadership/research-centres-institutes/bharti-institute-of-public-policy/JSI.html.

Kretchmer, H. (2021). *3 leadership lessons from the age of coronavirus.* World Economic Forum. www.weforum.org/agenda/2020/08/corona virus-leadership-women-leaders-jacinda-ardern.

Srivastava, R. K., Shervani, T. A., and Fahey, L. (1998). Market-based assets and shareholder value: A framework for analysis. *Journal of Marketing*, 62(1), 2–18.

Suneja, K. (2021). Indian economy to contract by 10.3% in 2020; to bounce back with 8.8% growth in 2021: IMF. *Economic Times.* https:// economictimes.indiatimes.com/news/economy/indicators/indian-econ omy-to-contract-by-10-3-in-2020-to-bounce-back-with-8-8-growth-in-2021-imf/articleshow/78641478.cms?from=mdr.

Taxila Business School. (n.d.). *Top 50 business schools in India.* https:// taxila.in/blog/top-50-business-schools-in-india.

9 | Strategic Continuity or Disruption? Adaptive Structures of Business Schools in Times of Crisis

BARBARA SPORN

The crisis has revealed challenges of different models for business schools. At the same time, as history shows, institutions of higher education are resilient organizations with a high adaptive capacity. Hence, responses to the crisis range from strategic continuity to disruption caused by financial impediments. It can be assumed that a new landscape of schools and programs will emerge.

In order to investigate the adaptive structures of business schools, this chapter has three objectives:

- Analyze the main uncertainties of the future.
- Present different scenarios of adaptive structures of business schools.
- Develop models of business schools in the future.

For this purpose, the chapter draws on the extensive literature of adaptation in higher education institutions and uses learnings from recent accreditation experiences. Implications for practice, with a special emphasis on structure and strategy, conclude this chapter.

Introduction: Uncertain Futures for Business Schools

Universities are among the oldest organizations in the world and therefore have always been subject to changes in their institutional environment (Bok, 2009; Hardy et al., 1983; Weick, 1976). In response to these changes, universities, like business schools, developed a resilient structural form and strong internal processes that make them successful institutions (Pinheiro and Young, 2017). Over time, scholars of organization theory and sociology have therefore characterized universities as professional bureaucracies (Mintzberg, 1989), loosely coupled systems (Weick, 1976), or organized anarchies (Cohen et al., 1972). Major features include a differentiated structure of independent and autonomous experts who are intrinsically motivated by the quality of their work and their professional standards in research and teaching; a relatively stable but complex environment with constant student demand and secured funding; a professional support structure administering services; and a relatively lean leadership cadre with a collegial and participative governance style. These features are complemented by a set of boundary-spanning activities that guarantee a translation of external demands into internal responses (e.g., technology-transfer units, interdisciplinary research institutes). With this, the constant exchange between the inside organization and the external environment has turned universities into institutions that are rather sensitive to societal developments.

The model of business schools has also evolved over time as an elaborate system of core processes and support services. From a value-chain perspective (Peters et al., 2018), they provide different degree programs (bachelor, master, PhD in all forms) with the help of sophisticated support activities ranging from faculty management to the learning infrastructure. Depending on their financial viability and market position, business schools have developed different business models. In recent years, the ecosystem of business education has changed dramatically with the rise of learning technologies, increased globalization, mobility and competition, the need for short-cycle education, heightened public expectations for relevance and impact, and more (Cornuel, 2007; Locke, 2020; Peters et al., 2018). Business schools – as a result – are in a state of flux.

The developments of 2020 and 2021 have added further. Universities arrived at volatility, uncertainty, complexity, and ambiguity (VUCA) challenges (Korsakova, 2019). VUCA challenges have been introduced to higher education markets by a combined appearance of different trends. Volatility is triggered by the fact that societal conditions are not constant (Meyer and Sporn, 2018). Demographics are changing, and the demand for education is constantly changing. Uncertainty encompasses the notion of the missing predictability of institutional development and, for example, employment arrangements moving from permanent to precarious. Without a doubt, the complexity has increased for higher education. There is not one challenge that is occurring but a facet of issues that need the attention of universities and schools. Ambiguity arises for higher education in the sense of multiple contradicting demands in the form of more impact and more innovation or more quality and more diversity. VUCA does create the need for a profound rethinking of the organization of universities and business schools. In a sense, they are moved out of their comfort zones of stable environmental conditions (Bennis and O'Toole, 2005).

Adding to the already-existing dynamic environment came the COVID-19 crisis. The consequences have included issues like online teaching competence; safety for students and faculty; research disruption as a result of the lack of opportunity to travel and network; and administrative threats caused by the rising costs of response, for example, new infrastructure needs, personnel challenges caused by the home office, or the impact of the pandemic on student learning and outcomes, thus influencing their qualifications for the job market (Baker, 2021; Marinoni et al., 2020).

All these changes can trigger financial restructuring and reorganization. Globally, schools are facing changes in student demand for educational programs. Those programs creating revenue for business schools are especially in jeopardy of financial restructuring. For example, some Australian and US schools have been downsizing their program offerings. Strategies have been revised as to the portfolio of program offerings, and mergings of different program types have been the result. The faculty has been restructured in the process as well, in the sense of replacing full-time faculty with colleagues who work on a part-time and flexible basis. Altogether, the COVID-19 crisis led to financial restructuring that scrutinized existing strategies and reformulated them in order to face a much more uncertain future (Lockett, 2020).

In this chapter, business schools and their adaptive capacity are the major foci. Along those lines, many business schools around the globe have chosen accreditation as a way to have a visible and sustainable tool at hand for quality management and continuous improvement. The European Foundation for Management Development (EFMD) is the major provider of formative evaluation schemes and strongly emphasizes – among other things – diversity, internationalization, and impact. Major accreditation systems include institutional assessment (under the name *EFMD Quality Improvement System* [EQUIS]) and program assessment (under the name *EFMD Accredited*). Hence, and because this volume is dedicated to 50 years of EFMD, this chapter also looks at EFMD accreditation when analyzing business schools.

The Role of and Impact on EFMD Accreditation

Accreditation at EFMD over the last 25 years has developed into a very successful system of assuring quality, on the one hand, and producing a visible global brand of excellently performing business schools, on the other hand. Today, there are some 200 EQUIS-accredited schools and some 130 EFMD-accredited business programs. Standards and criteria of accreditation encompass institutional factors like strategy, resources, faculty, networks with the world of practice, internationalization, research, and last but not least, students and programs. A peer-review system of colleagues from accredited institutions and representatives of corporates and nonprofit organizations regularly evaluates all these areas. Through the decades-long experience, a clear understanding of the different models of business schools developed within EFMD. Respect for diversity regarding different forms and market positioning has been a key element in this development and reinforces the understanding of business schools as a driver for societal change (Cornuel, 2005; Thomas and Cornuel, 2012).

Now, through the COVID-19 crisis, the accreditation system has become challenged as well. One aspect involves the actual delivery of the accreditation, which had to move online. According to the schools involved, this has worked rather well. The other aspect is certain standards used in accreditation that have turned into areas of major concern: digitalization; internationalization; and ethics, responsibility, and sustainability (ERS).

Digitalization is the most obvious area of change in recent months. From one day to the other, business schools worldwide had to move to virtual classrooms and offices. Within days, universities and business schools reorganized teaching and research and worked with administration remotely. In the assessment during an accreditation visit, digital venues played a bigger role and helped those that were able to build their activities on an already-existing digitalization strategy. Others were pressed to respond quickly without much preparation.

Internationalization is another standard of EFMD accreditation featuring prominently. The pandemic crisis put all efforts of mobility on hold. Schools have been in the process of responding with virtual internationalization, internationalization without mobility, online mixed teams, or virtual visiting professorships. Again, the business models of many accredited business schools have been challenged.

ERS is a third area where accreditation standards need to be developed further. Throughout the COVID-19 pandemic, business schools have paid more attention to the increased inequality of students and their access to online learning. Sustainable measures of resource use have become more widely discussed (e.g., travel regulations), and the integration of stakeholder diversity has increased in prominence (de Wit and Altbach, 2021).

Theory of Adaptive University Structures

The crisis has revealed the limits of university business models and available resources. At the same time, history shows that universities and business schools are resilient institutions with a high adaptive capacity. Hence, responses to the pandemic are expected to range from strategic continuity to disruption caused by financial impediments. Building on existing theories of adaptive university structures (Sporn, 1999) and entrepreneurial universities (Clark, 1998), this chapter presents scenarios and possible business models of the future.

The question of disruption or continuity of strategy uses the following definition:

In an organisational context, business continuity management (BCM) has evolved into a process that identifies an organisation's exposure to internal and external threats and synthesises hard and soft assets to provide effective prevention and recovery. Essential to the success of BCM is a thorough understanding of the wide range of threats (internal and external) and a recognition that an effective response will be determined by employees' behaviour during the business recovery process. (Herbane et al., 2004, pp. 435–436)

Although strategic continuity is important, business schools and universities need to be analyzed regarding their adaptive capacity. The notion of adaptation to environmental challenges has been debated in higher education research since the 1990s. Under the topic of entrepreneurial university (Clark, 1998) or responsive university (Tierney, 1998), research focused on describing the mechanisms of adaptation and the role of organizational aspects prevailed. Up until today – with the ever-changing turbulent environment for higher education institutions – these theories are of great importance.

The work on adaptive university structures (Sporn, 1999) seems especially fitting for the analysis in this chapter. The model proposes six factors of influence (see Figure 9.1): shared governance, committed leadership, professional management, clear mission, differentiated structure, and entrepreneurial culture. The interplay of these six forces shapes the ability of business schools to respond to their

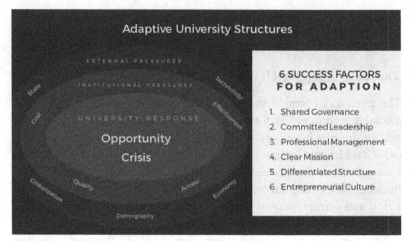

Figure 9.1 Adaptive university structures.
Source: Sporn (1999).

environment – an environment that is defined as a crisis or opportunity by the institutions. In this sense, the model also assumes an open-systems and institutional approach to university adaptation (DiMaggio and Powell, 1983).

Regarding the **external environment**, business schools and universities are viewed as embedded in an institutional context to which they have to respond. Clark has coined this as the *demand–response balance* – a condition where the university is aligned with the expectations of external stakeholders. For the sake of adaptive structures, it is important to note that the sense of crisis or opportunity is a necessary precondition for higher education institutions to respond.

A very important facet of adaptation is **shared governance**. Business schools, like universities, are bottom-heavy organizations with a dominant role of the experts (i.e., the professors). This group requests a key position in the functioning of the institution. Their contribution to teaching and research is the building block for the core value of business schools. The notion of shared governance is then interpreted as the involvement of the experts in all decisions in order to facilitate faculty buy-in and motivation. Basically, shared governance helps leaders to build their work on the support of the key players in the organization.

Following from that is the importance of **committed leadership**. In times of organizational transition, leaders are becoming the key drivers for change. Their understanding of the institutional environment can help to translate both threats and opportunities into strategies for the future. Leaders help to motivate internally in order to make necessary changes more transparent. At the same time, committed leaders are able to develop a vision that is shared by the university community. Thus, the interplay between faculty interest and leadership dedication can form an important alliance for successful adaptation.

The rise of **professional management** of business schools has contributed to the success of institutional adaptation. Over the last few decades, university administration has moved from a bureaucratic to a professionalized organization (Musselin, 2007). With this comes the evolution of a new class in schools and universities – the "third-space professionals" (Whitchurch, 2012). They are well educated in the field of their work (e.g., quality management, marketing, student services) and constitute a separate new group inside business schools – next to leadership, faculty members, and administration. Their work is characterized as service oriented, professional, and knowledge driven. Through their boundary-spanning capacity (e.g., entrepreneurship or technology-transfer centers), they are able to develop adequate responses to external pressures.

A **clear mission** has proven important for successful adaptation and change. Shared decision-making practices, committed leaders, and professional managers need to base their work on a clear mission and set of goals that are shared by the academic community and that combine past developments with future perspectives. A common understanding of the external challenges is a key feature of successful adaptive university structures. This clear mission is embedded in a vision and a strategy that help the institution to move forward.

A **differentiated structure** provides the higher education institution with different ways to respond to external needs. A business school could, for example, develop competence fields with different functions and services (undergraduate college, graduate school, entrepreneurship center). These differentiated units are relatively autonomous in terms of design and adjustments of their offerings and are at the same time accountable to central leadership.

The **entrepreneurial culture** is the remaining building block of adaptive structures. This refers to a set of institutional norms and values emphasizing opportunity-driven and solution-oriented behavior. Burton Clark, the famous higher education researcher, once talked about "joint institutional volition" (Clark, 2004) as the major driver for organizational transformation in institutions of higher education. This implicit openness for innovation paired with a common understanding of the future can help the institution to move through a disruptive period. The coherence makes change and adaptation successful.

Adding to the notion of adaptive structures is the importance of a **process view**. Clark (2004) presented three dynamics through which sustained change happens. First, *reinforcing interaction* is a key element in the process. The institution needs to provide enough opportunities to interact and exchange views on the issues involved. Decisions are in line with the envisioned future and enhance a change-oriented culture. Second, a sense of *perpetual momentum* is needed in order to support the – what he called – self-reliant university. Ongoing adjustments, negotiations, interactions, environmental scanning, and so forth should be in place to maintain organizational dynamics and agility. Third, the institution needs to develop an *ambitious collegial volition*. Clark makes a strong argument that only an "ambitious volition helps propel the institution forward to a transformed character"; he goes on to say that "inertia in traditional universities has many rationales, beginning with the avoidance of hard choices" (Clark, 2004, p. 94).

In order to discuss strategic continuity or disruption in the sense of adaptive structures of business schools further, it is necessary to look at the notion of strategic development versus disruption. For this, an example from the area of accreditation can help to illustrate how schools have responded to the challenge of maintaining a sense of quality improvement in times of severe societal crisis caused by the pandemic.

Back to the Practice of Accredited Business Schools: An Example

As was explained earlier in this chapter, business school accreditation is based on certain standards and criteria (see www.efmdglobal.org/). Among them are digitalization, internationalization, and ERS embedded in the main areas of strategy, teaching and research, and faculty and students, as well as connections to the world of practice. In all areas, EFMD defined a clear understanding of the meaning and implementation choices. At the same time, the COVID-19 crisis has challenged the accreditation system, and certain questions emerged that need to be addressed in order for the system to be fit for future quality-assurance exercises.

One recent example of a global business school – the Nottingham Business School China (NUBS China) – deliberating on the move from crisis management triggered by the pandemic to opportunities is informative. After a period of major disruption and immediate response to the COVID outbreak, the business school looked at the opportunities ahead and developed five opportunities for the future (Lockett, 2020) that resonate well with other accreditation experiences:

- Opportunity 1: Extending the use of digital learning
- Opportunity 2: Innovation in assessment
- Opportunity 3: Research and external engagement
- Opportunity 4: Reviewing the use of resources
- Opportunity 5: Challenging internal bureaucratic processes

As this list shows, digitalization can create an opportunity for business schools. New ways of learning within existing programs or new offers will evolve. This will include hybrid, virtual, or blended formats as well as flipped classrooms or cross-campus, cross-institution, and cross-country collaborations.

Assessment can be redesigned as well, in the sense of working more closely with students on their educational journey. Feedback can be provided online or through a link between faculty and students enhanced through technology.

Research and engagement require time and dedication. As the example shows, time can become available through the confinements and home-office arrangements. The future could possibly bring more opportunities to publish and to work on relevant topics in that way, creating an impact on society and the academic community.

The use of resources is also affected throughout the crisis. Resource needs that are decreasing in some areas (e.g., travel) can be used for investment in other, new areas (e.g., online delivery) in order to meet market demands.

As described earlier, decision making at business schools can be cumbersome and bureaucratic. The pandemic crisis showed new ways of working together in order to develop solutions. This could lead the way for more efficient and effective ways of management.

This example demonstrates the power of the pandemic crisis and its effects on the way business schools are run. In order to take this one step further, scenarios are presented that show different types of institutional responses.

Scenarios of Adaptive Structures Responding to Crisis

Scenarios are often used to give a plausible description of a possible "future reality," including some deliberations about the steps that lead to the future state and possible actions taken (Dean, 2019). Based on past research (Pinheiro and Young, 2017) and experiences during the last year, three responses to the pandemic crisis are suggested: resilient schools, reengineered schools, and reinvented schools. In this section, the major characteristics and conceptions of the most affected accreditation standards (international, digital, ERS) and the response patterns (disruption or continuity) are presented before moving to the description of the varying adaptive structures and business models of these types.

Type 1: The Resilient School

Resilience refers to the notion that lies at the heart of business schools and universities since their foundation. It is the ability to be prepared, adaptable, and responsive to an external demand – be it a crisis or an opportunity. The literature (Pinheiro and Young, 2017; Sporn, 1999) draws a picture of flat, expert-driven institutions that are firmly embedded in their institutional environment (Olsen, 2007; Pettigrew et al., 2014). Collegial leadership and a shared understanding of the functioning of the business school dominate decision making and action. A stable environment with secured funding and constant student demand is a prerequisite in this constellation. The power of the experts (professors of all levels) is based on a high degree of autonomy, the quality of the expertise, and individualized connections to the external environment. Resilient schools will mostly be found in public systems with a long tradition of higher education and a pledge for the "traditional model" of the university (Musselin, 2007).

Regarding the consequences for internationalization, the resilient school has invested sufficiently in the development of a functioning digital infrastructure, adequate teacher training, enhanced student services, and robust information technology (IT) support. Internationalization has been transformed in the sense of providing online opportunities for exchange through, for example, online inter-cultural learning teams and virtual visiting professors. ERS has been mostly concerned with acting responsibly in the manner of addressing rising inequalities and the widening digital gap; for example, according to a recent survey, 40 percent of students worldwide lack online access (Martin and Furiv, 2020).

Resilient business schools are apt for strategic continuity rather than disruption. Although the sudden crisis caused by the pandemic hit these business schools hard, they were able to respond sufficiently to address the most pressing issues in teaching and research. Further plans will most likely include "to move back to the classroom" and suggest the continued practice of existing strategies.

Type 2: The Reengineered School

On the contrary, reengineered business schools are more market dependent and driven by student demand. Hence, their functioning is dominated by a "business logic" where tuition-fee payments and a potential drop in enrollment numbers are major threats. The school leadership needs to respond with potential layoffs of faculty, closure of programs, or a combined set of measures that will "reengineer" the school in the sense of making it financially viable.

For reengineered schools, the changing pattern of internationaliza-tion represents a challenge caused by a drop in student mobility. Investments in this area will include solutions to satisfy demand through online offerings (e.g., exchange without mobility). Digitalization becomes the decisive tool in this scenario and will be used in all aspects of teaching and learning. The third area is ERS with respect to, for example, working students who lost their job and who will not be able to finish their degree programs. It is in the interest of those business schools to find a way to support those students and bring them back on campus (see global survey results in Marinoni et al. [2020]).

Strategic disruption features prominently at the reengineered busi-ness school. The leadership often exercises crisis management in order to reassess and review existing strategies, stressing program efficiency and cost management. Examples are business schools in Australia or the United States where faculty restructuring and program redesign have led to a new portfolio and structure.

Type 3: The Reinvented School

A third scenario describes a school that has had a pathway of innovation and is ready to respond to an unexpected crisis. These innovator business schools can demonstrate a history of innovation and redesign. Reinvented business schools are stakeholder centered (mostly students, employers, and public officials). Their teaching model is constantly adapting and has been using models like the flipped classroom and transformative approaches to learning. Outreach is global, and faculty is part of a community of "entrepreneurs." Connections with practice are key components to guarantee impact. Technology plays a large part in reinvented business schools as IT is used creatively to facilitate student and faculty work.

The reinvented business school is familiar with internationalization, digitalization, and questions of an ESR nature. The global outreach of these institutions has created a culture and structure that are built on the values of international mobility and exchange, with the objective of offering the best opportunities for graduates. Virtual and up-to-date technologies are part of their entrepreneurial tradition (Taylor, 2012). Innovation in the reinvented business school resembles the constant exploration of new opportunities and implementing them for the good of the institution. The impact of the reinvented school has included areas, such as, for example, ethics training, responsibility regarding health issues, or new sustainable infrastructure.

The reinvented business school is able to define the pandemic as a disruption that will create a revised strategy based on the sense of opportunity. Leadership has a strong entrepreneurial identity, the academic community believes in the value of exploration and experimentation, and the infrastructure is agile enough to adapt to new circumstances. This open mindset to newness paired with a strong foundation in institutional values and culture helps the business school to overcome the obstacle of a crisis in a way that will further develop and sharpen the strategic thrust.

The three scenarios are suggested categorizations of schools responding to the COVID-19 crisis based on certain assumptions (e.g., volatile environment, changed demand). Other types and

Table 9.1. *Models of Business Schools (based on Pinheiro and Young, 2017)*

	Resilient	*Strategic*	*Innovative*
External orientation	Cherish complexity	Control complexity	Use complexity
Core value	Robustness	Efficiency	Change
Resources	Allow slack	Maximize	Invest
Internal dynamics	Support variety	Rationalize	Capitalize
Locus of control	Networks: loose coupling	Hierarchy: tight coupling	Teams: independent actors
Modus operandi	Exploration	Exploitation	Innovation
Positional objective	Thriving – adapting to niche	Winning – being the best in the field	Creating – offering new solutions

different forms are certainly conceivable, depending on the institutional reality of business schools. For this chapter, these different types are taken one step further, with the goal of presenting models of business schools. This can sharpen the understanding of the diversity of business schools and their manner of responding to environmental changes.

Models of Business Schools in the Future

The modeling of business schools includes important aspects of organizational functioning (Pinheiro and Young, 2017): external orientation, core values, use of resources, internal dynamics of management and leadership, the locus of control, the modus operandi as the way to respond, and the positional objective or aspiration (see Table 9.1). When combined with the different types described in the previous section, three models of the business school emerge: the resilient, the strategic, and the innovative. These models of business schools will be combined with the elements of adaptive structures in order to provide a full account of their organizational characteristics (Sporn, 1999, 2018).

The Resilient Model of the Business School

The model of resilient business schools is built on the institutional tradition and past successes enabling a robust structure. Schools' organization shows an external orientation that appreciates complexity in a stable and predictable environment; that is, strategies make use of the complex nature of its diverse markets. Slack resources help to support all elements of a network of loosely coupled units (e.g., institutes, centers, individual professors and department chairs). The school explores opportunities as they emerge and adapts to niches in order to thrive.

Applying the approach of adaptive structures (Sporn, 1999), the resilient school will most likely react to a crisis with the understanding that it needs to be addressed and overcome. Internal functioning is very much dominated by shared governance involving academic stakeholders. Leadership and administration have a complementary role to play in this process. The focus is on transactional aspects with which the different involved parties agree on a strategic orientation. The structure is differentiated and allows the organization to respond to diverging environmental demands. An entrepreneurial culture is not dominant in this model but might exist in some of the differentiated parts. This model is most likely to be found in systems with public funding with less competition, such as those in some European countries.

The Strategic Model of the Business School

The strategic model of business schools features a hierarchical structure and tight coupling of the different elements; that is, leadership and management can work based on the notion of efficiency and rationalization. This model resembles an enterprise approach to schools' management. Environmental complexity needs to be controlled, and resources are scarce. Allocation is driven by the goal of developing a competitive advantage. A market position is exploited to the extent that the school is highly competitive based on its core competencies.

The adaptive structures of strategic business schools have a stronger commitment from leadership to successful change activities. Governance is geared towards professional values. Professional management needs be in place in order to guarantee the success of the programs. Entrepreneurial responses mainly encompass exploiting programs for economic value. The structure is focused on hierarchical arrangements. The strategic model of business schools often includes redesign and reengineering as a consequence of a crisis, as examples from more competition-oriented systems in the UK and the United States demonstrate.

The Innovative Model of the Business School

Innovative business schools are institutions with a strong entrepreneurial identity and an emphasis on change. The value of constantly developing existing programs further and designing up-to-date new offerings lies at the center. The organization is built around capitalizing on teams of creative actors and investing resources for innovation. Innovative business schools use the results of environmental complexity as opportunities. They are able and agile enough to respond quickly and successfully.

Regarding adaptive structures, innovative business schools combine the different areas for success. Their shared governance involves the relevant stakeholders to the extent necessary to secure the implementation of new initiatives. Committed leadership is a key building block – inspirational and visionary leaders help the business school to move forward. A professional infrastructure and staff help to develop feasible and sustainable solutions in a team-oriented fashion. The clear mission and vision act as the glue uniting the different groups and stakeholders behind a common idea and model for the future – based on a strong entrepreneurial culture. Differentiation is relevant in the sense that different actors are brought together to form networks and find creative ways to adapt. Innovative business schools can be found in all systems and often emerge from a financially independent position, with a history of change and widespread support for innovation of the academic community.

Concluding Thoughts

This chapter set out to analyze the adaptive capacity of business schools in the era of the COVID-19 crisis. For this, an account of the institutional environment was provided, followed by a description of possible theoretical foundations of adaptive structures. As a result, the chapter suggests three models of business schools based on their context, tradition, and structural arrangement: the resilient, the strategic, and the innovative. This analysis is not all-embracing or universal; depending on the viewpoint, different models could be developed. To conclude, areas for consideration by practitioners and researchers are presented.

First, business schools are complex organizations with the challenge of finding the right balance between resilience and change. The question arises as to how business schools can stay agile and resilient at the same time, given the complex internal environment of diverse stakeholders and their demands. These schools will most probably look for strategic continuity by following an agreed-upon plan and making adjustments where needed.

Second, business schools have the chance to develop the notion of innovation through crisis. In recent EFMD meetings of deans and directors, the pandemic was described as an opportunity for change. With this transformational view of leadership, business schools are able to capitalize on the ability to adapt. Schools can also become more innovative through a visionary strategy for the benefit of the institution.

Third, the question of strategic continuity or disruption of business schools is determined by multiple factors. The context and location play a role, as does the role of leaders, the faculty, and the students. For the analysis and practice, a key starting point would be to fully grasp the type and model of the business school and build the strategy accordingly.

EFMD, with its global presence, has a responsibility and a role to play in this situation. The continued belief in an open system characterized by diversity and inclusion while securing a high level of quality will provide business schools with the opportunity to learn from each other's practices. By understanding their specific contexts, benchmarking and mutual learning can be facilitated. With this, EFMD can help business schools to maintain their legitimacy and social impact in society.

References

Baker, S. (2021, April 15). Has the pandemic changed research culture – and is it for the better? *THE Newsletter*. www.timeshighereducation.com/features/has-pandemic-changed-research-culture-and-it-better.

Bennis, W. G., and O'Toole, J. (2005). How business schools have lost their way. *Harvard Business Review*, 83(5), 96–104.

Bok, D. (2009). *Universities in the marketplace: The commercialization of higher education.* Princeton University Press.

Clark, B. R. (1998). *Creating entrepreneurial universities: Organizational pathways of transformation. Issues in Higher Education.* Elsevier Science.

(2004). *Sustaining change in universities: Continuities in case studies and concepts.* Open University Press.

Cohen, M. D., March, J. G., and Olsen, J. P. (1972). A garbage can model of organizational choice. *Administrative Science Quarterly*, 17(1), 1–25.

Cornuel, E. (2005). The role of business schools in society. *Journal of Management Development*, 24(9), 819–829.

(2007). Challenges facing business schools in the future. *Journal of Management Development*, 26, (1), 87–92.

de Wit, H., and Altbach, P. G. (2021). Internationalization in higher education: Global trends and recommendations for its future. *Policy Reviews in Higher Education*, 5(1), 28–46.

Dean, M. (2019, November 27). Scenario planning: A literature review. Paper prepared as part of the MORE (Multi-modal Optimisation of Road-space in Europe) Project – Work Package 3 (Future Scenarios: New Technologies, Demographics and Patterns of Demand). Project Number: 769276-2. UCL Department of Civil, Environmental and Geomatic Engineering. https://cordis.europa.eu/project/id/769276.

DiMaggio, P. J., and Powell, W. W. (1983). The iron cage revisited: Institutional isomorphism and collective rationality in organizational fields. *American Sociological Review*, 48(2), 147–160.

Hardy, C., Langley, A., Mintzberg, H., and Rose, J. (1983). Strategy formation in the university setting. *Review of Higher Education*, 6(4), 407–433.

Herbane, B., Elliott, D., and Swartz, E. M. (2004). Business continuity management: Time for a strategic role? *Long Range Planning*, 37(5), 435–457.

Korsakova, T. V. (2019). Higher education in VUCA-world: New metaphor of university. *European Journal of Interdisciplinary Studies*, 5(2), 31–35.

Locke, W. (2020). Visions of higher education futures – the shape of things to come? In C. Callender, W. Locke, and S. Marginson, eds., *Changing higher education for a changing world.* Bloomsbury Academic, pp. 18–32.

Lockett, M. (2020). COVID-19: Crisis, lessons, and opportunities. *Global Focus – the EFMD Business Magazine*, 14(2). www.globalfocusmagazine.com/covid-19-crisis-lessons-and-opportunities/.

Marinoni, G., van't Land, H., and Jensen, T. (2020, May). *The impact of COVID-19 on higher education around the world. IAU global survey report.* www.iau-aiu.net/IMG/pdf/iau_covid19_and_he_survey_report_final_may_2020.pdf.

Martin, M., and Furiv, U. (2020, December 12). COVID-19 tests the resilience of higher education. *University World News.* www .universityworldnews.com/post.php?story=20201211130427131.

Meyer, M., and Sporn, B. (2018). Leaving the ivory tower: Universities' third mission and the search for legitimacy. *Zeitschrift für Hochschulentwicklung*, 13(2), 41–60.

Mintzberg, H. (1989). *The structuring of organizations: A synthesis of the Research*. Prentice-Hall.

Musselin, C. (2007). Are universities specific organisations? In G. Krücken, A. Kosmützky, and M. Torka, eds., *Towards a multiversity*. Verlag, pp. 63–84.

Olsen, J. P. (2007). The institutional dynamics of the European university. In P. Maassen and J. P. Olsen, eds., *University dynamics and European integration*. Springer, pp. 25–54.

Peters, K., Smith, R. R., and Thomas, H. (2018). *Rethinking the business models of business schools: A critical review and change agenda for the future*. Emerald Publishing.

Pettigrew, A. M., Cornuel, E., and Hommel, U., eds. (2014). *The institutional development of business schools*. Oxford University Press.

Pinheiro, R., and Young, M. (2017). The university as an adaptive resilient organization: A complex systems perspective. In J. Huisman and M. Tight, eds., *Theory and Method in Higher Education Research*, Vol. 3. Emerald Publishing Limited, pp. 119–136.

Sporn, B. (1999). *Adaptive university structures*. Jessica Kingsley Publishers. (2018). Adaptive university structures: From theory to practice and back. In M. João Rosa, A. Magalhães, A. Veiga, and P. N. Teixeira, eds., *Under pressure – HEIs coping with multiple challenges*. Brill Sense Publishers, pp. 37–54.

Taylor, M. P. (2012). The entrepreneurial university in the twenty-first century. *London Review of Education*, 10(3), 289–305.

Thomas, H., and Cornuel, E. (2012). Business schools in transition? Issues of impact, legitimacy, capabilities and re-invention. *Journal of Management Development*, 31(4), 329–335.

Tierney, W. G. (1998). *The responsive university: Restructuring for high performance*. Johns Hopkins University Press.

Weick, K. E. (1976). Educational organizations as loosely coupled systems. *Administrative Science Quarterly*, 21(1), 1–19.

Whitchurch, C. (2012). *Reconstructing identities in higher education: The rise of "third space" professionals*. Routledge.

III

Internationalization of Business Schools

10 | Reinventing the Internationalization of Business Schools in the Post–COVID-19 Era

YUAN DING

The dramatic spread of COVID-19 has disrupted lives, livelihoods, communities, and businesses worldwide. The collapse in global economic activity has ruptured the traditional arteries for school operations and international study, travel, and exchange. Yet, the need for international and interdisciplinary contact has never been greater. In this sense, the internationalization of business schools in the post–COVID-19 era will have two layers of new meanings.

First, international experience goes beyond constant overseas travel or exchange. Having recognized the COVID-19 crisis as a defining moment for transformation, business schools have now been called on to reset and rejuvenate their approach, explore the use of new resources to design rewarding and well-rounded curricula, and offer students ample exposure to international resources. They must establish a clear positioning and prepare hedging strategies to emerge stronger out of the wreckage of COVID-19.

Second, as corporate geopolitics becomes even more strategic, the international education agenda should encompass all the elements that equip students with the skills needed to navigate global companies and the world. Business educators must have a deeper understanding of how the world will be reshaped. Training must include solid geopolitical and economic elements for business leaders to engage in and support the transition to a fairer, more sustainable post–COVID-19 world. Both content creation and delivery are equally important: business schools must be quick to respond to the current context with agility and foresight.

As a result, the internationalization of business schools in the post–COVID-19 era is now being reinvented. New meaningful international opportunities exist, and as business educators, we all have to keep step with the accelerated pace of change.

The lessons learned by the China Europe International Business School (CEIBS), a business school in China, in the first 10 months of

2020 have given us a rare but real opportunity to reflect on risk mitigation in the event of lockdowns and travel bans. The experience of 2020 has been a chance to think about how we should equip ourselves today and tomorrow with streamlined learning approaches designed to engage, educate, ensure student program completion, and even enhance content creation and delivery.

This chapter therefore aims, first, to illustrate how external situations may affect business schools, and second, to share the initiatives explored by CEIBS to maintain its international education agenda.

Despite a general sense of uncertainty, one thing is for sure: we are not returning to an "old" or even a "new" normal. We believe business schools are going to be even more critical in reshaping the world's recovery in the aftermath of COVID-19. As such, the purpose of this chapter is to share our school's reflections and practices, with the hope that they may be relevant and, where relevant, transferable to others. Together, our efforts will add up to reset our world for a better future.

1. External and Internal Factors That Have Affected the Basic Operations of Business Schools amid the Pandemic

Geographic location has long been an important strategic factor for business schools. Schools based in countries with large populations can usually depend on a steady pool of domestic students. However, building a brand that is recognized beyond domestic borders and operating abroad are never easy, especially for schools based in developing countries. Therefore, to maintain a diversified student base and to give students the opportunity for greater cross-cultural exposure, schools must work hard to attract foreign students and provide international study and career opportunities.

COVID-19 confinement measures have largely turned this situation upside down. Fortunately, a large home base has offered a buffer to some schools suffering from a drop in enrollment during the pandemic. China was, of course, the first country to suffer from the virus. Today, however, it is also the first country to have succeeded in resuming normal life, and the impact of the pandemic on business schools has therefore been limited. A healthy supply of domestic candidates has also helped offset the slump in international applications (Moules, 2020).

In any crisis, it is often the large, successful companies, organizations, or institutions that survive and recover the fastest. Because the pandemic is fundamentally a crisis that has had an immediate and direct impact on workforces and workplaces, it is leading business schools that are more likely to successfully navigate the crisis and succeed in shifting to remote or hybrid learning.

CEIBS is fortunate to be in a strong position. It has access to a large supply of domestic students, is located in a country that has successfully controlled the outbreak, and is in a leading position in the business education industry. Incoming applications remain steady for the school, and CEIBS has even seen an increase in applications for degree programs, confirming the conventional belief that people turn to education to gain fresh knowledge to prepare for a new start amid economic downturns. In addition, offline campus life has returned to normal, at least for those students who live in China.

Yet, although external factors are critical for a business school to emerge stronger in the postpandemic era, they alone do not determine everything. The key factors lie in a school's resilience, which is comprised of its operations model, global resources, and hedging strategies. Another prerequisite, regardless of whether a school is for-profit or not-for-profit, is a healthy and diversified financial structure. Schools depending solely on government subsidies, donations, or high tuition fees from international students will suffer more than others.

That said, the driving forces behind CEIBS's successful turnaround amid the pandemic have always been its capabilities to evolve constantly and its continuous efforts to build and upgrade infrastructure. "Never sleep on the assets or wealth that founders or predecessors have created" is more than a guiding principle at CEIBS. It is a faith.

Since its establishment, CEIBS has sought to expand its influence and forge ties between the East and the West by building a global network of campuses, as well as through its teaching, research, and business practices. The past few decades have seen growing numbers of overseas universities partnering with local Chinese universities to provide executive education in China (Hodge et al., 2019). In most cases, however, the teaching is delivered in one way, with professors from around the world teaching Chinese students in China. As a result, there are still only very few truly global programs catering to both local and international students in China. CEIBS is the only business school based in mainland China with a student base composed of, according to CEIBS admissions data, approximately 40 percent international students studying business in China in English.

Before 2015, CEIBS had already realized that simple management knowledge dissemination and general business skills training were not enough for business leaders to deal with the complexity and changes occurring at the global level, especially as China began taking on a more important role in the global economy. CEIBS was aware that it was essential to build a platform for students from the East and the West to further engage in effective communication in order to foster mutual understanding and build synergy between global and local perspectives to find common ground for business practices.

Based on this premise, CEIBS extended its operations to Zurich, Switzerland, and integrated its campus in Accra, Ghana, into its global campus network in 2015. These initiatives were guided by five imperatives: **cultivate a global mindset, embrace inclusiveness, increase multicultural awareness, connect China and the world, and exchange excellence.**

Although neither overseas campus offers full-time degree programs, they are hubs of international exchange that are able to host short-term programs and modules. European and African students are able to complete their global executive MBA (EMBA) degree modules in Zurich and Accra, in addition to learning together with their Chinese peers in Shanghai and many other global centers around the world. Meanwhile, study trips, exchange programs, alumni events, forums, and local company visits hosted in Zurich and Accra are in high demand. Such two-way communication has been truly appreciated by students and the entire CEIBS community. In order to accommodate the influx of students, CEIBS doubled the size of the Zurich campus in October 2019.

It turns out that understanding the type of infrastructure required to build and update will not only support the school's growth but also help it mitigate the risk of uncertainties such as the COVID-19 pandemic. CEIBS must connect China and the world by building an integrated global campus network. The links the school has established through its campuses have made it possible for it to continue operating despite travel restrictions. The next section highlights how CEIBS has reconnected students in China and overseas, both online and offline.

2. From "Managing the Shift to Online" to "Restarting Life on Campus"

Although once considered a short-term aberration, the pandemic has now forced nearly everyone to adapt. The long-lasting effects of the pandemic on education remain unclear, but what is certain is that it has accelerated the development of online learning. Almost every school in the world has experienced a sudden shutdown and has had to adapt to remote or hybrid learning.

Online learning is an appealing educational option because it offers flexibility and convenience and eliminates the limitations associated with face-to-face teaching. Students and professors may enjoy a borderless campus and its convenience, as well as easy access to school resources that were previously constrained by physical distance. Some short-time-frame, led-by-speech, or presentation-dominant activities and events can be easily replicated online. The CEIBS Executive Forum series, for example, has been reorganized as a hybrid online/offline event, increasing its potential audience to include students and alumni around the world, offering them the hitherto nonexistent opportunity to interact with renowned business leaders. As for continuing business education, online learning can increase its impact and enlarge its circle of influence (Gallagher and Palmer, 2020).

For executive education, however, online learning can be viewed as a supplementary option rather than as a complete substitute. Online instruction can go smoothly as long as the teaching content is well designed and the instructor is well prepared. However, the learning result of business education is a total package of personal transformation. Moreover, the development of soft skills, such as leadership, communication, and strategic thinking, requires a lot of human contact, interaction, and on-site instruction and coaching. This cannot be completely replicated online.

In my opinion, the biggest difference between online and offline formats is not the channel or teaching method but the learning mood and motivation. A leading concern among scholars is how to keep students motivated and engaged in online settings. Human beings are social by nature, and engagement during class time can vary significantly depending on whether it is a highly interactive, responsive, and peer-bonded environment or a mute, hidden, easy-to-escape room with a screen. Moreover, according to an education researcher in the UK, the longer a higher education institution can retain a student on campus and in an academic environment, the greater the student's chance for academic growth and success (Tight, 2019).

While some schools are trying a variety of education technology platforms, some are pushing back start dates, some are testing various return-to-school efforts (such as partial re-openings) or limiting the number of students allowed back on campus, some are accepting credits taken in other schools in other countries that offer offline courses, and some are collaborating with third-party vendors that provide offline studying facilities (such as WeWork) in order to provide as much offline campus life as possible in the face of subsequent COVID-19 waves.

However, in terms of business school internationalization, aggravating an already difficult situation are the drastic differences in the border-control policies of different countries.

Although business schools in China have had the advantage of being allowed to resume normal campus life since September 2020, they have still been forced to bear the consequences of draconian entry restrictions and border controls. As a result, even students with valid visas have not been able to enter the country. For CEIBS, these restrictions have compounded the effects of the pandemic because almost 40 percent of the participants in its MBA program are international students. The decision for CEIBS to shift teaching and learning, and even some student activities and forums, online was relatively easy. The toughest problem for the school was how to maintain its diversified student body and retain students who remained overseas and were unable to enter China.

When CEIBS reopened and resumed normal offline MBA teaching in Shanghai in May 2020, many students and professors who were able to return to campus stated that face-to-face teaching, learning, and socializing was the most valuable part of school life. For those who had experienced both formats, the biggest difference between online and classroom learning was the level of peer-to-peer interaction. After all, schools are not just a collection of buildings, tables, and technology. At their most fundamental level, schools are about relationships. Educational research has also shown that students are more likely to excel academically and socially if their school fosters positive relationships and makes each class an enjoyable place to learn (Roffey, 2012). Consequently, CEIBS has done (and will do) everything it can to resume face-to-face communication and life on campus as soon as possible. Travel restrictions, however, still leave the problem of foreign students unable to enter China unanswered. This has served as a catalyst for CEIBS to begin exploring the possibility of reopening its Zurich campus to cater to students stranded outside China.

Although this step was a first for CEIBS, the school decided that it was necessary to explore these uncharted waters. After all, MBAs are all about breaking through new frontiers, challenging existing boundaries, and exceeding personal ambition.

The next section describes how CEIBS has mobilized resources to leverage the potential of its global campus network to overcome the risks and limitations brought about by the pandemic.

3. The "Twin-City" Model

Between May and July 2020, CEIBS internally discussed the possibility of enrolling new MBA students at both its Shanghai and Zurich campuses. For the program to be delivered in tandem on both campuses safely and equitably, the school would need to (1) implement the same curriculum, (2) open simultaneously, and (3) maximize opportunities for students to interact and create bonds between them.

Delivering such an ambitious twin-city program spanning two continents posed significant challenges in terms of leadership and governance – and in terms of risk management, funding, human resources, and communications. Tremendous efforts were made in order to cope with the administrative and logistical obstacles. The CEIBS Zurich team, first, had to overcome the hurdle of travel permits for students coming to Switzerland, then enable student visa holders to study on campus, live in student residence, and have access to quarantine facilities where needed. Furthermore, staff members at the Zurich campus were accustomed to organizing short modules and therefore had to be trained to transit effectively to supporting degree programs. The Shanghai campus, on the other hand, faced the challenge of designing a curriculum that could accommodate different time zones and balance teaching and student activities while ensuring continuity. The list of challenges was almost endless.

Despite the huge difficulties, CEIBS believed that organizing the program across two campuses was feasible and worth the investment in time and effort. Following this twin-city principle, Shanghai and Zurich therefore simultaneously launched the 2020 MBA program for new students on October 12, 2020. To ensure that the 10 core modules of the first semester (which include Financial Accounting, Data Analytics, Organizational Behaviour, Microeconomics, and Marketing Management) contained the same content and were taught in the same way, a hybrid curriculum was designed, and five professors were flown to Zurich to teach. In this way, although it created a busy faculty schedule and called for some modules to be taught twice (i.e., once online for Zurich and again offline in Shanghai), student interactions and academic quality could be ensured. As a result, students not only had the chance to learn and interact with each other in their groups but also had the chance to complete collaborative projects across campuses. Moreover, 2 hours each day were devoted to extracurricular activities for students to participate in simultaneously in both Shanghai and Zurich.

As a result, 41 out of 156 students were able to study in Zurich, attend face-to-face classes, interact with their peers offline, participate in student clubs, and even visit Chinese companies in Zurich to learn more about China and Chinese business culture. School leadership was therefore confidently able to declare, "We firmly believe that in-person classroom discussions with diverse peers and world-class faculty represent one of the true cornerstones of a leading MBA experience" (CEIBS, 2021, p. 49). This statement was affirmed by Sourav Panda, a member of the CEIBS MBA 2022 cohort: "During the Leadership Module kick-off, we looked sideways by knowing more about the team, we looked outside when we looked for inspiration, and we looked within when we looked for self-awareness. In a short span, CEIBS taught us the 360-degree view of leadership" (CEIBS, n.d., Part III, para. 2).

Even though fresh obstacles appear as policies continue to shift, CEIBS has guaranteed a degree of continuity in its training by developing its twin-city model. It has been a tough but worthwhile mission, especially because there are no clear signs to indicate when travel restrictions will be lifted. CEIBS Zurich campus CEO Dr. Robert Straw aptly pointed out during the opening ceremony that the campus hosting MBAs for the first time was a good practical example of the concept of VUCA – volatility, uncertainty, complexity, and ambiguity – a new norm in the post–COVID-19 environment.

Although this project presented many hurdles, it also generated valuable new experiences and revealed some of the schools' hidden strengths. First, inclusiveness: this has always been nurtured as a core value at CEIBS, and it proved to be a vital ingredient in ensuring that all those working for CEIBS felt empowered to do their jobs in challenging conditions, instilling a deep sense of pride with every achievement. Second, CEIBS's alumni and partner network: many of CEIBS's plans would have been impossible without the generous financial support of CEIBS EMBA alumnus and Tencent cofounder Jason Zeng and the support of the Swiss authorities. Finally, the sense of belonging that faculty and staff feel toward CEIBS: the twin-city plan would not have been possible without the willingness of faculty members to spend 2 long months away from home, the proactive work of faculty members to explore innovative online teaching and collaboration tools and approaches, and the dedication of staff working overtime to support both online and offline courses.

In terms of business school internationalization, the twin-city model has created new possibilities in the field of international education: classes included students from 20 different nationalities, who were able to interact with each other and with faculty in a truly diverse and multicultural environment. Within the framework of the twin-city program, students were able to explore their potential and reach out to business communities around them to gain on-site experience with local business practices. Meanwhile, in accommodating each other across time zones, students were trained to be open-minded and became skilled in building inclusive and cohesive virtual teams. In sum, students in the twin-city program have been able to practice firsthand the new skills that companies in the postpandemic era will require to rebuild themselves, on the basis of a new corporate social contract founded on care, trust, solidarity, and fairness between colleagues. These new skills are no longer just important; they are game-changers, given the new challenges that still lie ahead in the post–COVID-19 era.

Although the twin-city model has offered a convenient solution in the face of travel restrictions and constitutes a useful compromise between balancing online teaching and some degree of real campus life, it is still a suboptimal solution. As vaccines are rolled out, travel bans will be lifted, allowing international travel and exchange to resume, and mobility will remain a key part of business education. This could spell the end of the twin-city model. In reality, however, this model exposes students to a unique form of international exchange that amplifies classroom learning through one-of-a-kind experiences and cultivates students' skills in global networking. As such, the twin-city model is likely to be developed on another level to leverage a broader academic and professional network, creating more hybrid opportunities for academic engagement; encouraging students to discuss, collaborate, compete, and celebrate with one another; and fostering more common values in a shared community.

Another key ingredient behind the success of the twin-city model is student enthusiasm. Indeed, why did these 156 applicants decide to sign up for a full-time MBA at CEIBS amid all the uncertainty? Many will talk about the influence of location, alumni networks, and students already enrolled in the program (Jack, 2020). Of course, each of these factors plays a role, but the *strategic priorities of the school make a bigger difference*. CEIBS's leitmotif, "China Depth, Global Breadth," holds the foresight that drives the establishment of a global campus network and underpins its capacity to deliver a twin-city model. So, the answer to the previous question, in short, is CEIBS's uniqueness in providing students with both a China focus and a global reach, as well as the most up-to-date business knowledge about China and the world.

In the wake of the pandemic, business schools will play an ever more critical role as a platform not only for fostering international exchange but also for global experts to identify, better understand, and tackle the challenges emerging from the crisis. The internationalization of business schools, therefore, also means that knowledge creation in a global context has to be aimed at educating and engaging students in an effective approach to navigating the crisis and emerging stronger.

The next section outlines how the international education agenda has been redefined and what business schools need to do to prepare for this new frontier in teaching and learning.

4. Knowledge Creation in a Global Context

Over the past several decades, leading business schools have developed certain immutable assets, including a **solid knowledge base** with consistent intellectual output, a **transnational perspective** to cultivating students into business leaders committed to improving the state of the world, and a **boundary-free community** with a secure and trusted environment for all stakeholders to interact and connect.

The year 2020 saw the emergence of a global pandemic against a backdrop of world instability. Geopolitical tensions have persisted as the COVID-19 virus continues to spread, laying bare relations between countries and altering people's perceptions about each other in a way that is likely to continue in the wake of the crisis. This context has given rise to two new challenges for business schools.

First and foremost, business schools need to have the capacity to ensure nondisrupted knowledge creation to pool professional recommendations on the COVID-19 response and offer a clearer picture of the risks and solutions. Second, as educators, business schools need to understand the consequences of the growing sophistication and complexity of the global economy and adjust their international education curriculums accordingly.

Knowledge creation depends on faculty productivity. Maintaining continuity in productivity during the pandemic has required greater use of technology to efficiently deploy faculty resources. It has also required motivation, a sense of urgency, and dedication to being an engaged partner in the business community. The success of any community or region in the postpandemic world will hinge on whether higher education institutions, the business community, and civic partners can join forces to address corporate/workforce needs and societal needs.

At CEIBS, numerous webinars, online forums, cloud sharings, and live broadcasting lectures were organized immediately after face-to-face teaching was suspended. A series of surveys and reports was conducted to explore the impact of the COVID-19 pandemic on business operations in China. Meanwhile, faculty members immediately joined ongoing efforts to explore possible solutions for restarting disrupted supply chains and to identify trends in digital transformation, new retail and leadership, workforce management, and more. A new emphasis on technology has generated the unexpected positive consequence of helping the school reach more people. For example, an online lecture series featuring CEIBS professors in the fields of macroeconomics, mergers and acquisitions, corporate governance, and digital marketing was live-streamed by multiple mainstream media in China and received up to 2 million page views per session.

CEIBS faculty also led the way for the business community in connecting the dots on best practices related to reopening businesses and fostering economic recovery. As the first country to be affected by the pandemic, China was on the front line in terms of the actual outbreak and again for the post–COVID-19 economic recovery and related societal changes brought about by the crisis. CEIBS professors cooperated closely with industry leaders in retail, e-commerce, logistics, remote medical care, and telemedicine, among others, to conduct extensive research to examine responses to the crisis and to show how the pandemic accelerated several preexisting trends (notably, digitization and the increasing caution and health consciousness of Chinese consumers). The proprietary insights generated will not only explain how China fared compared to other markets but also generate findings that may be transferable to companies elsewhere in the world, sharing insight and strategies learned for thriving in such a challenging environment.

CEIBS professor of strategy Chen Weiru has researched how digitization combined with a value for satisfying people's pursuit of truth, kindness, beauty, and love can help corporations achieve sustainable development, as reported in his talk at the CEIBS Insights 2020 Europe Forum on November 26, 2020. A new series of business cases is also being compiled. For example, AstraZeneca's patient-centric innovation solutions piloted in China have made medical consultation, treatment, and recovery more available in third- and fourth-tier cities (China Daily News, 2020). At the same time, Ping An, a Shenzhen-based insurance company, launched its COVID-19 smart image-reading system in early 2020 to assist doctors with fast and accurate diagnoses to help control the epidemic. Ping An's system can generate smart analysis results in about 15 seconds, with an accuracy rate above 90 percent. It was used 22.04 million times by approximately 413,000 doctors in the first half of 2020 (Ping An Group, 2020).

CEIBS is working hard to share these lessons and practices from China with other parts of the world through its global platform. Students, alumni, and others have been able to learn about these developments through the school's Service Excellence Forum (hosted by CEIBS in collaboration with École hôtelière de Lausanne [EHL]) or from the CEIBS Insights Europe Forum series, which made virtual "stops" in Switzerland, Germany, the UK, and France in 2020 and featured insights from both academics and business leaders.

The more complex the emerging trend, the more it can drive innovation. A new initiative has been explored to establish multi-/cross-disciplinary research areas at CEIBS. This initiative will allow faculty members from different disciplines to create more synergy with other fields and introduce step-change solutions by combining developments in business administration with input from other disciplines and stakeholders. We believe that agility and flexibility in multi-/cross-disciplinary research will play an important role in promoting a different international education curriculum for future business leaders.

The pandemic has thrown into question conventional beliefs about the traditional global order and undermined trust in multilateral organizations, as well as how we conduct international trade and investment and forge partnerships. Although the United Nations (UN), World Trade Organization (WTO), World Economic Forum (WEF), Organization for Economic Co-operation and Development (OECD), and other international organizations have tried to showcase the power of cooperation, the world still faces the four "huge challenges" described by UN secretary-general António Guterres – namely, "climate change, the mistrust of leaders, increased geopolitical tension and the dark side of the technological revolution" (Guterres, 2020, para. 1). Furthermore, the WTO has remained stuck in a stalemate. First, inclusive multilateralism is an urgent need. Second, vision and practices for responsible and adaptive corporate governance are needed in a more volatile, multiconceptual, and post–COVID-19 context. This means that universal management frameworks are neither adequate nor effective enough to ensure business continuity in the face of surging national and regional interests. The corporate world needs to adapt to nonuniversal, culturally different, geographically segmented, and demographically diverse national and regional markets.

Against this background, it is incumbent on business schools to ground their teaching in a solid and inclusive understanding and awareness of current geopolitical tensions. *Inclusive* in this context refers to respecting diversity and exercising impartiality, where diversity is embraced along with strong accountability, and fair competition is assured along with transparency. To be able to manage across countries in a post–COVID-19 global context, managers and executives should become experts in one or two specific business environments or at least understand the specificities of one or two markets. Only when the specificities are understood and acknowledged can value be created through inclusive collaboration and cooperation.

As such, business schools need to be clear about their focus and how they want to position themselves. To become an enabler of global economic recovery, business schools should create and deliver content with regional depth and a global perspective in order to equip business leaders with the necessary knowledge and skills to understand changing dynamics, navigate through crises, and emerge stronger.

In the case of CEIBS, its unique strategic positioning of China depth and global breadth has made it the top expert on China with a global perspective. In the past few years, CEIBS has established itself as a knowledge hub and attracted many Chinese and non-Chinese professors to deep dive in China. As academic professionals, they received extensive and rigorous research training from top universities before joining CEIBS. What they are contributing to the overall business management field includes not only their in-depth explanation of China's economic transition and Chinese business models and practices but also their insights on how the corporate world can better engage with China and how experiences and innovations from emerging markets like China can also be drawn upon for growth and sustainability elsewhere.

As mentioned earlier, because the pandemic began in China, it was the first to face the crisis, but it has also played a leading role in the post–COVID-19 economic recovery due to its resilience and economic growth. As CEIBS leadership has put it: "[T]he demand from multinationals to come to China has dramatically increased as China has changed from being perceived as merely a manufacturing base to a driver of profit" (Yuan Ding, as quoted in Murray, 2019, para. 6). As such, CEIBS is the window for the world on China: demystifying perceptions, offering an interpretation of the country's unique cultural fabric across its different regions, and revealing the patterns and drivers behind its economic success.

5. The Cornerstone of Internationalization

In the postpandemic era, international cooperation, rather than unilateralism, will be the only sure way to avoid the risk of an increase in retaliation and reprisals between countries. It is therefore incumbent on business school students and alumni who go on to become important members of the business community to enhance international cooperation. We need more business schools to act as a bridge between China, Europe, the United States, and the rest of the world, one that provides practical experience and raises awareness among students of the diversity among geographical regions and fosters people-to-people dialogue, school-to-school exchange and communication, and greater mutual understanding between corporations. We believe global trust will be built by those who reach out to form partnerships. This is the type of international ambition that business schools should aim to instill in their students, and it is also the cornerstone of internationalization as a foundation for a better future.

References

China Daily News. (2020, June 18). AstraZeneca pledges holistic disease management and supports Chinese medicines. *China Daily.* https://global.chinadaily.com.cn/a/202006/18/WS5eeac14ea310834817253d16_1.html.

China Europe International Business School. (n.d.). *With love, from CEIBS Zurich.* https://europe.ceibs.edu/mba/student-life/19810.

(2021). Innovative response to pandemic sees Zurich campus host MBAs for first time. *TheLINK*, 1, 49. www.ceibs.edu/sites/portal.prod.dpmgr.ceibs.edu/files/import_images/pdf/thelink/50-51_4.pdf.

Gallagher, S., and Palmer, J. (2020). The pandemic pushed universities online. The change was long overdue. *Harvard Business Review.* https://hbr.org/2020/09/the-pandemic-pushed-universities-online-the-change-was-long-overdue.

Guterres, A. (2020, January 24). *Uncertainty and instability: The world in two words, says UN secretary-general.* World Economic Forum Annual Meeting 2020 News Release. www.weforum.org/press/2020/01/uncertainty-and-instability-the-world-in-two-words-says-un-secretary-general/.

Hodge, K., Garthwaite, A., and Chan, W. K. (2019, November 11). Asian business schools: Key data for prospective students. *Financial Times.* www.ft.com/content/8fcf8f0c-015e-11ea-b7bc-f3fa4e77dd47.

Jack, A. (2020, November 12). Answers to reader questions: "Should I study business in Asia?" *Financial Times.* www.ft.com/content/07fe57d1-e194-402c-a343-39df7b594cec.

Moules, J. (2020, November 11). Demand for MBAs rebounds amid economic crisis. *Financial Times.* www.ft.com/content/8c95a02d-f2a7-4dd7-be3c-08d0771a372c.

Murray, S. (2019, December 8). East meets West: China's business schools look to Europe. *Financial Times.* www.ft.com/content/a50a87b8-0c7c-11ea-8fb7-8fcec0c3b0f9.

Ping An Group. (2020, August 13). *Technology empowers Ping An's health care amid coronavirus.* https://group.pingan.com/media/news/News-2020/Technology-Empowers-Ping-An-s-Health-Care-Amid-Coronavirus.html.

Roffey, S., ed. (2012). *Positive relationships: Evidence-based practice across the world.* Springer.

Tight, M. (2019). Student retention and engagement in higher education. *Journal of Further and Higher Education,* 44(5), 689–704.

11 | The Face of Business Education in Africa Post–COVID-19: Gain or Loss?

ENASE OKONEDO

Introduction

On February 14, 2020, the first case of COVID-19 in Africa was recorded in Egypt, North Africa (World Health Organization [WHO], 2020), and by May 13, 2020, the virus had spread through all 54 sovereign African states. Following this, similar to countries in other parts of the world, almost all countries on the continent established measures aimed at curbing the spread of the virus. These included the closure of land borders, flight cancellations, travel restrictions, and school shutdowns that affected universities as well as business schools. Only a few business schools on the continent were able to transit seamlessly to online teaching as a result of several factors, which are discussed later in the chapter. For the majority, there were major disruptions to their activities as teaching effectively stopped, with negative implications both for the learners and the schools concerned. In this chapter, I discuss the impact of the COVID-19 crisis on business schools in Africa, the challenges faced by business schools, the risks and opportunities arising from the crisis, and the changes that have to occur in business schools across Africa for them to remain relevant.

Business and Management Education in Africa

Formal business education in Africa can be described as relatively recent because the predominant form by which skills for running businesses were acquired was through informal apprenticeship long established as an indigenous management practice or learning on the job. The first business school was established in the University of Pretoria, South Africa, in 1949, but across the continent, very few emerged following this until the late 1980s to early 1990s. During this period, several business schools were established across different regions in Africa, most within universities but a few others as stand-

233

alone business schools. By the 2010s, more business schools were being established, bringing the number of business schools on the continent to 144. The reasons for the establishment of these business schools were mainly to prepare managers for (1) the growing number of multinationals expanding into Africa following the global financial crisis of 2008/2009, which saw most countries in the developed world in a recession, and (2) the growth of numerous entrepreneurial ventures established across the continent spurred by a number of factors, including a strong entrepreneurial spirit among young Africans, a large and accessible market even within countries, and high unemployment levels. Howard Thomas, in his article "Management Education out of Africa," states that business schools exist in several countries across Africa in different forms – state-owned and private; stand-alone business schools and schools within universities offering business and management education with traceable unique cultural practices, contexts, and values that often shape their different curricula (Thomas, 2017). This remained true at the onset of the COVID-19 crisis in 2020, when there were numerous schools on the continent – mostly African business schools but also a couple of offshoots of foreign universities.

I would classify the business schools on the continent into three broad categories: first-tier, second-tier, and third-tier business schools.

First-Tier Business Schools

Business schools in the first-tier category aspire to be global schools, and in terms of their operations and programs, they are similar to well-developed business schools that have a longer history of operations. There are a good number of such schools in South Africa and others interspersed in countries such as Nigeria, Kenya, Egypt, and Morocco in North Africa.

These schools have achieved or are in the process of achieving global accreditations, which are the hallmark of well-established schools in the developed world; seek collaborations with top global business schools; aspire to attract international faculty as well as international students; and are deemed leading schools in their home countries. Prior to 2006, there were no African business schools accredited by the Association to Advance Collegiate Schools of Business (AACSB) International, and only one institution had obtained accreditation from the Association of MBAs (AMBA) and the EFMD Quality

Improvement System (EQUIS), the three of which form the top 3 global accrediting bodies. By 2020, the number of schools accredited by top global bodies had increased to 12, with 7 having two such accreditations (AACSB and AMBA) and 3 business schools achieving triple accreditations (AMBA, AACSB, and EQUIS). First-tier business schools are typically financially autonomous or semiautonomous and are usually independent of parent institutions in making decisions (Okonedo and Aluko, 2016).

Second-Tier Business Schools

Schools in the second-tier category are focused on developing managers and executives within their home countries. Typically, these schools are not financially autonomous and exist as part of schools of management or business within universities. Students and faculty in this category of schools are predominantly drawn from the home countries, and there is little or no effort given to attracting international students. Some of the schools in this category have aspirations to attain global accreditations in the medium to long term (Okonedo and Aluko, 2016).

Third-Tier Business Schools

Often referred to as the local majority, schools in the third-tier category serve local communities and exist within universities. They offer degrees in business, but many of the faculty members do not possess doctorate degrees, and the schools do not have independence in decision making. Students are almost exclusively from the home country because the focus is on preparing students to work in their respective domestic markets.

I will refer to the first-tier category as the "global few" and the second and third-tier categories as the "local plenty." Collectively, though, these business schools provide management education to students within the continent, many of whom remain within the continent upon completion of their degree programs. There are also concerns about the number of managers being developed within these schools compared to the needs of the continent, as well as the adequacy of the curriculum to address the needs of the continent. According to a qualitative survey conducted by the African Management Initiative

(2016), only a minority of African managers at low and mid-levels are well trained. Participants in the study, which comprised educators, large businesses, nongovernmental organizations (NGOs), training providers, and consultants from across Africa, highlighted poor management and a disconnect between theory and on-the-job practice as common.

The Impact of COVID-19 on Business Education in Africa

Typically, participants enroll in business schools to acquire more knowledge to function effectively as managers and executives within corporations, to effectively run their own businesses, or to attain higher degrees for career mobility.

Business schools in Africa have existed over the years with no major disruption in the sector, unlike in the United States and other developed nations, where the global financial crisis of 2008/2009 disrupted the sector and called business schools' curricula into question, given that a number of the principal actors who had a role in the lead-up to the crisis were graduates from top business schools in these countries. The COVID-19 crisis, however, was a major disruptor to the business education sector not only globally but in Africa as well.

Globally, the closure of schools across 184 countries has sent 1.5 billion students home, and this is equivalent to 87.6 percent of the world's students (Education Cannot Wait, 2020). In Africa, a 2020 survey conducted by the Mazawo Institute revealed that 72.5 percent of respondents reported interruptions in their research activities (Bayusuf et al., 2021). This is attributable to school closures, implying that only those schools that had the technology infrastructure in place were able to move programs online and continue classes.

I would classify the impact of the COVID-19 crisis on business schools under the following:

1. Limitations in access to learning
2. Increased competition
3. Effects on delivery mode
4. Faculty/Other staff limitations in the use of technology
5. Curriculum
6. Others

Limitations in Access to Learning

Almost all the first-tier schools moved, albeit at varying speeds, to adopt a combination of online and in-person instruction because prior to the pandemic, these schools had integrated digital learning into their delivery model. There were, however, challenges in some countries, even among the first-tier schools, as students were unable to access online learning as a result of limited bandwidth and connectivity, lack of access to electricity, and the high cost of data. Africa's internet penetration at the end of 2019 was 26 percent, well below the global average of 59 percent (GSM Association, 2019).

Among the other categories of business schools – second and third tier – activities were stifled by the unpreparedness of these institutions and the lack of technological infrastructure, which may be connected with inadequate funding because many of the schools get government subventions. These funding sources were affected as many countries in Africa grappled with dwindling revenues as a result of the COVID-19 crisis. In several countries, allocations to universities and publicly funded business schools were reduced. In Kenya, for example, funding to public universities was slashed in advance by $400 million for the new financial year, which was to begin on July 1, 2020, necessitated by the effects of the COVID-19 pandemic on the East African economy; this cut university allocations to $1.13 billion, versus the intended $1.53 billion that the government planned to spend on institutions earlier in the year (Nganga, 2020).

In other instances, cultural norms relating to female students being primarily responsible for domestic chores while at home affected their participation and adoption of online learning. Other problems, such as income reduction and job losses as a result of the pandemic, also contributed to students' inability to continue their learning programs.

Increased Competition

Prior to the COVID-19 crisis, the providers of business education were predominantly business schools in Africa. For the first-tier category of business schools providing degree programs and executive education courses, competition included foreign business schools because corporations often sponsor the programs. For second- and third-tier schools, which typically offer degree programs and are not active in the executive education sector, competition was limited to other local universities. With the COVID-19 crisis and the exponential increase in online courses being offered by a variety of learning providers, including tech companies, universities, and consulting companies, among others, the competition changed almost overnight to include all.

In the wake of the COVID-19 pandemic, massive open online courses (MOOCs) have increased exponentially since March 2020. Coursera, edX, and FutureLearn, which were the top 3 MOOC providers, registered more users in April 2020 than in the entire 2019, with total users of 20 million, 8 million, and 4 million people, respectively (Shah, 2020). The courses that had the most engagements were Personal Development (167,000), Business (167,000), Art and Design (117,000), and Management and Leadership (115,000) (Shah, 2020). And of the many geographical locations, the following were the top 3 cities: Bangkok (Thailand), Lagos (Nigeria), and Mumbai (India) (Shah, 2020). There is also the Quantic MBA, which has been accredited by the Distance Education Accrediting Commission. This program can be completed in 11 months, comes at no cost, and is typically completed by students who pass through three different admission stages. The program is funded by companies, which pay to hire graduating students through Quantic's career network (Shah, 2020).

In June 2020, Microsoft made public its vision to upskill 25 million people across the globe before the end of March 2021 (Smith, 2020). In the Middle East and Africa (MEA), an estimated 900,000 learners have engaged with one of the 10 learning paths that include software development, sales, project management, information technology (IT), customer service, digital market, IT support, data analytics, finance, and graphics design, which are statistically proven to have the greatest number of job openings globally, pay a livable wage, and require skills that can be learned online (Microsoft News Centre, 2020). All of these opportunities have sprung up because of the education and skill deficits made evident by the COVID-19 pandemic, and together, they pose stiff competition to traditional business schools in Africa.

Furthermore, as a result of the COVID-19 pandemic, with visa and travel restrictions and the overall need for safety, the number of international applications to first-tier schools in Africa has been greatly affected. With the massive offering of online courses, competition is no longer limited to providers within the region because students can assess learning from any of the global providers.

Effects on Delivery Modes

Many business schools all over the world adapted online modules for their students, and this may continue beyond the pandemic. Institutions are turning to blended-delivery alternatives, with providers also seeking to reduce the adverse effects of the pandemic by making admission schedules more flexible. However, an effect of these online trends could be the huge financial implications. For example, if a top global school offers a fully online MBA program and any of the first-tier business schools in Africa has a similar offering with costs in the same range, there is a high likelihood that students will go for the global brand. Business schools in Africa therefore need a clear value proposition to attract prospective students to such programs, failing which, the revenues will be affected.

Faculty/Other Staff Limitations in the Use of Technology

Earlier, I had alluded to the issue of funding in business schools, especially those dependent on government funding. With learning expected to be delivered online or using a blended format, such schools may lack adequate funding to adapt technology in their delivery modes. In addition, faculty not versed in the use of technology will have to be trained and must embrace the use of technology in delivery. With constraints on funding, this may prove difficult for many schools to do. A change in business model may be necessary to diversify funding sources. The adoption of technology could also be advantageous to schools that wish to recruit international faculty to teach or collaborate on research, projects, and programs.

Curriculum

The curricula of schools in the region were largely similar to those of leading business schools, covering the various functional areas of business and management. Often, these were nuanced with any peculiarities in the local environment. After the global financial crisis, when business education was disrupted in some regions of the world, almost all business schools began to include courses in ethics, sustainability, and corporate governance in their curricula and course requirements.

The COVID-19 crisis, however, has brought to the fore questions about what is being taught in business schools, the relevance to the world of today, and its ability to prepare students for the world in the future. Key areas that business schools, especially those in Africa, have to grapple with are risk management, globalization, and the concept of shareholder value maximization.

Managers being prepared for work in organizations operating in Africa need to have, in addition to other skills, keen risk-management capabilities, given the risks and uncertainties in the operating environment. The COVID-19 crisis highlighted the absence of a risk-management framework in many organizations, with business continuity being threatened in many businesses that were unprepared and whose business model was not suited to cope with the situation. Risk management, scenario planning, and business continuity, especially in an emerging-market context, are things that students preparing for the world of business today and in the future have to learn. In addition, as the pandemic caused a disruption in global supply chains as a result of measures taken by governments to stem the spread of the virus, Africa's imports and exports were projected to decline by 16 percent and 8 percent for 2020 (World Trade Organization [WTO], 2020). The whole concept of globalization, long taught in business schools around the world, is being reexamined. Should this be a concept that should be taught in business schools in Africa, given that the effects of global disruption had a manifold impact on companies and countries in Africa, especially those with a heavy reliance on imported goods? For example, Nigeria's value of imports, initially pegged at NGN 1.86 trillion as of January 2020, dropped to NGN 1.13 trillion in March as a result of the pandemic (PricewaterhouseCoopers, 2020). This indicates that there is a need to shift from globalization to domestication. As more countries in the developed world are tending away from globalization to domestication, what should be included in the curriculum? The challenges for business schools now include determining what should be taught to prepare students for a fast-changing world affected by global issues such as the COVID-19 pandemic.

A look at the business school curricula across the first-tier business schools in Africa shows that the key competencies and skills required by managers and employers are still not being taught. Courses such as sustainability and social responsibility, problem solving in structured and unstructured environments, and business analytics do not feature prominently in the curriculum. According to the World Economic Forum (WEF, 2020), the top skills required by employers in the wake of the pandemic are complex problem solving, critical thinking, creativity, emotional intelligence, people management, and so forth. Business schools in Africa should therefore integrate these courses into their respective curricula in addition to courses on ethics and sustainability, which will ensure that students are completely grounded in business technicalities and ethics.

Agility of Business Schools

There needs to be a reflection on how the business models of our schools have to change and how we can build structures that are adaptable to changes in consumer behavior and patterns caused by crises. According to the 2021 African Economic Outlook (African Development Bank, 2021), the real gross domestic product (GDP) of Africa shrank by 2.1 percent in 2020 as a result of the COVID-19 pandemic, culminating in the region's first recession in 25 years. The real GDP of Africa has, however, been forecasted to increase by 3.4 percent in 2021 (African Development Bank, 2021, p. 1). Through customized and executive education offerings, business schools can play a role in affecting business executives.

Future of Business Education in Africa

As we have seen earlier, reports alluded to the African economy making a rebound in 2021. In the interim, however, the decline in African economies affected many businesses, including small to medium enterprises and large businesses, as well as student enrollment, business school funding, and curricula, and as a result, these events should ideally lead to a reorganization of business schools.

In Africa, the pandemic also provides opportunities for businesses to commit to a low-carbon economy transition as issues of climate change have become increasingly important. By paying more attention to sustainability themes in their curricula, business schools can help participants identify potential opportunities in achieving a low-carbon economy. These schools can build more collaborations with environmental agencies in order to improve the learning experience of participants and to ensure that participants are fully prepared for the realities of the world. Overall, these actions tie into the ongoing discussions of purpose in business schools. "Purpose should not be mundane, neither should it be aspirational. It is not completely descriptive of the operations of a business or unrealistic of what the business seeks to do. It is about problem solving in order to produce profitable but lasting solutions to people and planetary problems, and not to profit from creating problems for people or planet" (Mayer, 2021, p. 888).

Conclusion

As a result of the COVID-19 crisis, business schools in Africa are facing a number of challenges, as discussed in this chapter. Consideration must be given to what has to change systematically to facilitate access to learning and develop managers who will contribute to not only the economic but also the social development of Africa. Despite these challenges, the crisis has brought forward opportunities for schools across Africa to consider their strategies with respect to their markets, their student and faculty recruitment, curricula, and partnerships in order to thrive.

Partnerships

Business schools have to consider the mode of delivery, and where online teaching is a big part of the delivery, careful thought has to be given to affordability for both the schools and the students. On the part of the schools, innovation in product offerings could be an opportunity for increased and diversified revenues that could go toward investment in technology. Partnerships could be sought with collaborators such as technology companies and other bodies to facilitate online teaching and learning. Where internet connectivity may pose barriers, what can business schools do? Overall, there is a call to work on partnerships that enable the provision of tools and the provision of bandwidth at reduced costs for institutions. For those schools that hitherto invested in brick-and-mortar resources, perhaps a shift to investment in technology may be well suited to the postpandemic era. The biggest impact and differentiator may be in those schools that invest in technology and are able to deliver education using a blended approach.

But it goes beyond acquiring the tools; from the decision makers in the school to the faculty and, in some cases, the students, the change from traditional classrooms to blended or fully virtual classrooms and learning requires a change in mindset to be embraced. Although the pandemic has accelerated the adoption of technology, there must be a concerted move to upskill faculty for virtual teaching and interaction. For the students, there has to be a change in mindset so that they can learn independently and see on-campus experience more as a way to foster interaction and networking rather than the only place learning can be achieved.

Collaboration

The COVID-19 crisis has heightened the awareness that schools in Africa have to work to attain world-class standards and relevance in their respective countries in order to attract potential students, many of whom now have a wider choice of institutions – local and international – that offer what they seek. Business schools, especially the second- and third-tier schools, may have to consider collaboration with other institutions – both within and outside Africa – to complement their strengths, as well as stronger interaction and partnerships with industry, not only to understand what skills employers are seeking in order to shape their curricula but also to improve job prospects for their graduates.

Regarding curricula, business school theories on shareholder capitalism may not be effective in the wake of COVID-19. In Africa, where income inequalities are high, should there be a different emphasis on a more inclusive society and how to achieve this? What has to change or be included in the curriculum to achieve this change in mindset? With the COVID-19 crisis, issues such as health-care provision and funding, inequalities in society, and access to learning being affected by income inequalities have highlighted the need for teaching in business schools to go beyond theories that focus on shareholder value maximization and emphasize managers' responsibilities to a broader group of stakeholders.

Especially in Africa, the need for high-level collaboration between governments, corporations, and citizens to achieve a more inclusive society has come to the fore. Business schools have to rethink their part in making this happen and should see their role as going beyond imparting function-specific knowledge to contributing in a broader way to the development of society.

Rankings

In terms of ranking, perhaps it is time business schools in Africa give careful consideration to which particular rankings are relevant in the environment and which ones enable schools to contribute to not only the personal development of the student but also society as a whole, in addition to the economic development of the individual countries. It may be that for second- and third-tier schools that have no aspiration to be global, a focus on rankings that measure societal impact and sustainability may influence the curriculum, create awareness in students, and serve as a call to action. Such a focus could also influence the research being done in business schools that speaks to these issues in developing- or emerging-market contexts in order to uncover insights that students can learn from and embody in their management practices.

Competition

Increasingly, with education being offered by a variety of providers with attractive value propositions to learners, business schools have to address the issue of how to deal with enrollment in the face of increased competition. The value and distinctiveness of a business education and what business schools offer must be clear. The challenge for business schools in Africa may be achieving this distinctiveness in order to communicate the value to prospective students and employers. The challenge may well be, though, that in the face of reduced employment opportunities brought on by the COVID-19 crisis, business schools have to consider what can be done to persuade students to invest in a long-term degree rather than the free courses widely available from a variety of providers.

African business schools have to be able to adapt to counter the rising threats and take advantage of emerging opportunities. In doing so, the skills of agility and nimbleness will be required. In addition, a new look at the business model is required, with consideration being given to the physical and technological infrastructure, faculty mix, and student learning. In doing this, business schools in Africa have to be ever mindful of what students are being trained for – function-specific knowledge for now or skills to thrive in an ever-changing, uncertain world of business?

References

African Development Bank. (2021). *African economic outlook 2021: From debt resolution to growth: The road ahead for Africa.* www.afdb.org/en/documents/african-economic-outlook-2021.

African Management Initiative. (2016). *Catalysing management development in Africa, identifying areas of impact.* http://gbsn.org/wp-content/uploads/2016/04/AMI_interim_report_.pdf.

Bayusuf, H., Hammouda, I., Vilakazi, Z. Z., Canavan, C. R., and Fawzi, W. W. (2021, February 20). Reasons to be optimistic about sub-Saharan HE after COVID. *University World News.* www.universityworldnews.com/post.php?story=20210216103536969.

Education Cannot Wait. (2020). *COVID-19 and education in emergencies.* www.educationcannotwait.org/covid-19/.

GSM Association. (2019). *Connected society: The state of mobile internet connectivity report.* www.gsma.com/r/wp-content/uploads/2020/09/GSMA-State-of-Mobile-Internet-Connectivity-Report-2020.pdf.

Mayer, C. (2021, May). The future of the corporation and the economics of purpose. *Journal of Management Studies*, 58(3), 887–901.

Microsoft News Centre. (2020, November 12). *Nearly a million people in the Middle East and Africa have embarked on a skilling journey with Microsoft.* https://news.microsoft.com/en-xm/2020/11/12/nearly-a-million-people-in-the-middle-east-and-africa-have-embarked-on-a-skilling-journey-with-microsoft/?ocid=FY21_soc_omc_br_tw_MEA_Skills.

Nganga, G. (2020, June 11). Government cuts universities' budget by 26%. *University World News.* www.universityworldnews.com/post.php?story=20200610144752328.

Okonedo, E., and Aluko, T. (2016). The role of accreditation in overcoming the challenges of graduate management programs in Africa. In H. Kazeroony, ed., *Sustainable management development in Africa: Building capabilities to serve African organizations.* Routledge, pp. 64–90.

PricewaterhouseCoopers. (2020). *Impact of COVID-19 on the supply chain industry.* www.pwc.com/ng/en/assets/pdf/impact-of-covid19-the-supply-chain-industry.pdf.

Shah, D. (2020, August 16). *By the numbers: MOOCs during the pandemic.* Class Central. https://www.classcentral.com/report/mooc-stats-pan demic/.

Smith, B. (2020, June 30). *Microsoft launches initiative to help 25 million people worldwide acquire the digital skills needed in a COVID-19 economy.* Official Microsoft Blog. https://blogs.microsoft.com/blog/ 2020/06/30/microsoft-launches-initiative-to-help-25-million-people-world wide-acquire-the-digital-skills-needed-in-a-covid-19-economy/.

Thomas, H. (2017). Management education out of Africa. *Asian Management Insights,* 4(1), 68–75.

World Economic Forum. (2020, October). *The future of jobs report.* www3 .weforum.org/docs/WEF_Future_of_Jobs_2020.pdf.

World Health Organization. (2020, April 7). *COVID-19 cases top 10,000 in Africa.* www.afro.who.int/news/covid-19-cases-top-10-000-africa.

World Trade Organization. (2020, April 8). *Trade set to plunge as COVID-19 pandemic upends global economy* [Press release]. www.wto.org/ english/news_e/pres20_e/pr855_e.htm.

12 | Creating a New Major Business School in the Times of COVID-19: The HSE-Moscow Way

VALERY S. KATKALO[1]

Robert K. Yin has written in a reference book that "case studies are the preferred strategy when, 'how' or 'why' questions are being asked. When the investigators have little control over events, and when the focus is on contemporary phenomenon within some real-life context" (Yin, 1994, p. 1). When the European Foundation for Management Development (EFMD) asked me to write a crisis-management chapter on the issues involved in the strategy of business schools in order to cope with the consequences of COVID-19, I decided to focus on a particular issue to which my professional practice brings me daily, namely, the leadership of a newborn management education institution. Indeed, it seems to me that these two fields of crisis management and of launching an academic institution have in common, in an exacerbated way, to use Yin's formula, the fact that they constitute fields in which "the investigators have little control over events" and are examples of a "contemporary phenomenon." In addition, the aim of my chapter is to detail the rationale for the project and describe how our schools faced the challenge of the COVID-19 crisis – in other words, the "how" and "why" questions. Therefore, structuring this chapter around a case study was an obvious choice.

In the recent decades, it became almost an axiom that any major university recognized as a champion in the national system of higher education – and especially one that is striving to become globally competitive – already has or is in the process of creating an in-house business school (sometimes as a school of economics and management). The drivers for this trend include the growth of the management profession in modern society; the maturation of management research as a recognized member of the university academic community; the

[1] Professor Valery S. Katkalo is the first vice rector of lifelong learning at the Higher School of Economics (HSE University) and the dean of HSE Graduate School of Business. He can be reached at vkatkalo@hse.ru.

need for developing entrepreneurial and innovation potential at the so-called *third-generation university*,[2] which is now the model for almost any top university; and a solid revenue stream generated by a b-school and CEOs among its alumni as an important addition to resource base for a university's strategic aspirations. All these arguments were considered in the late 2010s by the National Research University Higher School of Economics (HSE), Moscow – quite young (est. 1992) but already one of the top 3 Russian universities – in making principal decisions about creating a world-class business school at HSE as one of the key strategic initiatives in its 2030 Development Plan.

Creating a new business school inside an established university is always a challenge because of the need for semiautonomous governance and a much more entrepreneurial style in running a successful b-school as compared with the related administrative features at its other academic units. In the HSE case, on top of that, there were such challenges for the project in question as the need for turning around an existing old-fashioned and very fragmented system of business education at HSE, as well as the need to develop and execute a strategy for catching up with the leading Russian b-schools in the era of the Fourth Industrial Revolution, with its revolutionizing impact on management development in all its aspects. Although these challenges were well recognized, the COVID-19 pandemic has radically disrupted the context in which the new b-school was to start and progress. However, if one is in the business of developing new business leaders, then the more adventurous is the road toward ambitious goals, and the more exciting and inspiring is the venture of creating a new university-based b-school via creative destructions and leadership.

This chapter is organized into five sections. In the first section, the internal and external contexts for the new HSE b-school, the related university reorganization, and the key challenges for this project in the COVID-19 era are addressed. In the second section, the related changes in the business program portfolio and innovations in learning are discussed. The third section is dedicated to the new faculty policies and actions, whereas the fourth section covers the creation of the b-school's corporate ecosystem, including its operational, cultural, and business-model aspects. All these themes are examined with

---

[2] A detailed conceptualization of the third-generation university is provided in the work of Wissema (2009).

respect to an innovative approach and nonorganic growth strategy undertaken for successful implementation of the HSE b-school project in the times of COVID-19. This analysis is concluded in the fifth section with a summary of the lessons learned during the first year of this project and the vision for the road ahead in developing the HSE Graduate School of Business as an institution of international caliber.

1. The Context for a New B-School Project: Strategic Intent and COVID-19 Shocks

The unprecedented-for-Russia history of HSE University – which was built from scratch in late 1992 and in less than 30 years became one of the top 3 in the country and a globally highly recognized research university – is self-explanatory for the credibility of its ambition to create a world-class business school. The HSE was established by the Ministry of Economic Affairs of Russia on November 27, 1992, in Moscow as a public university, which initially was a small boutique institution for master in economics programs, designed in accordance with international standards and aiming to train a new generation of economists in support of Russian market reforms.[3] Soon after that, a partnership with the London School of Economics (LSE) was created, which resulted in 25+ years of a very successful – still flagship for HSE – double-degree bachelor (and later also master) program in

---

[3] Almost at the same time and with a similar mission, the Graduate School of Management (GSOM) was founded on January 25, 1993, at St. Petersburg State University as an alternative to its slowly reforming Faculty of Economics. Among the key factors for GSOM's success were the strategic partnership with Haas School of Business at the University of California, Berkeley (UC Berkeley) and the first-in-Russia international Advisory Board, chaired for its initial 10 years by John E. Pepper, CEO of Procter & Gamble. The Advisory Board has orchestrated a fundraising campaign (pioneering for Russia) for the renovation of a historical complex in downtown St. Petersburg to support GSOM growth. In 1999, GSOM launched the first-in-Russia fully English-language master in international business; in 2006, it became a Russian CEMS and Partnership in International Management (PIM) member and was selected by the Russian government to become part of the National Priority Project in Education. After receiving EFMD Programme Accreditation System (EPAS) and Association of MBAs (AMBA) accreditations, GSOM achieved EFMD Quality Improvement System (EQUIS) accreditation in 2012 – the first key international institutional accreditation for a Russian b-school. Today, the professional roads of the founders of HSE and GSOM (who collaborated since the early 1990s) have come together – several GSOM veterans are now leading the newborn HSE Graduate School of Business.

economics. In the 1990s, other additions to the HSE portfolio included programs in sociology, management (with a separate program in logistics), and later, law and political science. By the early 2000s, HSE became the prime socioeconomic university in Russia, widely respected for its dedication to the highest bar in the quality of education and continuous innovations in learning as integral elements of its DNA, and for the advanced expertise in socioeconomic reforms and policy-making that it provided for the Russian federal and regional authorities. In the 2000s, at its second evolutionary stage, HSE expanded (now also with regional campuses in such key cities as St. Petersburg, Nizhnyi Novgorod, and Perm), mostly in the socioeconomic areas, but it also pioneered in Russia some multidisciplinary areas, such as business informatics. Also, during its second decade, HSE was granted the status of a National Research University.

The third and strategically new stage in HSE's dynamic growth started in 2013 when it began to participate (among 21 other winners in an open competition of development plans) in the Russian Universities Global Competitiveness Project, also known as "5-100" because of the decree of President Putin that formulated a goal of bringing five Russian universities into the top 100 of global university rankings by 2020.[4] Although it initially seemed that HSE could potentially follow the model of LSE or Science Po as the only two institutions with a socioeconomic profile in these rankings, it soon became evident that a more realistic proposition would be to reshape HSE toward a multidisciplinary university. By the late 2010s, as a result of launches of new schools and departments in natural sciences, as well as the creation of a major Faculty of Computer Sciences and the development of other new areas (i.e., arts, communications, and design), HSE became a "Higher School of Everything" and repositioned itself internationally and domestically as "HSE University." These expansions – supported by a set of innovative faculty policies and organized research

---

[4] By the design of the 5-100 Project, the two oldest (established in the eighteenth century) and top Russian universities – Lomonosov Moscow State and St. Petersburg State – did not take part in it. In July 2013, the author of this chapter participated in the selection sessions of the International Expert Board of the 5-100 Project and witnessed the powerful presentation of the HSE development plan, which was competing only with those from the top 2 technical universities and was far ahead of other Russian universities regarding visions and action plans for achieving global competitiveness.

initiatives – resulted, by 2021, in dramatic growth of the student body (up to 50,000 in four campuses) and in radical progress in research output, with 70 percent of HSE faculty now publishing in international peer-reviewed journals as compared with 15 percent a decade earlier.

Evidently, such dynamic growth in scale and scope could not have been achieved organically and resulted mainly from bringing in teams of top scholars from the Russian Academy of Sciences and other leading universities, as well as through recruiting in the international job markets. The strong HSE brand – not only in academic circles but also in society at large, and increasingly beyond Russia – combined with a great executive team and unique organizational culture that fosters advanced studies and a spirit of innovation, along with its appetite for leadership in the profession and ambitious strategic goals, were among the key factors attracting the best talent in many fields. In addition to special government funding from the 5-100 Project, the creation of a Board of Trustees with a number of prominent Russian business leaders (led by German Gref, chairman and president of Sberbank), an HSE endowment fund, and an Alumni Association were instrumental in supporting this growth of human capital at HSE.

By the late 2010s, HSE had gotten into the top 50 and top 100 in Quacquarelli Symonds (QS) subject-matter world rankings (primarily for Sociology, Politics and International Studies, Economics, Education, and Mathematics), and in 2020, it became the second Russian university, after Lomonosov Moscow State, in terms of the number of positions (10) in the top 100 of these rankings (number 1 among other participants in the 5-100 Project), along with number 1 in Russia in 10 subjects; additionally, in 9 subjects, it is the only Russian representative in the world rankings. In the "QS – Top 50 under 50," HSE is ranked 31st among the best young universities globally. The HSE subject "Business & Management Studies" was only 131st in the QS (although number 1 in Russia) and largely deserved it as a result of contributions by scholars from departments and research units in economics, sociology, and others besides the business management area. This status reflected quite well the almost peripheral status of the business management area at HSE, despite its more than 20-year history at this university. In ShanghaiRanking's 2020 Global Ranking of Academic Subjects, HSE had positions of 101–150 for Political Sciences and for Mathematics, but only

301–400 for Business Administration and 401–500 for Management (number 2 in Russia here).

The gap between the caliber of the business management area at HSE and the fast-growing overall reputation of the university was steadily widening in the 2000s–2010s, thus limiting the ability of HSE to become a leader in the maturing Russian management education industry.[5] Among the reasons for that, on the one hand, was the lack of knowledge about the foundations of a modern business school, which resulted in a certain neglect of management research in developing this area as compared with academically "more serious" fields, such as economics or sociology, and low maturity of relations with business (without even a career center) and alumni at the Faculty of Business and Management (FBM) and a lack of internationalization of education, research, and faculty here. On the other hand, even more dramatic effects created systemic fragmentation of the business management area at HSE in three key aspects: (a) between university programs (bachelor, master, and doctoral – all at FBM) and continuous education (retraining, MBA, and some executive education [ExecEd] – all at other university units, specialized on this level of education); (b) between multiple units of continuous business education, the so-called "HSE business schools," which were 16 as of spring 2019 and operating independently from each other, with serious product cannibalism thus diffusing the HSE brand image in the market; (c) between teaching and research in business management – almost all HSE providers of business programs were more "teaching machines" than the modern business schools as professionally recognized by international accreditations. Not surprisingly, while the HSE umbrella brand and public interest in business education attracted large pools of candidates for FBM[6] and the "HSE business schools" programs, none of them had EPAS or AMBA accreditations; none of these "b-schools" evolved as a serious national player; and although some management

---

[5] For the institutional evolution and development challenges of Russian management education, see Katkalo (2011) and Krotov and Kuznetsova (2018).

[6] In the 2010s, FBM was the national leader in the Unified National Exam (UNE) grades of the newly enrolled students in the Bachelor in Management program; by 2019, two of its master programs – Master in Marketing Communications and Master in Big Data Systems – were recognized at 51st place in the respective global QS rankings.

professors had publications in Q1/Q2 and in FT50 journals, they formed less than one-fifth of the faculty body in the area.

By the end of the 2010s, this reputational gap became even more striking as the three top Russian business schools achieved major international institutional accreditations – EQUIS (St. Petersburg University GSOM in 2012; Moscow School of Management Skolkovo in 2019) and AACSB (Institute of Business Studies [IBS] at the Russian Academy of National Economy & Public Administration in 2019) – and got into the *Financial Times* and *The Economist* global rankings afterward. Three other factors in the radical upgrading of the business management area at HSE were (a) the new competition from corporate universities (CUs; there were about 50 CUs at Russian companies in 2020, with 5 CUs being EFMD members, and Sberbank CU with Corporate Learning Improvement Process [CLIP] accreditation) and newborn digital platform education companies (such as Skillbox, Netology, and Skyeng) that started to affect the positions of b-schools in almost every market segment; (b) the new requests for relevance of b-schools under the Fourth Industrial Revolution, with the disruptive effects of artificial intelligence, big data, blockchain, and the internet of things, among others, on business models and the related needs for digital transformation of any industry and organization, along with other economic, technological, and societal changes that are now central for successful business strategies and operations with a special focus on the sustainability/environmental, social, and governance (ESG) agenda; and (c) the new realities of lifelong learning, with rapid changes in professions and skills, and the need for mass customization of learning opportunities and experiences – all of which generate high expectations for b-schools' abilities to efficiently and effectively meet these demands.

Given the aforementioned, in 2019, the HSE leaders made a principal decision to launch an in-house business school through a major reorganization of existing internal business education units, with a strategic goal for that school to become a world-class one. Several Russian experts in creating and running business schools and corporate universities of international quality were invited to join the HSE management team in implementing this project. Three key elements of the concept for the new HSE b-school were identified as the following: (a) a university model of a b-school with an integrated portfolio of programs, from bachelor to executive MBA (EMBA) but with focus on graduate studies, and with a network of centers of research in advanced management topics; (b) systemic internationalization of learning and research; and (c) "corporate reorientation" of business education at HSE, with the priority of systemic corporate relations and corporate learning services, especially ExecEd. This vision has been incorporated into the HSE Development Plan (DP) 2030 that was, in its basic principles, accepted by the Conference of HSE faculty and staff in March 2019; its fully developed version was adopted by the HSE Academic Council in January 2020.

The new HSE business school concept and the roadmap for its implementation seemed well thought-through, but with the COVID-19 disruptions, it faced new critical dilemmas: To continue with or to postpone this strategic initiative? Whether and how to adapt the initial concept to new realities of COVID-19 context? How to overcome – if it is at all feasible – the new resource limitations resulting from pandemic effects? However, despite that, since March 17, 2020, HSE University, almost overnight, totally switched its programs to distance mode, there was not much hesitation on whether to go on or not with the Graduate School of Business (GSB) initiative, and on April 24, 2020, the University Academic Council accepted the concept of developing the GSB and gave the "green light" for launching this project.

In the following 4 months, an in-house organizational restructuring of an unprecedented (at least for the Russian universities) scale took place at HSE: its 11 units in business education and research (FBM, 9 semiautonomous "business schools,"[7] and the Innovation Management Institute) were reorganized and put under the umbrella of the newborn GSB. More than 400 full-time faculty and staff, 22 bachelor and master programs with 4,300 students, and about 160 programs of continuous education (including EMBA and doctorate of business administration [DBA]) with 5,000+ participants annually were in the perimeter of this organizational turnaround, which was successfully orchestrated by the executive team of the GSB project. And this was not just a sum of 11 units in question – all of them were

---

[7] Other semiautonomous "business schools" at HSE were merged with those entering GSB, went out of business, or mostly reoriented their portfolios toward other areas of education.

reshaped in their product portfolios and/or administrative modes during this reorganization toward structuring a coherent business school with many potential internal synergies. Not to forget that in this period, 22 faculty members left, and about 25 new ones came in from other top Russian universities and business schools. On September 1, 2020, the GSB started its first academic year with a unified portfolio of degree and nondegree programs covering most of the key segments in the national business education market, with a new set of 6 departments, which is typical for a modern business school instead of the FBM's post-Soviet structure of 14 "chairs/groups," and that housed all GSB faculty of both academic and nonacademic profiles.

Although this fundamental reorganization was the key prerequisite for launching the HSE GSB, the continuation of the COVID-19 pandemic appeared to be a major test for the b-school's abilities not only to successfully adapt its business model but also to continuously innovate in order to ensure the new qualities of HSE business education after this major strategic change. In spring 2020, under the first wave of the pandemic, there were some (naïve) beliefs that it would end by fall, and the 2020–21 academic year went almost totally online (with minor softness of anti–COVID-19 policies at HSE in September–October), thus creating the "new normality" of related rapid shifts in learning technologies, faculty teaching skills, and product offerings as the new self-selection mechanisms and powerful source of competitive differentiation in the business education industry. Needless to say, HSE GSB experienced most of the pandemic shocks that were typical to business schools worldwide in such critical aspects as financial revenues, international student mobility, academic faculty recruitment processes, and so forth. However, even under these conditions, the GSB managed to fulfill its aspirations for the 2020–21 academic year by effective capitalizing on the three key sources of its competitive distinction: being an integral part of the unique multidisciplinary and highly advanced academic environment of HSE, continuously innovating in learning modes and in orchestrating new combinations of available resources, and building a powerful business ecosystem. These three factors together explain the progress achieved by GSB in its first academic year in terms of learning, faculty development, and corporate relations, as will be shown in the following sections.

2. Renewal of Program Portfolio and Learning Innovations in Response to COVID-19

The key priority for any newborn educational institution is to ensure its impact through fresh and advanced approaches in program offerings and learning methods. In the case of GSB, such expectations from all of its stakeholders were initially very high. The GSB launch – through both turnaround of the old-fashioned HSE system of business education and adaptation to COVID-19 challenges – required effective mastering of large-scale restructuring and acceleration of learning innovations, almost simultaneously. For succeeding in this context, the following four cornerstone factors were of critical importance:

1. Formulating an inspiring GSB mission – as a business school at the top research multidisciplinary university – in the following way: "We advance management thinking to develop innovative and responsible leaders that are capable to change the world for a better one."
2. Setting very ambitious goals for the GSB to become (a) the prime partner for the key Russian companies in developing their managers, as well as management concepts and methods to succeed in the digital world, and (b) a world-class business school as recognized through international professional accreditations and global rankings. Although reaching such goals requires high competitiveness from a newborn school, the COVID-19 disruptions provided for it a new "window of opportunity."
3. Assembling and developing an international-level team of business school executives,[8] academic and practice-based faculty, and staff members that are unified by and dedicated to promotion (inside and beyond GSB) of the culture of leadership, continuous innovation, and lifelong learning. COVID-19 effects also accelerated such key

---

[8] The totally new GSB executive team was composed of experienced professionals with backgrounds in dean/associate dean positions at the top Russian b-schools with EQUIS and EPAS accreditations; top-management positions at the corporate universities of the major Russian and global companies (such as Sberbank, Danone, Mars); and board memberships at the European Foundation for Management Development (EFMD), the Association of Russian Managers, and the Russian Association of Business Education. Three out of eight members of the GSB executive team served as chairpersons and/or members of EPAS peer-review teams (PRTs).

aspects of lifelong learning in the digital era as mass personalization of opportunities for professional and personal development.

4. Selecting the right choice for the GSB business model, which was designed after (a) an open business model, in support of a nonorganic growth strategy through developing a network of partnerships with top companies and the global business schools; (b) multichannel financing from tuition, state funding, and fundraising; and (c) a new balance of offline/online learning, with an increasing role of blended, hybrid, and fully distant (synchronized and asynchronized) formats. In the postpandemic world, this balance will never return to a predominantly offline mode.[9] This "new normality" influenced investment choices for HSE GSB – the initial priority of a physical campus (which is a typical key project for a new b-school) was at least counterbalanced by solid financing of advancements in digital resources.[10] The new GSB investment policy to support high-quality learning will be in optimizing square meters while advancing digital technologies and services, including digital learning platforms and the learning marketplace.

Changes in the business program portfolio in the first 12 months of the GSB project were systemic and dynamic. All five bachelor programs (Business Administration, Marketing & Market Analytics, Logistics & Supply Chain Management, Business Informatics, Digital Innovation in Enterprise Management) went through an upgrade of the curriculum, both in content and in structure, to reflect the changes in business management competencies and skills under the Fourth Industrial Revolution, with a special focus on data-driven management, digital skills, and soft skills (teaming, design thinking, etc.), as well as on ESG agenda. Out of 17 master programs that were at the FBM in 2019, in 2021, only 2 continued without reinvention (both

---

[9] Across HSE University, starting with 2021–22 academic year, at least 25 percent of the curriculum in any bachelor and master program will be delivered online for all four of its campuses.

[10] The GSB operates in a distributed campus with three locations in downtown Moscow. Despite expected growth in students and participants, with the new offline/online balance, the focus will be not on expansion in physical infrastructure but on renovation of facilities to create new learning environments. Three locations will be specialized for clusters of GSB programs according to specific requests for bachelor and master programs, continuous education, and ExecEd.

industry-focused: Retail Management and Management in Tourism & Hospitality); 5 were brand-new; and 6 went through major curriculum renovations, in some cases through merging small programs into more solid ones; and others were eliminated. Also, in 2021, this new set of 13 master programs was organized into four clusters: Strategic Management (3 programs); Marketing (4 programs); Operations & Logistics (2 programs); Business Informatics (4 programs). Even more importantly, two of the brand-new master programs at GSB were fully designed as online programs – Master in Marketing Management and Master in Digital Product Management – which enrolled in 2021 their first classes of about 70 and 130 students respectively.

In the MBA and ExecEd segments at GSB, the portfolio-renewal trends were very similar. The previous family of 14 MBA programs at HSE (with strong cannibalization effects) was replaced in 2021 with only 4 MBA programs (in Strategic Management, Managing Digital Technologies, Investment Management, and Project Management), much more clearly positioned and divided in their most valuable players, clientele, and pricing policies and now all focused on digital transformation and related new business models. The completely new Online MBA and EMBA – both in partnerships with top international business schools – were in the design phase in spring 2021. The non-degree ExecEd sector at GSB, both open and customized, also experienced major reshaping and digitalization during 2020–2021. Whereas in 2020, the GSB revenues from the MBA/ExecEd portfolio almost did not drop below their 2019 level, which was a good result under COVID-19 shocks for the Russian business education market, in early 2021, the GSB enjoyed certain growth in revenues from this renewed portfolio. As some offline MBA programs switched to online and others – as well as some customized ExecEd programs – were postponed, the main drivers of business became newly designed open online programs and "digital twins" of previously successful offline programs.

A more delayed outcome is expected from the relaunch of the doctoral program, which went through complete reshaping for the 2021 intake and now is compatible in content and design with the PhD programs of the top European business schools. The DBA program (offered at HSE since 2007) also was renewed, and now the PhD–DBA pair at HSE GSB well reflects the same duos at such European schools as IE, Bocconi, Manchester Alliance, or Aalto and could be potentially used as another case for the ongoing international debate on the similarities and differences between these academic and professional doctoral studies.[11]

Innovation in learning experiences was another core focus of GSB's team from the inception of this new business school. In the contemporary technological, social, demographic, and economic environment, it became evident that a business school's capabilities for creative renewal and advancements in learning experiences are not less, if not more, important for the strategic success of the school than effective and efficient management of its program portfolio. The last decade witnessed not only the rapid growth of blended learning, flipped classrooms, and other new learning modes but also almost a request for any successful bachelor or MBA course to combine learning in three channels – offline, distance, and social. This trend was reinforced with the quick and total switch to online education under the COVID-19 pandemic – very soon after this transition, it also became quite evident that, on the one hand, the traditional Coursera-style massive open online course (MOOC) approach should be enriched by many innovations in the design (i.e., including media content, gamification, etc.), and on the other hand, almost everything in program delivery should be digitalized – not only to meet the expectations of students and participants but also to continuously ensure high-quality standards in the learning experience.

During its first 12 months, GSB introduced quite a few innovative solutions across its diversified product portfolio to ensure high-quality learning experiences in the online formats. The internationalization aspect of learning was one of the most disrupted during the COVID-19 pandemic. However, given that systemic internationalization of the newly created GSB was among its principal differentiators from the earlier traditions of business studies at HSE and one of the key drivers toward GSB strategic goals, it had to move fast and innovate here even with the closed national borders and other pandemic restrictions. In the 2020–21 academic year, the GSB not only (a) retained and even increased, through new enrollments, its body of 600+ full-time international students and (b) continued – although in limited numbers – its outgoing and incoming student mobility but also (c) revisited its

---

[11] See Maguire et al. (2013) and Pina et al. (2016) for reflections on these discussions in the European and US business education contexts, respectively.

international network of partner schools and signed a number of new agreements on student exchanges with the schools with EQUIS, AACSB, and EPAS, bringing the total number of such agreements to 41. The opportunities for double degrees (eight as of early 2021, including the ones with École Supérieure de Commerce de Paris [ESCP] and Lancaster University) were enriched by a new agreement with HEC Paris on a joint bachelor–master degree. In the ExecEd area, GSB started some new customized corporate programs in partnership with INSEAD.

In addition to evolving with these basic internationalization mechanisms, the GSB went on with a number of initiatives of so-called "internationalization at home." This endeavor essentially consisted of launching a fully English-language Master in International Management program, doubling the number of courses taught in English, and adding international professors.

Although online education has many attractive features and is instrumental in coping with pandemic restrictions, its major weakness is its lack of emotional contact, which is so important in a learning process at any level or age – between students and professors, between students and supportive staff, and between students themselves. This is not only about so-called "digital empathy" when communicating only via video profiles of students and professors (hopefully, not with their black screens) during classes in Zoom or MS Teams. The main concern here is with major hurdles that the online mode creates for the social interactions of humans and learning from each other through real-life personal exchanges. Negative consequences for learning (whether in master or EMBA programs) and other aspects of academic life may include the growth of ego-type personalities and difficulties in networking. Quite important proactive actions would include expanding project-based learning in teams and developing diversified services for students to involve them more intensively in professional- and personal-development activities. At GSB, immediately after its official launch, specific actions were undertaken in these directions: from a reorganization of academic program offices (toward a 2×2 "matrix" structure: bachelor and master for management and business informatics areas) that increased their effectiveness in student services to the institutionalization of a set of key student services with the creation of the Career Center, International Office, Office for Developing Project-Based Learning, and Student Affairs Office. Also, the number of teaching and research assistantships among doctoral, master, and bachelor students grew twofold.

Parallel to the creation of the new learning experiences for students and participants, the new support functions for adaptation to new professional challenges in teaching and course design in the time of the total switch to online, as well as additional professional development opportunities, were created for GSB faculty. These new faculty-development policies and actions are addressed in the next section.

3. New Faculty-Development Policies and Actions under COVID-19

Developing highly competitive human capital is one of the key priorities for a newborn business school with an ambitious growth strategy. In the GSB case, this effort started with a major structural reorganization of the faculty body of about 130 professors from the previously quite chaotic set of 14 chairs/groups with no mention of "Operations," "Finance," or "International Business" in their titles (and clustered into three "schools" of Business Administration, Logistics, and Business Informatics) into six new departments symbolizing a contemporary business school. Each of these departments was assigned responsibilities for the quality of the GSB faculty in its area, regular research seminars, and analytical reports on "hot" topics on the management agenda. The bar was initially raised high. For example, the first report from Organizational Behavior and Human Resource Management was on "hybrid offices" and received very good feedback from many top companies, given their current expansion in remote modes of work, and in spring 2021, among speakers at a research seminar in Strategic & International Management were such prominent international scholars as professors David Teece (at the Haas School, University of California, Berkeley) and Serguei Netessin (Wharton School).

The next steps in the first academic year of GSB included (a) a series of professional development seminars for its faculty, (b) introduction to the system of "three professional tracks" and other innovative faculty-development policies, and (c) launch of the new formats for organized research in priority areas and topics.

Professional-development seminars and programs are necessary for supporting faculty in COVID-19 times, when the role of professors is changing rapidly, digitalization is changing business schools as institutions, and teaching in Zoom is not only quite stressful but also very demanding in terms of permanent upgrading of content and learning methods in a newly balanced offline/online learning environment. In a certain sense, business schools have to prepare to manage a new wave of professors who are equipped with a new set of capabilities and skills to be adequate for postpandemic learning requests and expectations from students and corporate clients. Examples of the related seminars and programs for GSB faculty (all provided for free) in 2020–21 include the following:

- Seria of seminars, regular consultations, and a "hotline" service from its Center for Digital Learning Technologies on the design and delivery of online courses and on using the media lab for these purposes
- Two programs on developing case-writing competencies provided by the GSB Case Resource Center in cooperation with the Case Center at Cranfield Business School
- Several programs for upgrading English-language proficiency at various levels
- Seminars by Professor Desislava Dikova from WU on publishing in top research journals on business and management

The new faculty-development policies that were introduced at GSB in its first year happened to be innovations not only for Russian business schools but also for the national university system as well. Whereas GSB was among the pilot cases in HSE with the three-track model – this model was one of the key initiatives of the university's 2030 Development Plan – the other two new policies were pioneered at GSB for HSE at large.

- The model of three professional tracks effectively means a departure from the traditional unitary model of an academic track only, additionally introducing a teaching and methodology track and a practice-oriented track, thus providing faculty members with equal rights and promotion opportunities in any of these three areas. Each of them has its key criteria for faculty selection and assessment: publication in top peer-reviewed journals for the academic track, excellence in teaching and advances in pedagogy (including online courses and programs) for the teaching and methodology track, and high-caliber professional career and excellence in orchestrating project-based learning for the practice-oriented track. Given that each HSE School and Faculty has the right to specify these criteria for its subject area, the GSB not only made them quite high (i.e., a candidate for professor of practice has to occupy a position of the CEO or 1–2 levels below the CEO in a Fortune 500 company or in the top 200 Russian companies from the rankings compiled by *Expert* magazine) but also imposed a criterion for any faculty member to produce new "codified" knowledge in business management of high academic and/or professional quality. The target composition of GSB faculty is the following: 75 percent for the academic and teaching and methodology tracks and 25 percent for the practice-oriented track. In the 2020–21 academic year at GSB, there were 10 professors of practice with executive careers at ABB, VimpelCom, and VK (formerly Mail.ru}, among others.

- The required English-language criteria for faculty selection and assessment were officially introduced at GSB in February 2021, and for the first time in HSE and for GSB faculty only. The target level of proficiency was initially B2 as the "basic" level and C1 for those teaching in English; the level has to be proven by the Cambridge test or another recognized.

- The annual personal meeting of each full-time faculty member with the dean at the end of the academic year to discuss teaching and research plans for the next academic year, as well as professional-development plans for the next 3 years. This organizational ritual was introduced in May–June 2020, right after the HSE University's decision to go ahead with the GSB project, and included 123 personal meetings of the future GSB dean with management faculty members in the presence of the head of their respective academic unit. Although it is clear that this time-consuming exercise will eventually be replaced by such meetings at the level of departments, for the GSB starting phase, it proved to be a very effective tool of organizational change management, especially in the dramatic COVID-19 period.

The new formats of organized research that were implemented at GSB in its first year included faculty group projects and new research labs. This attention to promoting organized research was especially important in the COVID-19 context for supporting collective academic activities to prevent faculty from excessive atomization during pandemic self-isolation. All these new formats were launched on a competitive basis and focused primarily on four priority research areas: Digital Transformation and New Business Models; Transformation of Corporate Human Resource Management (HRM) Systems and People Analytics; International Business in the Times of New Globalization; New Trends in Business and Society Relations and ESG Agenda. In 2020, there were 26 group projects by GSB faculty formed with 1- to 2-year horizons and three new research labs created: Management of Creativity, International Business Strategies and Operations, and International Companies Doing Business in Russia. These three complemented the two other research units at GSB – the Lab on Network Forms of Business Organization and the Innovation Management Institute, both with solid publication records. Many of these research groups benefit from multidisciplinary collaborations across HSE, with applications of business logistics studies to city transportation management and business informatics joining forces with computer sciences as good examples of such cooperation.

Evidently, the new business school has to develop its human capital via recruiting new talent as well. In 2020, about 25 new faculty members, including three international colleagues, were recruited to GSB from the top Russian universities and business schools (and some of these also became new academic directors of programs in various segments); however, faculty recruitment slowed during the COVID-19 era. On the one hand, with many schools freezing their recruitment, the GSB made an initial appearance in 2020 on the international job market at the Academy of Management Annual Meeting and the EFMD job fair, as well as placing ads on Acadeus and other such platforms. This resulted in four or five final candidates, some of whom flew in; others presented for the faculty groups via Zoom. On the other hand, much more fruitful was a nontrivial way of broadening the spectrum of contractual modes for international recruitment for part-time engagements in teaching courses online, co-supervision of doctoral students, participation in research projects, and so forth. This sort of "cloud" strategy in developing faculty attached to the institution on a long-term basis might become a viable proposition. Also, this trend broadens the understanding of a business school faculty to a mix of "employees" in the traditional sense and "contributors" as just another type of faculty, that is, almost equally important for the overall success of the institution. The next section extends this logic to the practice-oriented faculty.

4. Creating the GSB Business Ecosystem: Operational, Cultural, and Business-Model Aspects

Achieving success in the business of management development almost inevitably requires a systemic approach to developing corporate relations. For the newborn HSE GSB, the creation of a unique and powerful business ecosystem is considered as one of its key strategic focuses and a source of (sustainable) competitive advantage. This also implies a conceptual move from a traditional, relatively static mode of business school to the dynamic model of an ecosystem. Cultivating a culture of openness to the external professional world is another fundamental principle for the design and operation of such a business school. Three prime aspects of GSB actions in creating its business ecosystem in its first year that contributed to its effective adaptation to COVID-19 disruptions are examined in this section: institutional formats for the involvement of business leaders in program development and teaching, initial fundraising projects, and the promotion of the ESG agenda together with corporate partners.

Corporate relations for ensuring the quality of learning may be productive in many alternative or complementary forms. At GSB, most efforts here are devoted to establishing and energizing the institutional formats of business-to-business (B2B) relations, thus providing for deep and long-term involvement of the corporate partners in the permanent renewal of the programs' design and substantial contributions to their successful delivery. Three main avenues for implementing these intentions are the following:

- Academic Boards for bachelor and master programs and Expert Boards for MBA and DBA programs have been formed by business leaders since GSB's inception. The basic assumption here is that industry leaders, not academic faculty, are better informed about the "most wanted by the market" profile of a graduate of a given program. With this, they may be involved in a program's development as its co-owners with an academic director and other core faculty of the program in question. The "academic" notion of such boards refers not to the status of its members but the purposes of this collective decision-making body, which include co-creation of the program's curriculum architecture, menu of electives, topics of the key projects and in-company internships, and so forth. Such boards have the majority of members from among GSB corporate partners and alumni, and the chairperson of the board is always a prominent business leader. These business leaders reinforce the reputation of the program, participate in teaching, and are prime employers for graduates. By March 2021, 14 out of 17 bachelor and master GSB programs already had such boards created and in action, and the first Expert Board for MBA in Strategic Management was created.

- Project-Based Labs (PBLs) and Business Learning Units (BLUs) that are created at the GSB by top companies are their hubs here for designing and delivering courses (at least two courses each) for particular programs and providing students with real-life projects. In the 2020–21 academic year, there were 10 BLUs and 2 PBLs at GSB. Examples include an SAP project-based lab in customer experience; Bank Openness, Accenture, and Kearney business learning labs; and a Huawei technology center.

- Jointly designed or redesigned programs that are co-branded with top companies are another very instrumental mechanism of attracting industry leaders to be involved in developing GSB toward the implementation of its goals. Great examples include a joint Master in Strategic Management and Consulting with McKinsey & Company, a continuous education program on Innovations in Retail with the X5 Retail Group, and the fully redesigned bachelor in business informatics offered together with the top enterprise resource planning (ERP) software company 1C.

Fundraising activities were culturally undeveloped in HSE business education units prior to GSB creation. By the end of quarter 1 of 2021, the fundraising tradition at GSB started to be cultivated, and the first million euros of restricted and nonrestricted donations were secured. These funding sources included a major donation from Bank Openness for developing teaching in risk management, funding from AFK Systema Holding for writing cases on its businesses, in-kind contributions from 1C for new computer labs, and naming opportunities for other companies. Taking into consideration the plan to form the GSB Advisory Board by mid-2022, this is only the beginning of fundraising efforts, and they will be intensified to contribute to the success of the

GSB business model and to compensate (at least partially) for the negative financial impact of the pandemic.

Promotion of the ESG agenda together with business is among the key focuses of GSB in ensuring its impact on society. Given that the purpose of corporations and of business in society is of growing importance, the development of understanding of this purpose is becoming one of the key value-added aspects of business education. Besides institutional moves in joining the Principles for Responsible Management Education (PRME) and attending Business School Impact System (BSIS) seminars, operational activities were also launched, such as recruitment of new faculty with research and teaching interests in ESG, the introduction of ESG-related courses and student projects in bachelor and master studies, and roundtables and seminars on the ESG agenda that were jointly organized with key Russian companies.

Thus, the development of systemic corporate ties for GSB has already shown results and has great potential for both serving its reputational and cultural strengths, operational uniqueness, and effectiveness and for closing resource gaps and creating additional opportunities in critically important human and financial capital provision for its ambitious growth strategy.

5. In the Way of Conclusion: Lessons Learned and a Road Ahead

This chapter presented an analysis of the rather unique (and not only for Russia) case of the HSE GSB project of creating a new major business school with an ambition of becoming a world-class one and implementing such intention in an era of radical disruptions in business education caused by the COVID-19 pandemic. An important aspect of this case is its scale and scope because the newborn school inherited a vast program portfolio, from bachelor to MBA and ExecEd, with 9,000+ students and participants in total and about 400 faculty and staff members. Certain path-dependence effects (and organizational resistance) were minimized at the initial stage of this project through systemic reorganization of the HSE business education landscape, innovations in learning experiences at GSB, the introduction of radically new faculty-development policies, and new cultural norms of learning and management research at international quality standards, as well as openness to integration with corporate partners in this institutional-building endeavor. These focuses on continuous innovation, cultural changes, and an open business model were among the key factors in making the first year of the GSB project a successful one, despite the challenges of COVID-19. This progress was symbolized in late 2021 by the start of customized ExecEd programs for six top Russian companies, and by receiving EFMD Accreditation for 5 years for the set of two bachelor programs – in Business Administration, and in Marketing and Market Analytics.

Probably the main lesson learned from this first year is related to the awareness of the tectonic shift in almost everything related to the conventional model of a highly competitive business school, which was previously mostly associated with offline education. Almost undoubtedly, face-to-face training and communication will still be prioritized in most of ExecEd offerings, where personal-experience exchanges are among the core value-added aspects of a learning experience. Otherwise, the digital transformation of business education will continue to reshape the offline/online balance, and most of the programs will soon become blended or hybrid. This requires a Chandlerian approach to redesigning structures and systems and introducing other organizational innovations at business schools following the disruptive technological innovations[12] of the pandemic that forced such schools around the world to pivot to delivering education over virtual platforms.

Another major lesson is that as new technologies create new learning experiences, we need to systemically retrain business school faculty members for them to fit with the realities of a postpandemic learning environment and the demands and expectations from students, participants, and corporate clients. Also, with the growing diversity of requests for learning modes and learning experiences, the faculty of the academic track will be complemented by faculty on other professional tracks, and even more, the pluralism of contractual modes for faculty will increase. This requires not only new approaches to strategic human resource planning at business schools but also a new set of skills for orchestrating such a new faculty body.

---

[12] For an excellent series of essays on Alfred Chandler's managerial revolution, see Lazonick and Teece (2012).

The third lesson learned involves the economics of online education, which proved to be not exactly as we expected. Although in principle online education is "cheaper" than offline, most online learning is in a synchronized format, and thus the number of faculty needed is not reduced. In fact, we have witnessed quite the opposite: the schools that are going to be on the top in the industry will have to invest massively in digital infrastructure and the production of online programs, especially nondegree ones or those for micro-degrees, both of which will grow in demand.

The vision for the road ahead for HSE GSB to become an institution of international caliber includes, at this moment, at least three key elements, each of which will be a source of GSB competitive advantage. First is developing its dynamic capabilities for sensing and seizing new market opportunities for advancing learning experiences and then transforming internal and external organizational assets of the business school accordingly.[13] It is critical to realize that GSB will not compete with other business schools only and will permanently face new competitions from corporate learning functions and digital learning platforms that may run faster, have a more solid resource base, and have more flexible management systems. This means that GSB should, on the one hand, not allow for major gaps here with its competitors in the segments in which it decides to do business, and on the other hand, it should have its own clear positioning in the market and distinctive features that are highly attractive to the clients of its product offerings.

Another strategically important area for creating unique learning opportunities at GSB is in intensifying multidisciplinary collaboration with other HSE schools and faculties. Although such cooperation is already an integral element of almost all GSB programs, two directions are worth exploring in the near future: (a) new program offerings based on the synthesis of business, computer sciences, and design, which well matches the requirement of business in the digital age and thus was reflected in recent developments at St. Gallen, IE, Aalto, and some other top European schools, and (b) developing joint projects involving students from GSB and HSE engineering and biotech

---

[13] The story of the institutional design of HSE GSB and of the evolution of its business model could be interpreted as a successful application of the dynamic capabilities concept of strategic management in the context of a university-based business school. For the nature of dynamic capabilities and their relation to business models, see Katkalo et al. (2010) and Teece (2018).

programs, as well as technology entrepreneurship, as one of the GSB competencies at large.

Finally, the open business model approach will most likely remain one of the key drivers for GSB progress toward reaching its ambitious goals and fulfilling its mission. A unique GSB ecosystem that involves, in various formats, top Russian and international companies, as well as some of the global business schools, will serve as an important source of tangible and intangible assets to support its growth. The GSB has to attract, assemble, and orchestrate these assets in the right way, which is key for its successful nonorganic growth strategy. If this strategy is wisely coordinated with developing and capitalizing on its internal resources, GSB has a good chance of becoming a world-class business school, in time, with its development plan and of contributing in this way to even further growth of HSE University's high global reputation.

References

Katkalo, V. S. (2011). Institutional evolution and new trends in Russian management education. In M. Morsing and A. Sauquet, eds., *Business schools and their contribution to society*. Sage, Chapter 4.

Katkalo, V. S., Pitelis, C. N., and Teece, D. J. (2010). On the nature and scope of dynamic capabilities. *Industrial and Corporate Change*, 19(4), 1175–1186.

Krotov, K., and Kuznetsova, A. (2018). Higher education in management: The case of Russia. In S. Dameron and T. Durand, eds., *The future of management education*. Palgrave Macmillan, pp. 185–211.

Lazonick, W., and Teece, D. J., eds. (2012). *Management innovation: Essays in the spirit of Alfred D. Chandler, Jr*. Oxford University Press.

Maguire, L., Revilla, E., and Diaz, A. (2013). PhDs & DBAs: Two sides of the same coin? *Global Focus*, 7(3), 32–35.

Pina, A. A., Maclannan, H. L., Moran, K. A., and Hafford, P. F. (2016). The D.B.A. vs. Ph.D. in the U.S. business and management programs: Different by degrees? *Journal for Excellence in Business Education*, 4 (1), 6–19.

Teece, D. J. (2018). Business models and dynamic capabilities. *Long Range Planning*, 51(1), 40–49.

Wissema, J. G. (2009). *Towards the third generation university: Managing the university in transition*. Edward Elgar.

Yin, R. K. (1994). *Case study research design and methods*, 2nd ed. Applied Social Research Methods Series, Vol. 5. Sage.

IV

Crisis Management with a Special Focus on COVID-19

13 | Going Beyond "Always Look on the Bright Side of Life" in Management Education Crisis Strategy

ERIC CORNUEL

E. Morin developed thinking on how important it is for the social sciences to study crises.[1] In particular, he showed that a crisis of endogenous origin reveals the tensions and contradictions in a social system that led to the crisis occurring – that determined it from within. Also, beyond its analysis (its course, its eventual means of resolution, its consequences), studying an endogenous crisis helps better understand the social system in which it occurs.

The book in which this chapter appears aims to develop thinking on management education institutions facing the COVID-19 crisis.

The question of the relevance of this thinking arises immediately; the COVID-19 crisis is, first and foremost, a public health crisis. There is little doubt that it has had consequences on many other spheres, including that of management education. But what can we learn for this sector from a crisis imported from another sector? It seems logical to assume that management education institutions reacted to this crisis by trying to operate as closely and consistently to the way they had been accustomed to operating before the crisis period. Studying such a situation makes it possible to better understand how the management education sector reacts to a crisis of exogenous origin. But to what extent can this tell us about the dynamics of the sector in question? A review of the very notion of crisis clearly shows the potential for developing such thinking.

The COVID-19 Crisis Reveals the Social Role of Business Schools

The expressions commonly heard in everyday language at the time of a crisis such as that of COVID-19 ("return to normality," "the new normal after the crisis," etc.) demonstrate the extent to which the very

---

[1] See, in particular, Morin (2020).

notion of crisis is strongly linked to that of "normal" and "normality." G. Canguilhelm approached the latter notion as consubstantial with that of abnormality, but above all, he highlighted the extent to which the normal is understood in relation to the implementation of a project

The abnormal, as ab-normal, comes after the definition of the normal, it is its logical negation. . . .. The normal is the effect obtained by the execution of the normative project, it is the norm exhibited in the fact. (Canguilhem, 1991, p. 243)

Thus, the notion of crisis describes a situation in which it seems as though one has left a situation of normality in which a project was being implemented.

The importance that one gives to the latter results in a will to return to normality (and is thus a "crisis project," the existence of which implies a "crisis strategy" that one tries to carry out in parallel to the project that justifies an organization's existence) and therefore to the previous situation. However, the realization of a crisis project can ultimately assert itself not as leading to the status quo ante but as revealing new possibilities to be implemented (Habermas, 1976). If an endogenous crisis provides information on the weaknesses of the past, the study of a crisis of exogenous origin makes it possible to analyze potentialities for the future.

These two attitudes – that of seeking a return to the previous situation and that of developing new ideas and their implementation – emerge from the examination of the strategies and actions of business schools in the face of the COVID-19 crisis. The analysis of this crisis makes it possible to appreciate the depth of the changes underway in management education and confirms Milton Friedman's assertion that "only a crisis – actual or perceived – produces real change" (Friedman, 1962/2002, p. xiv).

In other words, the study of the influence of the COVID-19 crisis on management education institutions leads not only to studying the way in which these institutions are organized in order to be able to continue to develop their management education but also, beyond management education, how they were able to structure themselves so as to help solve the constitutive social crisis which is that of public health.

Studying how management education institutions have responded to the COVID-19 crisis helps to shed light on how they see their mission.

Responsiveness to the Crisis in the Management Education Sector

Although some management education institutions had begun, as early as the start of 2020, to develop their thinking on how to react to the pandemic, the consequences of this did not really erupt into the management of business schools, except for those located in the Wuhan region, until February and March. Then, in management education institutions around the world, it suddenly became a question of responding to very concrete challenges. Examination centers being closed, it was impossible to take the Graduate Management Admission Test (GMAT) and the Graduate Record Examination (GRE) in China, and it very quickly became so in Bahrain, Mongolia, Kuwait, Thailand, Hong Kong, Singapore, and other places as well. It became necessary to cancel study trips and seminars in China even though "global experience," "immersion trip," "global consulting," and other such programs in which social-impact projects constituted a significant feature had been rapidly increasing in the country. In a now-globalized management education market in which Chinese students represent a very large proportion of international students, we observed a drastic decrease in international applications for the following academic year.

Very quickly, too, immediate daily management problems arose as a result of the consequences of the epidemic that was taking hold across the world. Thus, institutions in Europe and Asia (quickly followed by those in certain regions of Oceania and Africa) had to face confinement as of March. At this time, when the United States was not yet intensely affected by the epidemic, the first effects of it were being felt on campuses (e.g., starting at the very end of February at Tuck School of Business, after a student came in contact with a patient during an on-campus party, Dartmouth College had to deal with the first effects of quarantine). In addition, management schools and faculties have had to tackle major reorganization and rescheduling issues.

The way in which schools reacted to the occurrence of a crisis is very revealing, both of their management style and of their position in the societies in which they operate. It is particularly remarkable that in Europe, Asia, and South America (and a little less in the USA), schools anticipated the measures taken by their regional and national political and administrative authorities. The examples are too numerous to all be cited, but we can present a few from various continents.

On March 12, a day after the outbreak was declared a pandemic by the World Health Organization, 16 cases of COVID-19 were reported among Mexico's 128 million people. Although the number of cases was still very low in the country at this date, the IPADE Business School, sensitive to the global impact of the coronavirus, decided the next morning to temporarily suspend face-to-face activities in all of its national and international academic programs to protect the health and integrity of every member of its community. With the firm conviction that everyone must take part in the fight against the spread of the virus, IPADE implemented this precautionary measure even before the Mexican Ministry of Education decided to suspend all educational activities in the country (Alvarado and Romero, 2020).

At the Gordon Institute of Business Science at the University of Pretoria on March 16, all face-to-face teaching had ceased, and the bulk of employees had begun to work from home (Kleyn, 2020; while the first case of coronavirus detected in South Africa dated March 5, when there were in all only 27 cases in the whole of Africa). This decision long preceded the first measures taken by the South African government.

The Hong Kong University of Science and Technology was an even more specific case because, as a result of the troubled situation in Hong Kong, which had led some students to move away from campus, the school had been operating with hybrid teaching since fall 2019.

Grenoble Ecole de Management (GEM) decided to put an end to two essential activities – face-to-face teaching and work at school – 72 hours before the French government decided to initiate a national confinement strategy (Saviotti, 2020). The reasons for this reactivity are extremely revealing of the reality of business school activities: at the end of December 2019 and in the beginning of January 2020, GEM received feedback from exchange students in Asia and on its campus in Singapore indicating the development of a difficult situation. Thanks to the quality of this dialogue that arose as a result of the internationalization of its activities, GEM had started to prepare itself to face a major crisis. In February, the school banned travel to China for its students and staff and asked all staff and students in the country to return to their home countries.

These few examples were chosen arbitrarily from dozens of similar ones. They trace how the international activities of business schools helped found their crisis management and how they are in a position to coordinate their decisions with those of national administrations. These examples are all clues to the way in which business schools now connect a regional and national dimension to an international one.

Adapting Schools' Activity to Maintain Their Raison d'être

In general, the first responses of schools to the onset of the coronavirus crisis were situated in a reactive logic and centered around two priorities. These were, first of all, maintaining (or restoring, in the cases of institutions that had stopped teaching for a short period) their teaching activity as regularly as possible while also maintaining its quality (keeping in mind that they very quickly moved toward distance learning) and, second, recruiting students for the following academic year. (The globalization of management education had made it possible, for example, that even though in March the United States was still relatively unaffected by the coronavirus, business schools were already beginning to postpone the dates of their admissions rounds.)

The reactive attitude initially implemented by management education institutions is therefore typical of crisis logic; it involved maintaining, through a series of detailed responses to organizational needs and specific dysfunctions, operations that were as close as possible to those in effect in the "normal" situation before the crisis.

Although it was accepted that logistical *and* educational adjustments were necessary (caused in particular by the switch to distance education), these were not to affect the logic and the deep coherence of the system of management education. The objective of management education institutions seemed to consist of getting through the difficult moment of crisis, getting out of this abnormal situation, and returning to a normal one by perpetuating the main modes of operation and the logic of the system.

However, clues quickly appeared that made it possible to measure how difficult such an approach would be. An episode in the life of business schools that took place in March and April is a particularly revealing example of this difficulty. The high tuition fees at business schools are, particularly in the United States, a constituent element of the system. Talented candidates who have already accumulated significant savings or a high borrowing capacity as a result of their prior professional careers and the resulting social recognition are admitted to business schools following a strict selection process. There, they receive an education that subsequently enables them to accelerate their careers and increase their income (and thus to reimburse, if necessary, the very high cost of their studies). The quality and relevance of this education constitute the supreme justification for its high cost because they guarantee that the system functions properly.

It is thus very interesting that starting in the second part of March, in many business schools, including some of the most prestigious, a petition signed by a very large proportion of students (for example, 80 percent of students at the Stanford Graduate School of Business) demanded that the management of their school reimburse part of the tuition fees to students during their schooling because of the switch to distance education (Moules, J., 2020, April 12). These petitions particularly affected American universities (e.g., the Stanford Graduate School of Business; the Wharton School of the University of Pennsylvania; Columbia Business School; the University of California, Los Angeles [UCLA] Anderson School of Management; the New York University [NYU] Stern School of Business) but also schools beyond the United States, for example, in Europe (IE Business School in Spain) and in Canada (University of British Columbia [UBC] Sauder School of Business).

The signatories of the petition justified their request with two main elements: first, they presented distance education as being of inferior quality, and second, they argued that the tuition fees paid to schools cover not only the education provided but also campus life – the latter being a socialization process that includes starting a networking process for their future professional careers, both with the leaders and professionals with whom they might make contact through campus life and with the other students, who will later develop their own careers.

Switching to distance learning during an epidemic appears to be a logical and appropriate reaction; however, this change has had consequences on the operating logic of schools.

This episode has made it possible to measure the danger of a solely reactive approach that responds step by step to the difficulties caused by the COVID-19 epidemic and dispenses with a substantial reassessment of the practice and of the approach implemented. Such an approach risks losing the coherence of the functioning and activities of schools.

The pandemic presents some unique challenges to business schools because of their international character. Numerous business schools have experienced students and staff from a range of countries being forced to return to their home countries because of travel or visa restrictions (Krishnamurthy, 2020, p. 3). The top 20 MBA programs in the United States reported a 14 percent decline in the number of international students: compared to the fact that international students account for an average of 35 percent of students in elite programs, this indicates the magnitude of the challenge that COVID-19 poses to business schools. These students in the USA have the distinction of paying full tuition fees, which can be as high as $160,000 per year (Roth, 2020).

In many business schools, foreign students are an important source of income because they subsidize the tuition fees of domestic students (Brammer and Clark, 2020, p. 453). As the number of foreign students declines, institutions may be forced to change their financial models. Moreover, institutionally, many business schools are now part of universities, whose entire business model is threatened by the pandemic.

Moreover, the mere fact that COVID-19 has had a significant impact on business has profoundly affected business schools. Entire sectors, such as aviation and tourism, have been severely affected, without any prediction of when or even if an upturn will occur. Similarly, small and medium-sized enterprises are often in a particularly unstable situation and are threatened with bankruptcy. This will have an impact on the opportunities for students after their studies and thus on the academic paths followed and the curricula. At the same time, there is a growing interest in health-care management (Krishnamurthy, 2020, p. 4).

These changes, as well as the labor-market volatility that graduates will face in the coming years, are expected to have an impact on enrollments. But these changes are also having an impact within schools themselves: a survey of 172 senior university executives indicates that their main short-term concerns have been identified as the mental health and well-being of students and staff, unbudgeted costs, and high dropout rates. In the long term, their main concerns are about the financial future of their institutions.

Alongside the various challenges to be overcome, it is interesting to point out that the current crisis has also created opportunities. The demand for flexibility and adaptability has led to a significant acceleration of innovation in the academic world, which may generate opportunities to reimagine the future of resilient and sustainable academic institutions. Previous research carried out before the coronavirus crisis indicates that students study slightly better online than in a traditional classroom environment, indicating the possible benefits of moving to e-learning (Krishnamurthy, 2020, p. 2).

In addition, teaching staff members have proven their resilience and adaptability, committing themselves to research and teaching throughout the crisis. Communication channels, as well as teaching and assessment methods, have been reimagined. A major challenge faced by business schools is continuity of teaching, mainly through a focus on the continued availability of educational opportunities for the students during disruption. Business schools strive to make arrangements to provide students with education during this period. Emphasis is placed on finding a way to maintain services during the disruption period. During this period, business schools undertake "emergency distance education," with a focus on sustaining curriculum requirements (Hodges et al., 2020). At the institutional level, the consolidation of technology as a central aspect of higher education offers various opportunities for collaboration and even restructuring of academic institutions. The crisis has also accelerated and intensified existing trends, providing the conditions for a natural experiment in which adaptable institutions can test innovative methods and practices. It has also opened up opportunities for new areas of research on changes in consumption, communication, and market trends, as well as on adaptive and innovative capacities in times of international crisis.

Emergent Strategy and the Need to Maintain Consistency in the Face of the Crisis

Our purpose is certainly not to argue that the community of management education institutions has contented itself with being reactive to the coronavirus crisis. Not only have strategies to respond to the effects of the crisis (see the crisis strategies mentioned previously) been implemented, but so have strategies involving fundamental changes whose relevance became apparent during the crisis.

If strategy is defined as a pattern in a stream of decisions and can be conceived as a continuum going from deliberate to emergent strategies (Mintzberg and Waters, 1985), the latter can be defined as "patterns realized despite or in the absence of intentions" (Mintzberg, 1979, p. 257).

The notion of emergent strategy reflects the way in which strategies have been developed in business schools in the face of the situation created by the coronavirus. Although the decisions taken were made in response to given challenges, it is possible to highlight a consistency between these decisions that creates a strategic pattern. The implementation of an emergent strategy requires that the actors in organizations have developed sufficient empirical knowledge and practical wisdom forged in the field to allow them to make decisions that are compatible with the needs of the context. That is, they need to have a clear understanding of what it is possible to do and the consequences of making a decision. The notion of emergent strategy does not imply that the decisions taken within this framework are secondary decisions, whereas the important decisions are only the subject of deliberate strategies. The culture; the type of staff working for business schools; the balance between administrative and academic staff; and the presence, in many cases, of very committed leadership have led to the implementation of emergent strategies that go well beyond the blow-by-blow response of reactive decisions.

The question of selection tests, which is a central issue for business schools, is an example of how elements of emergent strategy have been formed. On the one hand, this question models the type of candidates, and therefore the students, that the school receives and thus, consequently, the character of the school. Moreover, to the extent that these tests require a great deal of preparation, they create expectations commensurate with the level of "suffering" they have generated in test-takers. At the same time, experience shows that the effort that students feel they had to make to be accepted is strongly correlated with their level of identification with their schools. In addition, the GMAT and GRE score requirements contribute to determining the schools' reputations.

Lastly, and above all, because these tests are deemed reliable, they constitute an important "safety net" for schools by guaranteeing the quality of candidates in a certain number of parameters considered fundamental. Even if the GMAT and the GRE are sometimes criticized because they produce too homogeneous a profile of students, giving them up is a difficult choice for the schools. In addition, these tests have demonstrated their undeniable quality over the years, and moreover, they have demonstrated their ability to evolve and improve with respect to all the challenges they have to face.

Additionally, most of the schools, in particular, most among the more recognized ones, had retained a GMAT or GRE requirement for candidates until extremely recently. We must therefore consider the current trend to exempt GMAT and GRE at its proper importance.

Following the June decision by the University of Virginia Darden to waive these tests, other universities made the same decision in August and September (Wisconsin School of Business, Rutgers Business School, Northeastern University Kellogg School, University of Texas at Austin McCombs School of Business, Emory University Goizueta Business School). The consequences of these exemption decisions were not long in coming. For example, in mid-July, Darden announced an increase in MBA applications of 364 percent (Byrne, 2020c).

The rationale put forward for these exemptions is that during the coronavirus epidemic, it was very difficult for applicants to be able to take the GMAT and GRE tests within a reasonable timeframe. The decision was based on the observation that it was impossible to continually push back the deadline for submitting applications. At one point in the process, universities also feared that they might face a shortage of applicants (which may explain, for example, why Northwestern Kellogg, alongside granting test waivers, also decided to revisit rejected applications).

But now Pandora's box has been opened. It is indeed difficult to think that after the eventual end of the epidemic, a return to the status quo ante in the selection process will be entirely possible. At the same time, no one can seriously imagine that this change will not have profound consequences for management education institutions. Indeed, this should upset the type of preparation done and change the level of investment in time and money in order to be a candidate. Schools will certainly not be satisfied with using the same selection process with one less evaluation parameter (the tests); they will have to completely rethink their selection process and take career profiles into account more.

Yet while some argue that this could give applicants from low-income families a greater chance of getting in (Byrne, 2020a), given the high cost of preparing for the GMAT and GRE tests, foregoing such a reliable and relevant tool does not appear to be an inevitable option. The Graduate Management Admission Council (GMAC), the company that designs these tests, has demonstrated its capacity for innovation and to face challenges that arise. Furthermore, one also imagines that GMAC will cooperate with the schools to limit the impact of the social environment of origin on the results of candidates' tests. And without the tests, the assessment of applications from foreign applicants would be much more difficult because it is traditionally complicated to assess career profiles from distant countries; this could lead to a change in the composition of the groups recruited, and it would become necessary to modify the pedagogy during studies. The conditions of competition have also been disrupted; can one seriously imagine, for example, that being able to apply to Kellogg without having to take the GMAT or the GRE would not have a huge influence on candidates in Chicago (and therefore force this university to change its criteria, which would likely lead to the same at other institutions)?

Finally, it is difficult to think that schools have made such fundamental choices in terms of selection by imagining that it was only a question of solving a temporary, one-off problem and not of reacting to and participating in a systemic change.

Developing Comprehensive, Integrated Approaches to the Crisis

The fact that this example of a shift in the selection process seems to be a possibly favorable development should not lead one to infer that all developments provoked by the coronavirus crisis are easy and devoid of danger. We stand in opposition to the many articles published in recent months arguing that the chief among these developments (the spread of online education, exemption from GMAT and GRE tests, the increase in the level of admissions selectivity, authorization for deferrals of beginning of studies, etc.) are only accelerations of trends that began before the COVID-19 crisis and that, being "in line with the movement of history," they are necessarily favorable.

We would like, on the contrary, to underline the difficulties that they carry with them, which attest to the fact that even if these developments were brewing and even if it was technically possible that they could be implemented, schools were careful not to spread them rapidly. They are only potentially favorable within the framework of approaches whose coherence we will present.

To highlight the issues, we will analyze a few examples of these supposedly fashionable developments that, in reality, were marginal before the COVID-19 crisis.

Even though online MBAs had experienced some development in recent years (Warwick, IE Business School, University of Massachusetts – Amherst, University of North Carolina [UNC] Kenan-Flagler Business School, Carnegie Mellon, Durham, Northeastern, Politecnico di Milano, Bradford, etc.), the majority of schools were careful not to rush toward this option.

The COVID-19 crisis has created a need to move toward this type of education. Examining the way in which schools have reacted to this imperative shows, however, that they have tried as much as possible to maintain outdoor or indoor teaching, at least in parallel to, and as much as possible side by side with, online education. Going online, if we want to combine it with quality education, requires significant investment, a fact that favors the most affluent and recognized schools. It is interesting to note that these have opted whenever possible for hybrid MBA education options rather than ones that are entirely online.

The approach adopted by INSEAD is indicative of schools' preferences in terms of teaching during the COVID-19 crisis. At the same time, it is particularly remarkable for its coherence and the choices it entails.

Despite a 58 percent increase in MBA applications, INSEAD decided to reduce admissions on all its campuses by 38 percent in September 2020 in order to carefully manage social distancing guidelines and to organize all its MBA courses as face-to-face offerings (INSEAD, 2021). It is particularly noteworthy that this decision to conduct as much of the 2020–21 academic year as possible in an in-person setting was taken in consultation with students. It should also be noted that all courses will also be accessible by distance learning, making INSEAD's approach a hybrid method with a preference for a classroom-based approach.

Similarly, at the beginning of July 2020, Harvard announced a move toward such a solution (at the cost of a reduction from 930 to 720 students in the entering MBA class) (Byrne, 2020b). Stanford is now moving toward an entirely online solution, as well, out of health necessity, specifying that if the situation vis-à-vis COVID-19 improves, its educational offerings will become hybrid. Even the institutions that have announced going online (Wharton; University of California, Berkeley, Haas School of Business; Georgetown; UNC's Kenan-Flagler Business School; etc.) indicate that it is only to avoid remaining in limbo for too long a period and note that as soon as possible, things will change. Likewise, the case of Georgia Tech Scheller is interesting because after management announced that teaching would be partly on campus, the institution finally, reluctantly, gave up on the idea in early July. In fact, it was the teaching staff who drew the attention of the management to the fact that the state of health in Georgia did not allow for such a reopening. Management viewed maintaining education on campus as a strategic and educational priority but responsibly acquiesced to the public health argument.

The reasons for reservations with respect to a change that technically appears to be positive are not just a problem of resistance to change. They are also due to the fact that such a change cannot be conceived in isolation by ignoring the need for consistency with the many other parameters of school management. Some difficulties experienced at the end of summer 2020 by Wharton are an illustrative example of this.

Faced with the sustained increase in coronavirus cases, the Wharton School at the University of Pennsylvania announced on July 31 that it had changed its mind (Wharton School, 2020). It had previously announced (on July 6) that the fall semester would be hybrid but ultimately opted for a completely virtual semester. It also announced that it would not be flexible on matters of deferral of studies or discounts on tuition fees.

The school did not communicate clearly enough, claiming until July 21 by press release that the semester would be hybrid, and many students lamented that it was only after they had paid tuition and declined the offers of other schools they had been accepted into that this news was announced.

They also regretted that the particular case of foreign students was not taken into consideration. While the latter had planned to come to the United States on the basis of Wharton's first indications of a hybrid semester, the sudden announcement that everything would be online put them in a difficult situation with respect to visas because the American administration is now making it difficult for students studying online to get them.

Students, management education professionals, and the press have thus insisted repeatedly on the poor management of the crisis at this eminent school.

Likewise, NYU Stern's decision to increase its tuition fees by 3.5 percent (Joung, 2020), announced in early August 2020, appears to pose a problem of consistency and adequacy in the current situation. It is true that business schools traditionally increase their tuition fees every year. But not to see that this increase was acceptable only because it was based on the implicit double assumption that the quality of education improves from year to year and that salary expectations at the end of the MBA were increasing constituted a serious lack of lucidity. Also, in the period of transition to online learning, which is producing a lot of uncertainty, continuing to increase tuition fees constitutes a dangerous temptation and a lack of coherence in management, to which a number of the schools that have renounced such increases (Harvard, Chicago Booth, etc.) have not succumbed. Although it is understandable that NYU's financial situation may require additional resources, to raise tuition fees (which prompted a petition from over 200 MBA students) is to omit the need for consistency.

Likewise, the manner in which Wharton switched to wholly online education risks damaging that school's credibility. This shows that even in a crisis situation, it is necessary to take a holistic approach to managing change. In this case, the question of virtual versus face-to-face education was raised in ignorance of the fact that it is linked to many other parameters of school administration, in particular to the management of foreign students and the question of tuition fees and related issues.

The Harvard or INSEAD cases mentioned previously, on the contrary, would seem to demonstrate a comprehensive awareness of the situation. Indeed, the loss of approximately 200 students for Harvard's 2020 entering class occurred because it was necessary to take into consideration the fact that a liberal policy in terms of deferral was needed, in particular for foreign students. (Harvard decided that any student, after having been accepted, could freely postpone their admission to the school by 2 years.) In addition, this choice can be explained by the decision-making logic holding that maintaining some amount of face-to-face education is very important and that, to that end, it was necessary to be able to follow the imperatives of public health and therefore initiate physical and social distancing among students.

The crisis situation places management education institutions in perilous contexts that are liable to jeopardize the future. Articles, books, and conferences devoted to the direction of academic management institutions in the face of the COVID-19 crisis that repeat that these adaptations constitute an opportunity, or that they validate favorable developments that had already been initiated and were ineluctable, call to mind the famous scene in Monty Python's *The Life of Brian* in which convicts sentenced to death by crucifixion joyfully sing, "Always look on the bright side of life." To accomplish their mission of training creative managers and agents of change and to maintain the sustainability of their institutions, the management of these establishments must develop global, integrated approaches, of which I have tried to give a few examples.

Business Schools: Social Actors in the Face of COVID-19

The elements analyzed previously show management education institutions that have responded to the COVID-19 crisis by attempting to create the conditions necessary to continue to accomplish their missions and fulfill their raison d'être by training students in management. In certain cases, the discussion has indicated how, in an effort of strategy and foresight, these institutions went even further by attempting to make the crisis an accelerator of change and a catalyst for improvements in the way they function. That these various shifts within schools tend to make them better able to accomplish their missions may seem very self-centered.

Yet in fact, one of their justifications is that business schools and management faculties have a high level of awareness of their social responsibility to train competent managers who, through their activities in companies and organizations in general, contribute to well-being and progress throughout society.

But beyond this important social contribution through their graduates, the COVID-19 crisis has helped to reveal how business schools themselves are real social actors. If the inclination already existed for business schools to act as a positive force for social progress, the COVID-19 crisis has greatly accelerated this trend (Cornuel and Hommel, 2012).

This is arguably the most remarkable aspect of the COVID-19 crisis in the management education sector. Beyond the fact that schools have deployed powerful mechanisms to maintain and improve their teaching activity and its quality, there are many cases in which business schools have stepped forward to provide answers to the social difficulties created by COVID-19.

For these schools, it goes well beyond educating students and executives – it is a question of engaging as a social actor contributing to society's response to the COVID-19 crisis by employing the skills present in the schools themselves, the research that is developed there, the social influence and mobilization capacity of these institutions, and so forth. The forms this commitment takes are diverse: offering assistance to companies by providing them with volunteer consulting; providing leadership support to help businesses meet the challenges created by the coronavirus crisis; creating labs for ideas and being a creative force in a region or for a network of for-profit or nonprofit organizations, in certain cases accompanied by a workforce commitment in the field; and so forth.

Occasionally, schools have mobilized to seek answers to the problems created by the coronavirus crisis at a particular organization. Thus, Wharton accentuated an existing partnership with the Philadelphia Zoo (Symonds, 2020). The university took the initiative to help the zoo find responses to the lack of visitors during the coronavirus crisis period, an issue that posed problems for zoo maintenance, for the mental and physical well-being of the animals, and especially for the educational programs of Philadelphia schools.

In many cases, schools made a commitment to the business community by identifying territories, particular branches, or even companies that could benefit from expertise in dealing with the COVID-19 crisis (and by providing them with students, professors, graduates, and/or business professionals with whom the school is in contact, to help deal with a particular problem). Sometimes, schools brought together representatives from these various groups to form a task force, a think tank, or a convivium on behalf of a company or a particular business community.

It is particularly remarkable that in almost all cases, the approach followed by the business schools was initiated by a clear desire to help the community and society through an action developed with (or in favor of) companies.

In most cases, it was the business school that offered its services, knowing that its integration into the business world and into society had put it in a position to spot a problem. It should be noted that the cases in which companies went to schools to ask for their support (less numerous, but they do exist) are no less revealing of the position occupied by the schools in the business community and in society.

It is also interesting to note that the schools based their intervention on already-existing systems (portals, webinar creation, project guidance, start-up labs, executive education activities, applied research, workshops, etc.) that, prior to the COVID-19 crisis, had developed expertise that proved to be relevant in the time of the crisis.

The mobilization of schools' assets to develop a response to the COVID-19 crisis was also achieved through the mobilization of graduates. In this respect, the China Europe International Business School (CEIBS) was a paroxysmal case in terms of both its scale and impact and the fact that being a Euro-Chinese school, with its historical base in Shanghai, China, an acute awareness of the importance of what was at stake was established very early on. However, CEIBS, through its action, has been a particularly successful example of schools mobilizing their graduates and also their students: by donating masks, raising funds, offering free services, providing medical equipment, and volunteering in the local communities, students and graduates have responded to the pandemic in Hubei with agility and compassion, as shown by the following examples (communicated via both personal communication with the dean and via news releases on the school's website):

- Within 24 hours, the CEIBS graduates' association collected 12 million RMB when the donation project was announced on January 30, 2020.
- By the end of May, CEIBS had collected a total of 1.285 billion RMB. The value of the donated materials reached RMB 474 million.
- With the coordinated assistance of 26 CEIBS alumni sections, the procured medical supplies were distributed to nearly 100 provincial and municipal medical teams in Hubei in just a few days.
- Alumni companies have also contributed (and continue to contribute) according to their capacity. For example, alumni companies have distinguished themselves by implementing the following examples:
  o The Fosun Group set up a global command center, which quickly delivered donated materials to the front line through its sourcing network covering 23 countries.

- o At JD Logistics, more than 100,000 employees across China made a concerted effort to ensure that emergency materials were reasonably coordinated, shipped in an orderly fashion, and delivered quickly.
- o Yuwell Medical mobilized its employees to work overtime to ensure the supply of medical materials.
- CEIBS alumni sections abroad also spontaneously organized to provide meals, masks, and travel assistance to those who were temporarily stranded.

The proactive approach of management schools, the desire to "do good" and contribute to resolving the problems posed by the COVID-19 crisis, is attested by the fact that the know-how (particularly in terms of hackathons and digital platforms) has led to particularly innovative approaches that are the reversal to those seeking to help a company, a business community, a region, or a particular employment area. That is, they seek to tackle a general problem (creating organizations that are resilient to the coronavirus crisis, strengthening health systems, developing social solidarity in the face of COVID-19, avoiding the exclusion of elderly people who must confine themselves, etc.). A platform makes it possible to solicit proposals worldwide while retaining or encouraging individual commitment from students, teachers, and the school. This involves facilitating the creation of start-ups (by providing a toolbox for such creation), giving support to actors already in activity who face a particular challenge, and so forth. In most cases, the project has a limited duration (on the order of 2 or 3 months), but the school supports certain projects over the long term (and it is assumed that for others, a decisive impetus was thus given). In addition, the objective of crisis-management training for students (and also for all participants) is also included in such projects.

All of this allows for both the type of social integration that business schools have been enacting in their new role as full social actors and the way in which the entire sphere of management education has faced the COVID-19 crisis.

Conclusion

The analysis of the consequences of the COVID-19 crisis on management education institutions reveals to what extent this crisis profoundly modifies our understanding of this sector.

Two types of particularly noteworthy lessons can be drawn, corresponding to the two levels at which the response of the management education institutions sector has been structured.

At the first level, a notable effort was made to allow the continuing education of management students and the populations of executives and managers. This happened in various ways, including switching entirely to distance education, attempting to maintain face-to-face teaching when possible and often preferentially, and moving to hybrid teaching styles. In addition, the response of the schools, which endeavored to maintain the most "normal" operations possible, focused as much on teaching questions and questions of selection for the following year as on research questions.

Yet it is remarkable that some schools have gone beyond the quest to operate as efficiently as possible. They have mobilized as full-fledged social actors to help respond to the difficulties caused by the coronavirus crisis at the societal level. This desire to intervene *hic et nunc*, as outlined previously, deserves to be highlighted. It resonates with a problem that emerged for business schools during another crisis – that of 2008. At the end of it, the observation that business schools had done a remarkable job in teaching the techniques, skills, and tools of business administration but had failed in their mission to instill ethics in their students sparked debates that have spread throughout the world of management education.

It appeared that Milton Friedman's position that "there is one and only one social responsibility of business – to use its resources and engage in activities designed to increase its profits" (Friedman, 1962/ 2002, as quoted by Fox, 2012, para. 2) best illustrated the approach that business schools were at that time teaching. They seemed to ignore the fact that the Friedman quote is truncated; Friedman went on to write: "so long as it stays within the rules of the game, which is to say, engages in open and free competition without deception or fraud" (Friedman, 1962/2002, as quoted by Fox, 2012, para. 2). In fact, the foundation of the education provided lay in a misunderstanding of Friedman that had led management education institutions to limit corporate social responsibility to the creation of profit (which was supposed to contribute to the future well-being of the company) by neglecting the present social impact of the company. The "*hic et nunc*" became properly unthinkable in the social domain.

To remedy this state of affairs, following the 2008 crisis, many institutions, among which the European Foundation for Management Development (EFMD) ranked first, as well as many thinkers and researchers in management and just as many business leaders, stressed the need to reintroduce ethics and social responsibility to business schools. But on the question of how, the responses and proposals hardly went beyond the suggestion of strengthening and enriching the ethics and social responsibility courses. The fragility and the lack of impact of this suggestion made the sphere of management education expect a more appropriate and powerful response to this major challenge.

The response to the COVID-19 crisis shows how far schools have come and how much progress they have made. Management education institutions are no longer satisfied with responding to the crisis by maintaining and deepening their standard operations. They position themselves as actors intervening directly to help solve social problems. They see their roles as including social responsibility and the need to act in response to it here and now.

Thus, the COVID-19 crisis shows that the management education sector has made progress and has moved into a new stage in its maturity.

At the second level, the COVID-19 crisis has changed the balance between regional and global development within management education. Obviously, in recent decades, the world of management education has placed great emphasis on the importance of internationalization. The EFMD itself has preached a great deal in favor of the internationalization of faculty, research topics, student recruitment, and so forth. The importance of following this development was evidently apparent, insofar as it enriched debate in the classroom while avoiding the obvious topics and commonplaces that are the subject of consensus only in a very reduced geographical and social framework. In such a context, the development forced research to gain ground and to take a breath of fresh air and made it possible to increase sensitivities and approaches among professors and others. For example, the need for a high level of internationalization has often arisen in order to obtain accreditation for a school or for a program.

The COVID-19 crisis seems to have marked the return of the territorial, the regional, and the national in the field of management education. This is not surprising because the same trend has emerged in many areas, including health, defense, and food: the need for territorial anchoring – to avoid being in a situation of strategic dependence and the impossibility of defining a policy – has reappeared in the light of the many tensions that our societies face because they no longer control their own production and supply chains. It is therefore not surprising that jointly in the field of education management, the importance of not sacrificing territorial, regional, and national anchoring for the benefit of international anchoring is reimposing itself. For example, the prospect that the flow of foreign students (which had seemed to want to increase steadily on campuses) would slow down, that their proportion in the student body would decrease, reappeared after having been forgotten for 30 years. There has been a sudden reemergence of the importance of the fact that management education institutions are often important local, regional, and national institutions – places that have shaped local leadership for years, institutions whose names enjoy an important local aura that partly guarantees the development of the institutions. In addition, the examination of the commitments of schools in favor of the resolution of social problems created by COVID-19, mentioned previously, shows that in most cases, this commitment took place at the level of the primary anchoring territory of the schools – that is, regional or national rather than international. All of this encourages a rebalancing of the approaches brought into play by the management education sector. This rebalancing is certainly the bearer of new developments for management education that are better anchored in the humanities because it avoids culturally disembodied and socially evanescent approaches.

References

Alvarado, G., and Romero, J. (2020, April 15). Taking care of its community: The way IPADE business school has handled the COVID-19. *EFMD Global Blog.* https://blog.efmdglobal.org/2020/04/15/taking-care-of-its-community-the-way-ipade-business-school-has-handled-the-covid-19/.

Brammer, S., and Clark, T. (2020). COVID-19 and management education: Reflections on challenges, opportunities, and potential futures. *British Journal of Management, 31*(3), 453–456.

Byrne, J. A. (2020a, September 2). *Class profile: Harvard enrolls smallest MBA class in decades.* Poets & Quants. https://poetsandquants.com/

2020/09/02/the-new-hbs-class-profile-harvard-enrolls-smallest-mba-class-in-decades/

(2020b, August 5). *Should MBA programs make the GMAT & GRE optional?* Poets & Quants. https://poetsandquants.com/2020/08/05/should-mba-programs-make-the-gmat-gre-optional.

(2020c, June 10). *UVA Darden extends pandemic accommodations into 2020–2021 admissions.* Poets & Quants. https://poetsandquants.com/2020/06/10/uva-darden-2020-2021-mba-application-deadlines/?pq-cat egory=admissions&pq-category-2=mba-essay-questions-and-deadlines &utm_campaign=PQNL&utm_medium=email&_hsmi=89323802&_ hsenc=p2ANqtz-_RlzimHRnoVYGjyeQcyXVmnIzQHbQ6fAqyBPS kOeyWqxuXDYnQygGFbbMPSI52sk-0oaBdnCpvo6ddWwLei8tm IIhlmA&utm_content=89323802&utm_source=hs_email.

Canguilhem, G. (1991). *The normal and the pathological.* Zone Books.

Cornuel, E., and Hommel, U. (2012). Business schools as a positive force for fostering societal change-meeting the challenges of the post-crisis world. *Business and Professional Ethics Journal,* 31(2), 289–312.

Fox, J. (2012, April 18). The social responsibility of business is to increase . . . what exactly? *Harvard Business Review.* https://hbr.org/2012/04/you-might-disagree-with-milton.

Friedman, M. (1962). *Capitalism and freedom.* University of Chicago Press.

Habermas, J. (1976). *Legitimation crisis.* Heinemann.

Hodges, C., Moore, S., Lockee, B., Trust, T., and Bond, A. (2020, March 27). The difference between emergency remote teaching and online learning. *Educause Review.* https://er.educause.edu/articles/2020/3/the-difference-between-emergency-remote-teaching-and-online-learning.

INSEAD. (2021). *The latest news on how INSEAD Master Programmes is responding to the COVID-19 situation.* www.insead.edu/covid-19-updates/students-participants.

Joung, M. (2020, August 17). *Students protest tuition hikes as universities continues online.* VOA. www.voanews.com/covid-19-pandemic/stu dents-protest-tuition-hikes-universities-continue-online.

Kleyn, N. (2020, April 9). How Gordon Institute of Business Science responds to the COVID-19 crisis. *EFMD Global Blog.* https://blog .efmdglobal.org/2020/04/09/how-gordon-institute-of-business-science-response-to-the-covid-19-crisis/.

Krishnamurthy, S. (2020). The future of business education: A commentary in the shadow of the Covid-19 pandemic. *Journal of Business Research,* 117, 1–5.

Mintzberg, H. (1979, December). An emerging strategy of "direct" research. *Administrative Science Quarterly,* 24(4), 582–589.

Mintzberg, H., and Waters, J. A. (1985, July/September). Of strategies, deliberate and emergent. *Strategic Management Journal*, 6(3), 257–272.

Morin, E. (2020). *Sur la crise*. Champs essais.

Moules, J. (2020, April 12). MBA students demand tuition fees refunds over campus closures. *Financial Times*. https://www.ft.com/content/d093664c-0381-487f-99e6-027230e2104f.

Roth, C. (2020, October 21). Elite business schools see surge in applications in lousy economy. *Bloomberg Business Week*. www.bloombergquint.com/businessweek/u-s-business-schools-mba-program-applications-are-up-amid-coronavirus-pandemic.

Saviotti, M. (2020, May 21). COVID-19, society, innovation & sustainable business review from Grenoble Ecole de Management [Interview with Loick Roche]. *EFMD Global Blog*. https://blog.efmdglobal.org/2020/05/21/covid-19-society-innovation-sustainable-business-review-from-grenoble-ecole-de-management/.

Symonds, M. (2020, August 3). What are B-schools doing to support businesses during the pandemic? *Forbes*. www.forbes.com/sites/mattsymonds/2020/08/03/what-are-business-schools-doing-to-support-businesses-during-the-covid-19-pandemic/?sh=6ea0defd2066.

Wharton School. (2020, July 31). *Community updates*. www.wharton.upenn.edu/coronavirus/.

14 | Developing Future Leaders with New Partners: Trends from a Business School Perspective

FRANK BOURNOIS

Introduction

The current COVID-19 crisis has triggered unprecedented upheaval on a global scale. From a strictly public health point of view, however, humanity has proven itself capable of joining forces and transcending political boundaries.

The Crisis Is Transforming Management and Leadership

Coming hot on the heels of our bicentenary year, the pandemic has had a severe impact on the work of École Supérieure de Commerce de Paris (ESCP) across all of our European campuses, affecting our faculty members and international students alike. The crisis has confounded forecasters completely and now raises serious questions as to the responsibilities of managers and the meaning attached to their work.

For the heads of higher education institutions, this issue takes on a dual significance. First and foremost, there is the question of the meaning, usefulness, value, and purpose of the knowledge we produce for society in general. Then, of course, there is the dissemination of actionable knowledge for the benefit of our stakeholders: students, alumni, businesses, organizations, and public administrations.

As deans of business schools, our duty reaches above and beyond the production and dissemination of knowledge, methods, and managerial practices. It also consists of guiding and responding to events and overseeing the constant adaptation of individuals within structured social systems.

Finally, as an academic specializing in leadership, I find myself wondering how business schools can best prepare the business leaders of the future for the challenges they will be facing.

I. Rethinking Leadership after the Experience of Multiple Lockdowns

1. ESCP as a Pan-European Business School

Our school was founded in 1819 and has rarely closed, even during the darkest periods of the three wars of 1870, 1914, and 1939. ESCP has 7,300 students in initial training, in programs ranging from bachelor to doctorate, and 5,000 managers in executive education (ExecEd). The school is unique in that it boasts campuses in six European countries, with national recognition as a *Grande Ecole* in France, as a university in Germany by the Berlin Senate, as a university in Italy, as a university in Spain, and as a British higher education institution. All of these campuses are managed and coordinated by a team that is united around European values and the ESCP culture: Excellence, Singularity, Creativity & Pluralism.

The pandemic has hit ESCP in several waves:

- **The first phase came in February–March 2020,** when our Turin campus was the first to be hit. The resilience and relevance demonstrated by the Italian entity in its reactions provided some good practices for the benefit of the school as a whole, as the Madrid, Warsaw, Berlin, and Paris campuses were then confronted in turn with the challenges of managing a school in lockdown. Finally, the London campus was the last to close. During this initial lockdown phase, the school capitalized on its previous experience of coordinating multiple campuses, and our faculty members built on their experience of using digital tools. There was a reconceptualization of the student recruitment process for the start of the 2020–21 academic year, with written tests but no oral interviews so as to place all candidates on an equal footing, whatever inequalities there might be in their access to good-quality digital facilities. We must salute the continued research efforts by the faculty who leaped into action and succeeded in producing *Managing a Post-Covid19 Era* (Bunkanwanicha et al., 2020), a collection of impact papers enabling students, employers and companies, and governments to better understand the global pandemic and its multifaceted implications for our societies.
- **The second phase came with the start of the new school year, from September 2020 through to the end of the year.** After a start to the

new school year with the students present in person, in compliance with the health regulations, a second partial lockdown was put in place with the introduction of a curfew. Because the various governments did not all make this decision at the same time, the organization of student mobility was disrupted, but it did provide an opportunity to put the new teaching facilities to use. At ESCP, we opened the Phygital (contraction of *physical* and *digital*) Factory, a place where our faculty can record their teaching modules easily. At the same time, increasing proportions of remote courses were organized, both synchronously and asynchronously. As an indication, whereas 3,070 courses were delivered online during the first lockdown, the second lockdown saw a significant increase to 4,200 online courses, representing more than 80,000 hours of teaching. ESCP has now entered a period of "Mobility and Motility" where students keep enjoying the experience of physical mobility and the experience of learning in just moving intellectually.

• **The third phase began in January 2021,** with the various states making different decisions regarding the physical presence of students in higher education institutions. The latter is currently in a hybrid phase, with the possibility for students to return, subject to a maximum of 20 percent of the students physically present. However, the schools have now mastered the digital tools for the courses and services they offer, which is a big difference compared to the first lockdown. In March 2020, the schools were unable to organize the recruitment orals. This year, however, they will take place digitally, which shows the confidence higher education institutions now feel in their adaptation to digital technology. However, there is a feeling of weariness at present – weariness with the digital world, as well as with the lack of social contacts for our young people at a very important time in their student lives. It is this psychological aspect that led President Macron to keep the schools open. This third phase has also brought an awareness that ExecEd will no longer concern the same services or same profiles, and we will come back to that in detail in Part II. Similarly, in the governance of higher education institutions, meetings are taking place with a high level of quality, especially board meetings, and the same goes for the governance of the EFMD board and the EFMD deans conference, which I was able to attend at the beginning of February 2021. The level of satisfaction of the deans was very high, despite the distance and lack of real contact.

2. Responding to the Pandemic: Our Eight Key Takeaways

In short, the school's internal stakeholders – students, faculty, adminis-trative staff – have been strongly mobilized, and from our vantage point today, at the beginning of 2021, we can outline eight practical lessons that will inevitably change the way a Business School is run, in a lasting manner.

1. Taking the 20-40 digital turn today: ESCP has become convinced that neither students nor management research has anything to gain from the uberization of the business school model. What is needed is more widespread use of the forms of blended learning that were already emerging before the pandemic. We have also chosen to give the teaching staff a great deal of pedagogical flexibility. Looking to 2040, it has been decided to have a minimum of 20 percent digital and 40 percent in-class teaching for all courses. This will allow some teachers to favor 80 percent of class time with their students present in person and 20 percent remote, for example, or others might prefer to divide their teaching into 40 percent face-to-face content and 60 per-cent digital. This will make it possible to adapt the pedagogy of management disciplines. The challenge now is to produce digital modules that can be integrated into a symbiotic face-to-face architecture.

2. Delivering premium asynchronous courses: The crisis has revealed the need to provide students with courses of the highest standard wherever they are in the world. This has led many business schools to produce prerecorded (asynchronous) modules to take account of the realities of time-zone differences. Pedagogically, the production of an asynchronous module is much more demanding than filming a syn-chronous course livened up by questions from students. The asyn-chronous module must captivate the learner from beginning to end by means of a teaching sequence that is punctuated with videos of illustrations and quizzes for midterm evaluations, along with impec-cable presentation materials.

3. Rethinking ExecEd: As will be discussed in Part II of this chapter, the changes underway in ExecEd are drastic. Corporate expectations will be radically different once the pandemic issues are resolved. The share of digital methods will increase, whereas the duration of sem-inars will be shortened considerably. Business school professors will be invited as expert witnesses, rather than as the half-day facilitators they were in the past, when they would give presentations with (albeit sophisticated) overhead transparencies and pass from one subgroup room to another to encourage executives to solve case studies. If the business school professor previously took the lead over the group of learners, it will now be the university or a pedagogical coordinator it has appointed who will lead the group of business school professors invited to the company's training.

4. Striking a new equilibrium between research and teaching: The rise of digital technology will require business school deans to speed up the production of educational capsules for students and continuing education managers in a short space of time. This will have consequences for business school rankings, where the quality of an institution will be measured in terms of research, student selectivity, the pedagogical quality of teachers, and the size of the business school's digital offering. Digital technology will not replace research; it will become an additional criterion for evaluation.

5. Launching a massive real estate plan despite the uncertainties: The question of business school real estate is being raised once again as we move from managing real estate to digital estate. The need will shift from managing classrooms, floor space, and teacher researchers' offices to questions of ergonomics, furniture, and equipment adapted to digital technologies and teaching resource storage capacity in terabytes.

6. Not resting on the success of our flagship programs: Digitization is reshuffling the cards when it comes to educational portfolios, with the expected flowering of specialized and regularly updated digital certificates. The accumulation and combination of these certificates can lead to lifelong diplomas.

7. Anticipating what Google, Apple, Facebook, Amazon, and Microsoft (GAFAM) and educational technology (EdTech) will be able to offer tomorrow: This will involve establishing a position for the major digital and EdTech companies in higher education. They have a technological advantage in the global spectrum and have the financial muscle to acquire renowned universities, but they also run the risk of being rejected by the governments that serve as regulators of higher education. In any case, business schools will not be able to avoid taking this potential new player, partner, and predator into account.

8. Positioning higher education institutions in relation to EdTech: It is striking that there is much more talk about the transformation and innovation of EdTech companies than about the transformation of

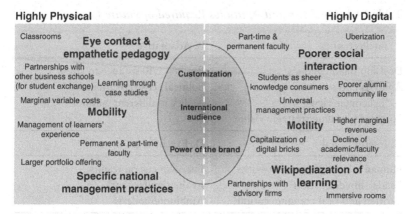

Figure 14.1 Finding the right pedagogical mix.
Source: Augmented from Bournois & Roussillon (1998).

business schools. EdTech companies tended to be seen as subcontractors for the business schools before the pandemic, and increasing digitalization should not reverse that relationship. It would be a bit like science being hosted by Wikipedia.

Business schools must therefore skillfully weigh up the advantages and risks when they engage in a pedagogical mix that combines physical and digital. Figure 14.1 shows the main elements to be taken into account, bearing in mind that there is no absolute "one best way" and that a balanced mix needs to be constructed according to parameters such as the duration of the training, the level of the participants, the size of the group, and the variety of the international audience.

3. Executive Profiles and Competencies

In a recently published work, Rebecca Henderson (2020) of Harvard Business School explains that managers now have no choice but to totally reinvent capitalism. In *La Prouesse Française* (French Prowess), published in 2017, I insisted on the defining characteristics of the French style of management, highlighting its strengths and the weaknesses in need of a rethink (Suleiman et al., 2017).

The COVID-19 crisis has thrust this debate front and center. Attentiveness to well-being at work, respect for individuality within groups, and a commitment to the greater good are all key pillars of European humanist culture. These values have come rapidly to the fore

Table 14.1. *Qualities and Aptitudes Required of Future Leaders*

A. Intellectual	B. Adaptative
Decision making/ethics	Resilience/Resistance to stress
Analysis and synthesis/	Political sense/governance
"helicopter view"	Agility in different cultures
Forward-planning/strategic vision	
C. Interpersonal	**D. Executive**
Human relations/teams/networks	Energy/focus on results
Leadership/delegation	Evaluation/feedback
Written and oral communication	Ambition/modesty
E. Digital	**F. Environmental**
Digital transformation	Construction of ecosystems
Interdisciplinarity/artificial	Integrating the interests of all
intelligence	stakeholders
Disruption	Focus on sustainable development

Source: Adapted from Bournois and Roussillon (1998), Bournois et al. (2010), and Bournois and Allary (2019).

through the decisive measures taken to protect citizens, respect individual liberties, and prepare for the economic recovery of the European Union.

Leaders in both the public and private sectors are acutely aware of the impact of this enforced pause, this moment of reflection on a global scale, and must learn the lessons of the current crisis. Going forward, the six major dimensions identified in Table 14.1 will be of primary importance by 2030.

The ESCP Community Rises to the Occasion Once Again

I could not be more impressed by, or proud of, the monumental work done by the ESCP faculty – and all in record time! Students, alumni, and decision makers will find herein a rich profusion of ideas, debates, and pragmatic proposals for the future of the post-2020 economy.

What variety and depth of talent we have in the academic community of our business school! All of our European campuses, all of the disciplines of management studies, and all of the principal dimensions of decision making are represented here. Six overarching themes emerge, corresponding to the major challenges awaiting managers:

the digital transformation (particularly at work); the limits of individualism and the rise of new forms of collective action; inclusive management/leadership; the resilience of businesses in times of crisis; uncertainty and the need for change (or stability) in the financial markets and the markets for goods and services; and finally, the challenges this crisis raises for higher education.

II. Business Schools Must Engage in Strategic Partnerships

During the past decade, large companies have made profound changes to the way they design programs within their corporate universities. Overall, they have shortened the duration of seminars for senior executives and managers, professionalized their program managers, internationalized the sourcing of their speakers, increased the variety of teaching tools, opened up the themes to include individual development and codevelopment, introduced metrics to systematically evaluate the added value perceived by participants, and so on.

This has led to the creation of much more varied ecosystems than in the past. The main idea behind this contribution is to show that the *Grandes Écoles* no longer have to do everything in-house, from collecting the company's needs to providing certificates once the seminar is over, including the implementation of face-to-face or distance learning sequences. The trend that is emerging for the new decade will consist of business schools creating, devising, and professionalizing partnerships with other business schools, with consortia of leading companies in certain sectors of activity, and most certainly, with the leading professional service firms (PSFs), the consultancy firms for which education is at the heart of their strategy.

The ExecEd environment will be different tomorrow, driven by new quality expectations, a new relationship to the workspace, and new organizational and time-management habits. New types of partnerships will flourish in the coming decade. They will deliver diplomas and certificates from largely digital offerings, and the highest-profile and most reputable of them will succeed in attracting corporate leaders to take on a doctoral thesis based largely on their professional expertise.

1. Digitalization and Customization as Partners

Among the major developments of the past decade, there is one absolute certainty: digitalization is going hand in hand with the customization of ExecEd needs. The interviews I have conducted with many directors of corporate universities underline the trend toward microlearning, that is, highly specialized, carefully customized modules. At first glance, this may seem paradoxical if we think that digitalization boils down to automation, the accumulation of teaching resources, and increasing storage of knowledge (knowledge accumulation). In fact, if we know how to identify the needs of each learner in detail (senior executives and managers), if we know their previous experience, their personal approach to the digital world, and the time they have available for their personal training, then digitalization will make it possible to (1) provide them with specific resources, (2) guide them in their choice of modules, (3) provide them with numerous self-assessments, and (4) provide them with points of reference in relation to other managers in their category, all while respecting their rate of progress in conjunction with their direct bosses and line management. To do this, three main conditions must be met:

1. The business school must have a vast pool of teaching resources at its disposal.
2. The business school must have an information system linked to its teaching; this does not exist in many cases because the information systems mainly manage the administrative life of the business school, leaving pedagogical matters in the hands of teachers. If the business school succeeds in establishing the connection between pedagogy and information system, this opens up numerous possibilities for tracing individual paths and maintaining the motivation of participants to go further.
3. Because of the faster obsolescence of management knowledge, it is essential to have knowledge that is constantly updated and targeted by sector of activity, company size, and management issue. This is all the more essential because ExecEd is increasingly committed to lifelong learning, with shorter programs that are more dispersed throughout the career.

Today's business school, taken in isolation, with its permanent faculty of between 150 and 300 professors generally, will not be able to provide the answers to this variety of needs requiring constant updating and dealing with heterogeneous business sectors and countries.

Alliances will be required, first to boost the revenues that will be increasingly necessary to finance investments (growing faculty size, digital development, rethinking buildings and real estate, etc.). Business schools will not disappear totally – there will always be a need for research production and teaching professionals (management faculty reproduction). The decade from 2010 to 2020 saw the Shanghai research ranking reach its acme, introducing a race toward high productivity in research, and business schools will continue to be ranked according to their ability to select the best students, their ability to produce research, and their ability to produce and market attractive and updated digital modules.

2. Partnerships at a Crossroads

In terms of alliances to be made, business schools are currently at a crossroads; according to the trendsetters, these alliances will be of four main kinds:

1. Alliances inside the existing network of business schools in order to provide a broad range of resources, combining materials from reputable business schools located in different geographies: the CEMS, with Bocconi, Cornell, Calcutta, and Keio, among others, is one illustration of a such a pioneering initiative.
2. Alliances with a consortium of companies (by sector, size, country). Business schools, mostly those with specialized know-how (supply chain, finance, leadership development, etc.), will thrive on a real-time connection with industrial partners. The latter will provide the expertise and high-caliber teaching leaders that will make the consortium extremely attractive to students.
3. Alliances with EdTech are also very likely, although there are risks of cannibalization. EdTech companies will be seeking academic legitimization, whereas schools will be in search of technological innovations.
4. Alliances with consulting companies will certainly be more promising because business schools and professional service firms (PSFs; consulting and advisory firms) are almost next of kin. Both are knowledge extensive and have education as a common differentiating factor. Business schools have the mission of grooming future leaders, whereas PSF or audit and advisory firms excel in tailoring management advice to the upper echelons of organizations.

My take is that it will be hard for business schools to establish sustainable alliances with all of these different players at the same time.

Business school deans and governance will find themselves facing strategic choices and having to weigh up the relative benefits of their newly wrought relationships: the likelihood of boosting ExecEd revenues, raising their profile and enhancing their reputation, creating a sustainable and inimitable advantage, and increasing outstanding faculty and selected students.

3. Partnerships for MBA and Doctorate Programs

Alliances may also develop on several specific program levels (bachelor, master/MSc, and PhD). I would take the example of the visionary Next MBA program that Mazars developed in 2012 with participants from six or seven leading international companies. In this spirit, Mazars is working with business schools to develop its top leaders through a PhD degree. It provides the experience of research, with the dissertation topic being aligned with the job profile of the future leaders. Whereas in the past, top leaders would not find the time to enroll in a time-consuming PhD program, in the 2020s, we will certainly see growth in executive PhDs for senior managers eager to look at their practice with hindsight and contribute to management science. Such doctoral undertakings are very likely to have the following features:

1. Academic production focused on the hot managerial issues the leaders have on their front burners. In the near future, corporate social responsibility may very well also include academic social responsibility (ASR), especially in business environments fraught with risks of fast knowledge obsolescence.
2. These PhD degrees will serve as markers to differentiate the development paths of high-caliber leaders who will be seen as able to translate knowledge into action. As PhD holders, they will obtain a token of in-depth investigation skills and a sign of helicopter-view abilities.
3. Their doctoral pieces may get published in journals because they will present guarantees of scientific regard, as well as transferability to practitioners.
4. These future "leaders and doctors" will ideally be mentored by a tandem of two PhD supervisors representing the two worlds of academia and practice, very much in the approach and spirit of Peter Drucker in *The Practice of Management* (Drucker, 1955/2007):

Above all, the new technology will not render managers superfluous or replace them by mere technicians. On the contrary, it will demand many more managers. It will greatly extend the management area, many people now considered rank-and-file will have to become capable of doing management work. The great majority of technicians will have to be able to understand what management is and to see and think managerially. And on all levels the demands on the manager's responsibility and competence, his vision, his capacity to choose between alternate risks, his economic knowledge and skill, his ability to manage managers and to manage worker and work, his competence in making decisions, will be greatly increased. (pp. 19–20)

5. PhD dissertations of this new kind will necessarily be innovation oriented. Disruptive methodological approaches must be encouraged.
6. It goes without saying that digital transformation aspects will be central to most dissertations of the 2020s.
7. The augmented "doctor and leader" is bound to play a key role in the dissemination of knowledge to peers internally and clients externally. This constitutes a radical change from the times when knowledge was reserved only for the learned.

4. The Making of the New Corporate University

From all of the previously discussed points, the profile of tomorrow's new corporate university will emerge. Broadly speaking, its characteristics will include the following:

1. **A close link with the company's strategy.** The role of the university will clearly be seen as a support mechanism for the company's global strategy. A specific budget will clarify the contributions of each participant (business units, central budget, the participants themselves, etc.), whether for training activities or for obtaining certificates and diplomas, because all this will be done in the framework of partnerships with business schools.
2. **Close coordination with career management.** More than ever, the corporate university will be linked in with the systems for identifying potential and career development. Several modalities will exist on the spectrum:
   - Option 1 – participants are sent by career management.
   - Option 2 – the university defines the profiles of the participants it hosts.

3. **Identification of target populations.** This presupposes the existence of a sufficient internal population to justify the existence of a dedicated structure. In terms of volume, we find the following:
   • Level 0 – COMEX and extended COMEX (top 300)
   • Level 1 – COMEX-1 staff and leading experts (top 2,000). Integrate expertise and functional aspects.
   • Level 2 – those considered capable of joining level 1 ("key players").
   • Level 3 – "key business lines of the company." The aim is to provide business units with training that is specific to their profession and know-how.
   • Level 4 – "customers, suppliers, and ecosystem." Corporate universities will also develop modules bringing together the different stakeholders in the company. In the extreme, participants from competing companies will reflect together on sector developments. The environmental, social, and governance (ESG) dimension will be more prominent than ever before in the modules and certificates issued.
4. **A range of offers.** There will be variety in the portfolio of education courses, their durations, e-learning methods, certification, and the possibility of combining several modules that will progressively earn credits towards obtaining a diploma. All the content will be updated very regularly. Participants will also be the developers of modules for others.
5. **A metric and permanent tracking.** Assessments will be carried out in an automated way to evaluate (1) the individual progress of participants, (2) the overall quality of a program, (3) the efficiency of the corporate university, and (4) the internal and external stakeholders. Obviously, a tracking system linked to information systems will make it possible to follow up with and motivate participants by tracking what they have received and read, or not, and so forth. This learner-centric approach will make it possible to provide highly individualized services. This is the advent of learning analytics, the main vocation of which will be to motivate and accompany participants in their learning. The electronic terminals (e-beacons) placed in the company will remind participants of their training duties.
6. **External recognition through accreditation bodies, such as Corporate Learning Improvement Process (CLIP)/European**

Foundation for Management Development (EFMD), partners of business schools, professional branches, and so forth. Just as there are business school rankings, the visibility of company universities will be reflected in rankings highlighting the triple added value for the individual, for the company, and for society.

Conclusion

Our community is particularly proud of the mission statement we set for ourselves a few years ago: "To inspire and educate business leaders who will impact the world." In that collective spirit, it falls to me to salute the initiative of three colleagues who have launched and steered this project with incredible energy and commitment. On behalf of our president, Philippe Houzé, and everybody here at ESCP, I would therefore like to take this opportunity to thank Pramuan Bunkanwanicha, Régis Coeurderoy, and Sonia Ben Slimane, without whom the project would never have risen to such heights. The call for contributions inspired a veritable flood of original scientific work, despite the fact that faculty members were already overburdened by the sudden need to create teaching materials for remote learning while also preparing for an unprecedented level of digital engagement in 2020–21. Once again, I would like to express my admiration and extend my sincere thanks to all the colleagues who have contributed to this wonderful outpouring of intellectual solidarity and stimulation. Thank you for sharing so generously the fruits of this prolific period of reflection, inspired by these uncertain times.

ESCP is a business school with a profound connection to the European humanist tradition. As we traverse this time of global crisis, I am reminded of a passage from the memoirs of Jean Monnet, one of the founding fathers of the European Union, published in 1978. His words ring as true now as ever, and they offer a beacon as we navigate these turbulent times: "When people find themselves in a new situation, they adapt to it and they change. But so long as they hope that things may stay as there are, or be the subject of compromise, they are unwilling to listen to new ideas" (Monnet, 1978, p. 344).

References

Bournois, F., and Allary, C. (2019, July 30). La coopération entre dirigeants: un ingrédient essentiel du leadership. *Harvard Business Review France*.

www.hbrfrance.fr/chroniques-experts/2019/07/27217-la-cooperation-entre-dirigeants-un-ingredient-essentiel-du-leadership/.

Bournois, F., Duval-Hamel, J., Roussillon, S., and Scaringella, J., eds. (2010). *Handbook of top management teams*. Palgrave MacMillan.

Bournois, F., and Roussillon, S. (1998). *Préparer les dirigeants de demain: une approche internationale de la gestion des cadres à haut potentiel*. Les éditions d'Organisation.

Bunkanwanicha, P., Coeurderoy, R., and Ben Slimaneecsp, S., eds. (2020). *Managing a post-Covid19 era*. https://escp.eu/faculty-research/erim/Impact-Papers/managing-a-post-Covid-era.

Drucker, P. (2007). *The practice of management*. Butterworth Heinemann. [Original work published in 1955]

Henderson, R. (2020). *Reimagining capitalism in a world on fire*. Public Affairs.

Monnet, J. (1978). *Memoirs*. Richard Mayne, trans. Doubleday & Company, Inc.

Suleiman, E., Bournois, F., and Jaïdi, Y. (2017). *La prouesse française: le management du CAC 40 vu d'ailleurs*. Odile Jacob.

15 | *Leading an (Unusual) Academic Institution through a Crisis: A Personal Reflection*

JEAN-FRANÇOIS MANZONI

The COVID-19 crisis was a perfect storm for an independent business school like International Institute for Management Development (IMD). On the positive side, we started the crisis on the wings of a substantial revenue-growth momentum – 2020 was going to be our best year ever by a mile! On the negative side, more than 80 percent of our revenues come – or rather, came then – from nondegree programs requiring one party to travel to another, overwhelmingly across national borders. Within the 20 percent of revenues coming from degree programs, more than half came from the executive MBA (EMBA) program, which also requires extensive international travel for students. In other words, as of February 2020, more than 90 percent of our revenues were suddenly at very severe risk.

On the organizational front, January 2020 was the launch of a new governing body called the Executive Committee, a larger group – nine members versus the previous five – including key staff function heads reporting to me. The year also started with us sharing with IMD's staff the pretty negative results of an internal climate survey conducted in late 2019. Faculty responses were very positive, but the staff (outnumbering faculty six to one) reported a very clear lack of trust in the management team – in terms of both competence and intentions. The report had made for very painful reading, and the town-hall meeting in which I reported the results and faced anonymous questions from more than 200 staff members was brutal.

Given our economic model, the crisis became very much of a reality for us quite early in the process, as Open Program executive education (ExecEd) participants and Custom Program corporate partners started calling us to ask for postponements. In the following weeks and months, I experienced a very interesting case of "theory meets practice." As a professor of leadership and organizational development, I had been studying and educating leaders for about three decades. So I "knew what to do," at least in theory. Having to "do it," especially

311

under the intense pressure created by the risk of revenues grinding to a halt (and nobody to bail us out if we failed), led to four major insights that I would like to share in this chapter.

I am acutely aware that I could have organized these insights differently, so I am not presenting them as "the way" to lead in a crisis. Please consider them as a humble personal reflection on what has been a fascinating – and so far, very successful – experience. Befitting this personal reflection positioning, the style of this chapter is conversational – I will be addressing you, the reader and the leader of your organization.

These four insights are not presented by order of importance – I think they are all equally important – but hopefully, the *sequence* in which they are introduced will appear logical to you and will make them more memorable.

Insight 1: Maintaining a Very Engaged and Aligned Leadership Team

As critical as the leader is, the performance of the *leadership team* (LT) is going to be at least as important. In particular, it is even more important during a crisis for the members of the LT to all be *engaged* and *aligned*.

You need all members of the LT *engaged* because in a crisis, you can't be everywhere at the same time, even less so than in normal times. If you try to do it all alone, you will exhaust yourself in addition to becoming a bottleneck. In addition, the troops would for sure notice that some LT members are not fully engaged, which would undermine their morale and your efforts.

You also need all the members of the LT to be even more *aligned* than during "normal times." Research has shown that human beings are fundamentally programmed to look for threats, even under normal conditions.[1] Unsurprisingly, this propensity to look for threats becomes even more salient during a crisis. As a result, faculty and staff

---

[1] See, among others, H. A. Rued, C. J. Hilmert, A. M. Strahm, and L. E. Thomas (2018), "The Influence of Stress on Attentional Bias to Threat: An Angry Face and a Noisy Crowd," *Psychonomic Bulletin & Review*, 26(2), 1–8. Or more generally, R. F. Baumeister, E. Bratslavsky, C. Finkenauer, and K. D. Vohs (2001), "Bad Is Stronger Than Good," *Review of General Psychology*, 4(4), 323–370, https://doi.org/10.1037/1089-2680.5.4.323.

analyze communications from the LT even more carefully than usual, actively looking for any sign of individual weakness in, and of lack of alignment between, members of the LT.

Outside of crises, most LTs have learned to look at least moderately (if not always perfectly) engaged and aligned. Crises ought to bring the best out of LTs, so why would they suddenly start underperforming individually and/or collectively? For two reasons.

The first reason is individual: While some members of your LT will immediately "step up" during the crisis, showing the confidence, the willingness, and the ability to take on more responsibilities, *other members of the LT will tend to wither* because they lack one or more of these qualities. This withering can manifest itself in different ways. Some individuals will seem to produce a lower – or at least a less-than-maximum – level of effort and engagement. Others will be "working hard," but their time and effort will seem to you to be misallocated (too much time and energy on lesser priorities, at the expense of real "must-win battles"). Another sign of withering is increasing indecisiveness/inability to make basic decisions.

An LT member's insufficient individual effort, incorrect prioritization, and/or growing indecisiveness will rapidly become problematic and potentially debilitating for employees reporting to them. It is also very frustrating for the leader and for the LT colleagues who are "stepping up." Frustrated leaders can react aggressively – increasingly berating the withering team member(s) – or more passively, by avoiding them and withdrawing from interactions. Both are suboptimal solutions.

The second reason why an LT's performance may decrease during a crisis is that *the crisis may reveal heretofore undetected fault lines within the team.* These fault lines are due to less-than-100-percent alignment on the organization's strategy and/or priorities. Less than 100 percent can still involve a relatively high degree of agreement, and that degree of agreement may be sufficient to go unnoticed in an environment that is not hyper-stretched. But in a crisis, where resources become very scarce, questions from staff become very pointed, and decisions need to be made very quickly, the imperfect alignment will start to become observable and problematic.

What can the leader do to contribute to a higher-performing LT?

1. One important step is to remain patient and compassionate toward the team members who wither. Understand, with empathy and

compassion, that their withering is not intentional and probably reflects forces that are currently overwhelming them. When you can accept your colleagues' difficulties with compassion, it becomes easier to see that the solution is neither berating them (which will only increase their fear of failure) nor disconnecting from them (which will simply trigger a vicious circle of decreasing perform-ance). The solution is instead to make sure you remain *engaged* with the withering team member(s) and spend *more* time with them rather than less. These discussions will enable you to help increase the individual's confidence, willingness, and ability to contribute more during this challenging period.

2. With respect to alignment, you should invest *even more time and energy* in making sure that you and your team are strongly aligned on the key parameters. (This was particularly true during the COVID-19 crisis because it forced LTs to work remotely to a large and often complete extent. The lack of ongoing, informal contact made it more challenging to stay organically aligned.)

In a way, the crisis acts as a dam that lowers the level of water in a river. When the water sits at, say, 1 meter high, the 60-centimeter-high rocks are not a problem. As the water level falls to 70 centimeters, the 60-centimeter rocks are not yet observable, but they start becoming a problem for the canoes. At 50 centimeters of water, the rocks are now observable. That's what the crisis does. By lowering the level of the water in the river, smaller rocks – including a small lack of alignment among LT members – become a problem.

Looking back, this is the one dimension on which I probably did the least well, especially during Q1 and Q2 of 2020 (i.e., until I identified this insight and realized that I had started withdrawing from inter-action with two of my ExCo members, which had only made things worse over time). I knew better than to berate them, but the method I (unconsciously) chose to prevent expressing frustration was to with-draw from it. That was decidedly a less effective approach than engaging consciously and compassionately with them, which I did thereafter.

Insight 2: Communicating with the Troops

As mentioned previously, research shows that human beings are fun-damentally programmed to look for threats, even under normal conditions. That's simply the result of evolution, where for the longest of times, our ancestors lived in a world where underestimating a threat could be deadly.

Very legitimately, crisis situations intensify this tendency. When things all around us are relatively positive, we're on the lookout for threats. But when things all around become unmistakably threatening, our amygdala becomes hyperactive, and we start to *really* scan the world for dangers.

In this context, it becomes clear that as a leader, one of your key objectives during a crisis should be to help everybody to *stay calm and focused*.

Clearly, you don't want to go to the other extreme and pretend that that situation is not problematic at all and that all is going to be well. If your people believe you, they won't act with the sense of urgency you need them to have in this crisis. More likely, they won't believe you, and they will think that either you're a fool or you're taking them for one. Neither alternative is a good basis for a strong, positive relationship.

Rather, your goal ought to be to acknowledge that "there are indeed some threats, but (1) these threats are well understood and we have a plan. (2) Executing on this plan is our best bet to get through this crisis."

This, of course, requires you – the leader and the LT – to have such a good understanding of the situation and such a plan to guide productive action. Clearly, this is more likely to happen if, as per the first insight, you have a very engaged and aligned LT.

At IMD, we understood and acknowledged immediately that this crisis could become highly problematic for us, but we also rapidly identified *productive actions that we could take to mitigate the problem*. We placed these actions in the context of our ongoing strategy to highlight the fact that they were very *credible and feasible* actions.

LT members had clear ownership for categories of actions, but they also made sure they engaged their first reports and encouraged these first reports to engage their own staff in the fine-tuning of these actions. The architecture of the plan came from the top, but a lot of ideas and suggestions came from the "bottom up" through a series of connections with subgroups within the organization.

The COVID-19 crisis added an unusual element to a typical crisis: the overwhelming majority of our staff was working from home and was hence deprived of regular physical human contact. We understood that *these conditions of relative isolation would be conducive to a lot of rumors and anxiety.*

As a result, we made two important decisions: First, we immediately named a *Task Force* to gather information on the crisis and its various components. We simply did not want hundreds of people to feel they needed to spend several hours every day just to keep up with the news. So we explicitly gave that role to a few carefully selected individuals. Two, this Task Force and the LT gave very regular updates to the troops on the evolution of the crisis and its impact on us.

Again, the *frequency of communication matters.* We started with weekly "community meetings," then moved to bimonthly (virtual) connections, with updates in between as and when needed. Overcommunicating is dangerous because it feeds everyone's anxiety and devalues the LT's words. But you must still communicate enough and often enough to *maintain this strong sense of calm and deliberate action.*

We even coined a phrase to remind ourselves of this desired state. "At IMD," we say, "we don't get worried; we get busy." And this phrase has now become part of our common folklore.

If keeping the troops calm and productively busy is your first object-ive, your second objective must be to *inspire them.* To do so, we focused on two aspects.

First, we *highlighted the opportunity* that this crisis represents. Yes, the COVID-19 pandemic had the potential of having a very negative impact on IMD, but it could also be a great opportunity. For example, in our case, the downtime that the crisis imposed on us enabled us to dramatically accelerate our investment in technology-enabled learning. We had already started going in that direction, but with this crisis, (a) we suddenly recovered time to do it, and (b) our clients became increas-ingly open to it. In fact, increasingly, they asked us what we could propose to them on this front.

Our second lever to inspire the troops was to consciously and consistently reinforce our staff's *sense of community, shared purpose, and shared destiny.*

In particular, we used every piece of communication to connect actions and activities to our purpose. IMD exists for a reason: *challen-ging what is and inspiring what could be, we develop executives who transform organizations and contribute to society.* All of our faculty and staff know this purpose, but on a daily basis, what each of us does is typically a lot less glamorous. So we needed to remind ourselves that although this or that action may feel mundane or even uninteresting, it is one component in a multiplicative model that leads to value creation for executives, organizations, and society.

Also connected with the purpose, we emphasized the importance of the IMD community. Whereas some organizations around us used this crisis to implement cost-cutting measures that they were thinking of but heretofore had not dared to put in place, we chose instead to emphasize *solidarity within the community* by resorting to partial unemployment and Voluntary Salary Reduction (VSR; starting with a 25 percent VSR by the LT). We encouraged employees to use the intranet to stay connected at a personal level; we supported and celebrated their charity activities; with the help of our IMD coaching community, we also offered staff members free coaching sessions to give them an opportunity to express their concerns and possibly discuss them with a professional.

Our staff understood that IMD's financial means were not infinite and that if the situation worsened, we would have to resort to more painful cost-cutting measures.

Actually, we did end up reducing about 10 percent of our staff positions at the end of the year. By then, most companies in our region had started laying off employees, we had exhausted our ability to use government-sponsored furloughs, and our staff could clearly see how much program activity had dropped and how much money we were losing. The inevitability of layoffs to reduce our cost base was hence very clear by then. Still, to maintain the sense of community in spite of layoffs entirely directed at the staff, we also obtained a near-unanimous vote from faculty accepting a reduction in their 2021 ExecEd rate.[2]

---

[2] As I reread this chapter one last time, I am struck again the importance and helpfulness of the faculty's willingness to (a) contribute over and above the call of duty on the teaching and revenue-generation side and (b) contribute to the cost-reduction effort by accepting some reductions of compensation in 2020 and 2021. Staff working in academic institutions often feel a significant "faculty–staff divide," which can obviously reduce their sense of community and shared purpose. The IMD faculty's unambiguous and immediate "stepping up" was a key component of keeping the IMD community – including its staff and alumni – committed to our collective success.

In the meantime, we think that we maintained our organization at the peak personal and professional levels by pursuing two complementary objectives: First, we communicated frequently, candidly, and resolutely on the challenges and the solutions to ensure that our staff remained *calm and focused on their tasks and their priorities*. Second, we made sure that our communication also *inspired our staff* by (a) highlighting the opportunity that this crisis represented (if we do X and Y, we will come out of the crisis a stronger organization), (b) connecting all our actions to IMD's purpose, and (c) nurturing our employees' sense of community by sharing financial sacrifices for long enough to allow the inevitability of layoffs to become clear.

Insight 3: Balancing Offense and Defense

During a crisis, numerous stakeholders reinforce very regularly to the LT the need to "play defense" – that is, to protect liquidities, line up financing sources, and reduce cost as much as possible. In our case, our alumni, our Foundation Board, and the bank(s) from which we borrowed made sure that my LT colleagues and I remained very focused on this dimension.

But alongside playing defense, you and your LT must also ask a very important question: *Will you come out of the crisis a stronger organization, fit for the post-crisis world, or will you survive but exit the crisis pretty depleted?*

There are two major reasons why an organization could come out of the crisis *weaker* than it started it: One reason is the future impact of the sacrifices you may (feel you) have to make in order to survive the crisis – reduced investment in people, in systems, in research and development, and/or in business-development activities.

For example, during the 2008–2010 global financial crisis, most organizations and most countries made pretty severe cuts in these areas in order to survive the crisis and/or to maintain their financial performance during that period. In contrast, the Singaporean government decided to draw on its reserves to support companies and help them to upgrade their human capital by retaining and retraining their employees during the crisis.[3] Singapore came out of the crisis much

---

[3] See, for example, https://eresources.nlb.gov.sg/infopedia/articles/SIP_1489_2009–03-20.html.

faster than most – and with a momentum that contributed to Singapore's remarkable success over the last 10 years.[4]

As IMD's Executive Committee and with the support of our Board, we decided that as much and as long as humanly possible, we would pursue a Singaporean strategy, and we would avoid, as long as possible, making cuts in areas that would reduce our medium- to long-term success.

The second reason why an organization might come out of the crisis weaker is by failing to make the *additional investments* needed to succeed in the post-crisis world.

Some crises bring about a major disruption but do not fundamentally change the rules of the game. Other crises do change the rules of competition, and if you don't make the decisions needed to excel in that new world, you may survive the crisis, but you won't thrive thereafter.

At IMD, we decided pretty rapidly that this COVID-19 crisis would change the rules of the future game to a nontrivial extent. In particular, we felt that after months of using technology-mediated interactions (TMIs) increasingly effectively, executive-development participants and clients would want to continue to use TMIs in the future, at least for part of our activities.

This meant that we should take advantage of this crisis to accelerate our investments into (a) new technologies enabling us to support executives at a distance and (b) developing our faculty's and our staff's capability to design interventions and interactions that make the most of these technological possibilities.

So we decided that alongside playing defense, we would also play offense by using this crisis as an opportunity to prepare ourselves for the world that will follow. Our rallying cry became: "Let's innovate as much on technology-mediated pedagogy over the next 3 months than we would have otherwise done over the next 3 years."

This effort included significant investments in "technology" (hardware and software). We outfitted most of our classrooms with state-of-the-art equipment, equipped another 15 or so smaller rooms for individual faculty members to "teach from," and accelerated the development of a state-of-the-art classroom and system enabling us to interact

---

[4] See Sanchita Basu Das (2010), *Road to Recovery: Singapore's Journey through the Global Crisis* (ISEAS Publishing), https://doi.org/10.1355/9789814311045.

in a very engaging way with up to 120 individuals at a time. Over the next few months, we also developed a new multimedia studio to enhance our capabilities in this area. We also acquired two very professional "self-recording booths" to enable faculty to record short videos by themselves.

Looking back, I realize that although I was part of the discussions on playing defense, I (somewhat unconsciously) decided to take a leading role on the "playing offense" front. I think this was a good idea because "defense" already had quite a few natural champions – our chief financial officer (CFO), several members of our Board, several senior faculty members – all quite vocal on the need to cut down, hunker down, and retrench. Playing offense needed a strong champion, and in our case, the best champion was probably the dean.

Having a champion for "offense" is a necessary, but not a sufficient, condition for success. I gave two of my strongest LT members a very clear "innovation mandate," encompassing the launch of new programs, the acceleration of pedagogical innovation (especially on TMIs), and the scaling up of effective practices across all our programs. We also identified a few innovative colleagues willing and able to be at the forefront of innovation, and we secured support from key opinion leaders.

One of the key decisions we made was to launch, in June 2020, a liVe (synchronous technology-mediated) version of our signature Orchestrating Winning Performance (OWP) program, which normally gathers between 400 and 500 executives, coming from all over the world, for a week on campus. We resolved to design, market, and deliver a liVe version of this program and gave ourselves 10 weeks to do so. We really had no idea how to make this happen when we made the decision, so this was a real "man on the moon" moment for us.

Although faculty and staff understood the revenue-generation impact of this program, the LT had three major objectives more important to us than the financial one. First, we could feel the energy of our faculty and staff dissipating after 2 months of confinement, and we wanted to create another burst of collective energy by giving ourselves a risky collective project. Two, we knew that planting such a stick in the ground would help accelerate pedagogical innovation at a time when our faculty didn't have enough opportunities to innovate and practice. Third, we wanted to show to ourselves and to our clients that this kind of liVe program could be satisfying and impactful for participants; this was a proof-of-concept endeavor.

The program gathered 350 executives from all over the world. It was not a financial boon – we decided to double faculty compensation for this program because it required substantial additional investment on their part. Much more importantly though, OWP liVe was a major energy boost, an effective innovation accelerator, and a very successful proof of concept. It has since then been repeated several times.

We also spent significant time keeping our Board informed and engaged to ensure that they remained confident in the strategy and in the LT's ability to implement it successfully. For 2021, we even negotiated a special additional investment budget for TMIs.

Managing up effectively is potentially even more important during a crisis than in normal times. Your bosses and your board are probably facing anxieties of their own in their respective areas, and they have much less understanding than you do of all the good decisions you and your team are making. So keep them informed and engaged to help them remain, like your staff, calm and focused on their job instead of trying to do yours.

On the investment front, we also maintained marketing investments, increased communication expenditures, and hired several individuals to help us to innovate faster.

It has been very interesting, over the last few months, to work this balancing act between short-term survival and longer-term preparation. The balance between these two poles has varied up and down over time and will probably continue to do so as the crisis continues to evolve, hopefully toward a resolution. In the meantime, maintaining our focus on "offense" has required a strong resolve and discipline on my part. The "playing defense" forces are strong, and they can easily slow down even agreed-upon key investments if you take your eye off the ball and your foot off the gas. At the same time, you must also play enough defense to maintain support from the board and fund some of the key investments. It's been an interesting balancing exercise.

I don't know how high the return on our investments will be, but I do know one thing for certain: in the meantime, our decision to keep playing offense has been a powerful energizing force for the LT, as well as for all our faculty and staff.

Faculty and staff engagement are particularly important dimensions during crises because crises reduce slack resources, and world-class performance hence requires significant "beyond-role," "over-and-above" efforts from the organization. By staying clearly focused on our purpose and supporting our community, by giving everyone a clear path forward and reasons to be confident in our ability to survive the crisis and then thrive in the post-crisis world, we reduced the rise of individualistic, parochial, short-term-maximizing behavior.

Napoleon said that leaders are "dealers in hope." Leading through a crisis does require that you give your troops a reason to keep fighting together toward a common goal. In the absence of such a sense of shared destiny, centrifugal forces will ensure that the whole becomes less than the sum of the parts.

Insight 4: Why and How Leaders Actively Need to Manage Themselves

This fourth insight comes last *not* because it is the least important or because, from a timing point of view, you must address it after the others. In fact, quite to the contrary. *It is probably the most important insight* because, as highlighted in the first three sections, so much rests on the leader's shoulders during a crisis. Granted, there's also a lot resting on the leader during normal times, but crises reduce the time available to decide and execute, as well as the amount of redundant resources available to pick up and compensate for errors. In a crisis, everyone's paying a lot more attention to what you say and do, and the decisions that are being made have very high stakes. During a crisis, the sensitivity of the system to your and your LT's actions is very high, and a drop in performance on your part can hence have even more massive consequences. As a result, your goal shouldn't be to maintain yourself in *functional* order; it should be to maintain yourself at *peak performance*!

Managing yourself to remain at peak performance through a crisis involves a range of dimensions – some *physical/physiological*, others *cognitive and emotional*. These two domains are obviously linked; in particular, your level of physical energy influences your ability to think straight and to manage your emotions productively. In the other direction, feeling productive, engaged, and connected will, in turn, nurture your level of physical energy.

But connected as they are, these two domains still involve different sets of action. On the more *physical side*, many books are now available discussing how leaders can manage their energy levels. Tom Rath's (2013) book provides a good analysis of the interplay between nutrition, exercise, and sleep to help leaders to maintain a high level of productive energy and a positive attitude across good and bad times.[5] I imagine that by now, most of you have developed a point of view and probably also some practices and even rituals in this area.

Interestingly, a crisis introduces two additional challenges on this front: (a) time pressures, which may lead you to feel that you don't have as much (discretionary) time as usual to dedicate to self-care, and (b) a likely sense of guilt over taking valuable time away from your colleagues or even your family to "take care of yourself."

These are very fair concerns, and they may lead you to make some trade-offs; at the end of the day, leadership is about trade-offs. But as you consider these trade-offs, do keep in mind that there is a reason why airlines tell us to put the mask on ourselves first before we help someone else. Throughout a crisis, your team, your staff, and your family will rely and depend on your ability to think clearly, to have enough energy to power yourself and inspire them, to deal with your and their emotions, and to do so every day and throughout the crisis. So you must place a high enough level of priority on managing your own energy-generation system.

In particular, you should be mindful of your sleep patterns. It is easy for leaders to develop sleep disorders, in part because it is harder to manage thoughts and feelings while we sleep. Research shows very clearly how quickly and how significantly human beings' intellectual performance and emotional mastery decrease when we are sleep deprived, even in relatively minor ways.[6] So you may want to pay particular attention during these times to your sleep rituals – how you prepare yourself for sleep. There are excellent resources on this topic

---

[5] See Tom Rath (2013), *Eat, Move, Sleep: How Small Choices Lead to Big Changes* (Missionday).

[6] See, for example, June J. Pilcher and Allen I. Huffcutt (1996), "Effects of Sleep Deprivation on Performance: A Meta-Analysis," *Journal of Sleep Research & Sleep Medicine*, 19(4), 318–326; W. D. Killgore, E. T. Kahn-Greene, E. L. Lipizzi, R. A. Newman, G. H. Kamimori, and T. J. Balkin (2008), "Sleep Deprivation Reduces Perceived Emotional Intelligence and Constructive Thinking Skills," *Sleep Medicine*, 9(5), 517–526; C. M. Barnes, L. Lucianetti, D. P. Bhave, and M. S. Christian (2015), "You Wouldn't Like Me When I'm Sleepy: Leaders' Sleep, Daily Abusive Supervision, and Work Unit Engagement," *Academy of Management Journal*, 58(5), 1419–1437.

that you can easily access online. Too many people complain that they don't sleep well and treat this condition as an exogenous one – "It's genetic" and/or "It's not my fault." And there's no doubt that genetics plays a role in this area, as it does in most areas. But that doesn't mean that we cannot improve our lot in this realm by taking more effective actions.

Again, *you cannot use or give to others the energy that you don't have,* and your ability to get the cognitive and emotional dimensions of your job right relies in significant part on your ability to get the physiological component right as well.

Beyond minding your physiology through nutrition, exercise, and sleep, leading in a crisis presents leaders with *emotional challenges.* Leaders' emotions tend to be quite contagious under any circumstances, but they are even more so during a crisis, when so much depends on the leader's ability to remain calmly and resolutely positive. Unfortunately, remaining calm and positive is bound to be much harder than it normally is because in a crisis, you will have to deal with a lot of emotions – both yours and theirs.

One powerful emotion you and your staff will have to deal with is *grief,* that is, the psychological-emotional experience following a loss of any kind, from physical losses (e.g., the death of a loved one) to symbolic or social ones (e.g., divorce or loss of a job) or even simply the loss of a future that we desired or expected. In addition to the functional loss (i.e., the loss of the benefits associated with the expected outcome), the situation also highlights one's (partial or total) powerlessness vis-à-vis the situation, which magnifies the sense of frustration.[7]

---

[7] This unexpected crisis led to many dimensions of loss for all of us: loss of normalcy; loss of physical and emotional connection; loss of freedom (of going where we want when we want and meeting with whomever we want to meet with); loss of safety, of security, as a result of the uncertainty related to our health and the health of our loved ones, as well as the economic situation. This COVID-19 crisis has been tough on people! More generally, see www.alzinfo.org/articles/bereavement-and-grief for a simple explanation of the difference between grief, bereavement, and mourning. See also the excellent article "The Hidden Perils of Unresolved Grief" by my colleagues Charles Dhanaraj and George Kohlrieser in *McKinsey Quarterly* (September 2020) for a discussion of the pervasive presence of grief in organizations and how leaders can help, available at www.mckinsey.com/business-functions/organization/our-insights/the-hidden-perils-of-unresolved-grief.

Another emotion leaders experience during crises is *fear*. "Am I going to be able to do this? Am I going to be up the task?" For some leaders, this crisis awakens or reenergizes their "imposter syndrome"[8]: "Is this the time they will realize I'm not as good as they think I am?" The fear can also pertain to the fate of the organization: "Are we going to be able to come out of this crisis on top? Or will it bring us to our knees, or worse?"

Yet another emotion you have probably been experiencing is *frustration*, and potentially anger, because some people don't perform the way they should and/or some outcomes fall short of your expectations. That's always frustrating, but it is *particularly* frustrating when you are working at or slightly beyond your own maximum.

Compounding your own emotional challenge is the fact that *as the leader, you must also help your colleagues*, starting with your LT colleagues, *to deal with their emotions*. At a minimum, you will be exposed to their emotions, which may further intensify yours.

Ignoring your emotions, pretending that you don't have them, or trying to suppress them is unlikely to help. The emotions *will* resurface – tomorrow, next week, next month, during the day or at night when you're trying to sleep. Ignoring them won't help. Managing them *will*.

Managing one's emotions is obviously a skill that can be developed. Here are a few helpful avenues.

First, it really helps to be aware of the emotions that you are experiencing. For part of the day, particularly when you're interacting with others, you are managing your state – you are leading yourself to feel and act calm, confident, and resolute. Remember that this process takes effort, and *make sure you have moments where*, by yourself or with a close confidant, a mentor, or a coach, *you can connect with and acknowledge your underlying emotions*. Naming these emotions is a first step toward managing them.[9]

---

[8] The term *imposter syndrome* was first coined in 1978 by P. R. Clance and S. A. Imes in "The Imposter Phenomenon in High Achieving Women: Dynamics and Therapeutic Intervention," *Psychotherapy: Theory, Research & Practice*, 15(3), 241–247, https://doi.org/10.1037/h0086006. See also Manfred Kets de Vries (1990), "The Impostor Syndrome: Developmental and Societal Issues," *Human Relations*, 43(7), 667–686, https://doi.org/10.1177/001872679004300704.

[9] Research using brain-imaging technology shows that naming emotions reduces activation of the amygdala (the part of the brain associated with fear and other emotions). See, for example, M.D. Lieberman, N. I. Eisenberger, M. J. Crockett,

Research also shows that writing about your emotions and experiences in a journal can be a very effective way of processing negative emotions.[10] So if you can discuss with a trusted advisor, great, but you can also become a quasi-trusted-advisor for yourself when you write to yourself.

Beyond naming and potentially writing about your emotions, you could also consider three very powerful practices. The first and most powerful practice of all is *conscious breathing*. Conscious deep breathing has two very fundamental benefits: One, physiological benefits. Breathing deeply sends a message to your brain to calm down and relax. Your brain then sends the same message to your body, which helps decrease the stress symptoms we often experience, such as increased heart rate, shallow breathing, and high blood pressure. So first, your stress level goes down.[11] Second, conscious breathing helps to bring you back to the here and now; it is a very simple but very powerful mindfulness training exercise.

Bringing yourself back to the here and now is a very effective way to manage anxiety about the future: "I don't know what may happen later, but for now, I'm OK."

It also helps you to choose your response in specific situations. *If you're not present in the here and now, the habit wins.* But if you are here, now, then you have a choice, and you can choose to craft your behavior more productively than you would if you were on autopilot.

S. M. Tom, J. H. Pfeifer, and B. M. Way (2007), "Putting Feelings into Words: Affect Labelling Disrupts Amygdala Activity to Affective Stimuli," *Psychological Science*, 18, 421–428. More recently, psychologist Dan Siegel referred to this practice as "name it to tame it." See Daniel J. Siegel and Tina Payne Bryson (2012), *The Whole-Brain Child: 12 Revolutionary Strategies to Nurture Your Child's Developing Mind* (Bantam).

[10] Writing down thoughts and feelings about personal, meaningful topics or events has been shown to have many benefits. See J. Frattaroli (2006), "Experimental Disclosure and Its Moderators: A Meta-Analysis," *Psychological Bulletin*, 132, 823–865; B. C. DiMenichi, A. O. Ceceli, J. P. Bhanji, and E. Tricomi (2019), "Effects of Expressive Writing on Neural Processing during Learning," *Frontiers in Human Neuroscience*, 13, 389. Or see the interesting historical perspective in James W. Pennebaker (2018), "Expressive Writing in Psychological Science," *Perspectives on Psychological Science*, 13(2), 226–229, https://journals.sagepub .com/doi/pdf/10.1177/1745691617707315.

[11] For a short and easy introduction to the impact of (different types of) conscious breathing, see the video by Stanford neuroscientist Andrew Huberman at www .youtube.com/watch?app=desktop&v=S3oZ5dp5wfk&feature=emb_title.

Finally, bringing yourself back to the here and now enables you to manage your state to bring it to where you need it to be right now. You may not feel very confident as you're about to appear in a virtual meeting with dozens or hundreds of employees, but they need you to look and come across as confident, so now's the time to make yourself feel this way.

Second important practice: when we feel frustrated or annoyed, it helps a great deal to be able to *maintain a strong sense of compassion* for the individuals we are interacting with. Notice that I referred to the need for compassion rather than empathy.

Over the last few years, leaders have been strongly encouraged to develop their empathy for their staff. But research actually shows that empathy (which involves adopting the perspective of the other party and feeling similar emotions) is not necessarily the best approach. Over time, it can even prove damaging for oneself, leading to emotional distress and even burnout.

A more effective approach is to show compassion, which, "in contrast to empathy, ... does not mean sharing the suffering of the other: rather, it is characterized by feelings of warmth, concern and care for the other, as well as a strong motivation to improve the other's well-being. Compassion is feeling *for* and not feeling *with* the other."[12] In a crisis situation, you may well have to inflict pain on parts of the organization (e.g., by ordering layoffs or otherwise reducing investments or opportunities). When inflicting pain, actively feeling this pain (empathizing) won't be as helpful as you being able to relate to it and being intent on doing your best to reduce it.

Concretely, maintaining your compassion for people starts with you reminding yourself that they are very probably doing their best. Yes, this best may not be enough for you, but it is still their best right now. In addition, this best may not be enough, but it's generally not completely crappy either; there are typically some areas that are still going well. Connecting with their good intentions and their partial good performance will help you to be more patient and more helpful toward them.

---

[12] In T. Singer and O. M. Klimecki (2014), "Empathy and Compassion," *Current Biology*, 24(18), R875–R878 (quote is from p. R875). For a less scientific and perhaps more easily readable treatment, see Robin Stern and Diana Divecha (2015), "How to Avoid the Empathy Trap," *Greater Good Magazine*, https://greatergood.berkeley.edu/article/item/how_to_avoid_the_empathy_trap.

You may still decide that this won't be enough and that you will have to make more drastic decisions somewhere down the road, but again, *for now*, your compassion will help you to get the best out of them – and to create a more supportive atmosphere for all your other colleagues who are watching these interactions.

The third powerful practice that can greatly help you to stay at your best during a crisis is to *nurture your sense of gratitude* via a gratitude practice. Yes, some things are very tough right now, and you deserve better. Yes, this crisis is requiring you to step up considerably, at some cost to yourself and maybe your family, and it's forcing you to make up for the underperformance of some of your faculty and staff colleagues. Darn, this is frustrating and annoying!

It certainly is (frustrating and annoying), but do try to *also pay some attention to all the things that are going well* in your life. Start with all your body parts that are working relatively to very well. Then, are your family members healthy and well? Well, that alone is a great blessing. Look also at all the folks around you who are going over and above the call of duty to help you, their colleagues, and the organization. Some of them are even finding time to volunteer outside the school to help their communities! You can also be grateful for the client who will stand by you or the supplier who's giving you a break. Think of all the things that went well today and all the people who were admirable. Actually, no matter how difficult the situation is, we always have so much to be grateful for!

Gratitude helps leaders on several fronts. First, research shows that a regular gratitude practice contributes to better physical and mental health.[13] Also, by helping you to place your setbacks and frustrations in a proper perspective, gratitude can help you to deal more philosophically and calmly with these setbacks and frustrations – which will lead to better outcomes. Gratitude can hence be a foundation for resilience (the ability to rebound after a setback), a quality that leaders can greatly benefit from in times of crisis.

---

[13] See, for example, A. L. Boggiss, N. S. Consedine, J. M. Brenton-Peters, P. L. Hofman, and A. S. Serlachius (2020), "A Systematic Review of Gratitude Interventions: Effects on Physical Health and Health Behaviors," *Journal of Psychosomatic Research*, 135, 110165, https://doi.org/10.1016/j.jpsychores .2020.110165. Or see Summer Allen (2018), "The Science of Gratitude" (White Paper prepared for the John Templeton Foundation), https://ggsc.berkeley.edu/ images/uploads/GGSC-JTF_White_Paper-Gratitude-FINAL.pdf.

Summarizing this fourth insight: during a crisis, your role as a leader is more critical – and also more challenging – than ever. This combination of high stakes and high challenge means that you must be consciously looking after yourself to make sure you remain in peak performance throughout the crisis. This "self-care" has a physiological foundation building on the interdependent tripod of nutrition, exercise, and sleep.

Maintaining yourself in peak performance throughout the crisis also requires you to understand and manage your (and your colleagues' and staff's) key emotions. You cannot manage what you're not aware of; being able to identify and name your emotions will hence be very helpful. So will developing a mindfulness practice (starting with conscious breathing exercises), nurturing your compassion for others, and developing a gratitude practice to remind yourself regularly of how lucky you are.

Wrapping Up

It is important to acknowledge that some of the ideas proposed in this chapter do *not* feel "natural" to most of us. In fact, in many cases, they feel almost like the opposite of what we would be inclined to do. And that is *precisely* why leaders need to discuss and practice these ideas. Leaders do not need help to feel stressed and to become inhibited or frustrated; we can all do that pretty easily and pretty naturally! What is more challenging is to develop practices that are sometimes counterintuitive and oftentimes quite challenging, in order to become better versions of ourselves as leaders and as human beings. A crisis is a great opportunity to do so.

One last thought: rereading this chapter, I imagined some readers thinking that our situation at IMD was greatly helped by the clear sense of urgency we developed early in the crisis as a result of our dependency on non–degree-program activities. There is no doubt that faculty and staff understanding the severity of the situation was indeed helpful for the IMD LT, but please allow me to point out two elements in return.

First, a sense of urgency can and must be nurtured. In speaking with some colleagues at other schools over the last 18 months, I have been surprised at how many of them are looking forward to life post–COVID-19 "returning to normal." I do *not* think that life will return to what it was pre–COVID-19, certainly not on all fronts. This crisis created a real discontinuity in the evolution of business schools, and I think smart deans will follow Rahm Emanuel's admonishment to "never waste a good crisis"[14] and will use this one to introduce fundamental changes to their model.

Second, the slight benefit we may have gotten on the initial sense-of-urgency front was paid dearly when more than a third of our revenues disappeared, considerably reducing the resources available for continued operations and for investment. The point, I believe, is that smart leaders make the most of the situation they're in and leverage whatever advantage they may have to "make happen what otherwise would not," as Sumantra Ghoshal was fond of saying.[15]

Crises reshuffle the cards and raise the stakes. They put leaders under enormous pressure and require even more dedication and commitment on their part. I hope these modest reflections will stimulate yours and will help you prepare for the next crisis.

[14] See a November 19, 2008, *Wall Street Journal* video interview of Rahm Emmanuel at www.youtube.com/watch?v=_mzcbXi1Tkk.
[15] In Sumantra Ghoshal and Don Sull (1997), "A Crisis of Faith in Management?" in James Pickford, ed., *Financial Times: Mastering Management* (Pearson), pp. 1–10 (quote is from p. 3).

16 | "Real Change Comes from the Outside": COVID-19 as a Great Opportunity for the Revival of Business Schools and Management Education

GRZEGORZ MAZUREK

About the Change

Everything flows, as Heraclitus used to say. Business schools and the entire socioeconomic environment alike are changing rapidly before our very eyes. Schools are preparing their graduates to enter a labor market that we know nothing about yet. We educate students to take up professions that don't even exist, only knowing how big of a role transformation technologies are already playing. The overall atmosphere is changing, the ongoing digital transformation is gaining momentum, and the need for support not only in professional but also in more general development is getting bigger. Where is the place of management education in this landscape?

Change is a natural state – our environment is changing, and so are the organizations existing in it. The changes that occur usually take the form of more or less acceptable efforts to adapt to the transforming reality. They occur gradually, on an evolutionary basis. Changes of this type can be implemented in organizations effectively, but many conditions have to be met first. First, it is important to have a good, clear vision and a strategy to support it. The strategy has to be good as well – meaning appropriate, well thought-out, and feasible. The second condition is for the management board and the entire team of an organization to be able to turn this vision into reality effectively – and this is where problems resulting from limited and incompatible resources, regulatory aspects, or excessive costs determining compromises limit the original dreams and ideas start to appear. This multiconditional evolutionary nature makes real changes remain only an option, feasible in the long run, implemented slowly, carefully, and conservatively. Evolution brings about only correct changes – all too late and all too costly, but less daring, less risky. And this is how most business schools acted in terms of online teaching in the pre–COVID-19 years when trying to adopt new, more agile organizational cultures. Many discussions have not translated into any real change because they upset the existing ecosystem of stakeholders and because the current operating model has been working just fine despite its many flaws.

But there are also sudden changes caused by new, often unexpected, disruptive developments and circumstances. They can come from inside an organization (e.g., changed business model, loss of liquidity, and the resulting drastic cutbacks in the amount of resources and a structural reorganization), but they can also originate from the outside – an example of which is the COVID-19 pandemic, which has forced almost all business schools in the world to redefine their operations in a very short time, at least in the area of online teaching and remote management of their institutions, research projects, and relationships with students.

In this case, we can speak of a **radical change** – one that brings about a significant transformation of the ways in which an organization functions and operates. Such changes take place more quickly and suddenly because they are not optional but necessary; they are the only way possible – which eliminates the problems typical of evolutionary changes, such as lengthiness or compromising on solutions that don't provide answers to urgent strategic matters.

The most important question is whether the radical changes that have taken place in business schools worldwide as a result of COVID-19 are permanent and systemic; whether they respond to the expectations voiced many times in discussions at the institutional level; or whether they are just a temporary, makeshift dressing applied for the duration of a difficult period – something named by Hodges and colleagues (2020) as an "emergency stage," which we want to get out of as soon as possible and return to the "old normal." In the years to come, we will see if the ongoing changes become common and permanent, or if they appear to be one-off, isolated cases of individual institutions – global business school brands – which, just like successful online platforms, will prove the digital business perspective of "winner takes all." We will see if these changes become rooted in the rules and standards of rankings and accreditations as well as in the practice of domestic policymakers.

It is difficult to answer such questions. This will require many years of analyses, in fact. It is surely easy to fall into the trap of getting stuck in the middle of transformation at this point. What is the nature of this trap? And what is to be expected of the transformation of business schools forced by COVID-19?

A Changing Landscape

COVID-19 is, as already said, a natural contributor to the rapid implementation of radical changes in business schools (Jonathan, 2020). This involves, for example, adopting methods of synchronous and asynchronous online teaching, new forms of classes, new teaching content, and new channels used to reach stakeholders (an example of such a new format is collaborative online international learning [COIL] – which makes possible the effective use of technology in teaching in the domain of internationalization); implementing new software to stimulate in-class interaction (e.g., Mentimeter, Kahoot!); using learning management systems (LMSs) or massive open online course (MOOC) systems; and/or employing artificial intelligence (AI) to provide students with opportunities for long-term development.

Discussions on whether business schools are losing their monopoly on the knowledge and education market have been going on for a long time (e.g., Davidson, 2017; Eyring and Christensen, 2011; Kaplan, 2018). There are claims that universities do not create knowledge that is of relevance to and could find practical application in society (Tourish, 2019), that they nurture the culture of egoism and greed (Parker, 2018). The credibility of business schools as the dominant source of knowledge, competencies, and solutions for enterprises and executives is being questioned (Collinson, n.d.).

New players are appearing on the education market, a new force to be reckoned with – educational platforms (Kaplan and Haenlein, 2016), corporate universities, entities offering certification programs supported by globally recognized brands, especially from the information technology (IT) or educational technology (EdTech) sectors. This also concerns the creation of valuable and quickly applicable knowledge, which is produced in the existing think tanks, research departments of global corporations, or renowned knowledge portals and data aggregators, all with access to the best and most recent sources of information.

The monopoly on the business education market has also been a result of the common and globally recognized currency in the form of a diploma granted by a good higher education institution, which has been considered proof of a graduate's level of knowledge and competence. In addition, the system has been solidified by the standard labor-market practice, where a diploma of higher education has, for years, been a key to opening the door to interviews and, eventually, a career. This ecosystem has been kept alive and strong by the regulator, meaning the state, which determines the conditions to be met by a higher education institution to have the right to grant such diplomas. We thus have a system of cause-and-effect relations, encased in a rigid framework: state regulations, accreditation-supervisory bodies, and employers' requirements and expectations. This has always been accompanied by the lack of alternative formal ways to acquire knowledge and skills outside the university classroom and by the strong impact of rankings, making the existing rules and principles even stricter.

Nowadays, the model in question is undergoing a big transformation. First, the "diploma" monopoly is crumbling – employers are increasingly more willing to hire individuals with nonformal or alternative evidence of their professional preparation, meaning not only knowledge but also skills and competence. Because such signals come from the most wanted employers in the world, for whom many young people would like to work (Musk, 2020), it can't be ruled out that the conventional model of bachelor-level, master-level, and MBA-level education will go out of date over time. Employers and students alike will come to terms with other forms of proving one's level of knowledge, skill, expertise, and overall competence. These forms will include a range of various certificates, completed master classes, annual or semiannual training courses, development programs, and even one's achievements or scores in certain computer games or simulations. And they can be provided – even now, as we speak – not only by universities. If such alternative and innovative solutions are to be accepted, they need to be acknowledged by and incorporated into the existing education system and its principal outposts: ministries, universities, and accreditation bodies alike. The sooner these solutions are accepted and embraced by the current system, the quicker the existing structures governing our education will transform, to the benefit of both students and business schools.

Second, access to knowledge served in an interactive and attractive way is at our fingertips, not just because it's possible to serve it online but because business entities operating in the EdTech sector already provide solutions that make it possible to take advantage of sophisticated, reliable software, techniques, and methodologies enabling instructors to teach classes in an effective way in virtual settings. And although the pandemic has taught us that online education cannot replace its traditional form, online teaching can be very useful in some areas and disciplines – especially when it comes to acquiring practical knowledge – and may stay with us for good.

Third, thanks to the globalized market of online education and knowledge, there is greater competition for students and attention based on the uniqueness of the competing brands – brands of higher education institutions and brands of individual academics. This observation is of great significance in the context of the management activities undertaken by business schools and the changes taking place in the digital world featuring scientific influencers – individuals with millions of followers forming their target audience, popularizing knowledge and lifestyles, or scientists whose bold and often future-oriented statements enjoy record-breaking numbers of views, and they themselves suddenly become media celebrities, promoting themselves but also the brand of the universities or other institutions they are involved or affiliated with (Korzyński et al., 2020). Are we to expect knowledge and science to become "marketized"? Are we to see research teams becoming assembled like boy bands, where each band member is a marketing product designed for a particular target audience in the world of science and business? Surely, the desire for attention and brand recognition, the urge to popularize the knowledge one has created, juxtaposed with the existing rules governing the media world, may lead to a number of scenarios of development of the knowledge – or pseudo-knowledge – market. The existence of such phenomena as scientific influencing and the emergence of scientists-celebrities should be discussed further in more detail, especially in the context of business schools building their position, image, and trustworthiness. After all, as argued by Davis and Farrell (2016), as higher education institutions, we compete not in a knowledge or education market but in a prestige market.

Last but not least, in the light of the rapid changes taking place in the social and environmental sectors, business schools need to redefine their mission, the role they play in society. Especially in times as difficult and challenging as the present, entities such as business schools are expected to become examples to follow and creators of positive change, promoting changes that have to be implemented – among the younger generations in particular. Universities should aim to become spaces for development, not just for acquiring specific competencies for career building, especially in the times when we don't know what professions in business will look like in 5 to 10 years. This very utilitarian, inflexible perspective of higher education (career, profession, work-related skills) is actually a threat to the concept of the university and to society as a whole in the long run. A university should inspire students to become valuable contributors to a reality that is yet to come. This means that apart from the "hard" core competencies and skills required for professional development in a given field, students also should be encouraged and enabled – preferably by means of experiential learning – to acquire qualities like natural curiosity, entrepreneurial flair, critical thinking, leadership, care for others, social awareness, and care for the natural environment. An important thing to consider here is that in the technology-infused, digitally transformed world of today, students pursuing different fields of study, particularly from the STEM area, should be offered a curriculum containing elements of the humanities (psychology, sociology, philosophy, etc.) – and the other way around, of course. Every student in the world should be well familiar with notions and ideas such as digital transformation, circular economy, technological unemployment, sustainability, and well-being. They should be aware of the implications these phenomena carry for every human being and for the entire planet alike.

Easily said, of course, but this is, in fact, about a radical cultural change in many business schools, which is a big challenge for the leaders of these organizations. A lot is expected; the new world appearing after COVID-19 is in desperate need of new answers.

What Is Expected

The turbulence and the concern about the future – including its economic aspects – are the main challenges for the identity of business schools, for their own future, and for the promise they make to society and try to keep.

Although the discussion on what business schools should teach has been going on for many years, the usual standard still involves silo-like, function-oriented teaching based on old teaching programs and curricula, described in detail in tables with accompanying performance indicators, known unfortunately very often only to the most ardent evaluators from administrative staff. We teach marketing, finance, accounting, or strategy. This approach is additionally grounded by the practice of assigning scientific disciplines and categorizing scientific journals. Leaving the need for a serious discussion about the interdisciplinarity in educating contemporary managers aside, it's very important to stress what should be inside the "package" of knowledge and competencies offered to graduates of a good business school – apart from a collection of certain subjects. The most important thing should be for them to know that the volatility, uncertainty, complexity, and ambiguity of the world make it really difficult to make managerial decisions. **Complexity** and uncertainty are actually the main characteristics of the world of today (Pucciarelli and Andreas, 2016). This complexity makes it necessary for managerial plans, strategies, and decisions to take unexpected events – appearing suddenly, often unrelated to the operations of a given organization, coming from areas and disciplines far away from those we deal with – into account. The same applies to how managers of business schools perceive reality. Complexity determines the quickness and speed of action and reaction. At present, the number of networks of connections and networks of influences is constantly growing. Add to that the virtual networks that overlap with the former, as well as the strong impact the parallel – virtual – world has on us and on our environment. For business schools, responsible for the education and development of young managers, the complexity and ambiguity of the contemporary world should be a starting point for the creation of new scientific knowledge offering a sort of compass to guide the actions of their socioeconomic environments and to organize not only the right curricula but also individual paths of education and development for students and managers alike, or for anyone who wishes to embark upon the journey of personal development but isn't necessarily determined to officially be a student. Today, everyone is a student, in fact. And studies are any possible dose of development, not just two or three formally obtained degrees – lifelong learning is not an option anymore but a necessity. It's time it became obvious to everybody, not just because of the pressure of changes originating outside, but also because of an inner, spontaneous will to develop – and a business school should support the fulfillment of this need by all means.

Another crucial element of both the operation of a business school and the vision of education in such a school, be it on-site or online, is **the sense of purpose.** The many questions appearing in the development of societies today explain the search for authorities – including institutions ready to take on the responsibility for setting new paths and providing new patterns of action, based not as much on economic performance or a success–failure perspective as on the overall value for society. That's why a higher education institution should be an individual's life partner, so to speak, and that's why it is so important for it to be credible and trustworthy and have considerable social standing.

What Business Schools Have on Their Conscience

When it comes to changes in higher education, including in business schools in particular, it is mandatory to break free – at least to some extent – from certain "cardinal sins," especially three of them. The first of these sins is **the lack of identity based on values,** which results from treating the success measured by rankings as a goal in itself – not as a consequence of an adopted value-based and value-driven strategy. Such focus on all kinds of rankings leads to a certain "other-directedness," involving a mechanistic, index-oriented view of the university. What drives such a university is success for the sake of success, and its identity is a result of the subservient approach to strategically selected ranking lists. Such a university becomes Frankenstein's monster, a cluster of elements, which may seem powerful and well performing but is actually a hollow form, without an identity, uniqueness, and always-upheld values.

The second sin is the **measurement of success** – high-earning graduates and top-tier scientific articles are the two most crucial indicators of a business school's position and prestige nowadays. The first aspect nurtures the individualistic, opportunistic modus operandi of both students and headhunters alike. Is it worth recruiting an applicant who dreams of working for a nongovernmental organization (NGO) where they're not going to earn enough, or a keen young entrepreneur who will fail in business a number of times before they actually achieve what they dream of? The other aspect usually sees years of effort and hard work of brilliant researchers and scientists wrapped up forever in six typed pages, four of which will discuss the adopted sophisticated research method, followed by a few lines of conclusions and implications for business, which won't be of use to anyone because they're written in an overly hermetic language and get published 3 years after the question that they answer has first appeared. This exaggerated perspective illustrates the risks that the world of business schools now has to face and deal with.

In the post–COVID-19 times, marked by uncertainty, isolation-induced trauma, economic slowdown, and accelerating digital transformation, business schools should not promote the idea of business Darwinism but instead advocate looking for and applying solutions to problems of relevance to as many groups of beneficiaries as possible – this is manifested in, for example, corporate social responsibility (CSR) practices; measurement of the real impact of a business school on its environment using new measurement systems (e.g., Business School Impact System [BSIS]); consideration of teaching and attempts to measure its quality in a systemic way, using measures other than graduates' earnings only; research into contemporary – often interdisciplinary – problems; professional dissemination of the findings of such research in the media; and incorporating as many courses discussing social responsibility, mindfulness, or defining one's own happiness – not through slides but through experiential learning – into the adopted curricula as possible.

Business schools need to understand that their greatest and most important role is to "produce" and shape not egoistic plutocrats but socially conscious individuals, leaders, managers, and specialists who are aware of the challenges the world is to face; educated in an interdisciplinary way; proficient in the digital domain; and most of all, sensitive to other people, caring for the natural environment and their milieu.

The third sin is convenient inertia – **staying in a comfort zone**, which is often a result of a school's decent performance, which may also result from operating based on public funds granted on the grounds of simple measures, such as, for example, the number of students enrolled. This is also where a certain cultural context comes into play, especially in Europe. Universities, particularly European ones, are historically based on some influences, or bad habits, which include the following: a hierarchical structure, natural delay in decision making because of the number of decision makers involved in the process, application of formal, overly regulated and bureaucratized rules, fossilized communication structures, silo-like functioning of both administrative staff and faculty members, and a natural reluctance and reactive approach to the challenges of the reality. The deceptive pleasure of being in a comfort zone may easily make us blind to the need for changes, which, in the case of the acquisition of funds required for a business school to operate without implementing the necessary adaptation measures, can lead to the further erosion of trust in higher education institutions. The "wait-and-see" strategy is like the band playing on *Titanic*, and its business perspective has been addressed by Christensen (1997) in his in-depth theory of disruptive innovation.

Dimensions of the Main Vehicle of Change in Business Schools – Digital Transformation

Digital technologies have long been affecting the way in which business schools operate, but nowadays, we can see their impact to be even greater, with new technologies emerging and taking the form of digital transformation. Digital transformation is a phenomenon affecting organizations horizontally and affecting the strategic foundations of the functioning of business schools, where the crucial areas of this functioning undergo significant qualitative changes as a result of the employment of digital technologies – including emerging technologies (artificial intelligence [AI], machine learning, social media, big data, cloud computing, etc.). Digital transformation differs from digitalization in that the former doesn't aim to improve organizational performance, reduce operating costs, or accelerate or shorten processes; its goal is to change how organizations operate, including finding new areas of operation, especially in the digital environment (Vial, 2019).

Digital transformation has already disrupted many areas of human life, including business and education, which is a consequence of the occurrence of strongly developed drivers of digital transformation – digital technology, easily accessible for all market players; digital competition; and digital customer behavior (Verhoef et al., 2021). In education, parallel to other spheres and sectors, effective digital transformation manifests itself through strategic imperatives such as digital resources (hardware, software, content), organizational structure (implementation in crucial areas of a business school's operation – education, teaching, and management), growth strategy (which sets the purpose of the transformation), metrics, and goals (Verhoef et al., 2021). It's reasonable to get a deeper insight into the three crucial – key – areas in which business schools can or should already see digital transformation taking place.

Management

A major transformational challenge is managing a university in the age of digital transformation. The COVID-19 pandemic has accelerated changes that have already been occurring – these are changes in the area of managing higher education institutions, the curricula themselves, dealing with stakeholders, and the approach of higher education universities to their environments. As an organism functioning based on a range of complex processes, stakeholders, and objectives, a business school should itself be an example to follow when it comes to self-management in the context of digital transformation. And this means, for example, the adoption of a culture of data, business intelligence, data-driven decision making, agile management, algorithms that enable the prediction of the behavior (e.g., of students or researchers), and eventually, customizing the individual paths of education and development, which can't happen without the right technology and logistics (Canals and Heukamp, 2020). This is described in an accurate way by Krishnamurthy (2020), who speaks of the role of AI-enabled algorithms that will prepare personalized learning experiences. It also means developing the digital competencies of employees and embracing a culture of quality work, understood as the elimination of unnecessary decision-making links and the simplification of procedures through digitalization. The customer service offered to students needs to be digitalized, with the particular consideration of such elements as automation (e.g., the use of chatbots), mobile technologies (mobile apps), or social media platforms (e.g., LinkedIn). In the case of tech-savvy students, used to the provision of excellent customer service on an everyday basis and the top-notch user experience (UX) offered by their beloved corporations, business schools are doomed to minimizing the gap between the level of customer service they can offer – instead of focusing on a forced "wow!" effect, which corporate brands have already achieved long ago.

The fundamental role in helping a business school get through the process of digital transformation intact is played, according to Krishnamurthy (2020), by the IT infrastructure and financial constraints. It is important to also consider the area of management related to leadership in projects aimed at a digital change, which can be characterized as a process of choice and effective employment of the right information communication technology (ICT) solutions, for example, social media platforms, to enable an organization's leaders to pursue and achieve their personal and organizational goals (Van Wart et al., 2016). The technological changes caused by digital transformation are, in fact, a cultural – and often generational – change, and they not only require a plan, a strategy, and resources (e.g., the right IT infrastructure) but also call for strong transformational leadership on a business school's end, which involves a good sense of the role of technology and of its constraints, traps, and consequences for the school's operations. Such phenomena as reluctance to change, technological debt and tech legacy, short-term thinking over long-term planning, and organizational silos make digital transformation turn, in fact, into a huge challenge in terms of management – and only then in terms of technology.

Curriculum

Digital transformation in the domain of teaching is, of course, a new approach to education – which is usually equated with curricula designed to last a few years. This new approach involves, for example, offering courses in different forms: completely online, in a hybrid form, in an asynchronous online model with the use of learning management system (LMS) platforms, courses available on massive open online course (MOOC) types of platforms, and supplementing or adding value to the traditional curriculum (Kaplan and Haenlein, 2016). The biggest transformational change that may occur to curricula is that they become dynamically "shaped" based on a given student's personality, expectations, or current academic performance. Such a dynamic view of the path of education is possible thanks to the employment of algorithms. Still, the barriers that remain include the logistics and the management of university resources. But this is a quite obvious direction of the evolution of education – to become customized, personalized, tailor-made on a mass scale (Krishnamurthy, 2020).

The digital transformation taking place in the area of curricula pertains not only to the form and the channels through which education is offered but also to the content taught and the goals to be achieved in the process of learning. Surely, in the context of the post–COVID-19 world, a world that has gone digital – and one socially conscious on top of that – a business school should aspire to educate and inspire students to be valuable contributors to the human–machine world of the future; they have to be skilled all-rounders, literate in their language, words, data, technology, and the humanities but also possessing a very high level of digital skills and competencies. Apart from these aspects, we should focus on promoting curiosity, critical thinking, entrepreneurial spirit, leadership skills, and caring for others.

Therefore, the real and greatest change does not concern the methods applied to transmit knowledge or teach skills. It focuses on the promotion of a specific model of the outlook on the world – we have entered a paradigm of a different understanding of the word *success*. The aspect that is emphasized now, and that will probably continue to be emphasized for many years to come, is sustainability through digital transformation, climate change, and equality. Sustainability calls for the balancing of three fundamental dimensions: environmental protection, societal progress, and economic growth (Wilson and Schlegelmilch, 2020). This can take on the form of the increasingly common slogan of business schools forging a new type of leader, focusing their actions on the said participatory, socially responsible view of business activity.

This changed viewpoint may concern not only advertising slogans or catchy names of the subjects taught – this has to be incorporated into every aspect of teaching, including the applied case studies. After all, this shows and proves the significant role of business schools in the shaping of attitudes and perspectives toward the world. If the first thing we teach our undergraduate-level students is that the main objective of a company is to make a profit at any price, to outsmart competitors, and to employ a sophisticated range of tricks to encourage consumers to buy some product, we shouldn't be surprised by the fact that when this outdated perspective clashes with the reality of today, it fails to get approval or acknowledgment, and the value of the business schools teaching such an approach becomes questioned; actually, business schools tend to be considered as harmful to the development of society.

Research

Digital transformation has found a home most quickly in the domain of science and research. The scientific collaboration of today is usually virtual and international. Similarly, the dissemination and popularization of scientific knowledge have been taking place for a long time now in the digital world, where information spreads quickly, mainly through social media, including platforms for researchers, scientists, and other academics, which may be of great importance to the formation of international research teams (Korzyński et al., 2020) or making publications more popular through a growing number of citations (Mazurek et al., 2020a).

However, the digital transformation of science and research practices does not solve two fundamental problems affecting the domain in question. The first of them is the frequent irrelevance of research to societies and to important societal problems. The second is the insufficient promotion of research content. Concerning both challenges, they are even more dangerous as universities are losing their monopoly on knowledge creation and dissemination. Research is more and more often created by companies/corporations for which it has a strictly utilitarian value – research output is aimed at reaching the greatest audience possible. Scientific research, especially in the area of management, is not promoted strongly enough among the representatives of the business world, which results in its hermetic nature – society (and business) in such a case ceases to trust business schools, which requires undertaking an in-depth discussion on the relevance of research in the discipline of management sciences and the usefulness of its results for society (Tourish, 2019).

The Trap of Feigned Digital Transformation – a Digital Myopia

A clear distinction is needed between the digitalization of education and the digital transformation of education.

First, the rapid, obligatory switch to online teaching cannot be called the digital transformation of education. Using remote teaching tools has made it possible to make teaching digital, but in a situation in which the teaching practice simply copies the model of teaching applied so far, it has nothing to do with a true digital transformation of teaching. It's just one of the stages of the development of remote teaching (Norris and Lefrere, 2011). The situation has been aptly defined by Hodges and colleagues (2020) as "emergency remote teaching" (ERT), which is a temporary switch in the domain of teaching to an alternative method of instructional delivery in response to the occurrence of some crisis. It involves the employment of fully remote solutions to teach classes that would otherwise be taught face to face/on-site or in the form of blended learning or hybrid courses. It is also expected that once the crisis or emergency ends, the original format of delivery will be restored.

The key idea that needs to be underlined in such a scenario is the temporariness of the online model.

Indeed, a real, long-lasting digital change involves transformations of the ways, the methods, and the modes applied in equipping students with knowledge, competencies, and skills through the optimal utilization of digital technologies in the process of education based on selected forms of both teaching and learning. This means, in turn, that the most crucial area of development is not technology itself but teaching involving the use of new technology. The digital transformation of education therefore means fundamental changes in the adopted model of teaching classes and in the teaching techniques and aids used. This is what Norris and Lefrere (2011) speak of, claiming that a digital transformation of teaching actually means a great transformation of entire universities, involving, among others, the following: unbundling and reinventing teaching, learning, assessment, and certification; a focus on value, not just quality; a change in the use and roles of faculty, mentors, and peer-to-peer learning; and a transformation of the existing business models.

Digital transformation is a long-term process – a permanent process, in fact. It takes place with such objectives in mind as quick management, good working conditions, less bureaucracy, and making students better prepared to face the labor market. But both high-tech solutions and the digital era need to be confronted with the most important aspect there is – the benefits offered to stakeholders such as people, society, and climate, as well as the human and resource-related potential of each business school.

The Role of Policymakers

We shall not forget here that this digital transformation is, in fact, made possible and supported by not only the management boards of business schools, aware of the changes necessary to be made and having all the instruments necessary to implement them, or the faculty actually implementing these changes, but also the regulators, defining the very essence of studies, of ideas such as part time, full time, and so forth. Regulations are necessary. But they have to adapt to the circumstances of the present as quickly as the entities creating this present. Otherwise, the regulatory constraints will prevent real changes in education from actually taking place, which will only accelerate the processes of the decomposition of education – offered increasingly often by entities from outside the sector of education but aware of the existing (and widening) gap between the expectations of all stakeholders and universities, with their hands tied by regulations, unable to operate in these difficult conditions.

It seems reasonable to underline the big role played by institutions such as the European Foundation for Management Development (EFMD), which is a meta-regulator, by all means, but also a supporter of the best practices of change – one quite advanced when it comes to the awareness of its role in the creation of new standards and expectations. A similar role is played by ranking institutions. In the case of the business education sector, they have a great impact on how business education changes worldwide. Local domestic laws and regulations governing the sector of education in each market are equally important. This means that the regulatory awareness of the authorities of a given country translates directly into the level and extent of innovations that can be implemented and incorporated in the local ecosystem of education.

On the one hand, the flexibility of business schools in their efforts to adapt to the expectations of regulators carries a risk of homogeneity in the development of these schools, with each one of them operating according to the same rules, the same guidelines, suggestions, or even expectations, losing their identity and individual nature along the way. On the other hand, it makes it possible to consciously promote certain attitudes and expectations among game-makers.

The progress in the transformation of universities can be measured by analyzing their mission statements. The studies from previous periods show clearly that the catchphrases and slogans that were sort of buzzwords in the global system of business education in the second decade of the twenty-first century were reflected in the adopted mission statements, which were – in turn – determinants in the design of strategic goals and plans. This means they were implemented and enforced by business schools in practice on the level of their everyday operations (Mazurek et al., 2020b). It is therefore vital to identify how the present reality is articulated in these key definitions of progress and the development of universities – as quickly as possible.

An alternative to the conscious support of the transformation offered by all sorts of regulators and makers of standards is not stagnation but a quick development of "third-party" entities, existing outside the system of education but offering a similar or even better, faster, more innovative value. Although in the case of primary education it's difficult to think of nonstandard, "extracurricular" alternatives implemented on a large scale, it's quite easy to imagine such a course of action in the case of tertiary – higher – education, especially business education. The vision of higher education institutions losing their authority and the role they play in society over the next dozen years to come if they don't transform and evolve is not that abstract anymore.

Conclusion – the Business School of the Twenty-First Century

Will the time of the COVID-19 pandemic be used to skip – or leap over – the magical status quo of the transformation of business education around the world, which has been discussed for so long? Or will it become the fuel for the discussion held within the framework of pre–COVID-19 rules and regulations? These questions can't be answered right now, of course. The months and years to come will show how the evolution of business education progresses and if the time of the pandemic has been used wisely. It is clear that to make the necessary changes real, it is essential to see at least two groups of stakeholders involved in a systemic way: business schools and regulators on both international and domestic levels, including ranking institutions. Rapid changes in higher education policies shall be proposed and promoted by accreditation bodies, ranking institutions, and governments.

Business schools should aspire to be spaces for development, closely connected with many other key players in the social and economic landscape; they should be inclusive and accessible, ready to welcome the thought-challenge born within their networked structures; they should be environments encouraging the development of one's personality, regardless of age; they should be organizations that understand the volatility, uncertainty, complexity, and ambiguity (VUCA) world and the idea and implications of digital transformation; they should be institutions that are not afraid to be socially responsible. A business school of the future is where meaningful social attitudes are born, where research of relevance to society (and business) is conducted to provide answers to urgent issues. The business schools of the twenty-first century need to become authorities, act as role models for societies, and create a new kind of leader because this is something much expected and hoped for.

And maybe this urgent global demand for new thoughts, new solutions is a great opportunity for business schools, enabling them to respond appropriately to the global needs, proving that a crisis is a chance to break a deadlock and set a completely new, bold vision and path of development. Perhaps it's the very first time in dozens of years when business schools are actually needed and may prove really useful to societies – we need to educate and create thought leaders, leaders for new times, who will be able to create new standards, new models, and new patterns of actions, like pioneers, trailblazers with a fresh view of business and entrepreneurship in general. Graduates of business schools shall be role models in society.

References

Canals, J., and Heukamp, F. (2020). *The future of management in an AI world. Redefining purpose and strategy in the fourth industrial revolution*. Palgrave Macmillan.

Christensen, C. M. (1997). *The innovator's dilemma: When new technologies cause great firms to fail*. Harvard Business School Press.

Collinson, S. (n.d.). *Are business schools fit for the future?* Chartered Association of Business Schools. https://charteredabs.org/business-schools-fit-future/.

Davidson, C. N. (2017). *The new education: How to revolutionize the university to prepare students for a world in flux*. Basic Books.

Davis, J. A., and Farrell, M. A. (2016). *The market oriented university. Transforming higher education*. Edward Elgar.

Eyring, H. J., and Christensen, C. M. (2011). *The innovative university: Changing the DNA of higher education*. American Council on Education.

Hodges, C., Moore, S., Lockee, B., Trust, T., and Bond, M. (2020, March 27). The difference between emergency remote teaching and online learning. *Educause Review.* https://er.educause.edu/articles/2020/3/the-difference-between-emergency-remote-teaching-and-online-learning.

Jonathan, Z. (2020, March 10). Coronavirus and the great online-learning experiment. *Chronicle of Higher Education.* www.chronicle.com/art icle/coronavirus-and-the-great-online-learning-experiment/.

Kaplan, A. (2018). A school is "a building that has four walls ... with tomorrow inside": Toward the reinvention of the business school. *Business Horizons*, 61(4), 599–608.

Kaplan, A. M., and Haenlein, M. (2016). Higher education and the digital revolution: About MOOCs, SPOCs, social media, and the Cookie Monster. *Business Horizons*, 59(4), 441–450.

Korzyński, P., Mazurek, G., and Haenlein, M. (2020). Leveraging employees as spokespeople in your HR strategy: How company-related employee posts on social media can help firms to attract new talent. *European Management Journal*, 38(1), 204–212.

Krishnamurthy, S. (2020). The future of business education: A commentary in the shadow of the Covid-19 pandemic. *Journal of Business Research*, 117, 1–5.

Mazurek, G., Gorska, A., Korzynski, P., and Silva, S. (2020a). Social networking sites and researcher's success. *Journal of Computer Information Systems.* Advance online publication. www.tandfonline .com/doi/abs/10.1080/08874417.2020.1783724?journalCode=ucis20.

Mazurek, G., Korzynski, P., Gorska, A., and Pałyga, A. (2020b). Mission statements in FT ranked European business schools – a content analysis. *European Research Studies Journal*, XXIII(1), 639–649.

Musk, E. (@elonmusk). (2020, February 2). *Tesla will hold a super fun AI party.* Twitter. https://twitter.com/elonmusk/status/12240894449633 11616?s=20.

Norris, D. M., and Lefrere, P. (2011). Transformation through expeditionary change using online learning and competence-building technologies. *Research in Learning Technology*, 19(1), 61–72.

Parker, M. (2018). *Shut down the business school: What's wrong with management education.* Pluto Press.

Pucciarelli, F., and Andreas, K. (2016). Competition and strategy in higher education: Managing complexity and uncertainty. *Business Horizons*, 59(3), 311–320.

Tourish, D. (2019). *Management studies in crisis: Fraud, deception and meaningless research.* Cambridge University Press.

Van Wart, M., Roman, A., Wang, X., and Cheol, L. (2016). Integrating ICT adoption issues into (e-)leadership theory. *Telematics and Informatics*, 34(5), 427–537.

Verhoef, P. C., Broekhuizen, T., Bart, Y., Bhattacharya, A., Dong, J. Q., Fabian, N., and Haenlein, M. (2021). Digital transformation: A multidisciplinary reflection and research agenda. *Journal of Business Research*, 122(C), 889–901.

Vial, G. (2019). Understanding digital transformation: A review and a research agenda. *Journal of Strategic Information Systems*, 28(2), 118–144.

Wilson, A. M., and Schlegelmilch, B. (2020, July 23). *Future-proofing global business education*. Sustain Europe. www.sustaineurope.com/future-proofing-global-business-education-20200715.html.

17 | *The Extreme Situation, a Challenge for Management Education*

PIERRE KLETZ

Introduction: The Challenges Posed by the COVID-19 Crisis for the Management Education Sector

The expectations of business school and management faculty students go well beyond obtaining a degree and are defined around four essential elements:

- Acquiring theoretical and technical knowledge in the field of management and leadership
- Learning a manner of approaching problems and a mindset
- Developing a professional network with fellow program members (given that business school graduates are destined for a career in the field) and potentially entering the social circles of leaders once the degree is earned
- Social recognition of intellectual potential associated with an aptitude for accomplishment in action

Analyzing these four elements in conjunction with some of the consequences of COVID-19 makes it possible to appreciate the importance of the impact of this crisis on management education institutions.

For example, it seems obvious that its first effect is to have enormously accelerated virtual education, which affects both teaching methods and selection processes in educational management institutions.

In this new context, it is conceivable that management education institutions will succeed in meeting the requirements of the first of the previously listed elements – that is, the acquisition of knowledge – at the cost of immense work. A great deal of creativity will be required in order to adequately address the second and third of these, i.e. to inculcate a way of approaching problems and to develop networking, in the context of widespread virtual education.

The fourth element, the recognition of potential, is undoubtedly the one for which the new context in which business schools find themselves poses the most serious challenges. Indeed, although a business school degree is often seen by companies as a guarantee of the potential of graduates, this positive postulate is largely based on their having successfully passed the selection process for admission to a business school. To illustrate how companies perceive the importance of the selection process in elite management education institutions, Henri Tézenas du Montcel (1985) compared it to high-jump events for athletes. Successfully passing a difficult selection process is like an athlete successfully clearing a 2-meter-high bar. If they have succeeded in doing so once in their life, we can reasonably assume that these individuals, if well supervised and well looked after, will continue to be able to jump over a 1.8-meter-high bar very regularly for a long time to come.

Tézenas du Montcel (1985) went on to postulate that, on the other hand, in general, success during studies proper at a business school or a faculty of management is comparable to being able to systematically jump over a 1.5-meter-high bar. Using this metaphor, Tézenas du Montcel showed the fundamental role of selection in the process of social validation of the potential of business school graduates. Thus, COVID-19, which strongly affects the selection process of these institutions, poses a major challenge for the consistency of the management education system.

In addition, by quickly diverting the teaching of management education institutions toward distance education, COVID-19 not only poses a major challenge in terms of educational and curriculum reorganization, but it also obliges the collective of business schools to rethink the competition from those among them that had already moved to entirely distance education, insofar as these had represented controlled competition. This crisis appeared at a time when new challenges were manifesting themselves in business schools, foremost among which was the emergence of wholly new projects that followed completely rethought logic. Large companies were embarking on management education for audiences that extended well beyond their own employees (e.g., AI Business School, developed by Microsoft, and EY Business Academy, developed by Ernst and Young). Some ambitious projects were free (e.g., the University of the People, which allows students to obtain degrees in business administration entirely online), whereas others (e.g., JOLT) presented original business plans that were different from those of business schools or particularly innovative teaching methods (e.g., Quantic, a mobile, flexible executive MBA).

Management Education, COVID-19, and Extreme Situations

This chapter offers an analysis of the response of management education institutions to the conjunction of these profound changes by viewing the situation of such schools caused by the coronavirus epidemic as an extreme situation (Bettelheim, 1943). Obviously, managers, teachers, and administrative staff in business schools are used to facing an array of challenges that range from the most operational (e.g., facing a lack of classrooms at a time during the week when the entire campus is full of students) to the most complex (those with short- and medium-term educational and financial consequences; e.g., managing the establishment's recruitment and admissions campaign), and even societal and long-term challenges (e.g., how to answer the question that periodically arises about the social function of business schools and their relations with businesses).

All of these issues are multifaceted and important, but they arise periodically and normally in the life and management of a school. Contrarily, however, Bettelheim characterizes extreme situations by their complete exceptionality and their highly destabilizing character, and moreover, he underscores the fact that facing them successfully implies very strong adaptability (Bettelheim, 1943, p. 419). When management education institutions were first affected by the coronavirus crisis in February, March, and April of 2020, it looked like an extreme situation. During this period, a strong feeling of concern for the health and even the lives of students, teachers, and administrative staff existed, which attested to the exceptional nature of the situation for institutions that generally do not have to consider this kind of eventuality. In addition, these institutions had to very quickly face up to strongly destabilizing factors (e.g., new obstacles to the recruitment of international students, increased difficulty in developing international programs, and the need to rethink the selection process). But especially, in their response to the crisis, they found themselves faced with the need "to adapt themselves entirely and with the greatest speed" (Bettelheim, 1943, p. 419). The methods and requirements of this adaptation are the subject of this study.

One possible objection to an "extreme-situation approach" to analyzing an organizational situation is that Bettelheim (1943) formalized his theory to analyze the behavior of prisoners in concentration camps when he himself was returning from the one at Dachau. When we use this approach to analyze organizations, do we not take the risk of falling into anthropomorphism? No. Bettelheim, anxious to clarify the scope of his work, himself indicated that this approach was relevant for individuals, groups, organizations, and the masses (Bettelheim, 1943, p. 419).

Bettelheim's definition of the priorities essential in the case of extreme situations reinforces the relevance of this approach to the analysis of the way in which management education institutions have faced COVID-19 and its consequences. These priorities are twofold for Bettelheim: on the one hand, to preserve one's integrity and, on the other hand, to continue to accomplish one's mission.

He further specifies that the examination of how these two priorities are articulated provides an excellent tool for analysis, including the analysis of organizations.

These priorities correspond to the way in which the management education sector reacted to the outbreak of COVID-19; the two priorities that characterized the start of the crisis consisted, on the one hand, of preserving the integrity of schools by protecting the health of students, teachers, and administrative staff – very often by closing establishments at least for a specified amount of time – and, on the other hand, in accomplishing their missions by seeking the means to teach despite the impossibility of teaching face to face.

How Management Education Institutions Can Adapt to Extreme Situations

The centrality of the notion of adaptation in the context of an extreme situation has been underlined earlier. Faced with the mounting coronavirus epidemic, management schools largely distinguished themselves by reacting quickly and seeking to adapt.

The determining factors of the management education sector's rapidity in taking into account the challenges posed by COVID-19 are easily spotted. The international has taken such a prominent position in the life and management of schools, whose activities and recruitment reach all corners of the world, that they are in a position to appreciate the importance of problems even if they take place in an environment far from the historical headquarters of an establishment. Thus, even though the countries in which their teaching activities were located were not yet affected by COVID-19, schools had to think about issues such as whether to go ahead with student study trips. (From the beginning of March, the question of whether it was necessary to go ahead with study trips to China was raised in an acute manner, given the importance of this country for international seminars and learning expeditions for students as well as for executives in training.) Similarly, the difficulty that could exist in welcoming international students for the following year quickly became apparent, especially given that for some schools, the number of such students greatly exceeds half of the student body. Among these international students, students from Asia constitute a major portion. Schools were also quickly alerted to the importance of the challenge (Graduate Management Admissions Council [GMAC], 2020; Lister, 2020; McKie, 2020).

But above all, beyond the questions raised by the international, management schools also had to very quickly determine whether to continue activity on their campuses. The EFMD Global Focus review provided many interesting examples of how management schools have not only been able to use their international experience to anticipate and take stock of the COVID-19 problem but also often made the decision to close their campuses for several days before the public authorities imposed such conditions (Saviotti, 2020). This ability to position themselves as a source of information, coupled with their strong institutional image, has even, in many cases and many regions of the world, led them to advise and inspire public authorities on the decisions to be made and actions to be taken.

In addition, although the health situation in different countries led to the closure of many campuses, the speed with which teaching resumed via distance learning demonstrated impressive responsiveness. To take just one example among many, when the lockdown was put in place, thanks to the prior work of the university's rectorate, the management faculty of Ben-Gurion University of the Negev moved from a pedagogical style in which face-to-face education was overwhelmingly dominant to 100 percent virtual teaching, with only one day of interruption. In general, the management education sector has asserted itself through its ability to adapt in a crisis situation.

Management education institutions, like other faculties, have had to adapt their teaching practices.

This was not a careful or planned renovation but simply a response to the challenge created by the epidemic. The diversity of responses provided by the various faculties around the world to the challenge posed by the different stages of the pandemic has been accompanied in many cases by an impressive capacity for action and, above all, by a remarkable will to implement strategies. After realizing that the COVID-19 crisis would also affect the next school year (2020–21), some business schools decided to combine the two learning methods – face to face and virtual – as part of a hybrid education program. For example, lectures are given online in large auditoriums, and face-to-face meetings are held in small groups. This is the case, for example, with the Cambridge Judge Business School and the London Business School. At Cambridge, it is even required to physically go to school as soon as the situation allows. Each response to the crisis leads to further adaptation efforts. Thus, some students felt, already in the summer of 2020, that because of the virus, they could not commit to going to campus, which increased the rate of postponement of the start of studies. In addition, it was also decided to adapt the physical environment of the school in order to comply with the directives relating to the fight against the virus; thus, measures such as one-way elevators and stairs, physical distancing signs and procedures, and new self-service rules for the cafeteria, among many others, were put into place. Being very concerned about the fight against the spread of the virus, the health of staff and students, and the sustainability of learning, other schools (such as HEC Paris and EDHEC) asked everyone coming to campus to take periodic COVID-19 tests or routinely have their temperature measured on arrival (Nugent, 2020). To enable all students to have a good start to the school year, the opening of the school year was postponed in some schools by 14 days in order to allow the isolation period requested of students to be completed. Finally, some postponed the start of the school year so as to give themselves the best chance of delivering the program face to face and to allow students from different countries around the world to arrive. For example, Alliance Manchester Business School delayed the start of its school year from September to December (Nugent, 2021).

Many schools also created arrangements for students to arrive on campus in maximum safety within the framework of hybrid programs.

For example, WHU in Düsseldorf put in place a meticulous health and safety plan to ensure safe and harmonious education. Plexiglas walls were installed in classrooms, one-way systems were put in place, and the campus was extensively equipped with disinfectant dispensers. Access to the school premises is electronically controlled. Each student is registered via their electronic card when they come onto campus. Students receive detailed instructions prior to arrival and are encouraged to download and use the official coronavirus app, which the federal government promotes. No parties are allowed, and strict rules also apply to extracurricular and social activities. At the Bologna Business School, the pavilion was divided into eight classrooms to accommodate 370 students in a space that can typically accommodate 10,000. Every hour, an air-recirculation system brings fresh, clean air into the pavilion (BusinessBecause, 2020).

The Frankfurt School of Finance and Management invested in coronavirus tracers. Small devices are given to each student and each staff or faculty member (Nugent, 2020). Each device has a unique tracking ID linked to its owner, and using Bluetooth technology, it records the details of every device that is within 2 meters of it. This information is then kept in a system for 14 days, making it easy to spot potential infections if a student, staff member, or faculty member tests positive for COVID-19.

Types of Reactions to Extreme Situations

The very notion of an extreme situation seems to intuitively lead to behavior based on the assumption that it is not destined to last. However, in such a situation, it is quite possible to adopt an attitude that takes into account that an extreme situation can be prolonged, as it is the situation in its essence that is extreme in the difficulties that it generates, the contradictions it entails, the tensions it gives rise to. However, this does not say anything about its ability to last over time. For example, the state of extreme poverty experienced by 11 percent of the world's population puts these individuals in an extreme and unfortunately lasting situation.

To better understand the present situation for management education institutions, it is useful to compare it to loss. Loss is the extreme situation par excellence because it arises suddenly and puts the individual or organization in a difficult situation that must be faced. Three attitudes that religious literature has echoed (Grossman, 2016) since ancient times and can be described under various terms emerge when facing a situation of loss: coping, mourning, and resilience.

The attitude of coping involves coming to terms with the new, unpleasant situation, even when it is an extreme one – trying to do what it takes to "live with" the situation while still supposing that it will disappear. It is thus, above all, a matter of being in the best possible situation "afterward," when things return to normal, because the central assumption of coping is that the extreme situation is not destined to last.

The work of mourning, however, consists first of all in accepting the fait accompli, admitting that what was will not return, and that therefore, we must make it so that we can live *in* the new situation, which is the new reality.

Resilience occurs after having carried out and then moved beyond the stage of mourning, and it therefore implies having accepted that the present reality will persist. It also consists of trying to create the conditions to influence this situation by making it better and therefore more acceptable, creating new opportunities.

This section describes how, faced with the challenge of COVID-19 and the extreme situation that it created for the management education sector, schools reacted with attitudes, decisions, and actions relating to these three behaviors – coping, mourning, and resilience.

Obviously, sorting the behavior of business schools in response to COVID-19 into three categories is part of an approach that seeks after Max Weber's ideal types. Weber himself clarified that these are not found as such in the social reality; rather, it is a question of indicating the main features that help to think about the subject being studied. Thus, none of the ways in which business schools and management faculties have dealt with COVID-19 are linked totally and uniquely with a single attitude of coping, mourning, or resilience. Instead, they mix together elements belonging to each of these categories. However, the description of these three ideal types makes it possible to lay a foundation for the analysis of the impact of COVID-19 on management education institutions.

Coping

The consequences of the coronavirus epidemic for business schools and management faculties were felt almost cataclysmically in March 2020.

The difficulties seemed to accumulate. Many Graduate Management Admission Test (GMAT) and Graduate Record Examination (GRE) test centers had closed in many parts of the world as of February and March, which made it practically impossible to obtain these important test scores for applications. International travel became problematic or even impossible, which posed a serious obstacle for organizing international seminars, learning expeditions, student exchanges, and so forth, as well as for the recruitment of international students. And very soon afterward, in the specific case of the United States, visa problems for foreign students added to the surrounding difficulties. Thus, the months of March and April showed themselves to be not just difficult in and of themselves with the closure of campuses, one after the other, but also the bearers of difficulties for the future.

The adaptability of the management education sector, when faced with these difficulties, has been remarkable. Most high-level schools extended their final rounds of admissions or added additional ones. They lowered, and in some cases even did away with, their requirements in terms of GMAT and GRE test scores. The effect on the number of applications for the following year was significant (Byrne, 2020c; GMAC, 2020) – and all the more so because it was coupled with another unexpected factor: the COVID-19 epidemic, by causing the volume of business and economic growth to decline, reduced the promotion possibilities for young managers, as well as the number of interesting jobs in the labor market.

The labor-market situation, coupled with the easing of admission conditions for business schools, has led to a sharp increase in the number of applications in master's programs (Byrne, 2020a; Moules and Jack, 2020), which has even greater significance because in the previous 3 years, business schools, and in particular MBAs, had been faced with a regular decline in the number of applications.

This increase in the number of candidates was marked on all continents; it has been particularly spectacular in the United States, where despite visa restrictions, some schools have seen an increase of more than 50 percent in the number of applications for their MBAs (Ethier, 2020c).

These elements indicate that management education institutions have, in many respects, remarkably adapted to the new constraints created by the coronavirus epidemic and have succeeded, for example (also taking advantage of socially favorable circumstances), in increasing the number of applicants and turning around the somber situation that had been looming in which they would have suffered a decrease in the number of applications for the fourth consecutive year.

This observation must, however, be supplemented by an examination of the way in which management education institutions have reacted to this increase in applications. In the preamble of the analysis of how the increase in applications was managed, it is useful to underscore that with a few exceptions, which we will examine, the reactions of management education institutions have been remarkably similar on the six continents. In general, these institutions have not resisted the temptation to maintain an equivalent number of enrolled students as the previous year or even to increase the number of admitted students.

However, we must distinguish the case of management faculties belonging to universities, in particular public ones, from the case of business schools, where a significant portion of the budget comes from very high tuition fees. As regards management faculties, faced with an influx of candidates, they have tended to fill their classes as much as possible, taking into account the limit that their supervisory authority almost always sets for them.

Some business schools have gone much further in the same direction by increasing the number of successful applicants and, in many cases, recruiting classes of new students for the 2020–21 academic year that were significantly larger than the previous year.

Internationally, it appears that many business schools have followed the same pattern in the admissions sequence of MBA students and, more generally, in business schools. As schools around the world became aware of the negative potential of the COVID-19 epidemic in March–April 2020, they were led to try to adapt their admission requirements, both in terms of deadlines and dates to present applications and, often, in terms of the content requirements of the applications themselves, be it by waiving or postponing test results or even academic requirements.

From the month of May, they became aware of the fact that, far from declining, the number of candidates was increasing. Therefore, in many cases, the cohorts starting at the end of August/September/ October 2020 and in January 2021 are larger than in previous years. The reasons that led educational management institutions to accept more students than in previous years stem from the particular context of the COVID-19 epidemic, which has forced them to switch to distance education. Peter Johnson, assistant dean of the full-time MBA program and admissions at the Haas School in Berkeley, in an interview given to the Poets & Quants website, sums up perfectly the logic followed by many institutions: "In a normal year, if we were fully in-person, we wouldn't be able to have a class this large" (Ethier, 2020b, para. 3).

Schools have therefore often freed themselves from referring to the physical and educational limits that they would have had to follow if they had not switched to distance learning. Peter Johnson's statement implicitly means that schools have given up on the idea that they could go back to face-to-face learning if the situation improves on the coronavirus front in the months to come.

This observation necessitates two comments. First of all, it implies that a major shift in the teaching at business schools has taken place, even if this is not clearly stated and is not necessarily something schools have become explicitly aware of; schools are putting themselves in a situation of no return, at least in the short term, with regard to face-to-face education. This transition to virtual education will have enormous implications in terms of pedagogy, relationships with students, the use of premises, and school policies for investment in equipment, among other areas.

Second, the sphere of management education is faced with a major contradiction. Indeed, it seems that there is a consensus that distance education needs to make huge strides to be as good as face-to-face education. Thus, the numerous articles and declarations emphasizing the merits of hybrid education and calling for its rapid generalization constitute just as many positions according to which purely virtual education is not a panacea. However, to the extent that hybrid education includes a not-insignificant share of face-to-face teaching, the large number of students in this year's classes would require huge investments and major decisions to be made in order for it to be possible. Thus, schools seem to have put themselves in a system of paradoxical injunctions where their actions are out of step with their real situations and their stated objectives. They spread the message that it would be desirable to return to at least a small amount of face-to-face education, all the while incurring situations where this option is no longer possible.

This type of behavior raises another question, especially for the more reputable schools. Indeed, by putting themselves in a position to take the risk of suffering degradation of teaching, schools expose themselves to having their contributions questioned, in particular, in relation to lessons offered for a lower cost at more recent and less prestigious institutions that, from their conception, had turned to the virtual. It seems that schools are counting on the fact that their names, their reputations, and their branding will continue to support the demand for their degrees. Although this reasoning is undoubtedly correct in the short term, the sustainability of this type of behavior in the long term is problematic. The many ambitious new projects mentioned in the introduction, which are at the same time marginal compared to traditional academic education and totally supported by teaching on the internet, expect to be able to create different but effective branding that will put classic business schools in a difficult position.

In addition, the need to maintain an excellent educational level, pedagogically speaking, is therefore emerging in a precise and urgent manner for schools. Technological solutions have been sought in the context of the various lockdowns to try to avoid prohibiting the normal reception of students on campuses, doing "the same thing, but via Zoom" and risking offering students a degraded MBA experience. As a result, schools have tried to find online techniques to fill this gap. For example, the MIP Politecnico di Milano in Italy adopted FLEXA, an e-learning platform developed in partnership with Microsoft. FLEXA's machine-learning technology enables the creation of a personal online study program for each student based on data from online sources, which enables students to pursue effective learning. Another example is Prendo Simulations, which creates business simulations for schools like INSEAD, Wharton, and Kellogg. These simulations are specially developed for home students during quarantine (Novellis, 2020).

Although distance learning has undergone a huge acceleration as a result of the COVID-19 epidemic, school management is focusing on the acquisition of equipment, leaving educational innovation to the initiative of teachers in the field, who are now facing significant pressure. The need for pedagogical change is felt enormously in almost all institutions because they feel that distance teaching cannot be reduced to simply doing the same thing as face-to-face teaching, only mediated by a camera.

Thus, this need for change and the adjustment of pedagogy puts significant pressure on teachers, who are on the front lines when it comes to the adaptation of institutions to the constraints induced by COVID-19.

After two decades during which the centrality of questions of internationalization, accreditation, and so forth led to a focus on the deans of business schools, COVID-19 represents a return of the figure of the professor as a central element in the lives of business schools.

This also has consequences for the central approaches and concepts in the world of management education; where focusing on the figure of the dean had led us to focus on strategy, its concepts, and its rationality, the return of the professor's visible centrality could, as a result of the modes of adaptation the professor bears, well cause a renewed interest in practical wisdom, iterative adjustments, and the importance given to experience.

The Work of Mourning

In the description of coping, we considered the case of institutions that believed the crisis caused by COVID-19 was not sustainable and that we had to live with it, to cope with it, for as long as it lasted, as best as possible, by not refraining from seeking the effects of opportunity.

Faced with a difficult situation or with a loss, the attitude of submitting to the work of mourning is seen as an alternative to coping. The work of mourning consists of admitting that the loss that has occurred, that the disastrous change that has taken place is irreversible, which determines both behavior and subsequent actions. Similarly, to face up to the coronavirus crisis, some management education establishments have reacted in a way that is close to the work of mourning by integrating the idea that the consequences of this crisis were destined to last into their decisions as well as their activities.

Therefore, in opposition to the behaviors induced by coping, which consist of seeking short-term benefits even at the cost of long-term risks, it is here a question of admitting and taking into account the lasting nature of the effects of COVID-19 on management education institutions, even if doing so entails short-term costs and constraints.

An excellent example of this attitude is represented by the decision of certain schools, such as INSEAD and the Harvard University School of Business, to decrease the number of students recruited in the fall of 2020. INSEAD decided to decrease the number of accepted students by more than a third, although the school had a record number of applicants. Likewise, Harvard recruited the smallest incoming class in decades, with 732 students, compared to 938 the previous year (Byrne, 2020b).

The management of both INSEAD and Harvard thus considered the fact that in order to develop hybrid education, it was necessary to account for the fact that any face-to-face education would occupy more space on their premises, which made it necessary to reduce the number of students. Maintaining the same number of students as in previous years was tantamount to choosing entirely distance education.

One of the reasons for the relatively small number of students studying in the fall 2020 cohort is that Harvard Business School has given all admitted students the option to defer their enrollment for 1 or 2 years without any penalty while not compensating for these post-ponements by admitting a greater number of wait-listed candidates. In making this choice, the Harvard Business School recognized that face-to-face studies better corresponded to the very high Harvard standard and that this was a right for accepted students. The leaders of the institution were faced with a particular challenge that consisted of preserving classroom teaching, which was necessary for the institu-tion's famous "case-study method." However, COVID-19 restrictions prevented students from completely filling classrooms.

As well, Harvard Business School accepted that in order to maintain the constituent elements of its identity (the case-study method, the quality of teaching, etc.), it was necessary to mourn financial income.

It should also be noted that Harvard has also already indicated that if the world health situation returned to normal, it would recruit a record number of students at the start of the 2021 and 2022 school years. This is specific to a work of mourning that consists, above all, of recognizing and accepting a loss but that, at the same time, leads to the postulate that at some point, the situation will find a new normal. Finally, although it is easy to imagine that Harvard wants to return to its usual number of students when the health situation returns to normal, a sudden and sharp increase in its number of students would be a major challenge. It would seem that it will be achieved by capital-izing on the lessons learned from the COVID-19 epidemic and by maintaining a small amount of hybrid teaching.

Many other examples have emerged in which management educa-tion institutions recognized that the coronavirus crisis had led to situations it was necessary to face, even if responding to them was difficult and had a short-term cost, because the situations were going to persist in the long term, and schools had to be prepared to deal with them as best as possible.

Networking is an important asset of attending a business school. However, student separation from campus has greatly hampered networking possibilities, which are first realized face to face. We are seeing many efforts on the part of schools to make some of these activities happen online. At the Massachusetts Institute of Technology Sloan School of Management, virtual student networking includes quiz nights, hackathons, and a coding boot camp (Bartleby, 2020). Activities at the Haas School in Berkeley, California, also include distance yoga and mindfulness classes. At INSEAD, students meet in virtual meeting rooms for more in-depth discussions, with groups chosen at random to ensure interaction with a larger group of classmates (Bartleby, 2020).

The investment in time, energy, and money that management education institutions devote to this development is indicative of the awareness that networking activities will be carried out after the coronavirus crisis in a different way from the way they were carried out before.

The primordial importance of approaches that stem from what we have called "mourning" in the sphere of management education as it faces up to COVID-19 is largely because the effects of the epidemic have caused a sharp increase in uncertainty. Indeed, many analysts have pointed out that the epidemic has led to a global economic and financial crisis that has had a strong impact on unemployment rates and that will durably affect small businesses in particular because they are often no longer able to function (Skok and Owen, 2020). This general situation is causing a drastic increase in uncertainty, which blurs representations of what economies will look like when this crisis is behind us (Altig et al., 2020).

However, uncertainty should logically have an enormous effect on programs and curricula, insofar as it accelerates the obsolescence of teaching: the more quickly and significantly the future is different from the past and the present, the more the knowledge acquired is blamed. To illustrate this, Jaime Weinman (2020) recounts that in the novel *A Semester in the Life of a Garbage Bag* by Canadian author Gordon Korman, the protagonist writes a political science report on the governmental structure of an obscure monarchy whose ruler is overthrown and executed on the day the report is due. All the hero can do is add "until yesterday" to the title.

Likewise, the COVID-19 crisis seems to have largely indicted (not to mention made obsolete) strong trends in the global economy and the social evolution that is taking place – trends that had been seen as basic concepts of business school education. However, they must absolutely avoid providing teaching that would be relevant until yesterday. Two examples, among many others, illustrate this phenomenon:

- The until-recently-ultra-dominant idea of an increasingly intercon- nected world economy seems to have been largely demolished. The concept of the open economy of the Western world began to be questioned in 2016 with the announced desire of US president-elect Donald Trump to weaken globalized market policies, as well as to strengthen border restrictions. The British "Brexit" was also a signal of this tendency for countries to move toward economic independ- ence (McMahon and Hartigan, 2018). There is no doubt, however, that the sudden appearance of COVID-19 has given a boost to this notion of market fragmentation in parallel with that of the return of national sovereignty in the economic field. This change should have consequences in the teaching provided in business schools and should lead to changes in perspective.
- The global coronavirus pandemic has exposed and worsened social disparities in human societies and pushed millions of people into poverty (Ashford et al., 2020). COVID-19 has given renewed acuity to these themes. Further addressing the problems of socioeconomic inequality in business school classrooms and courses is now seen as an urgent need.

To be able to take into account such cardinal changes, it is necessary that business schools do the work of mourning the previous situation, which is over. Nothing can be more disabling than to stick to approaches supposing that when the effects of the coronavirus are no longer felt, we will return to the previous situation – this approach prevents us from putting ourselves in a situation to respond effectively to new challenges.

This is particularly glaring if we take the case of foreign students at American universities: while their numbers had been steadily increas- ing, in 2020, they decreased. Studying with international students from all over the world and working with them on assignments is an experience that will not be familiar to the students of American business schools this year. It is particularly noteworthy that the percentage of international students who study at American business schools will be significantly lower as long as the virus remains around because these students will not pay the high tuition fees that such establishments charge for an educational experience that consists only of e-learning. The paradox is that the spread of distance education has turned many students away from foreign universities and made them prefer local universities (Moules, 2020). But above all, contrary to what seems to be the fundamental hypothesis of the great American universities, nothing says that these students will return once the COVID-19 crisis is over.

Likewise, although it is commonly underlined how COVID-19 has had a strong impact on the ways of teaching in management education institutions and how quick and, in many respects, how successful the transition to distance learning has been, it is nonetheless clear that this development has not been accompanied by changes of the same magnitude in the curricula.

Likewise, teaching methods have often remained practically the same, and it is commonly reported that no review of technical aspects such as the length of sessions or the ideal number of students in each class has been performed, and students feel the lack of human connection with their faculty, school staff, and their peers (Liguori and Winkler, 2020). All these elements constitute enormous methodological challenges to overcome.

It would be excessive to draw conclusions that are too extreme and claim that pedagogy has not been affected by changes wrought by the coronavirus. Institutions have profoundly rethought their methods. The example of the South Korean Sungyunkwan University is particularly interesting: starting from the belief that fatigue is a major challenge of e-learning in many business schools, the decision was made not to record classes to increase student attention and involvement. The principle behind this decision is that watching the video is insufficient and that active watching is necessary not only to fully understand the course but also to ensure its quality (GBSN Emerge, 2020). To encourage active learning, some other schools recommend dividing the lesson into short segments of about 15 minutes, with a short activity between them; obviously, the length of teaching time slots in educational institutions is a contingency factor for organizations.

On another level, Weinman reports that when COVID-19 hit, McGill University's Bensadoun School of Retail Management was opening a 2,300-square-foot retail innovation lab to study the retail business experience; the lab was redesigned to take into account that the coronavirus has ushered us into the age of physical distancing, allowing students and faculty to simulate "how customers can make their shopping journeys without interacting with anyone or touching a single item in the store" (Weinman, 2020, para. 5).

In addition, noting how much of a general influence the coronavirus crisis has had on the curricula of business schools should not lead us to neglect the cases where, to the contrary, special courses were created to deal with questions raised by the COVID-19 crisis, considering that schools cannot afford to stick to old curricula and not react or update themselves to take into account the effects of the crisis. For example, the Wharton School at the University of Pennsylvania launched a course called "Epidemics, Natural Disasters, and Geopolitics: Managing Global Business and Financial Uncertainty." The London Business School will soon be organizing a course titled "The Economics of a Pandemic."

This underlines even more how much mourning is necessary to lead people to understand that management education will not return to the status quo ante of the situation before the pandemic. It is understandable that until such work is done, management education institutions and their teachers will be reluctant to really change their curricula and psychoeducational practices to meet a need that they feel is temporary.

Resilience

The two attitudes mentioned previously to represent the reaction of business schools to the extreme situation into which the COVID-19 epidemic has plunged them are based on radically different assumptions. Coping is based on the fundamental assumption that this extreme situation and the crisis that caused it are not going to last – that it is just a matter of waiting to return to the previous situation. On the other hand, the work of mourning consists of taking note of the fact that the consequences of the crisis are lasting and that a return to the status quo ante is not possible. This approach – for which examples were given in the previous section – consists of defining one's decisions, one's actions, and one's attitudes by being faithful to one's identity and one's objectives and by acknowledging the new situation.

The reaction of business schools to the extreme situation generated by the COVID-19 crisis has led to a third type of response that is also based on the recognition of the lasting nature of the consequences of the crisis. But this response is not satisfied with merely taking note of such durability and determining its attitude to best preserve the objectives and identity of the institution. Rather, it strives to act on the context in which the crisis has put schools in order to improve it. This type of reaction can be grouped together under the generic term of *organizational resilience*, which initially involves an accomplished grieving process.

An example of this is provided by the Stanford Rebuild initiative of the Stanford Graduate School of Business (GSB), for which the Startup Garage at Stanford GSB has been a key resource in an 8-week innovation sprint to design or scale up post–coronavirus-crisis economic stimulus plans. In this context, the school is entirely playing its role because this initiative is, first and foremost, a large-scale brainstorming session focused on large-scale problems and guided by eminent specialists from the business and academic worlds. The 8-week program began on June 22, 2020, and ended with a high-profile event in September (Ethier, 2020a). Stanford Rebuild is not limited to Stanford students; it is an event open to students, entrepreneurs, innovators, and business leaders from around the world. The school calls it a "focused investigation of ideas and solutions to accelerate the path to a better post-COVID future" (Ethier, 2020a, para. 6). Stanford's voluntarism is reflected in how, to give the project maximum impact, Stanford trains the participants by allowing them access to Stanford Embark, "an interactive entrepreneurial toolkit designed to help people explore if they can turn their idea into a viable business" (Ethier, 2020a, para. 6).

The intention of the project is manifested in the enunciation of the four sectors to which it relates: Reimagine Organizations, Reinforce Healthcare Systems, Revitalize the Workplace, and Redesign Human Wellbeing. Even more precisely, this intention is expressed by the type of challenges faced by the participants, which include not only challenges directly related to COVID-19, such as the implementation of scalable, socially responsible tests and contact tracing, but also major societal issues like rethinking childcare and preschool education; the impact of social distancing on mental health; and support for small businesses to recover and, in many cases, reinvent themselves. Finally, it is important to underline that for the projects considered most remarkable, the university has helped entrepreneurs find financing.

The Stanford example is one among dozens of others in which management education institutions are not content to merely take the consequences of the COVID-19 crisis as given but instead are embarking on processes intended to contribute to the reconstruction of post-crisis society. This example has in common with the examples of the grieving process provided earlier that it highlights instances in which the institutions of management education, far from making sacrifices to opportunistic processes to confront the crisis, remain faithful to their identities and their objectives.

The Stanford Rebuild project is presented as an initiative in which the management education institution mobilizes its teachers and students in an extra-academic framework. Certain other institutions have integrated an approach aimed at reacting to the consequences of COVID-19 as part of their curriculum. Many voices from both faculties and business school students call for engaging management and business administration students in actions related to their role as students and future managers in such a crisis. For example, Nyenrode Business University has realized how important it is to involve students in this resilience process and has launched programs in which students help small businesses and families with financial advice, all as part of their study program.

Likewise, an interesting example is the MBA Response project (Garner, 2020; MBA Response, n.d.). Harvard University has recognized that many struggling organizations, from those directly battling the pandemic to those devastated by the economic fallout, could benefit from MBA skills – marketing, finance, strategy, and so forth – to help face the challenges of the COVID-19 pandemic. The MBA program started a project that brings together businesses that need help and students who want to volunteer and help. The initiative spread to Georgetown University and became an inter-business school initiative called the MBA Response (Garner, 2020; MBA Response, n.d.).

Some business school projects facing the COVID-19 pandemic are trying to cope with global instability to launch progressive projects. For example, within the London Business School is the Wheeler Institute for Business and Development, which started a whole new business in India during the pandemic (Keller and Kwag, 2020). Rural areas of India were most at risk from the COVID-19 situation, not only from the health risks it entails (which also affect the rest of the world) but also because of the disease's impact on development and investment in new opportunities for the underdeveloped society of this country. The Wheeler Institute has established culturally sensitive and professionally empowering "labs" for female entrepreneurs. Knowing that this population was the most likely to be most affected by the pandemic, investing precious resources in times of global crisis is a message of solidarity and courage aiming at systemic progress.

Conclusion

The debates on the vocation of business schools traditionally oscillate between their responsibilities toward their students, which consist of educating them in management, and those toward companies in terms of training qualified personnel. They induce numerous developments for the way in which these two responsibilities complement and oppose each other and for the obligations toward each other that all of these stakeholders share.

The analysis of the consequences of the COVID-19 crisis for management education institutions via the notion of the extreme situation leads to the highlighting of another aspect of the raison d'être of these institutions. The coronavirus epidemic, like any crisis, is not limited to, on the one hand, "dealing with it" and attempting to operate in the manner closest to what was in effect before the crisis (even if it means disregarding it), nor, on the other hand, taking note of the fact that many aspects of the crisis are irreversible and trying to adopt behaviors that take into account the new situation in order to try to carry out one's mission.

This chapter has underscored how the notion of the extreme situation makes it possible to characterize the two attitudes described previously as relating to coping for the first and mourning for the second. But it has also highlighted a third alternative, resilience, which is characterized by acting proactively on the environment in which we operate. This analysis of the extreme situation through these three modalities reminds us of an element whose relevance is not limited to crisis situations: if management education institutions have a mission to educate students and meet the human resources needs of companies, then they are also a social place whose raison d'être is also to train elites for the society in which we operate and to influence the state of society as a whole. The leadership of management education institutions is enriched by also taking this third dimension into account. In addition, it thus contributes to the social legitimacy of business schools.

In its analysis of the consequences of the COVID-19 crisis on the management education sector, this chapter went through the notion of the extreme situation, borrowed from Bruno Bettelheim. Bettelheim (1943) argued that because extreme situations imply the need for adaptation, they act as accelerators and therefore revealers of the ongoing and desirable development pursued by an individual, a community, or a society.

The description and analysis of the responses of business schools to the crisis brought about by the pandemic have shown that alongside the two traditionally recognized missions of business schools and management faculties (training students in management and business administration and meeting the need for trained managers in companies), a third responsibility that had already emerged is now essential.

Indeed, the types of responses that can be given to an extreme situation (coping, mourning, and resilience), which have all been implemented by management education institutions, have demonstrated the increasing importance of a third mission of the management education sector, according to which business schools take note of the irreversibility of the consequences of the pandemic but use all their potential to contribute as social actors[1] to a reconstruction of the social environment and therefore to a way out of the crisis. We have seen that management education institutions, by letting companies in difficulty benefit from their knowledge, organizing forums in which skills are aggregated, training their students and participants in their executive education activities, and being immediately operational in confronting the crisis by adapting their teaching and so forth, work toward resilience for society in general and for the various communities. Obviously, this role of structuring society, or even, to paraphrase Berger and Luckmann (1966), of social construction of reality, had already

---

[1] See, in the present volume, Eric Cornuel's Chapter 13, "Going beyond 'Always Look on the Bright Side of Life' in Management Education Crisis Strategy."

emerged well before the coronavirus crisis. But this crisis, by demonstrating that the recognition and exercise of this social responsibility have a primordial role in the "post–COVID-19" world, also indicates an important direction of development for business schools, "in peacetime" as well as now.

References

Altig, D., Baker, S., Barrero, J. M., Bloom, N., Bunn, P., Chen, S., Davis, S. J., Leather, J. Meyer, B. H., Mihaylov, E., Mizen, P., Parker, N. B., Renault, T., Smietanka, P., and Thwaites, G. (2020). Economic uncertainty before and during the COVID-19 pandemic. *Journal of Public Economics*, 191, article 104274.

Ashford, N. A., Hall, R. P., Arango-Quiroga, J., Metaxas, K. A., and Showalter, A. L. (2020, July). Addressing inequality: The first step beyond COVID-19 and towards sustainability. *Sustainability*, 12(13), 1–37.

Bartleby, J. (2020, May 16). The pandemic increases the challenges facing business schools. *The Economist*. www.economist.com/business/2020/05/16/the-pandemic-increases-the-challenges-facing-business-schoolis.

Berger, P. L., and Luckmann, T. (1966). *The social construction of reality: A treatise in the sociology of knowledge*. Anchor Books.

Bettelheim, B. (1943). Individual and mass behavior in extreme situations. *Journal of Abnormal and Social Psychology*, 38(4), 417–452.

BusinessBecause. (2020, November 10). *Updates: Coronavirus impact on business schools*. www.businessbecause.com/news/live/coronavirus?page=2.

Byrne, J. (2020a, May 30). *2020–2021 MBA application deadlines*. Poets & Quants. https://poetsandquants.com/2020/05/30/2020-2021-mba-application-deadlines/?pq-category=admissions.

(2020b, September 2). *The new HBS class profile: Harvard enrolls smallest MBA class in decades*. Poets & Quants. https://poetsandquants.com/2020/09/02/the-new-hbs-class-profile-harvard-enrolls-smallest-mba-class-in-decades/.

(2020c, May 31). *Could 2020–2021 be the biggest MBA application season ever?* Poets & Quants. https://poetsandquants.com/2020/05/31/could-2020-2021-be-the-biggest-mba-application-season-ever/.

Ethier, M. (2020a, June 9). *How Stanford GSB plans to create a COVID-19 recovery blueprint*. Poets & Quants. https://poetsandquants.com/2020/06/09/how-stanford-gsb-plans-to-create-a-covid-19-recovery-blueprint.

(2020b, September 8). *Applications are up at UC-Berkeley Haas, but acceptance rate jumps too*. Poets & Quants. https://poetsandquants

.com/2020/09/08/applications-are-up-at-uc-berkeley-haas-but-accept
ance-rate-jumps-too/?pq-category=business-school-news.

(2020c, September 10). *Massive jump in apps, enrollment for the Rice Jones MBA*. Poets & Quants. https://poetsandquants.com/2020/09/10/massive-jump-in-apps-enrollment-for-the-rice-jones-mba/?pq-category=business-school-news.

Garner, B. (2020, July 17). *This Georgetown MBA is helping businesses overcome their COVID-19 challenges*. BusinessBecause. www.businessbecause.com/news/coronavirus-latest/7086/georgetown-mba-helping-businesses-overcome-covid-19-challenges.

GBSN Emerge. (2020, April 13). *COVID-19 lessons from South Korea* [Video]. YouTube. www.youtube.com/watch?v=Wcbki6eu2mw&feature=emb_logo&ab_channel=GlobalBusinessSchoolNetwork.

Graduate Management Admissions Council. (2020, November 10). *Application trends survey*. www.gmac.com/market-intelligence-and-research/market-research/application-trends-survey.

Grossman, J. (2016, November). Review of the book *Mourning in the Bible: Coping with Loss in Biblical Literature* by Shemesh, Y. *AJS Review, 40* (2), 397–399.

Keller, S., and Kwag, M. (2020, December 7). *UN Women and Dharma Life Foundation join to help marginalized women in rural India*. https://asiapacific.unwomen.org/en/news-and-events/stories/2020/12/un-women-and-dharma-life-foundation-join-to-help-marginalized-women-in-rural-india.

Liguori, E., and Winkler, C. (2020). From offline to online: Challenges and opportunities for entrepreneurship education following the COVID-19 pandemic. *Entrepreneurship Education and Pedagogy, 3*(4), 346–351.

Lister, A. (2020, September 22). *The 15 best business schools for international students*. BusinessBecause. www.businessbecause.com/news/best-business-schools-for/7175/international-students.

MBA Response (n.d.). *About*. https://mbaresponse.com/our-story.

McKie, A. (2020, January 24). French business schools attract Chinese students with luxury – students want to learn about Chanel, Louis Vuitton and Dior. *Times Higher Education*. www.insidehighered.com/news/2020/01/24/french-business-schools-attract-chinese-students-learn-about-luxury-brands.

McMahon, J., and Hartigan, J., eds. (2018). Brexit, the Trump effect, and de-globalization [Special issue]. *Journal of International Trade Law and Policy, 17*(1/2).

Moules, J. (2020, May 18). Coronavirus pandemic accelerates shift in MBA market. *Financial Times*. www.ft.com/content/f2d91aca-8933-11ea-9dcb-fe6871f4145a.

Moules, J., and Jack, A. (2020, September 27). Record numbers apply to top business schools. *Financial Times*. www.ft.com/content/5492262c-c566-42a5-a3f7-f153620460fd.

Novellis, M. D. (2020, March 27). *How business schools are battling coronavirus*. www.aacsb.edu/blog/2020/march/how-business-schools-are-battling-coronavirus.

Nugent, T. (2020, September 29). *The COVID-19 track and trace systems keeping business schools open*. BusinessBecause. www.businessbecause.com/news/coronavirus-latest/7204/covid-track-and-trace-systems-business-schools.

(2021, June 21). *COVID-19 campus updates for European business schools*. Business Because. www.businessbecause.com/news/coronavirus-latest/7156/covid-19-campus-updates-european-business-schools.

Saviotti, M. (2020, May 21). Covid-19, society, innovation & sustainable business review from Grenoble Ecole de Management [Interview with Loick Roche]. *EFMD Global Blog*. https://blog.efmdglobal.org/2020/05/21/covid-19-society-innovation-sustainable-business-review-from-grenoble-ecole-de-management/.

Skok, D., and Owen, T. (2020, May 21). *On a post-COVID-19 economy* [Podcast interview with Joseph Stiglitz]. Big.Tech. https://rb.gy/34wics.

Tézenas du Montcel, H. (1985). *L'Université ? Peut mieux faire*. Éditions de Seuil.

Weinman, J. (2020, September 8). *How the pandemic may change how MBA programs are taught*. MacLean's. www.macleans.ca/education/mba/how-the-pandemic-may-change-how-mba-programs-are-taught/.

Conclusion

ERIC CORNUEL

This book is a collective work comprising 17 chapters by the deans and leaders of important business schools from six continents.

Its conception occurred as the coronavirus crisis was in its beginnings and we were starting to sense its enormous consequences. The chapters themselves were written at a time when the pandemic was hitting societies all over the world and creating a new reality by having a strong impact on the systems in which business schools operated and on their prospects.

At the time of writing the conclusion to this book, everything suggests that we are, however, at the end of the coronavirus crisis; several vaccines have had their effectiveness demonstrated and are gradually being distributed throughout the world. Many astute observers foresee the end of the effects of this crisis in the months to come.

One might thus worry about the relevance of this book, which could be seen as little more than a work about a crisis that has ended, whereas marketing-inspired behavior could give rise to the temptation to shift the subject of the book from how to face the coronavirus crisis toward a reflection on the consequences of COVID-19, the latter being considered a violent but time-limited exogenous shock.

We feel, however, that the present work retains its strong relevance because of the fault line that it reveals in the way two groups of authors apprehend the consequences of COVID-19.

On one side lie the analyses that underscore how the COVID-19 crisis has brought to the fore trends that were already underway and have simply accelerated – that is, trends one could have all the same expected to establish themselves at a later date. A good example of this is distance education, which was progressing slowly but very surely.

On the other side are the authors who, to the contrary, feel that the coronavirus crisis has created possibilities for business schools that would never have been able to emerge in such a strong way without the crisis. Many are the chapters in this book that maintain that

COVID-19 has induced a recombination of possibilities in the world of management education. Trivial but relevant examples of this development include the upheaval experienced by business school selection systems and the increase in the number of students admitted to the most reputable business schools – developments that nothing prior to the pandemic had previously hinted at.

Thus, this book highlights a split and a classic opposition in business strategy between those approaches in which organizations must adapt to respond to constraints and conditions created by their environment (which is considered an exogenous datum) and approaches that, on the contrary, hold that companies may not even be able to influence the market conditions in which they operate and that this must constitute an integral part of their strategy.

These two attitudes are found in many major, highly recognized works of business strategy. They are not limited to this work. Literature is an excellent way to understand the gap between the two approaches, which are generally considered to be radically opposed.

They can be understood through the distance between the declaration of principle that Shakespeare puts in the mouth of the character of Page in Act V, Scene V of the *Merry Wives of Windsor*, "What cannot be eschew'd, must be embraced," and the modern, proactive stance of Antoine de Saint-Exupéry (1950) in his posthumous work *Citadelle* (or *The Wisdom of the Sands*), paraphrased as, "The future is only the present to be put in order."

This opposition, found in both business strategy and in literature, can be spotted just as well in many other areas where human thought is exercised. Remarkably, it always consists of a strong opposition between an opportunist attitude that renounces acting on the world but wants to take advantage of the latter's conditions and a voluntarist attitude that, on the contrary, aspires to influence its environment and society.

Our teaching in universities and business schools often makes it a point of honor to insist on the incompatibility between these two positions; the academic approach would designate such a rapprochement just the sort of paradigmatic dissonance that we teach our students to beware of.

On the contrary, reading this book makes the two attitudes coexist. Reading the contributions that make it up leads one to think that when faced with the COVID-19 crisis, the best attitude for business schools to adopt to meet both their educational mission vis-à-vis their students and vis-à-vis the need of companies for human resources training and to face their own constraints regarding their sustainability consists, conversely, of finding a compromise between these two attitudes.

To meet the challenge posed by COVID-19, business schools have had to both adapt to the constraints imposed on them by the conditions of the crisis and, at the same time, develop policies aimed at inducing market and social conditions that are different from those encountered during the crisis.

But above all, this book shows that the theoretical posture that emerges as an adequate response to the challenge posed by the COVID-19 pandemic is not limited to this particular crisis. To the contrary, through the dialogue that underlies it between the different chapters, this book establishes that the bias that consists of *both* accommodating the constraints of the crisis and creating the conditions for overcoming it by acting on the social system constitutes a mode of crisis management whose validity goes well beyond the COVID-19 crisis. In particular, it conveys the message that the attitude that seeks adaptation corresponds in particular to the sustainability needs of educational institutions, whereas the movement that seeks to act on the system corresponds more to the educational mission. In general, such a dual attitude is affirmed as constituting the very mission of business school leadership.

The scope of this important message makes this book not simply one more book on "management education and COVID-19" but, rather, a treatise on management education strategy that the European Foundation for Management Development (EFMD) is happy to have initiated.

References

de Saint-Exupery, A. (1950). *The wisdom of the sands*. Stuart Gilbert, trans. Harcourt, Brace & Co.